WRITERS
J. MICHAEL
STRACZYNSKI &
DWAYNE MCDUFFIE

PENCILER
MIKE MCKONE

INKERS
ANDY LANNING,
KRIS JUSTICE, &
CAM SMITH

COLORIST
PAUL MOUNTS

IF THIS BE ...
ANNIVERSARY!

WRITER
STAN LEE

PENCILER
NICK DRAGOTTA

INKER
MIKE ALLRED

COLORIST
LAURA ALLRED

A DAY AT THE RACES

WRITER/ARTIST
PAUL POPE

COLORIST
JOSE VILLARRUBIA

LETTERER
VC'S RUS WOOTON

ASSISTANT EDITORS
MOLLY LAZER &
AUBREY SITTERSON

EDITOR
TOM BREVOORT

COLLECTION EDITOR
JENNIFER GRÜNWALD

ASSISTANT EDITORS
MICHAEL SHORT &
CORY LEVINE

ASSOCIATE EDITOR
MARK D. BEAZLEY

SENIOR EDITOR,
SPECIAL PROJECTS
JEFF YOUNGQUIST

SENIOR VICE PRESIDENT
OF SALES
DAVID GABRIEL

PRODUCTION
JERRY KALINOWSKI

BOOK DESIGNER
DAYLE CHESLER

VICE PRESIDENT OF CREATIVE
TOM MARVELLI

EDITOR IN CHIEF
JOE QUESADA

PUBLISHER
DAN BUCKLEY

WAR
NTASTIC FOUR

CIVIL WAR
FANTASTIC FOUR

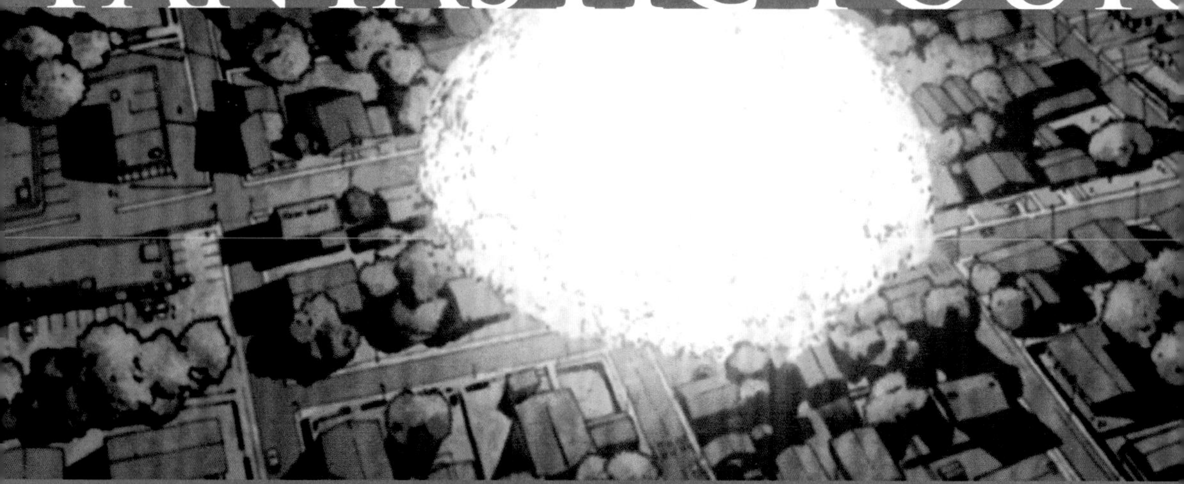

PREVIOUSLY...

Hoping to boost their ratings, four New Warriors--young super heroes and reality television stars--attempt to apprehend a quartet of villains holed up in Stamford, Connecticut. When confronted, the explosive Nitro employs his self-detonation ability, blowing the New Warriors and a large chunk of Stamford into oblivion. The entire incident is caught on tape. Casualties number in the hundreds.

As a reaction to this tragedy, public sentiment is turning against super heroes. Johnny Storm, the Human Torch, is attacked outside a nightclub and beaten into a coma. On Capitol Hill, a Superhuman Registration Act is debated which would require all those possessing paranormal abilities to register with the government, divulging their true identities to the authorities and submitting to training and sanctioning in the manner of federal agents.

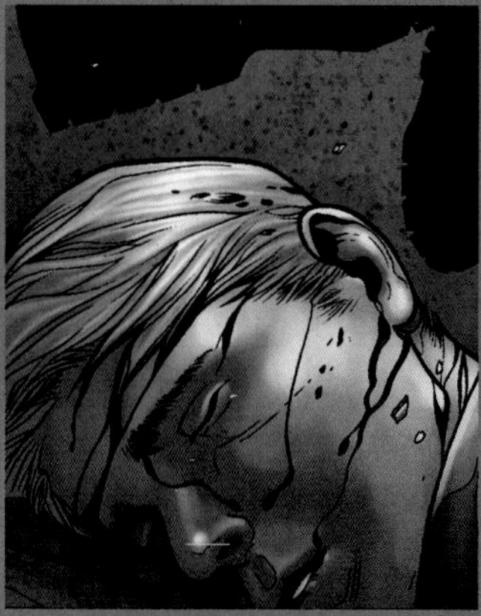

Some heroes, such as Iron Man, see this as a natural evolution of the role of super heroes in society, and a reasonable request. Others, embodied by Captain America, take umbrage at this assault on their civil liberties.

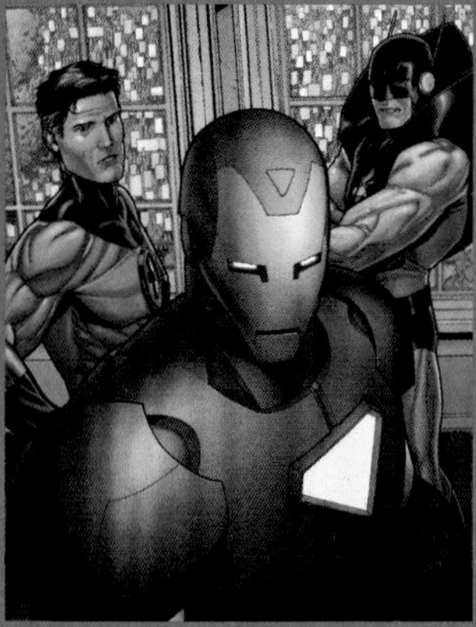

When Captain America is called upon to hunt down his fellow heroes who are in defiance of the Registration Act, he chooses to go AWOL, becoming a public enemy in the process. Meanwhile, Reed Richards has chosen a definite side for the Fantastic Four, as he teams up with Iron Man and Yellowjacket to bring Cap and other unregistered heroes to the ground.

A MARVEL COMICS EVENT

CIVIL WAR

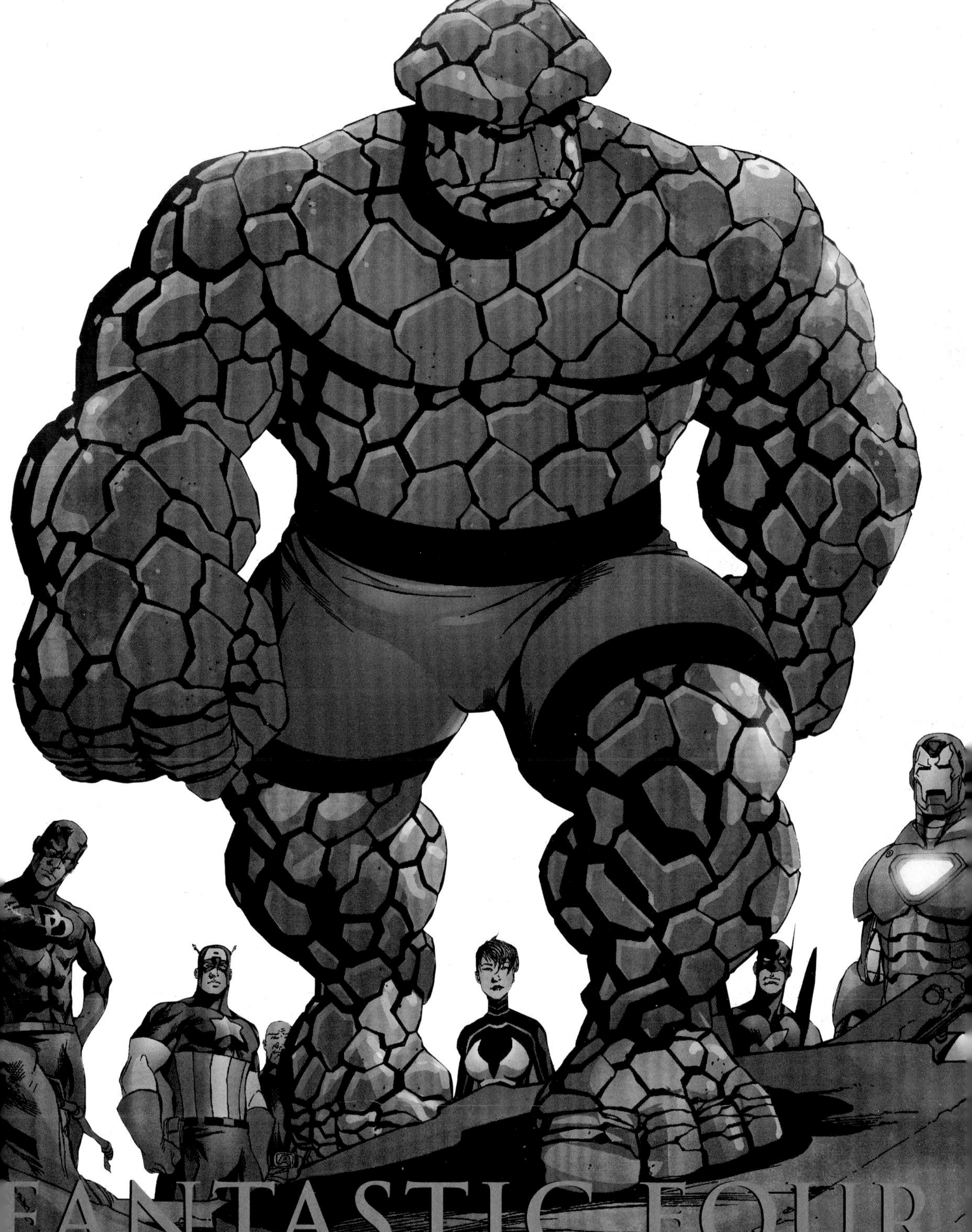

FANTASTIC FOUR

A

MARVEL COMICS

PRESENTATION

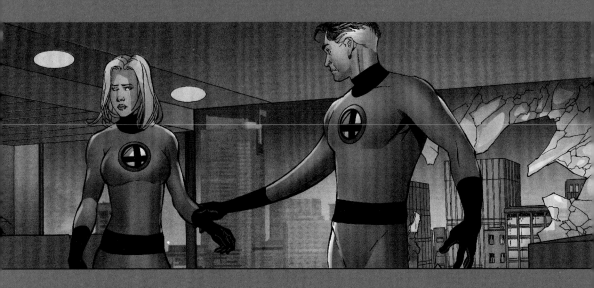

CIVIL
FA

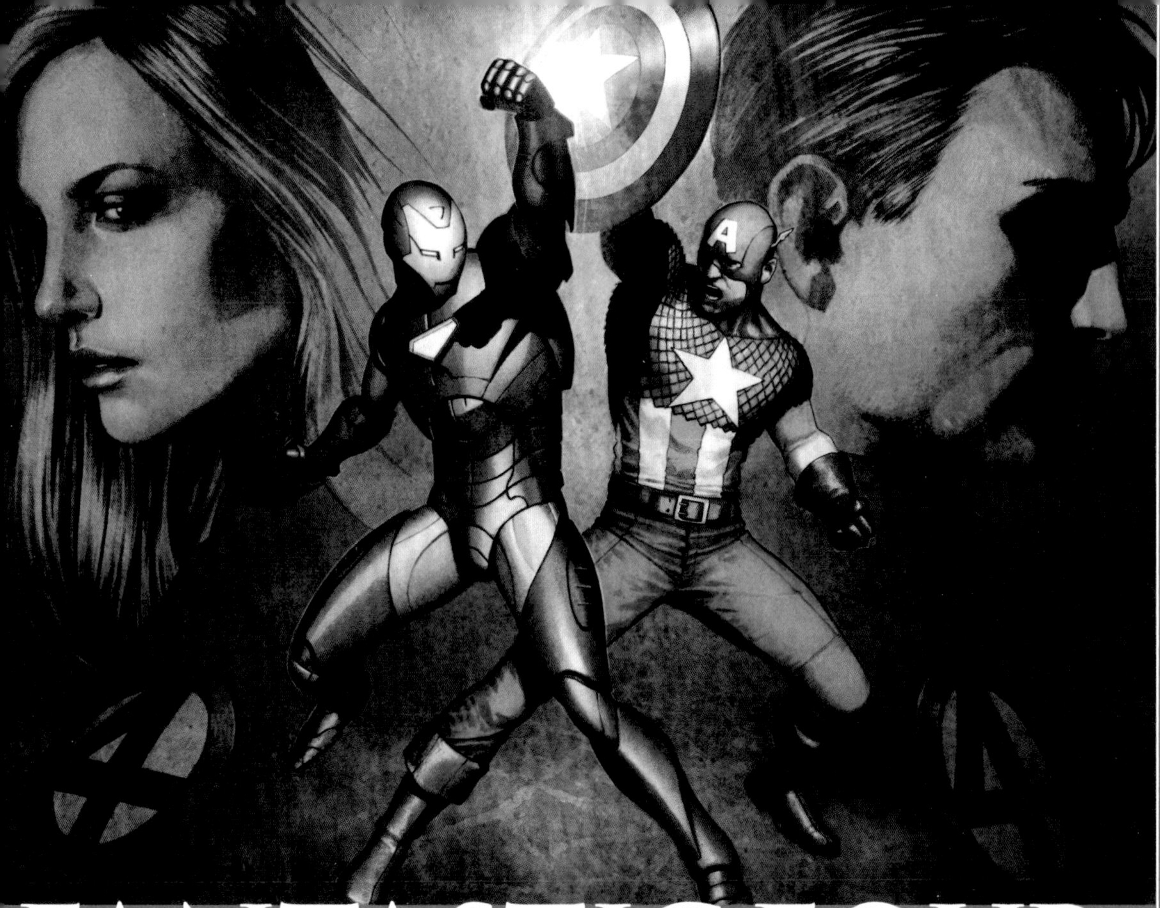

FANTASTIC FOUR

A MARVEL COMICS EVENT

CIVIL WAR

FANTASTIC FOUR #538

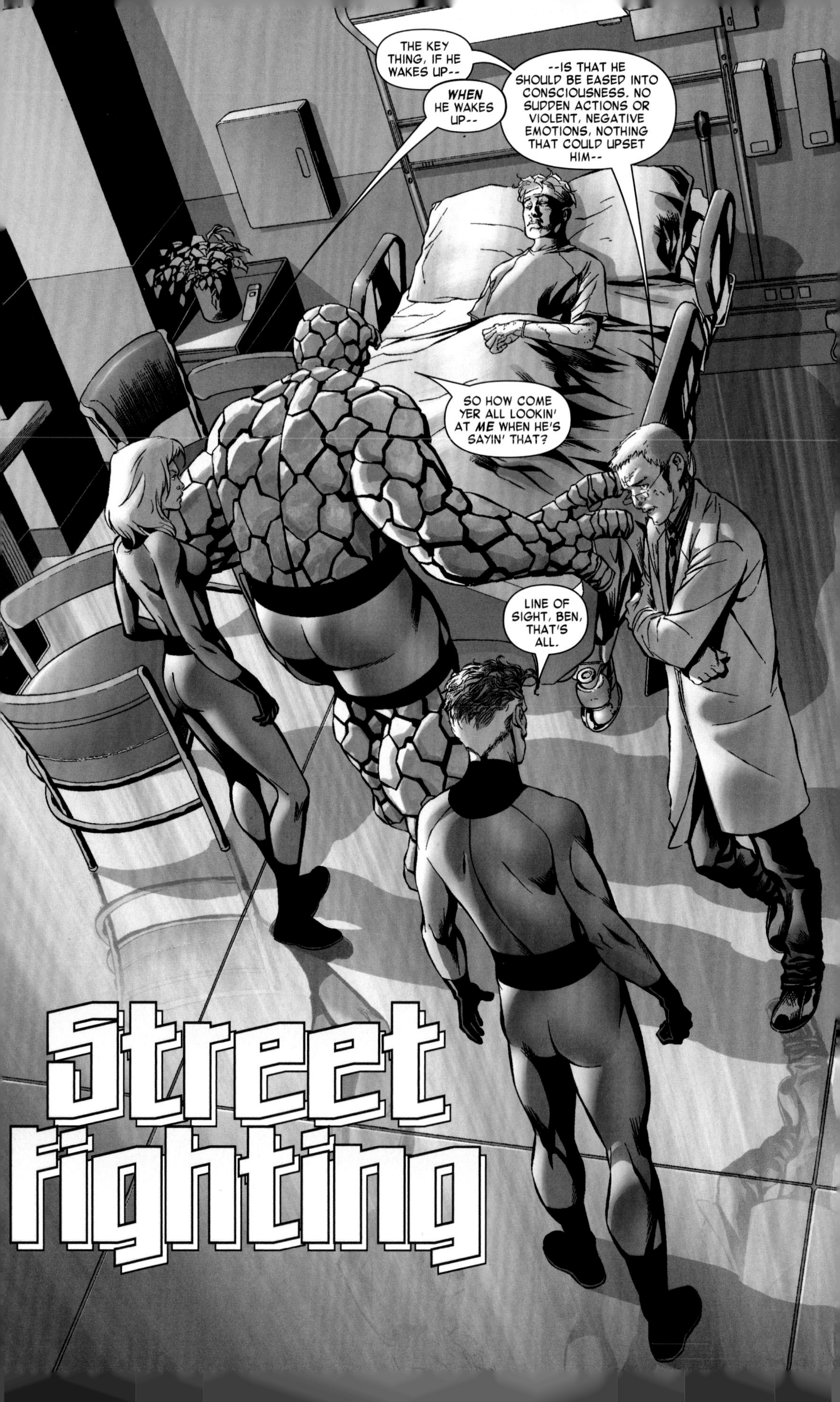
THE KEY THING, IF HE WAKES UP--
WHEN HE WAKES UP--
--IS THAT HE SHOULD BE EASED INTO CONSCIOUSNESS. NO SUDDEN ACTIONS OR VIOLENT, NEGATIVE EMOTIONS, NOTHING THAT COULD UPSET HIM--
SO HOW COME YER ALL LOOKIN' AT ME WHEN HE'S SAYIN' THAT?
LINE OF SIGHT, BEN, THAT'S ALL.
Street fighting

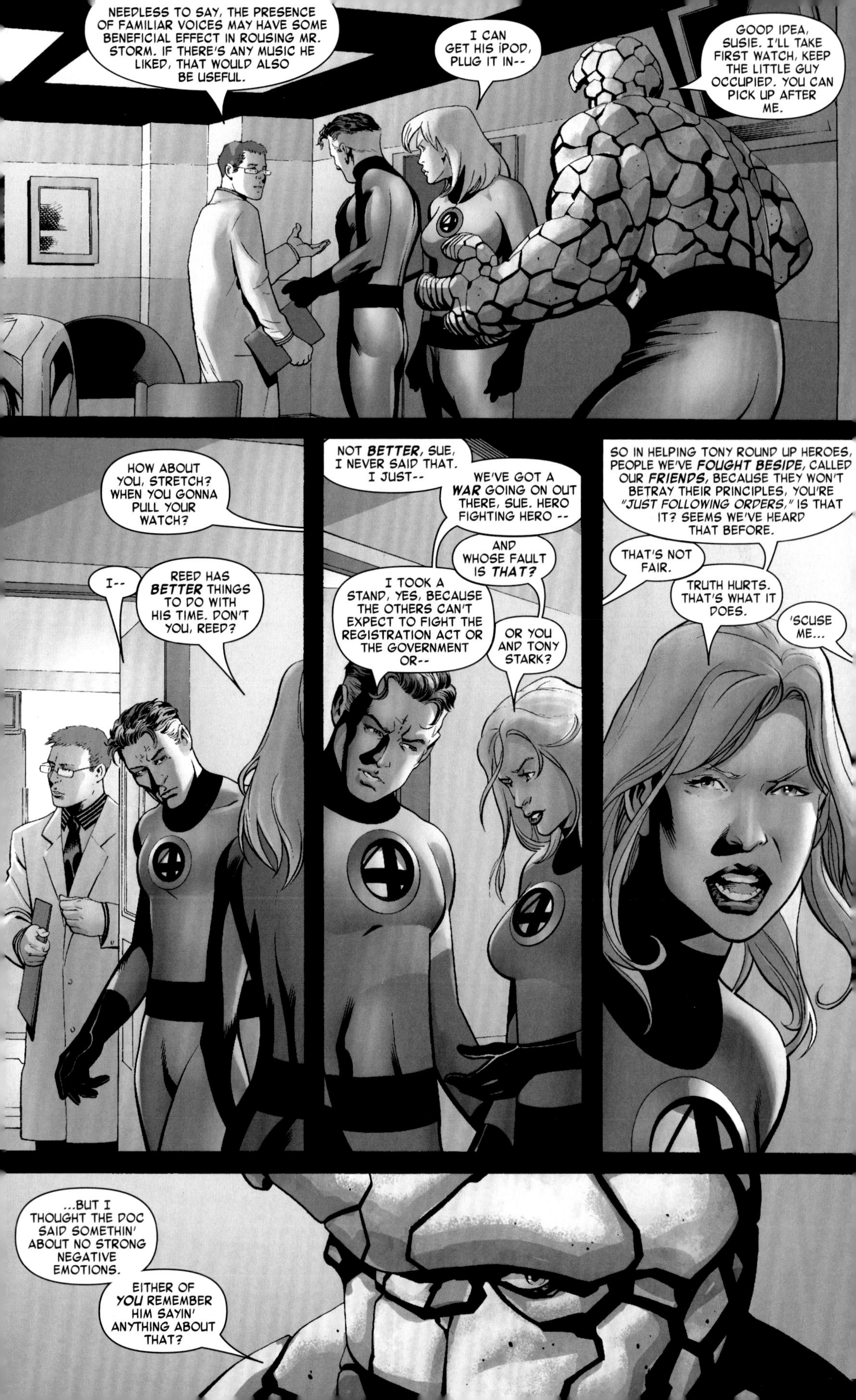
NEEDLESS TO SAY, THE PRESENCE OF FAMILIAR VOICES MAY HAVE SOME BENEFICIAL EFFECT IN ROUSING MR. STORM. IF THERE'S ANY MUSIC HE LIKED, THAT WOULD ALSO BE USEFUL.
I CAN GET HIS iPOD, PLUG IT IN--
GOOD IDEA, SUSIE. I'LL TAKE FIRST WATCH, KEEP THE LITTLE GUY OCCUPIED. YOU CAN PICK UP AFTER ME.
HOW ABOUT YOU, STRETCH? WHEN YOU GONNA PULL YOUR WATCH?
I--
REED HAS BETTER THINGS TO DO WITH HIS TIME. DON'T YOU, REED?
NOT BETTER, SUE, I NEVER SAID THAT. I JUST--
WE'VE GOT A WAR GOING ON OUT THERE, SUE. HERO FIGHTING HERO --
AND WHOSE FAULT IS THAT?
I TOOK A STAND, YES, BECAUSE THE OTHERS CAN'T EXPECT TO FIGHT THE REGISTRATION ACT OR THE GOVERNMENT OR--
OR YOU AND TONY STARK?
SO IN HELPING TONY ROUND UP HEROES, PEOPLE WE'VE FOUGHT BESIDE, CALLED OUR FRIENDS, BECAUSE THEY WON'T BETRAY THEIR PRINCIPLES, YOU'RE "JUST FOLLOWING ORDERS," IS THAT IT? SEEMS WE'VE HEARD THAT BEFORE.
THAT'S NOT FAIR.
TRUTH HURTS. THAT'S WHAT IT DOES.
'SCUSE ME...
...BUT I THOUGHT THE DOC SAID SOMETHIN' ABOUT NO STRONG NEGATIVE EMOTIONS.
EITHER OF YOU REMEMBER HIM SAYIN' ANYTHING ABOUT THAT?

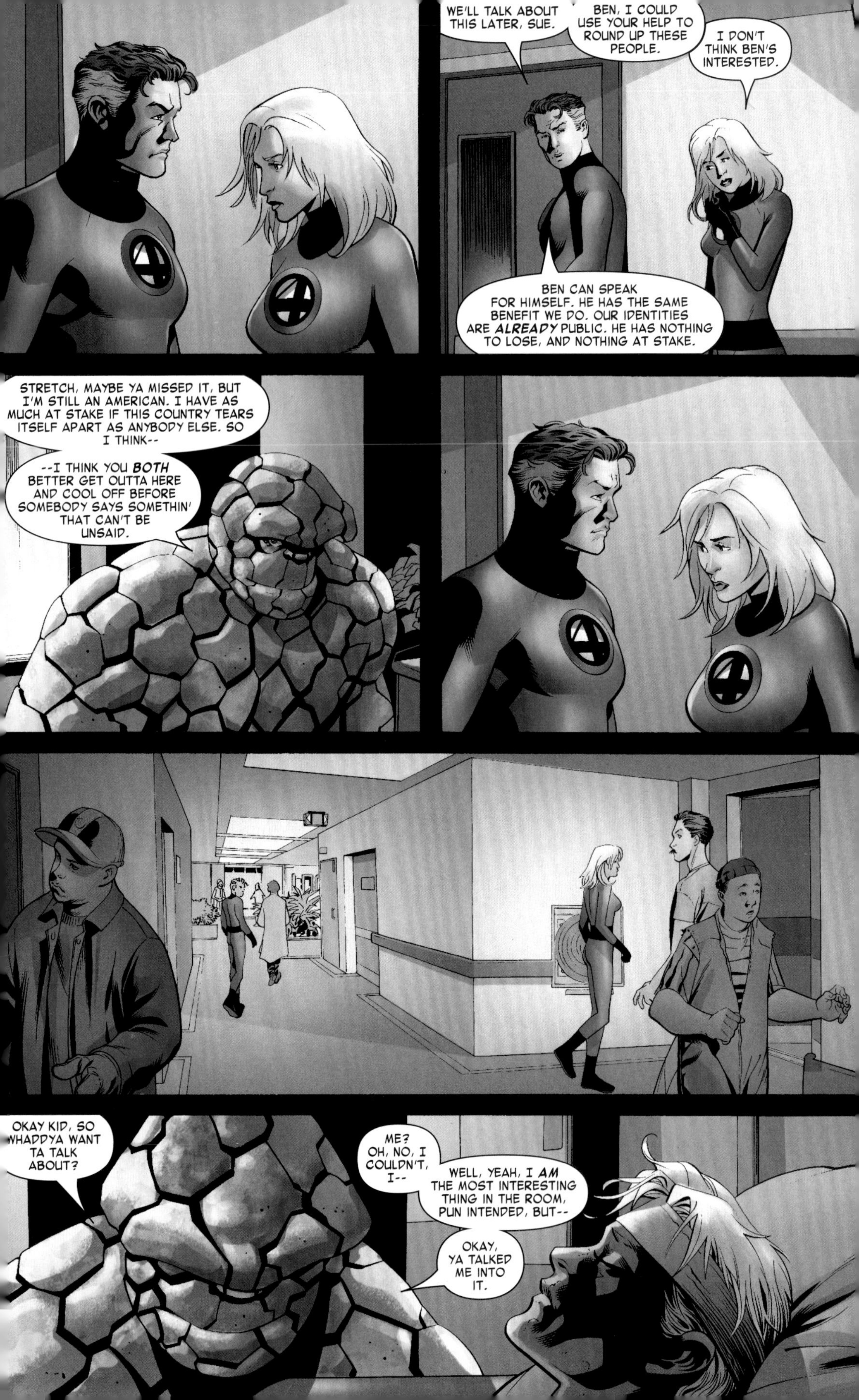
WE'LL TALK ABOUT THIS LATER, SUE.
BEN, I COULD USE YOUR HELP TO ROUND UP THESE PEOPLE.
I DON'T THINK BEN'S INTERESTED.
BEN CAN SPEAK FOR HIMSELF. HE HAS THE SAME BENEFIT WE DO. OUR IDENTITIES ARE ALREADY PUBLIC. HE HAS NOTHING TO LOSE, AND NOTHING AT STAKE.
STRETCH, MAYBE YA MISSED IT, BUT I'M STILL AN AMERICAN. I HAVE AS MUCH AT STAKE IF THIS COUNTRY TEARS ITSELF APART AS ANYBODY ELSE. SO I THINK--
--I THINK YOU BOTH BETTER GET OUTTA HERE AND COOL OFF BEFORE SOMEBODY SAYS SOMETHIN' THAT CAN'T BE UNSAID.
OKAY KID, SO WHADDYA WANT TA TALK ABOUT?
ME? OH, NO, I COULDN'T, I--
WELL, YEAH, I AM THE MOST INTERESTING THING IN THE ROOM, PUN INTENDED, BUT--
OKAY, YA TALKED ME INTO IT.

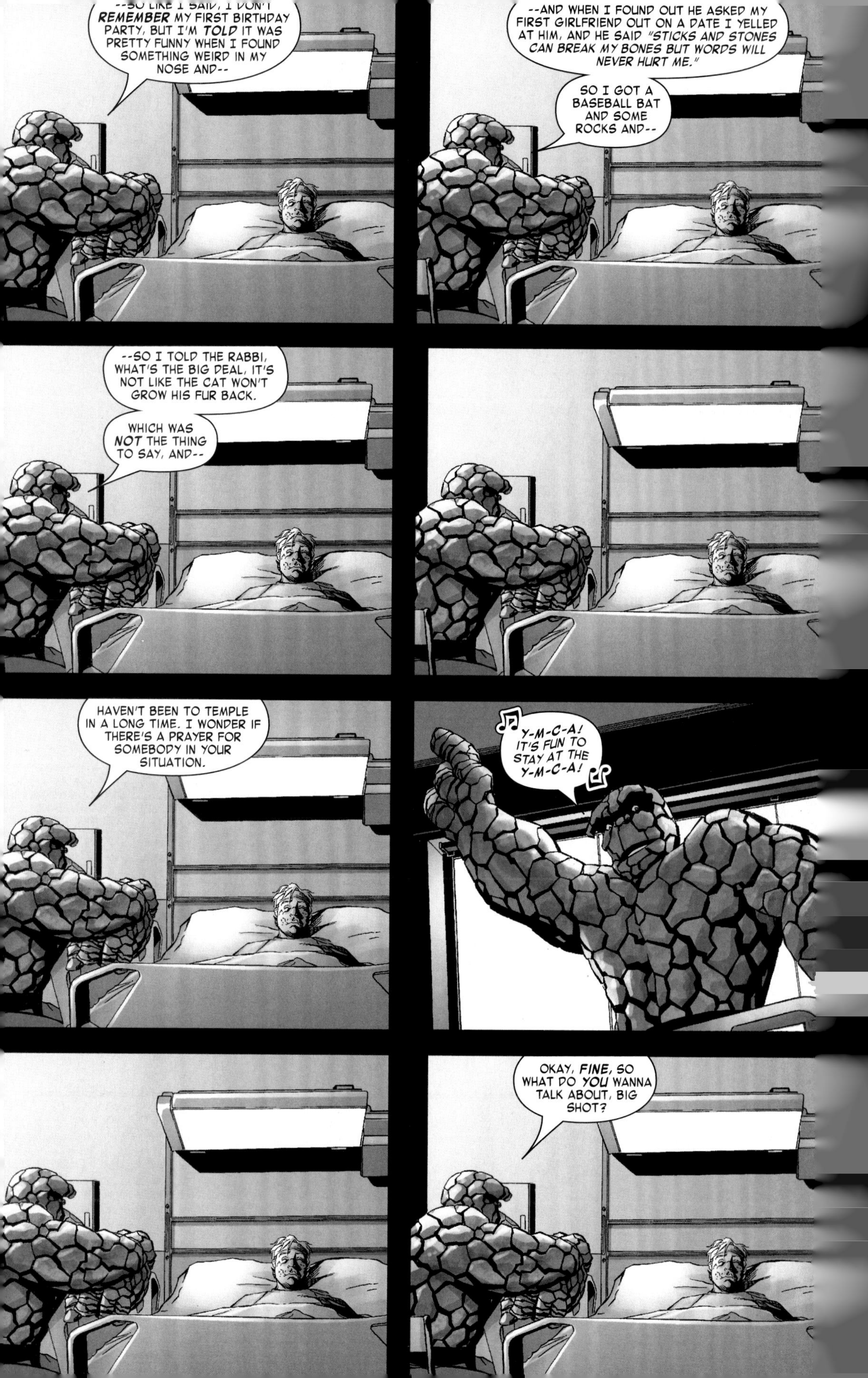
--SO LIKE I SAID, I DON'T REMEMBER MY FIRST BIRTHDAY PARTY, BUT I'M TOLD IT WAS PRETTY FUNNY WHEN I FOUND SOMETHING WEIRD IN MY NOSE AND--
--AND WHEN I FOUND OUT HE ASKED MY FIRST GIRLFRIEND OUT ON A DATE I YELLED AT HIM, AND HE SAID "STICKS AND STONES CAN BREAK MY BONES BUT WORDS WILL NEVER HURT ME."
SO I GOT A BASEBALL BAT AND SOME ROCKS AND--
--SO I TOLD THE RABBI, WHAT'S THE BIG DEAL, IT'S NOT LIKE THE CAT WON'T GROW HIS FUR BACK.
WHICH WAS NOT THE THING TO SAY, AND--
HAVEN'T BEEN TO TEMPLE IN A LONG TIME. I WONDER IF THERE'S A PRAYER FOR SOMEBODY IN YOUR SITUATION.
Y-M-C-A! IT'S FUN TO STAY AT THE Y-M-C-A!
OKAY, FINE, SO WHAT DO YOU WANNA TALK ABOUT, BIG SHOT?

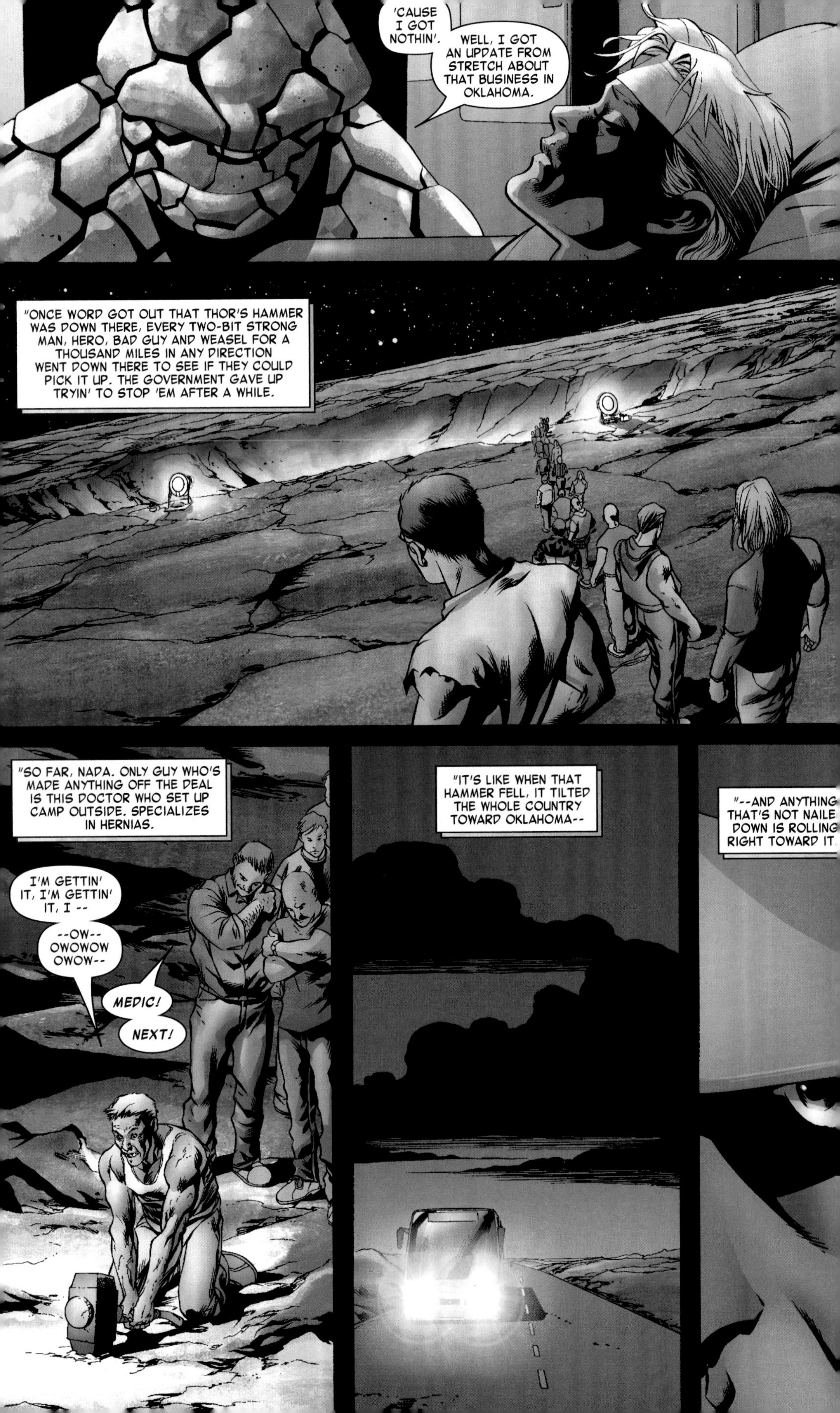
'CAUSE I GOT NOTHIN'.
WELL, I GOT AN UPDATE FROM STRETCH ABOUT THAT BUSINESS IN OKLAHOMA.
"ONCE WORD GOT OUT THAT THOR'S HAMMER WAS DOWN THERE, EVERY TWO-BIT STRONG MAN, HERO, BAD GUY AND WEASEL FOR A THOUSAND MILES IN ANY DIRECTION WENT DOWN THERE TO SEE IF THEY COULD PICK IT UP. THE GOVERNMENT GAVE UP TRYIN' TO STOP 'EM AFTER A WHILE.
"SO FAR, NADA. ONLY GUY WHO'S MADE ANYTHING OFF THE DEAL IS THIS DOCTOR WHO SET UP CAMP OUTSIDE. SPECIALIZES IN HERNIAS.
I'M GETTIN' IT, I'M GETTIN' IT, I --
--OW-- OWOWOW OWOW--
MEDIC!
NEXT!
"IT'S LIKE WHEN THAT HAMMER FELL, IT TILTED THE WHOLE COUNTRY TOWARD OKLAHOMA--
"--AND ANYTHING THAT'S NOT NAILE DOWN IS ROLLING RIGHT TOWARD IT.

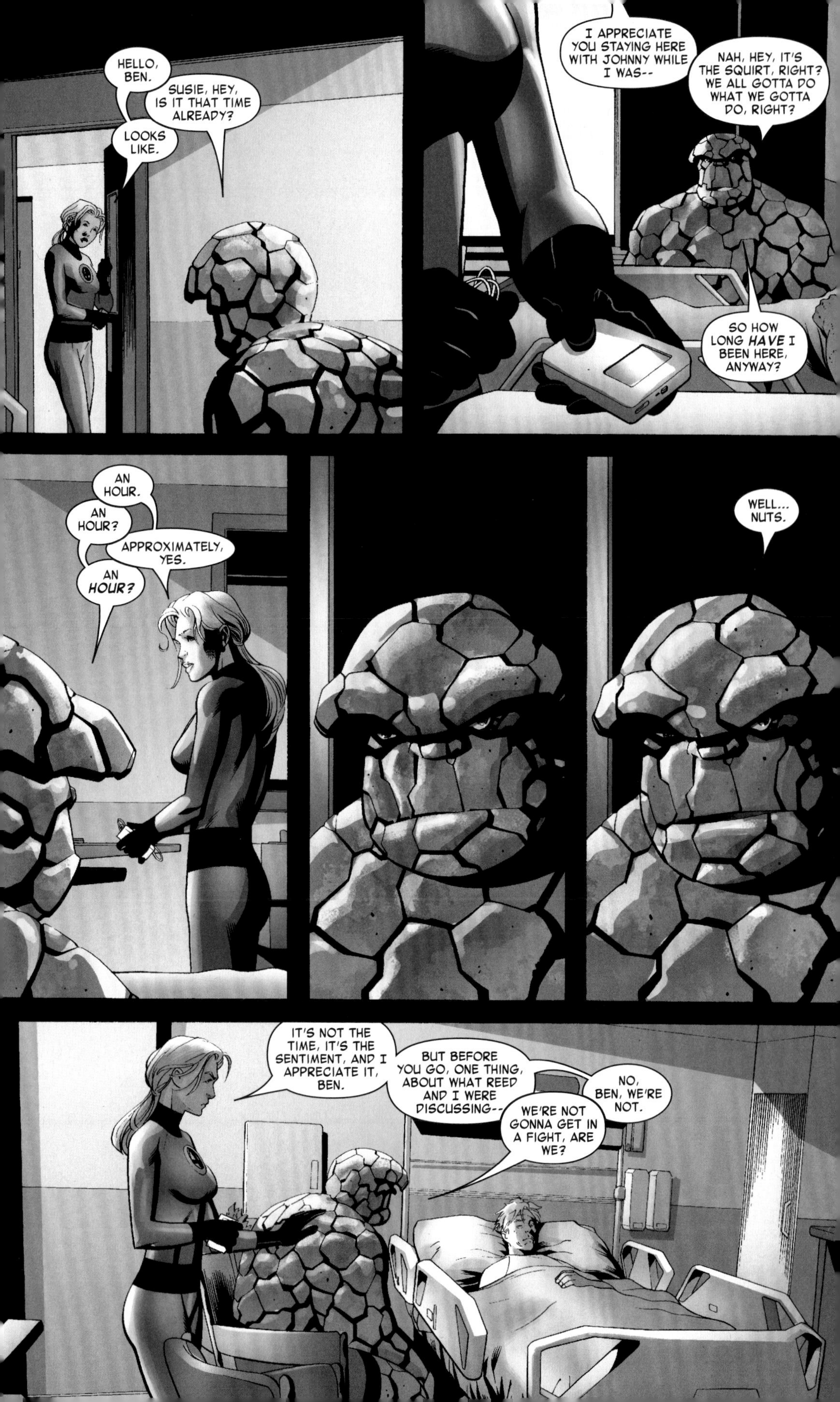
HELLO, BEN.
SUSIE, HEY, IS IT THAT TIME ALREADY?
LOOKS LIKE.
I APPRECIATE YOU STAYING HERE WITH JOHNNY WHILE I WAS--
NAH, HEY, IT'S THE SQUIRT, RIGHT? WE ALL GOTTA DO WHAT WE GOTTA DO, RIGHT?
SO HOW LONG HAVE I BEEN HERE, ANYWAY?
AN HOUR.
AN HOUR?
APPROXIMATELY, YES.
AN HOUR?
WELL... NUTS.
IT'S NOT THE TIME, IT'S THE SENTIMENT, AND I APPRECIATE IT, BEN.
BUT BEFORE YOU GO, ONE THING, ABOUT WHAT REED AND I WERE DISCUSSING--
WE'RE NOT GONNA GET IN A FIGHT, ARE WE?
NO, BEN, WE'RE NOT.

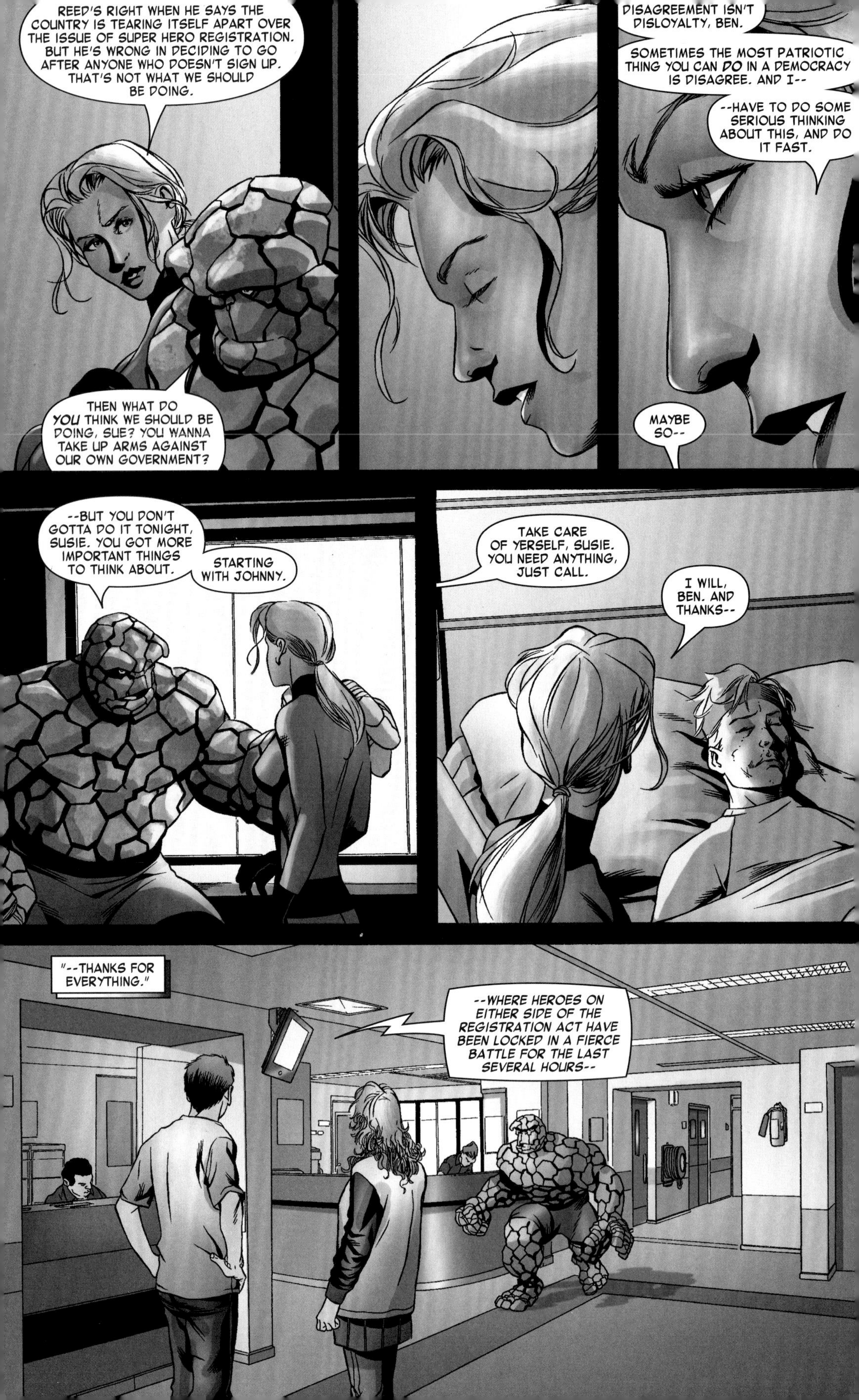
REED'S RIGHT WHEN HE SAYS THE COUNTRY IS TEARING ITSELF APART OVER THE ISSUE OF SUPER HERO REGISTRATION. BUT HE'S WRONG IN DECIDING TO GO AFTER ANYONE WHO DOESN'T SIGN UP. THAT'S NOT WHAT WE SHOULD BE DOING.
THEN WHAT DO YOU THINK WE SHOULD BE DOING, SUE? YOU WANNA TAKE UP ARMS AGAINST OUR OWN GOVERNMENT?
DISAGREEMENT ISN'T DISLOYALTY, BEN.
SOMETIMES THE MOST PATRIOTIC THING YOU CAN DO IN A DEMOCRACY IS DISAGREE. AND I--
--HAVE TO DO SOME SERIOUS THINKING ABOUT THIS, AND DO IT FAST.
MAYBE SO--
--BUT YOU DON'T GOTTA DO IT TONIGHT, SUSIE. YOU GOT MORE IMPORTANT THINGS TO THINK ABOUT.
STARTING WITH JOHNNY.
TAKE CARE OF YERSELF, SUSIE. YOU NEED ANYTHING, JUST CALL.
I WILL, BEN. AND THANKS--
"--THANKS FOR EVERYTHING."
--WHERE HEROES ON EITHER SIDE OF THE REGISTRATION ACT HAVE BEEN LOCKED IN A FIERCE BATTLE FOR THE LAST SEVERAL HOURS--

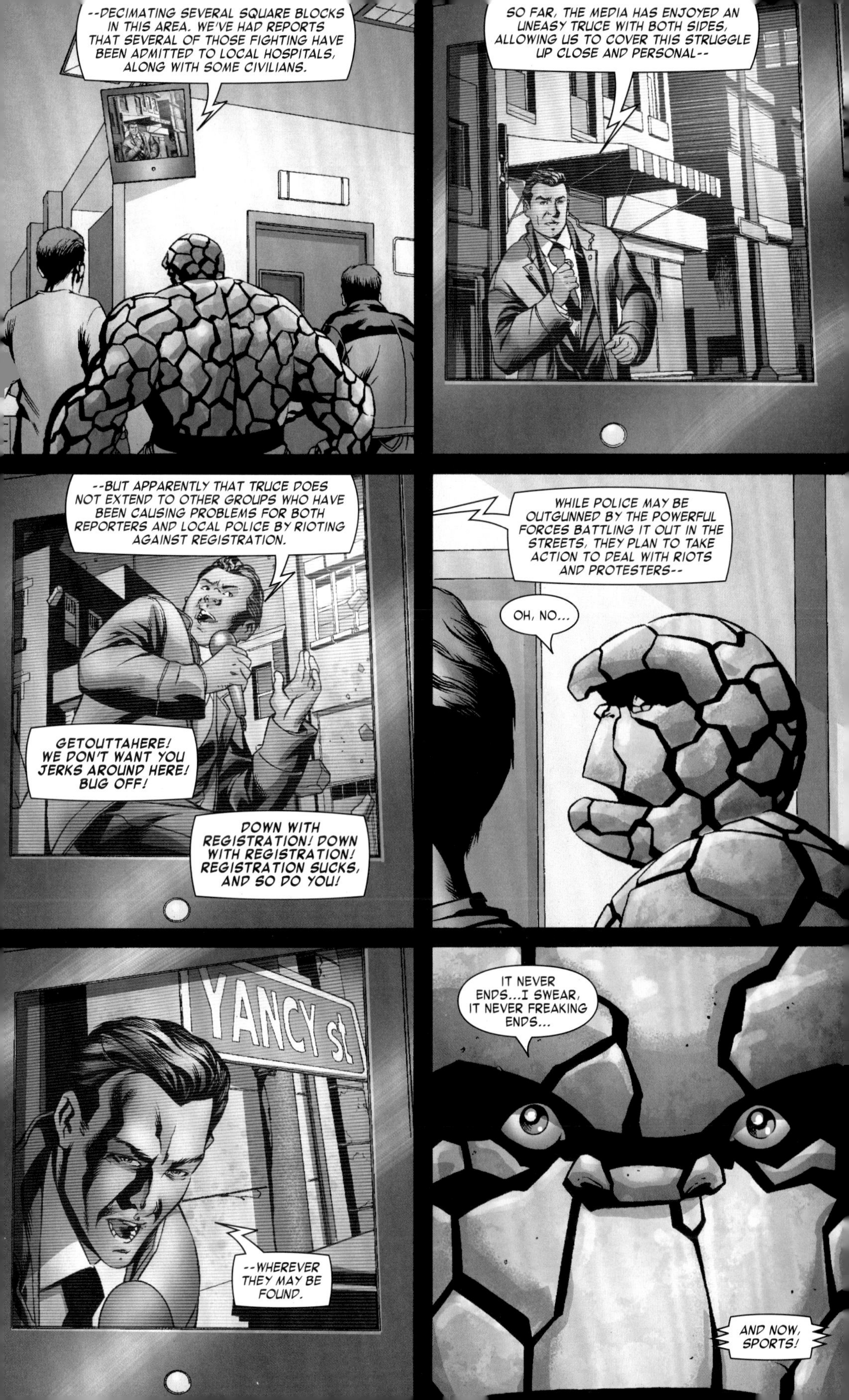
--DECIMATING SEVERAL SQUARE BLOCKS IN THIS AREA. WE'VE HAD REPORTS THAT SEVERAL OF THOSE FIGHTING HAVE BEEN ADMITTED TO LOCAL HOSPITALS, ALONG WITH SOME CIVILIANS.
SO FAR, THE MEDIA HAS ENJOYED AN UNEASY TRUCE WITH BOTH SIDES, ALLOWING US TO COVER THIS STRUGGLE UP CLOSE AND PERSONAL--
--BUT APPARENTLY THAT TRUCE DOES NOT EXTEND TO OTHER GROUPS WHO HAVE BEEN CAUSING PROBLEMS FOR BOTH REPORTERS AND LOCAL POLICE BY RIOTING AGAINST REGISTRATION.
GETOUTTAHERE! WE DON'T WANT YOU JERKS AROUND HERE! BUG OFF!
DOWN WITH REGISTRATION! DOWN WITH REGISTRATION! REGISTRATION SUCKS, AND SO DO YOU!
WHILE POLICE MAY BE OUTGUNNED BY THE POWERFUL FORCES BATTLING IT OUT IN THE STREETS, THEY PLAN TO TAKE ACTION TO DEAL WITH RIOTS AND PROTESTERS--
OH, NO...
YANCY st
--WHEREVER THEY MAY BE FOUND.
IT NEVER ENDS...I SWEAR, IT NEVER FREAKING ENDS...
AND NOW, SPORTS!

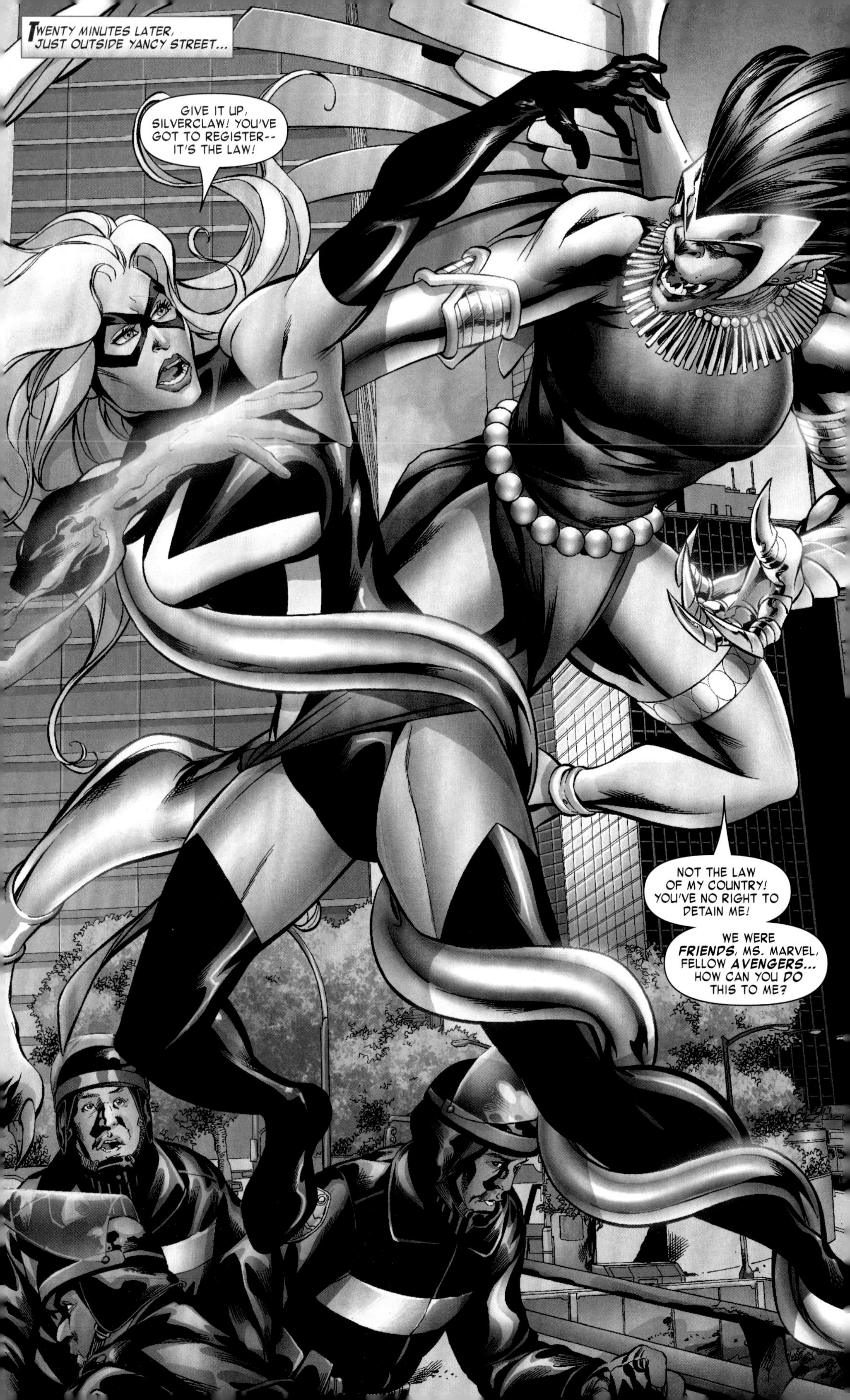
TWENTY MINUTES LATER, JUST OUTSIDE YANCY STREET...
GIVE IT UP, SILVERCLAW! YOU'VE GOT TO REGISTER-- IT'S THE LAW!
NOT THE LAW OF MY COUNTRY! YOU'VE NO RIGHT TO DETAIN ME!
WE WERE FRIENDS, MS. MARVEL, FELLOW AVENGERS... HOW CAN YOU DO THIS TO ME?

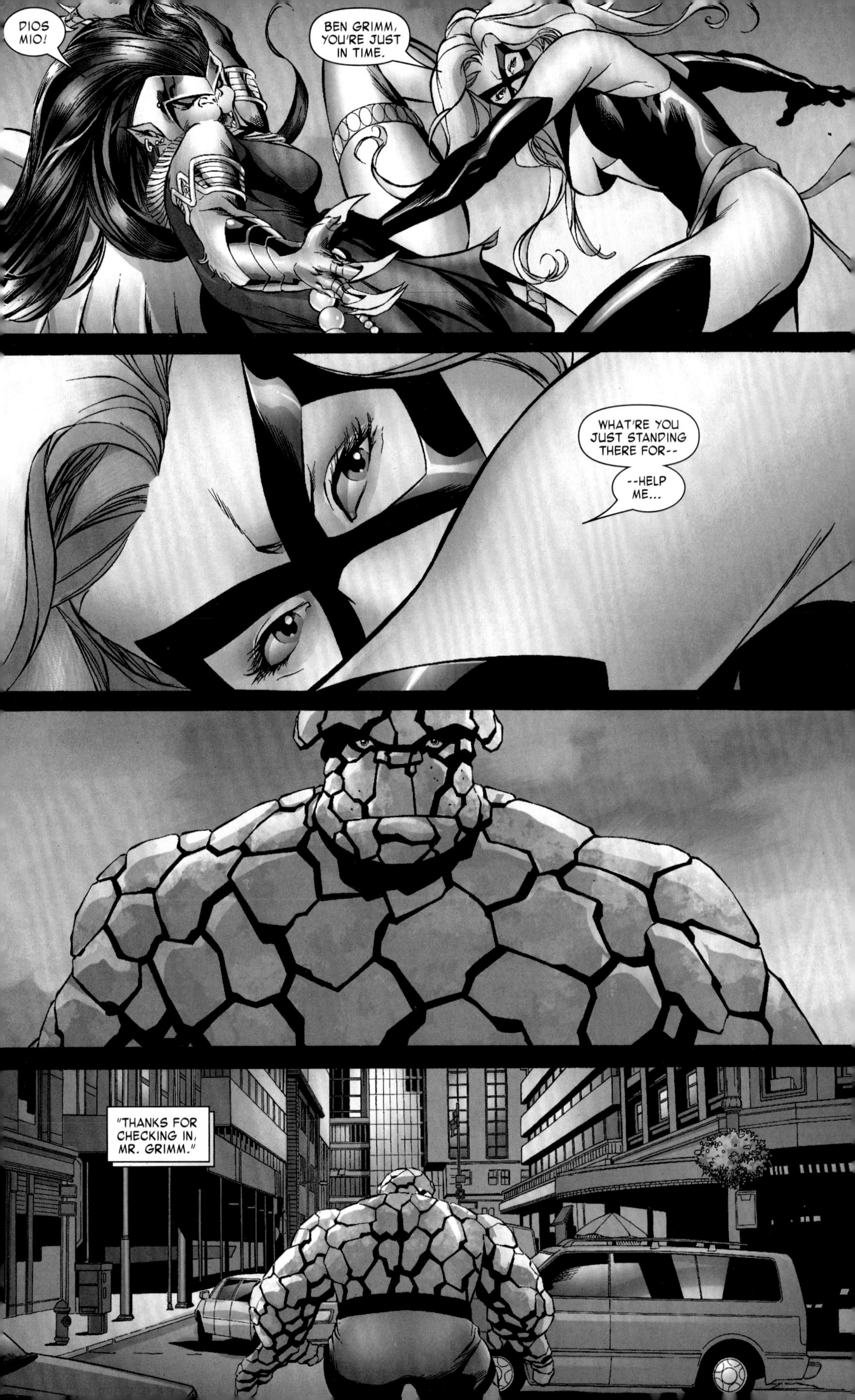
DIOS MIO!
BEN GRIMM, YOU'RE JUST IN TIME.
WHAT'RE YOU JUST STANDING THERE FOR--
--HELP ME...
"THANKS FOR CHECKING IN, MR. GRIMM."

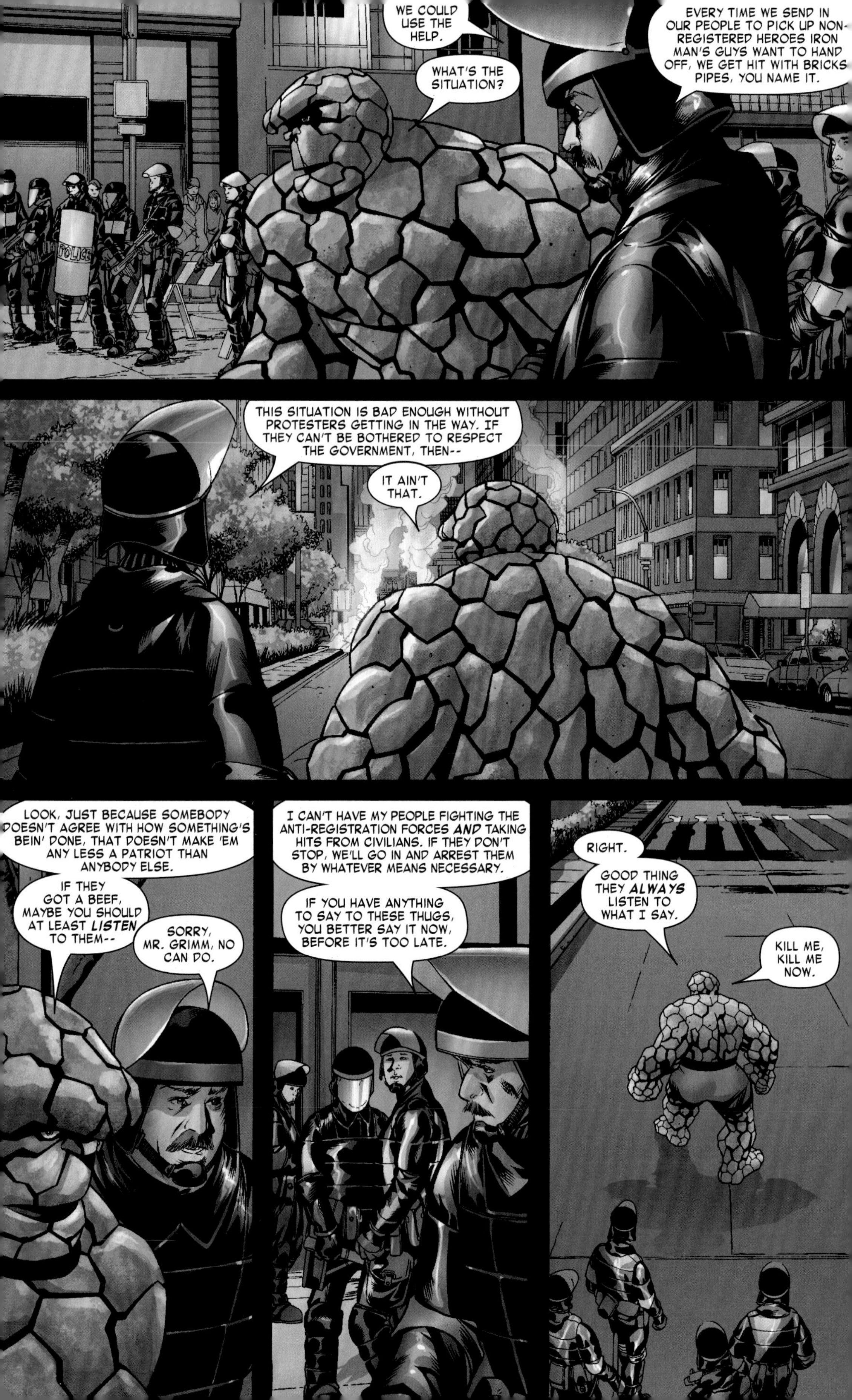
WE COULD USE THE HELP.
WHAT'S THE SITUATION?
EVERY TIME WE SEND IN OUR PEOPLE TO PICK UP NON-REGISTERED HEROES IRON MAN'S GUYS WANT TO HAND OFF, WE GET HIT WITH BRICKS PIPES, YOU NAME IT.
POLICE
THIS SITUATION IS BAD ENOUGH WITHOUT PROTESTERS GETTING IN THE WAY. IF THEY CAN'T BE BOTHERED TO RESPECT THE GOVERNMENT, THEN--
IT AIN'T THAT.
LOOK, JUST BECAUSE SOMEBODY DOESN'T AGREE WITH HOW SOMETHING'S BEIN' DONE, THAT DOESN'T MAKE 'EM ANY LESS A PATRIOT THAN ANYBODY ELSE.
IF THEY GOT A BEEF, MAYBE YOU SHOULD AT LEAST *LISTEN* TO THEM--
SORRY, MR. GRIMM, NO CAN DO.
I CAN'T HAVE MY PEOPLE FIGHTING THE ANTI-REGISTRATION FORCES *AND* TAKING HITS FROM CIVILIANS. IF THEY DON'T STOP, WE'LL GO IN AND ARREST THEM BY WHATEVER MEANS NECESSARY.
IF YOU HAVE ANYTHING TO SAY TO THESE THUGS, YOU BETTER SAY IT NOW, BEFORE IT'S TOO LATE.
RIGHT.
GOOD THING THEY *ALWAYS* LISTEN TO WHAT I SAY.
KILL ME, KILL ME NOW.

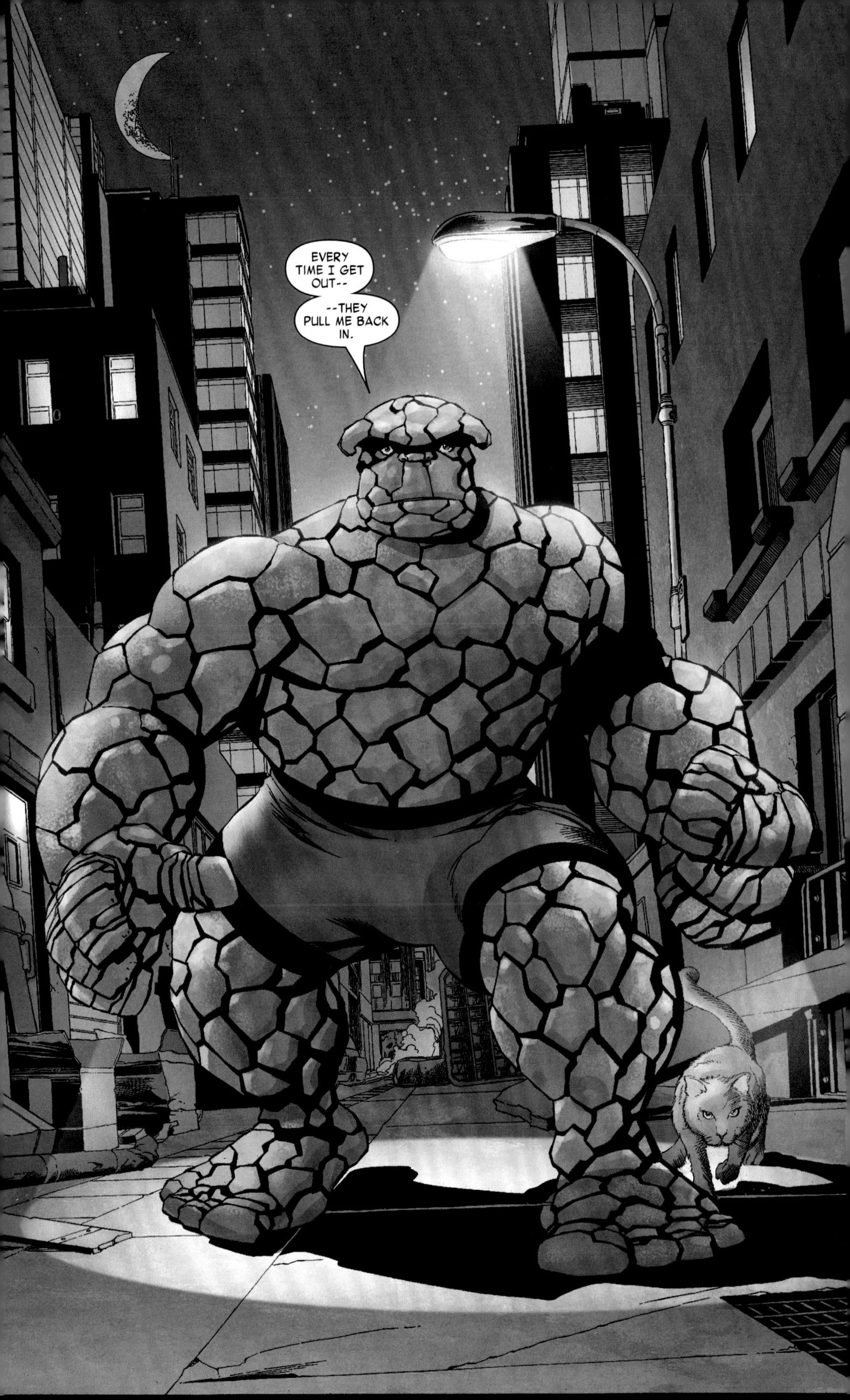
EVERY TIME I GET OUT--
--THEY PULL ME BACK IN.

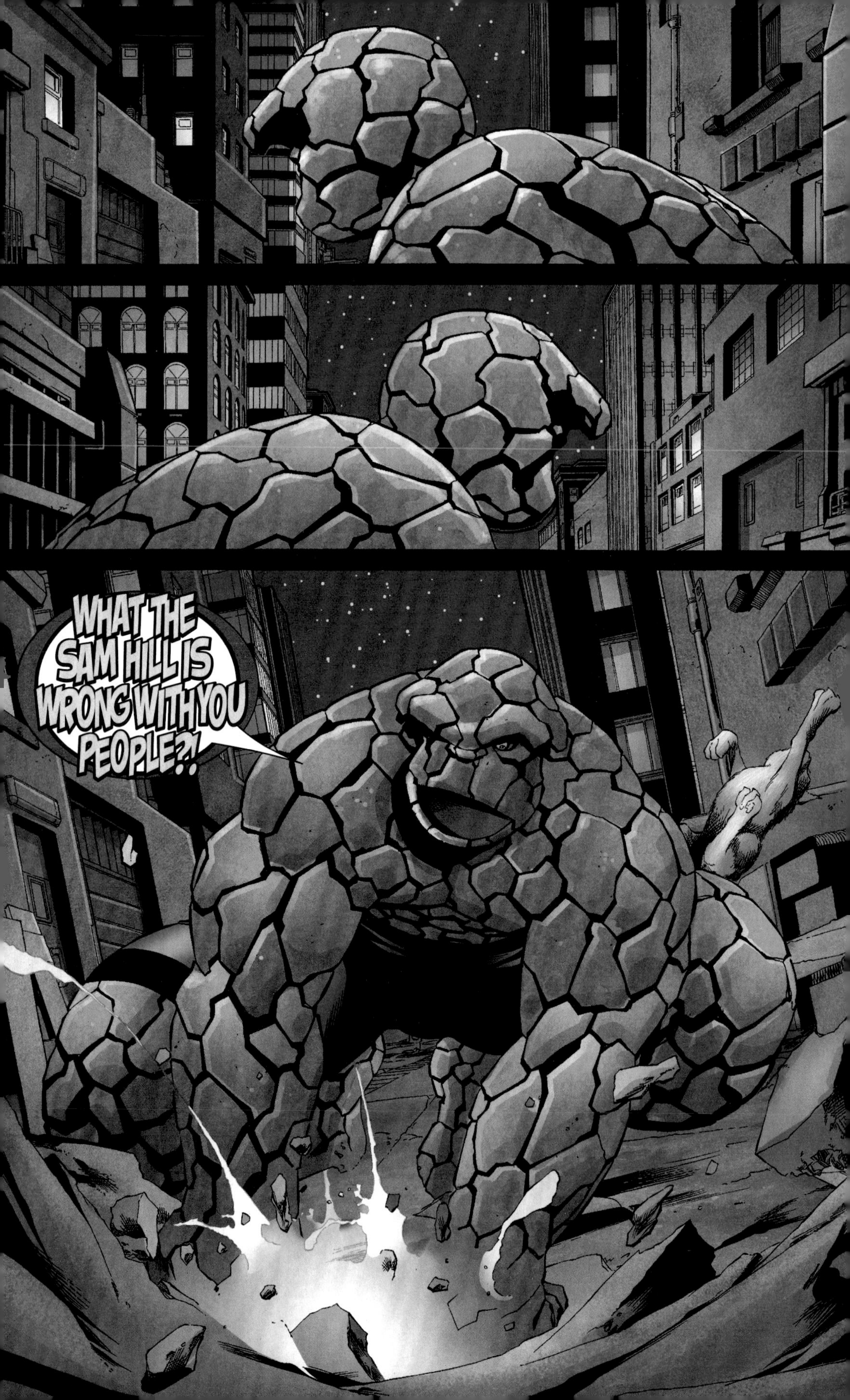
WHAT THE SAM HILL IS WRONG WITH YOU PEOPLE?!

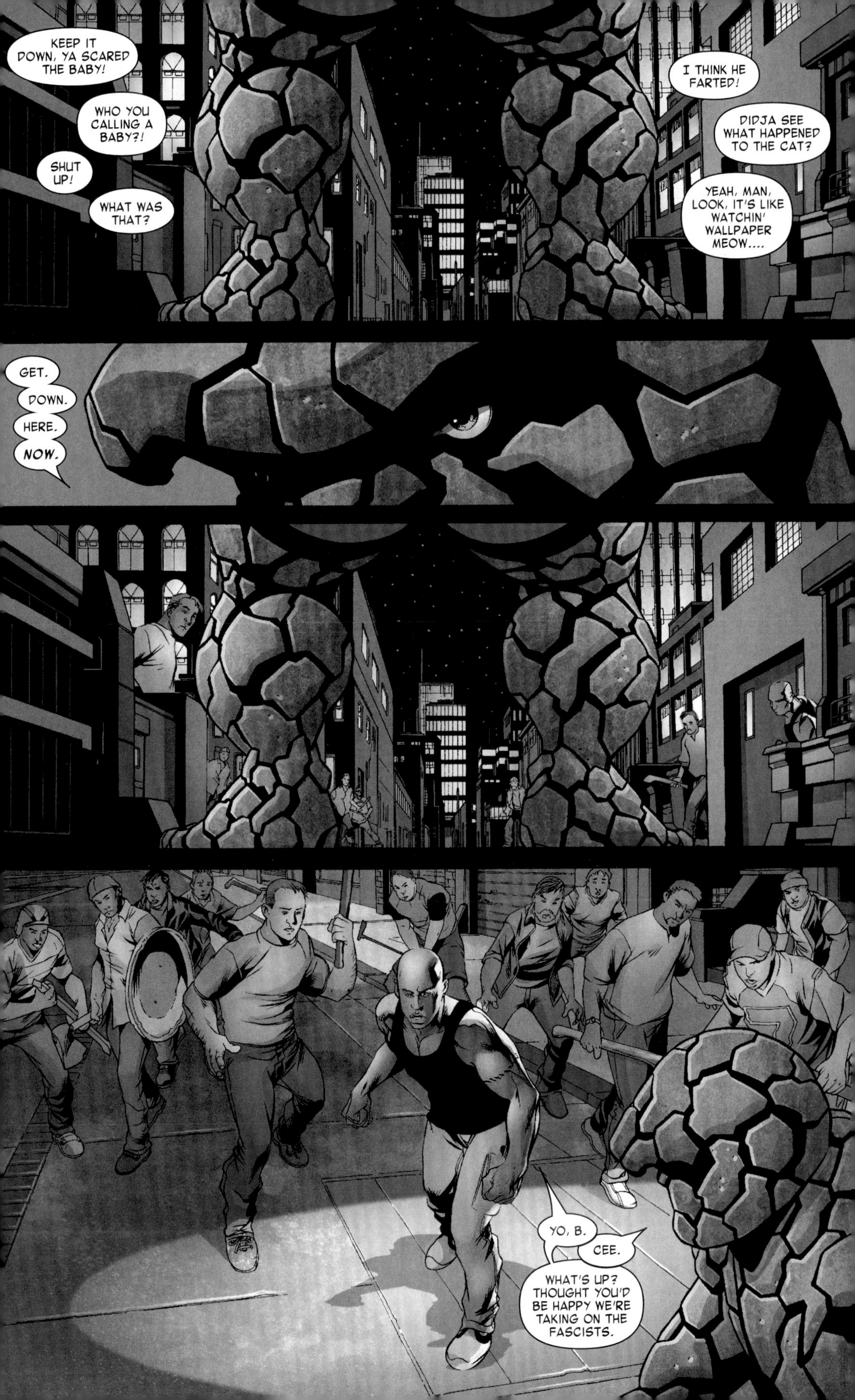
KEEP IT DOWN, YA SCARED THE BABY!
WHO YOU CALLING A BABY?!
SHUT UP!
WHAT WAS THAT?
I THINK HE FARTED!
DIDJA SEE WHAT HAPPENED TO THE CAT?
YEAH, MAN, LOOK, IT'S LIKE WATCHIN' WALLPAPER MEOW....
GET.
DOWN.
HERE.
NOW.
YO, B.
CEE.
WHAT'S UP? THOUGHT YOU'D BE HAPPY WE'RE TAKING ON THE FASCISTS.

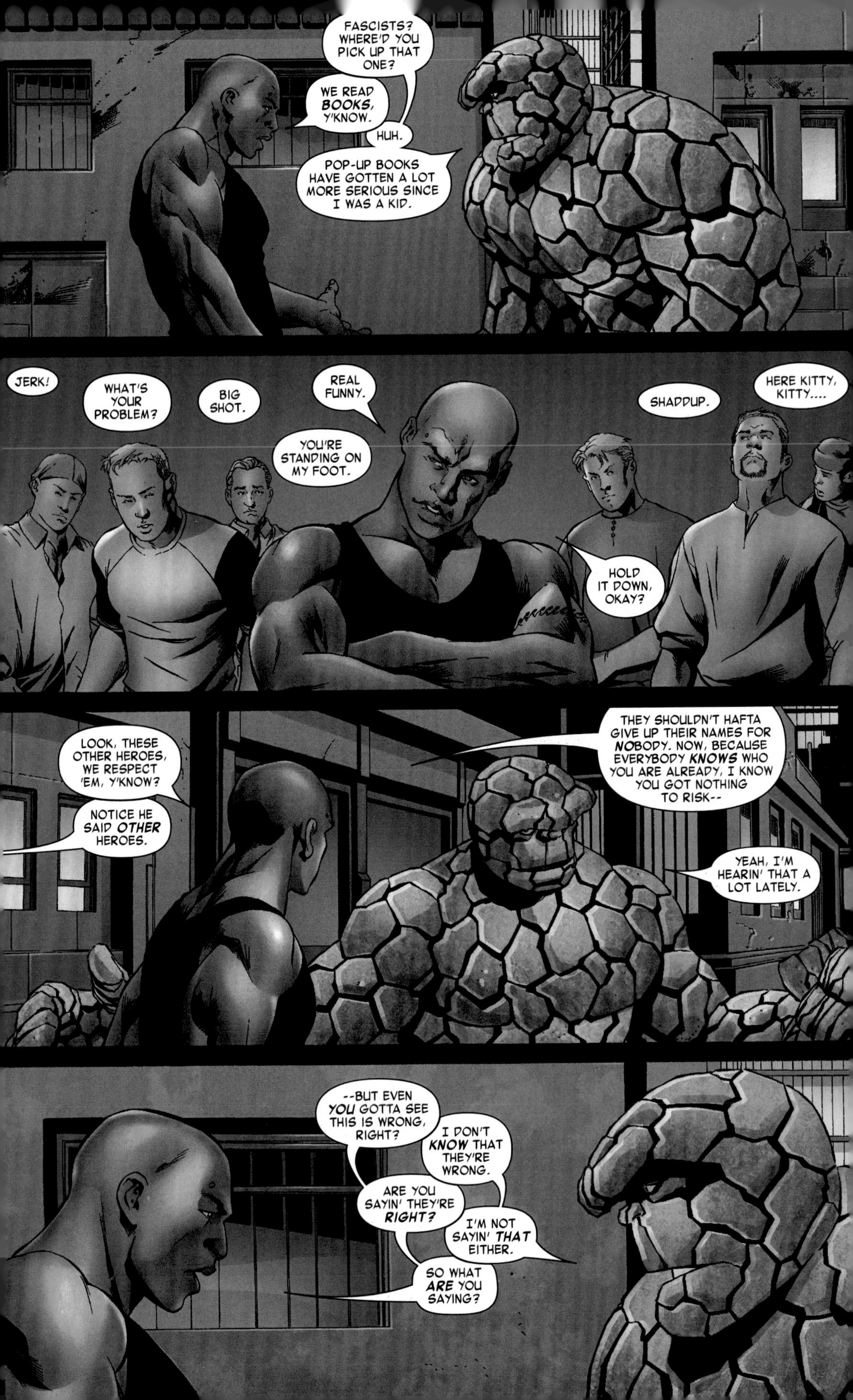
FASCISTS? WHERE'D YOU PICK UP THAT ONE?
WE READ BOOKS, Y'KNOW.
HUH.
POP-UP BOOKS HAVE GOTTEN A LOT MORE SERIOUS SINCE I WAS A KID.
JERK!
WHAT'S YOUR PROBLEM?
BIG SHOT.
REAL FUNNY.
YOU'RE STANDING ON MY FOOT.
SHADDUP.
HERE KITTY, KITTY....
HOLD IT DOWN, OKAY?
LOOK, THESE OTHER HEROES, WE RESPECT 'EM, Y'KNOW?
NOTICE HE SAID OTHER HEROES.
THEY SHOULDN'T HAFTA GIVE UP THEIR NAMES FOR NOBODY. NOW, BECAUSE EVERYBODY KNOWS WHO YOU ARE ALREADY, I KNOW YOU GOT NOTHING TO RISK--
YEAH, I'M HEARIN' THAT A LOT LATELY.
--BUT EVEN YOU GOTTA SEE THIS IS WRONG, RIGHT?
I DON'T KNOW THAT THEY'RE WRONG.
ARE YOU SAYIN' THEY'RE RIGHT?
I'M NOT SAYIN' THAT EITHER.
SO WHAT ARE YOU SAYING?

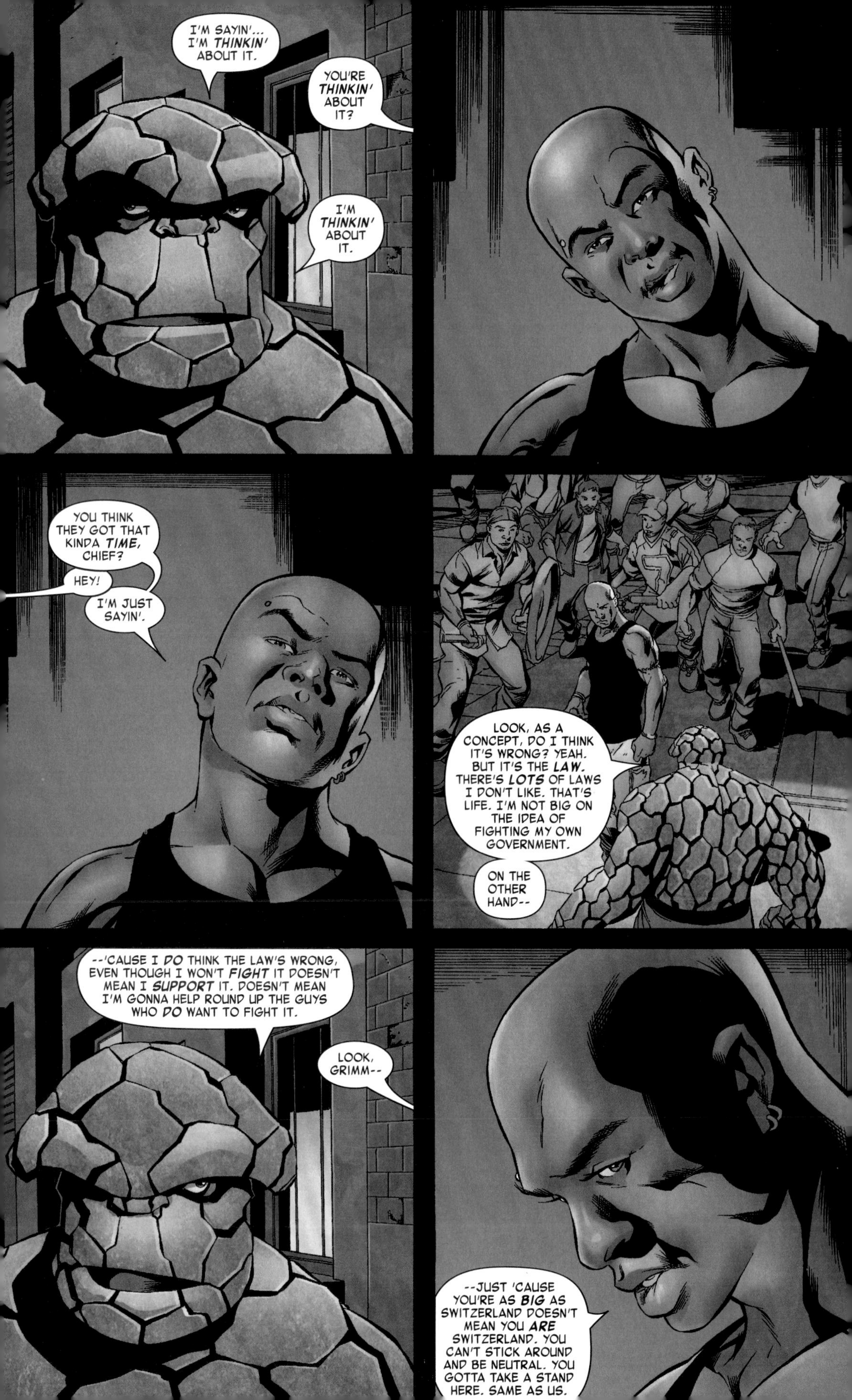
I'M SAYIN'... I'M THINKIN' ABOUT IT.
YOU'RE THINKIN' ABOUT IT?
I'M THINKIN' ABOUT IT.
YOU THINK THEY GOT THAT KINDA TIME, CHIEF?
HEY!
I'M JUST SAYIN'.
LOOK, AS A CONCEPT, DO I THINK IT'S WRONG? YEAH. BUT IT'S THE LAW. THERE'S LOTS OF LAWS I DON'T LIKE. THAT'S LIFE. I'M NOT BIG ON THE IDEA OF FIGHTING MY OWN GOVERNMENT.
ON THE OTHER HAND--
--'CAUSE I DO THINK THE LAW'S WRONG, EVEN THOUGH I WON'T FIGHT IT DOESN'T MEAN I SUPPORT IT. DOESN'T MEAN I'M GONNA HELP ROUND UP THE GUYS WHO DO WANT TO FIGHT IT.
LOOK, GRIMM--
--JUST 'CAUSE YOU'RE AS BIG AS SWITZERLAND DOESN'T MEAN YOU ARE SWITZERLAND. YOU CAN'T STICK AROUND AND BE NEUTRAL. YOU GOTTA TAKE A STAND HERE. SAME AS US.

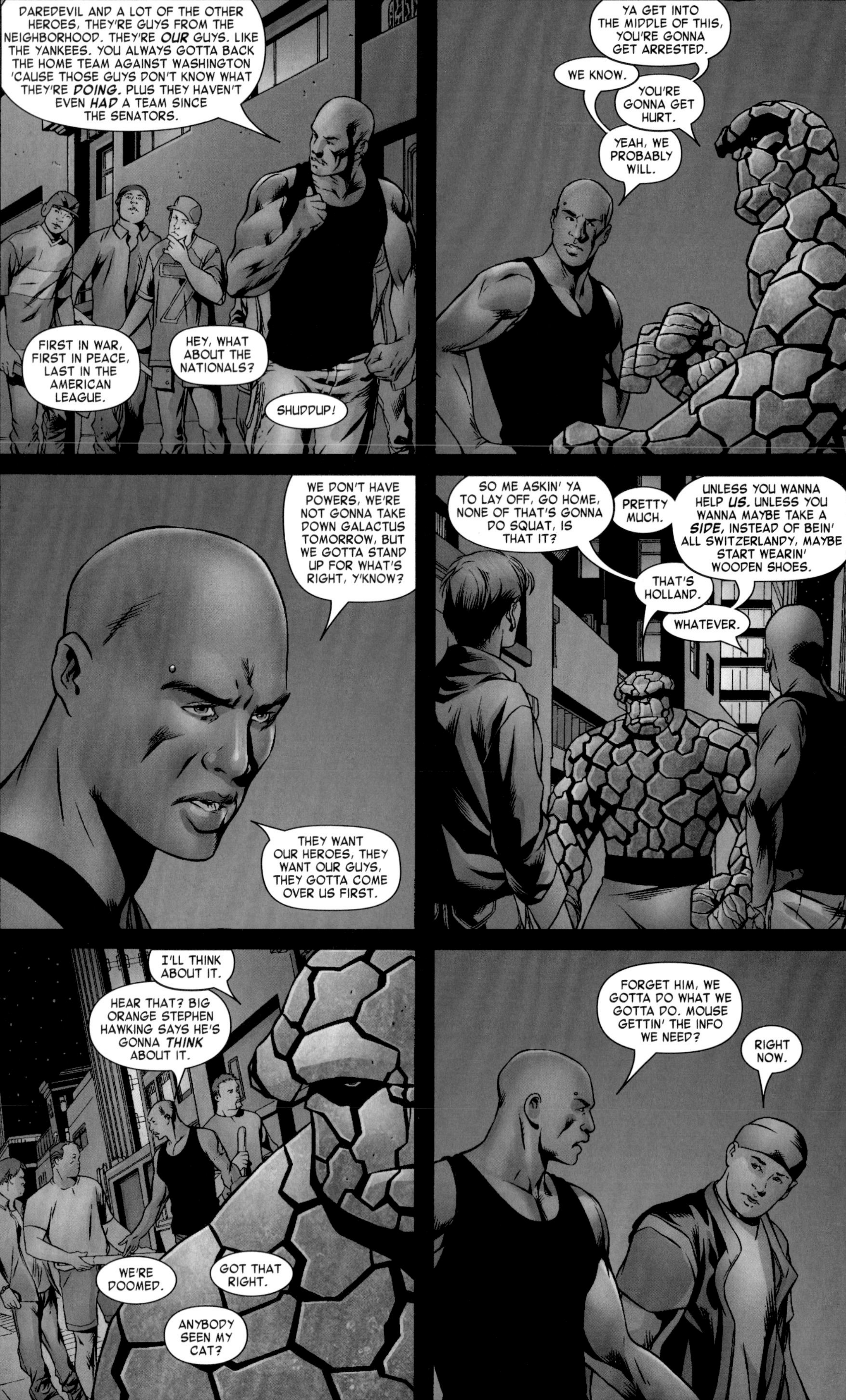
DAREDEVIL AND A LOT OF THE OTHER HEROES, THEY'RE GUYS FROM THE NEIGHBORHOOD. THEY'RE OUR GUYS. LIKE THE YANKEES. YOU ALWAYS GOTTA BACK THE HOME TEAM AGAINST WASHINGTON 'CAUSE THOSE GUYS DON'T KNOW WHAT THEY'RE DOING. PLUS THEY HAVEN'T EVEN HAD A TEAM SINCE THE SENATORS.
FIRST IN WAR, FIRST IN PEACE, LAST IN THE AMERICAN LEAGUE.
HEY, WHAT ABOUT THE NATIONALS?
SHUDDUP!
YA GET INTO THE MIDDLE OF THIS, YOU'RE GONNA GET ARRESTED.
WE KNOW.
YOU'RE GONNA GET HURT.
YEAH, WE PROBABLY WILL.
WE DON'T HAVE POWERS, WE'RE NOT GONNA TAKE DOWN GALACTUS TOMORROW, BUT WE GOTTA STAND UP FOR WHAT'S RIGHT, Y'KNOW?
THEY WANT OUR HEROES, THEY WANT OUR GUYS, THEY GOTTA COME OVER US FIRST.
SO ME ASKIN' YA TO LAY OFF, GO HOME, NONE OF THAT'S GONNA DO SQUAT, IS THAT IT?
PRETTY MUCH.
UNLESS YOU WANNA HELP US. UNLESS YOU WANNA MAYBE TAKE A SIDE, INSTEAD OF BEIN' ALL SWITZERLANDY, MAYBE START WEARIN' WOODEN SHOES.
THAT'S HOLLAND.
WHATEVER.
I'LL THINK ABOUT IT.
HEAR THAT? BIG ORANGE STEPHEN HAWKING SAYS HE'S GONNA THINK ABOUT IT.
WE'RE DOOMED.
GOT THAT RIGHT.
ANYBODY SEEN MY CAT?
FORGET HIM, WE GOTTA DO WHAT WE GOTTA DO. MOUSE GETTIN' THE INFO WE NEED?
RIGHT NOW.

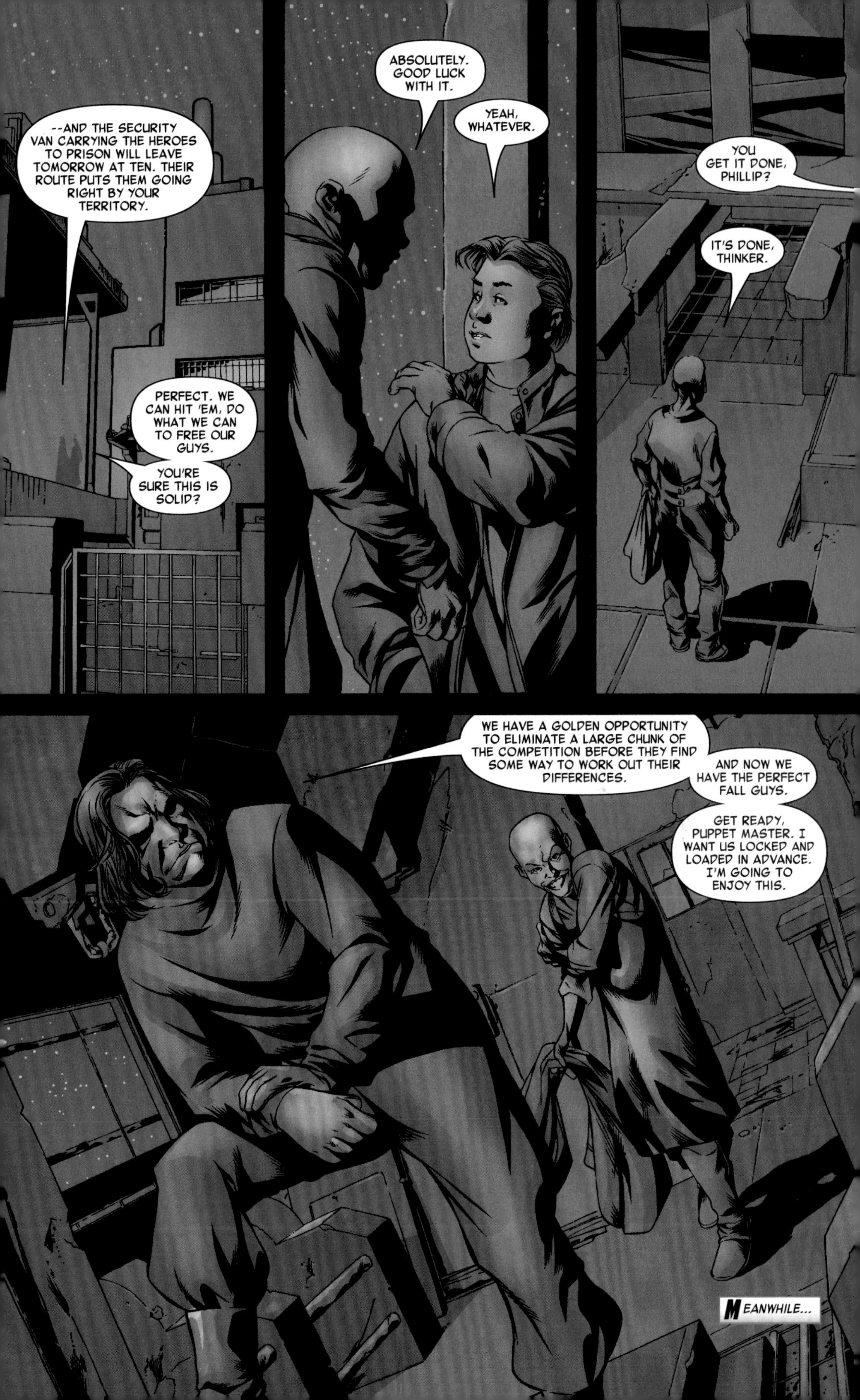
--AND THE SECURITY VAN CARRYING THE HEROES TO PRISON WILL LEAVE TOMORROW AT TEN. THEIR ROUTE PUTS THEM GOING RIGHT BY YOUR TERRITORY.
PERFECT. WE CAN HIT 'EM, DO WHAT WE CAN TO FREE OUR GUYS.
YOU'RE SURE THIS IS SOLID?
ABSOLUTELY. GOOD LUCK WITH IT.
YEAH, WHATEVER.
YOU GET IT DONE, PHILLIP?
IT'S DONE, THINKER.
WE HAVE A GOLDEN OPPORTUNITY TO ELIMINATE A LARGE CHUNK OF THE COMPETITION BEFORE THEY FIND SOME WAY TO WORK OUT THEIR DIFFERENCES.
AND NOW WE HAVE THE PERFECT FALL GUYS.
GET READY, PUPPET MASTER. I WANT US LOCKED AND LOADED IN ADVANCE. I'M GOING TO ENJOY THIS.
MEANWHILE...

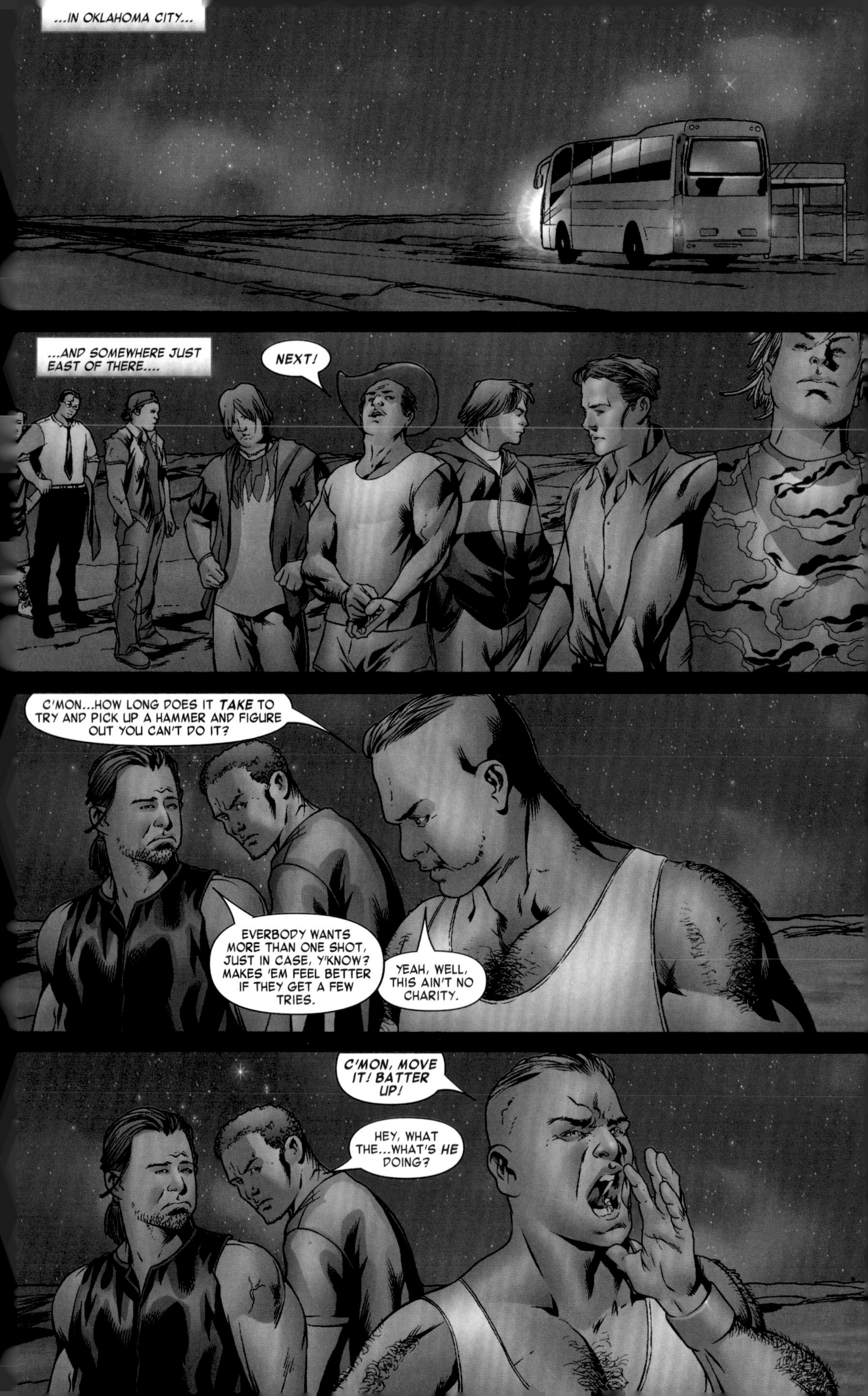
...IN OKLAHOMA CITY...
...AND SOMEWHERE JUST EAST OF THERE....
NEXT!
C'MON...HOW LONG DOES IT TAKE TO TRY AND PICK UP A HAMMER AND FIGURE OUT YOU CAN'T DO IT?
EVERBODY WANTS MORE THAN ONE SHOT, JUST IN CASE, Y'KNOW? MAKES 'EM FEEL BETTER IF THEY GET A FEW TRIES.
YEAH, WELL, THIS AIN'T NO CHARITY.
C'MON, MOVE IT! BATTER UP!
HEY, WHAT THE...WHAT'S HE DOING?

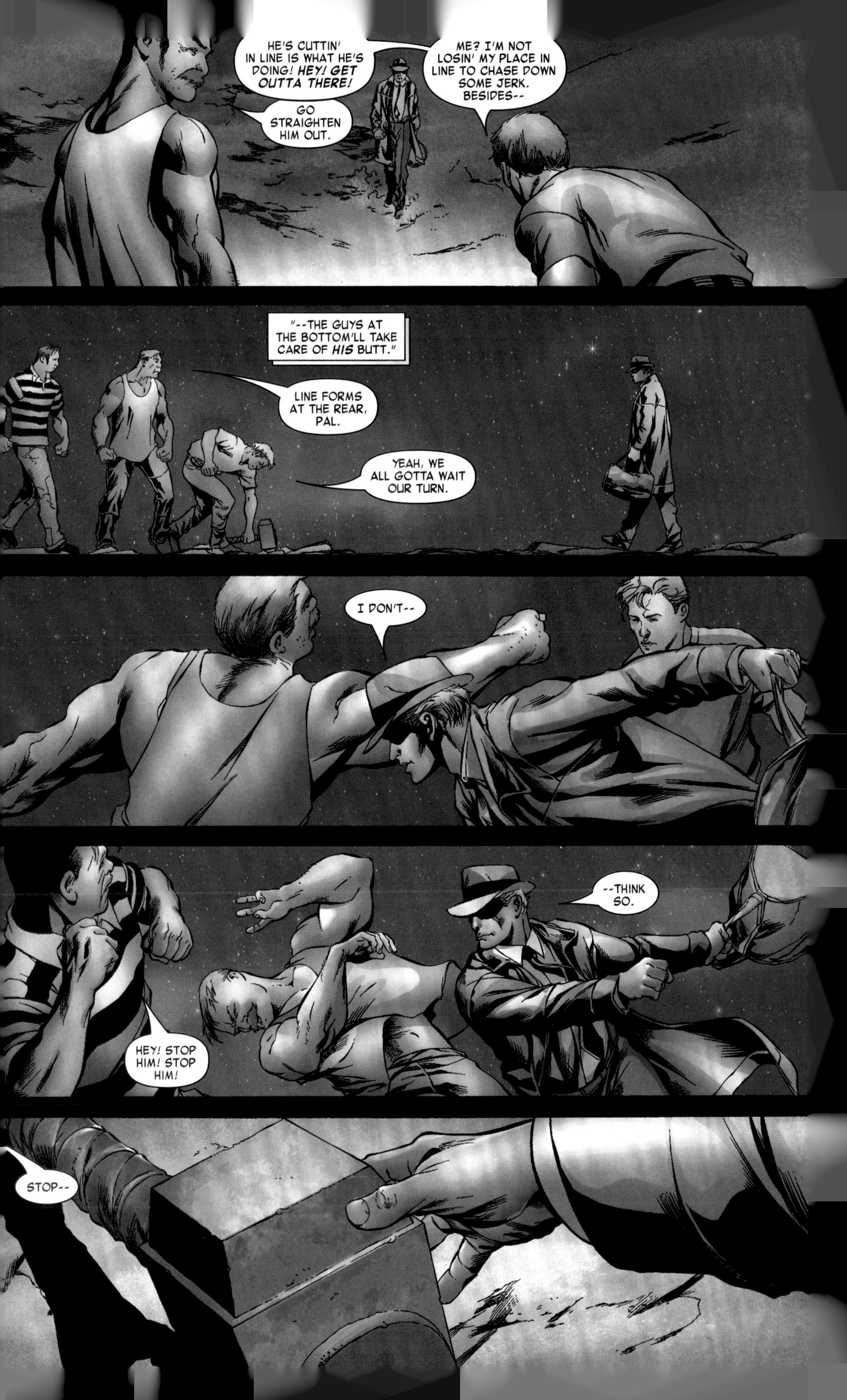
HE'S CUTTIN' IN LINE IS WHAT HE'S DOING! HEY! GET OUTTA THERE!
GO STRAIGHTEN HIM OUT.
ME? I'M NOT LOSIN' MY PLACE IN LINE TO CHASE DOWN SOME JERK. BESIDES--
"--THE GUYS AT THE BOTTOM'LL TAKE CARE OF HIS BUTT."
LINE FORMS AT THE REAR, PAL.
YEAH, WE ALL GOTTA WAIT OUR TURN.
I DON'T--
--THINK SO.
HEY! STOP HIM! STOP HIM!
STOP--

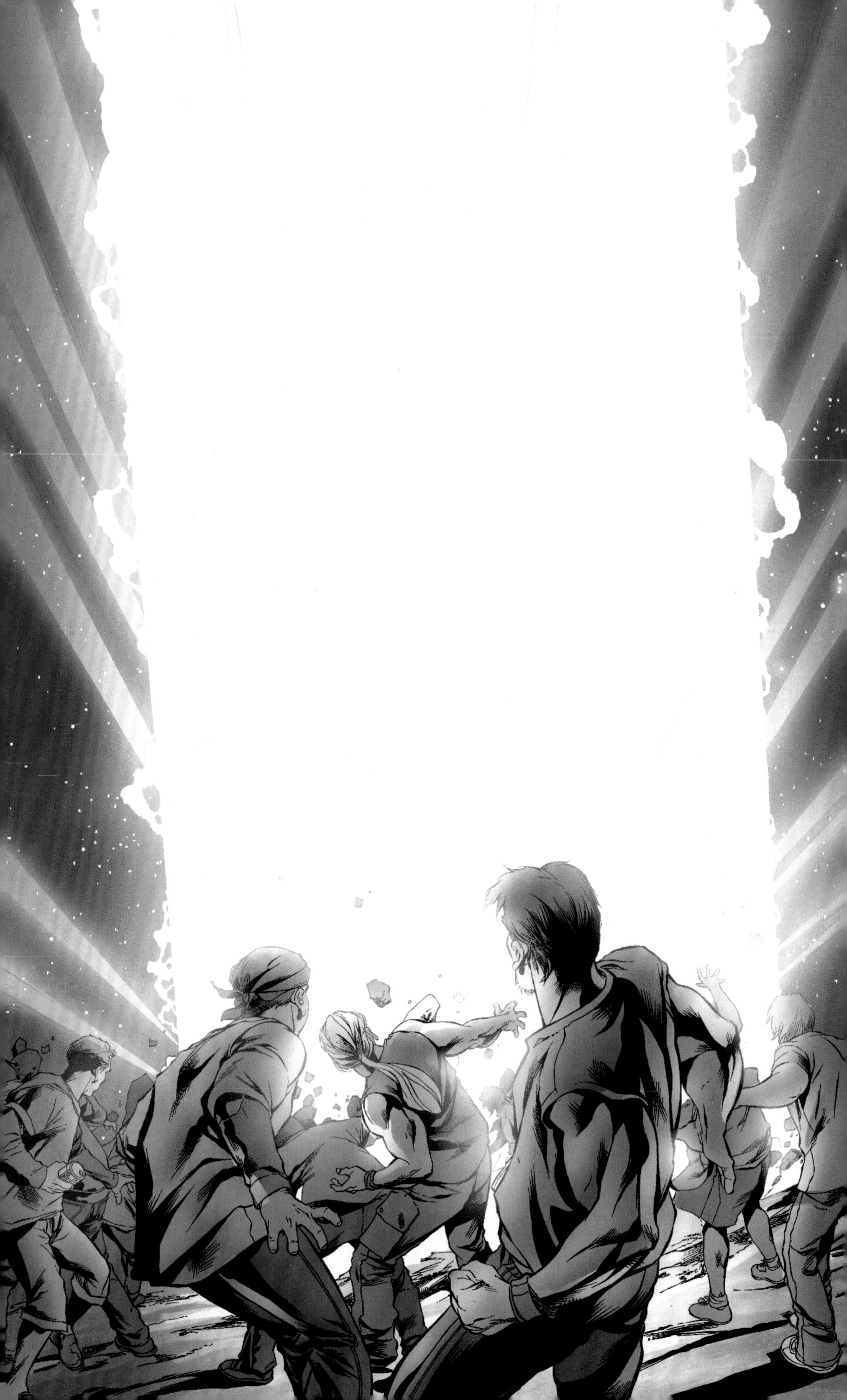

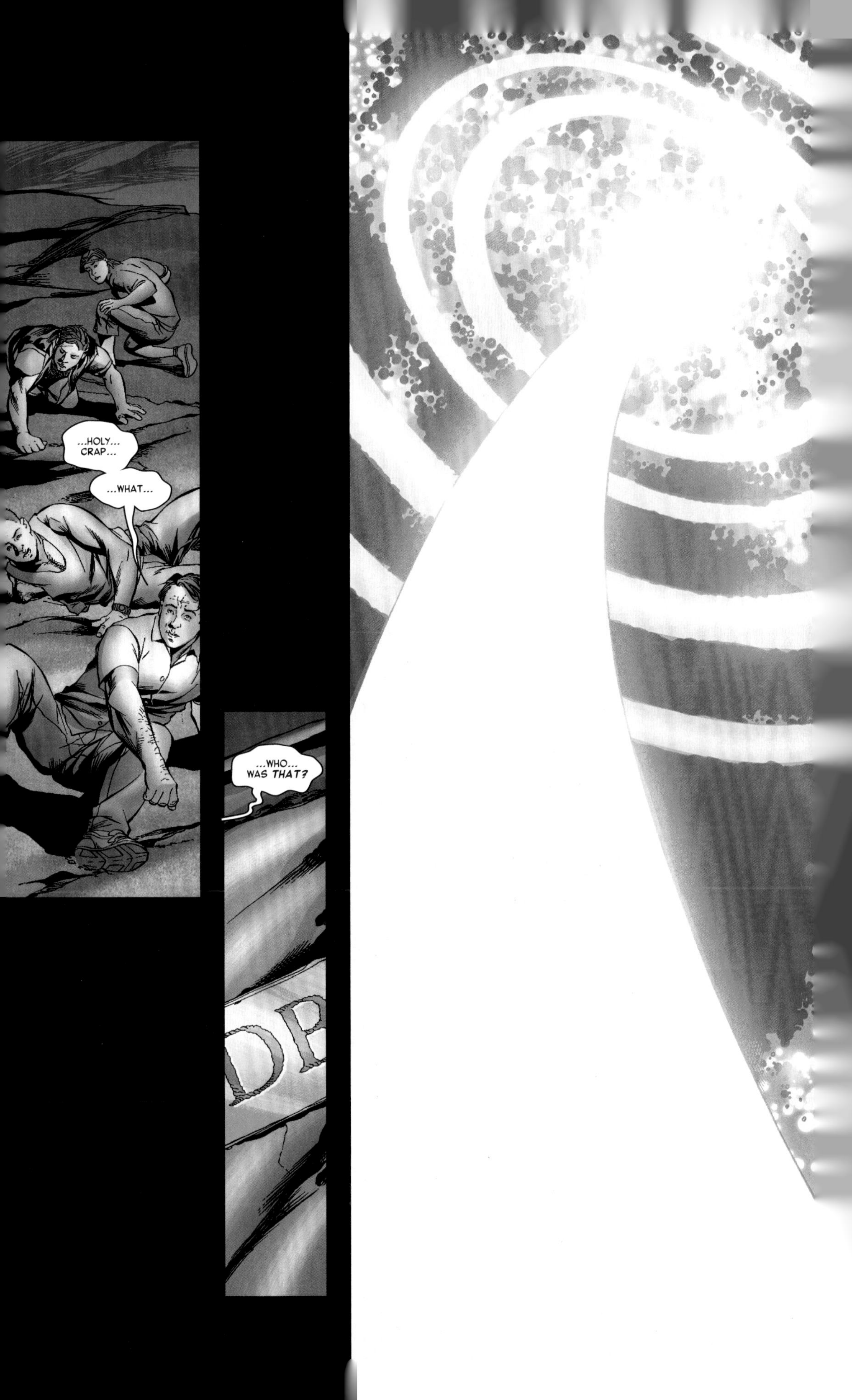

...HOLY... CRAP...
...WHAT...
...WHO... WAS THAT?

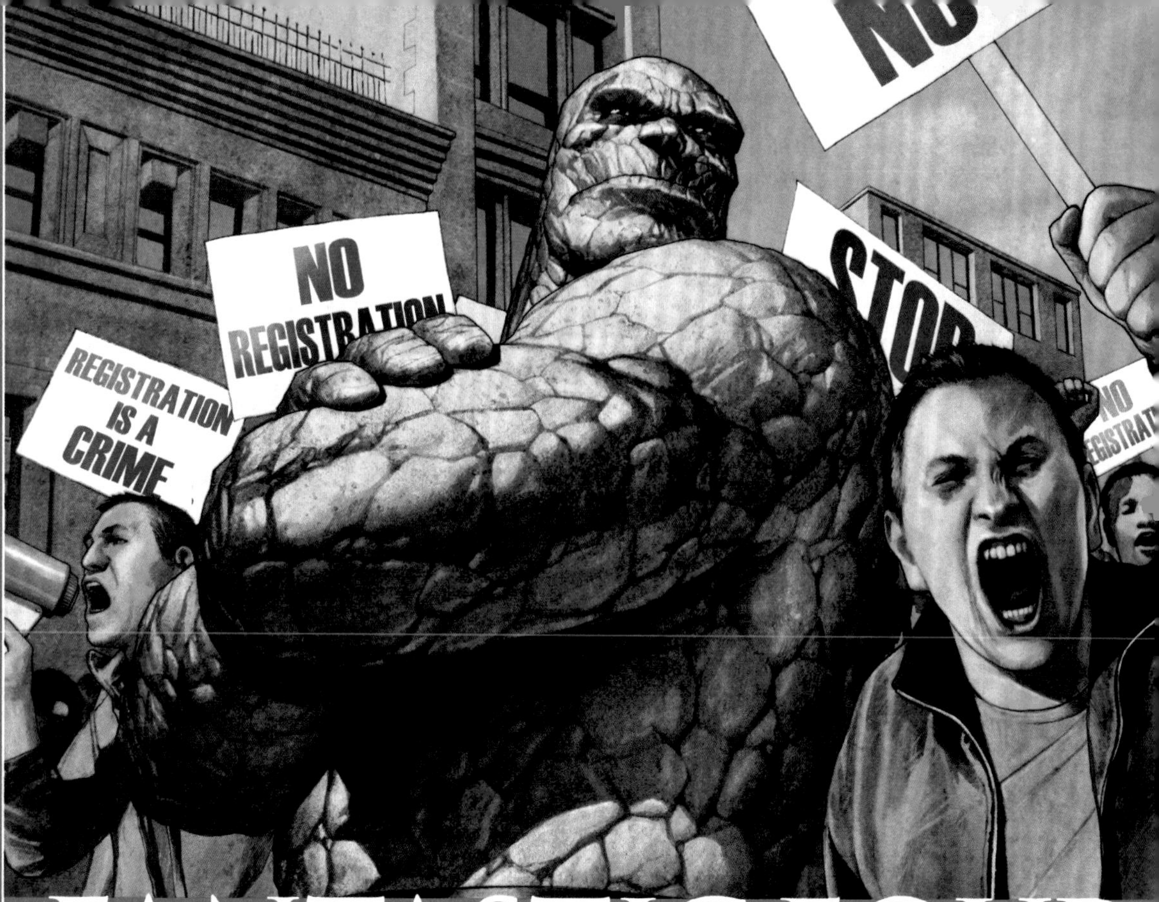
NO REGISTRATION
REGISTRATION IS A CRIME

FANTASTIC FOUR

A MARVEL COMICS EVENT

CIVIL WAR

FANTASTIC FOUR #539

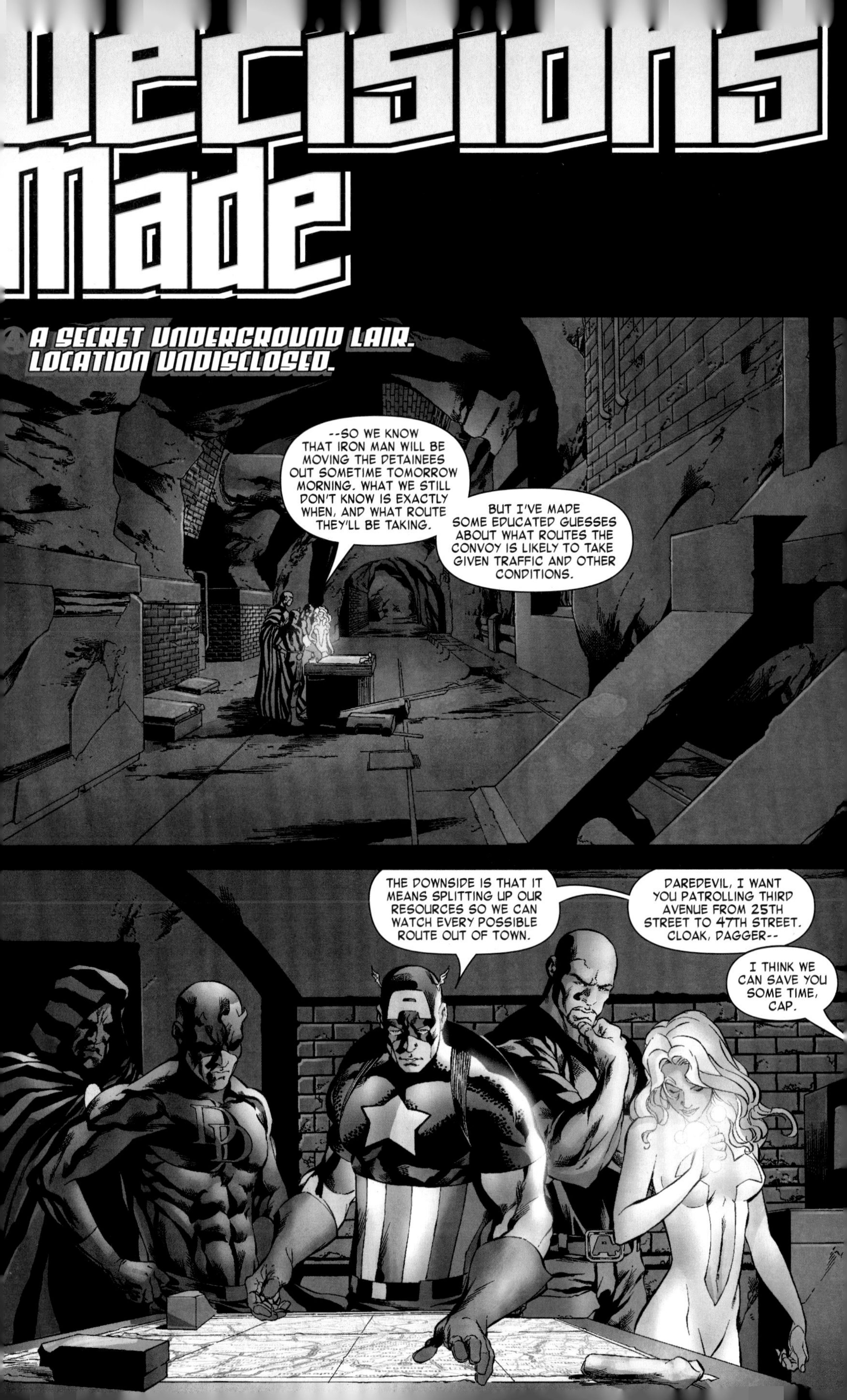
DECISIONS MADE
A SECRET UNDERGROUND LAIR. LOCATION UNDISCLOSED.
--SO WE KNOW THAT IRON MAN WILL BE MOVING THE DETAINEES OUT SOMETIME TOMORROW MORNING. WHAT WE STILL DON'T KNOW IS EXACTLY WHEN, AND WHAT ROUTE THEY'LL BE TAKING.
BUT I'VE MADE SOME EDUCATED GUESSES ABOUT WHAT ROUTES THE CONVOY IS LIKELY TO TAKE GIVEN TRAFFIC AND OTHER CONDITIONS.
THE DOWNSIDE IS THAT IT MEANS SPLITTING UP OUR RESOURCES SO WE CAN WATCH EVERY POSSIBLE ROUTE OUT OF TOWN.
DAREDEVIL, I WANT YOU PATROLLING THIRD AVENUE FROM 25TH STREET TO 47TH STREET. CLOAK, DAGGER--
I THINK WE CAN SAVE YOU SOME TIME, CAP.

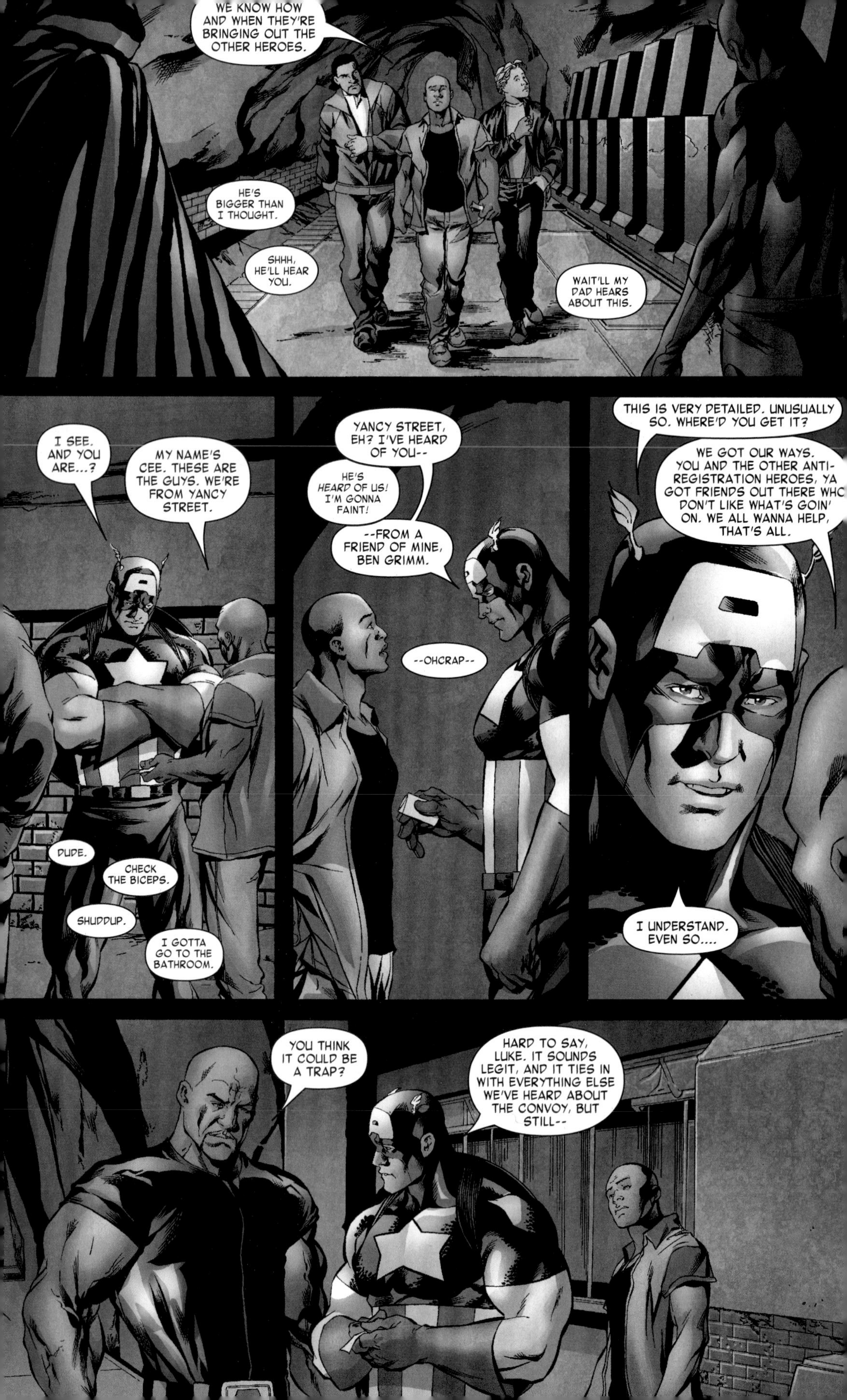

WE KNOW HOW AND WHEN THEY'RE BRINGING OUT THE OTHER HEROES.
HE'S BIGGER THAN I THOUGHT.
SHHH, HE'LL HEAR YOU.
WAIT'LL MY DAD HEARS ABOUT THIS.
I SEE. AND YOU ARE...?
MY NAME'S CEE. THESE ARE THE GUYS. WE'RE FROM YANCY STREET.
DUDE.
CHECK THE BICEPS.
SHUDDUP.
I GOTTA GO TO THE BATHROOM.
YANCY STREET, EH? I'VE HEARD OF YOU--
HE'S *HEARD* OF US! I'M GONNA FAINT!
--FROM A FRIEND OF MINE, BEN GRIMM.
--OHCRAP--
THIS IS VERY DETAILED. UNUSUALLY SO. WHERE'D YOU GET IT?
WE GOT OUR WAYS. YOU AND THE OTHER ANTI-REGISTRATION HEROES, YA GOT FRIENDS OUT THERE WHO DON'T LIKE WHAT'S GOIN' ON. WE ALL WANNA HELP, THAT'S ALL.
I UNDERSTAND. EVEN SO....
YOU THINK IT COULD BE A TRAP?
HARD TO SAY, LUKE. IT SOUNDS LEGIT, AND IT TIES IN WITH EVERYTHING ELSE WE'VE HEARD ABOUT THE CONVOY, BUT STILL--

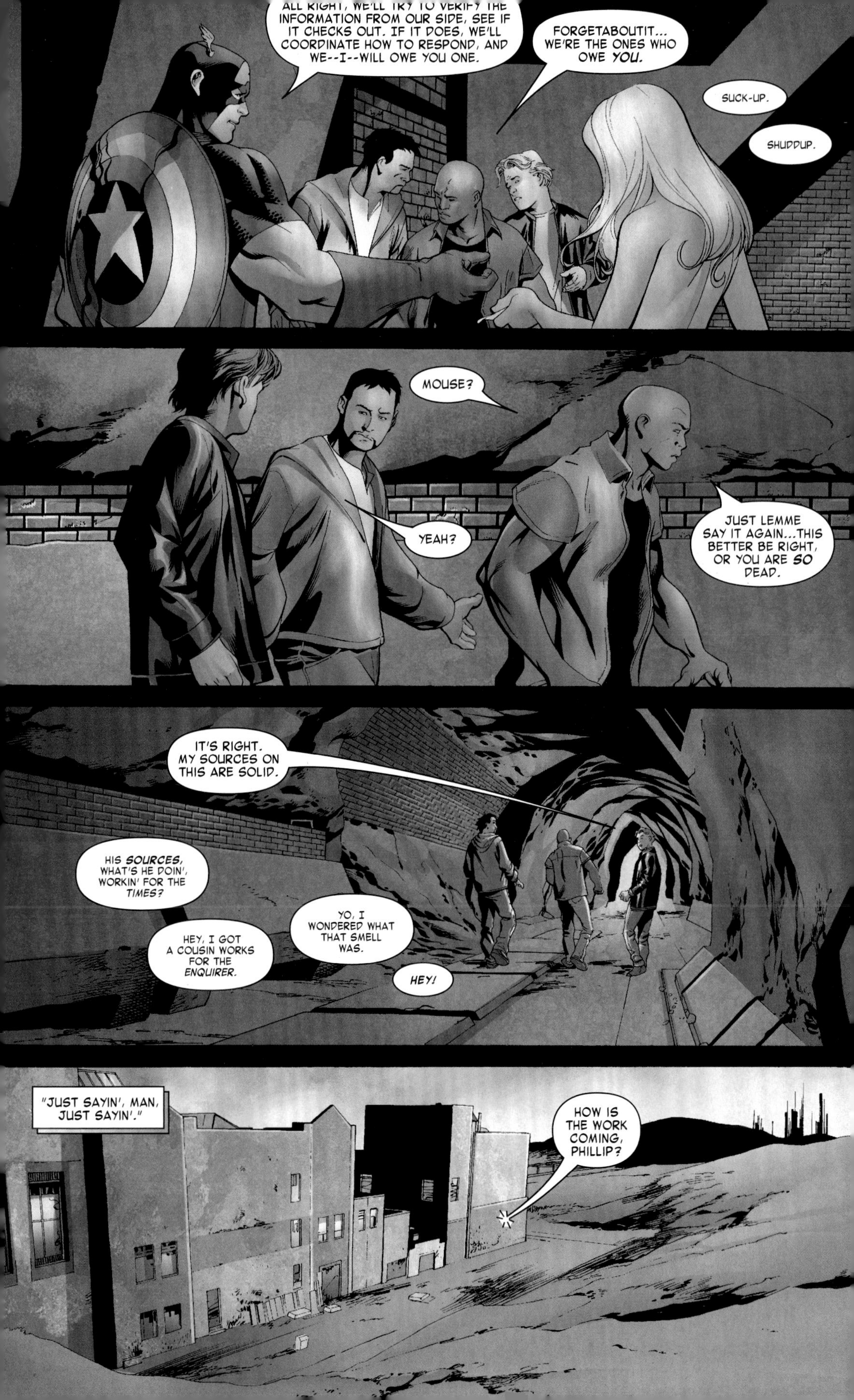
ALL RIGHT, WE'LL TRY TO VERIFY THE INFORMATION FROM OUR SIDE, SEE IF IT CHECKS OUT. IF IT DOES, WE'LL COORDINATE HOW TO RESPOND, AND WE--I--WILL OWE YOU ONE.
FORGETABOUTIT... WE'RE THE ONES WHO OWE *YOU.*
SUCK-UP.
SHUDDUP.
MOUSE?
YEAH?
JUST LEMME SAY IT AGAIN...THIS BETTER BE RIGHT, OR YOU ARE *SO* DEAD.
IT'S RIGHT. MY SOURCES ON THIS ARE SOLID.
HIS *SOURCES*, WHAT'S HE DOIN', WORKIN' FOR THE *TIMES*?
YO, I WONDERED WHAT THAT SMELL WAS.
HEY, I GOT A COUSIN WORKS FOR THE *ENQUIRER*.
HEY!
"JUST SAYIN', MAN, JUST SAYIN'."
HOW IS THE WORK COMING, PHILLIP?

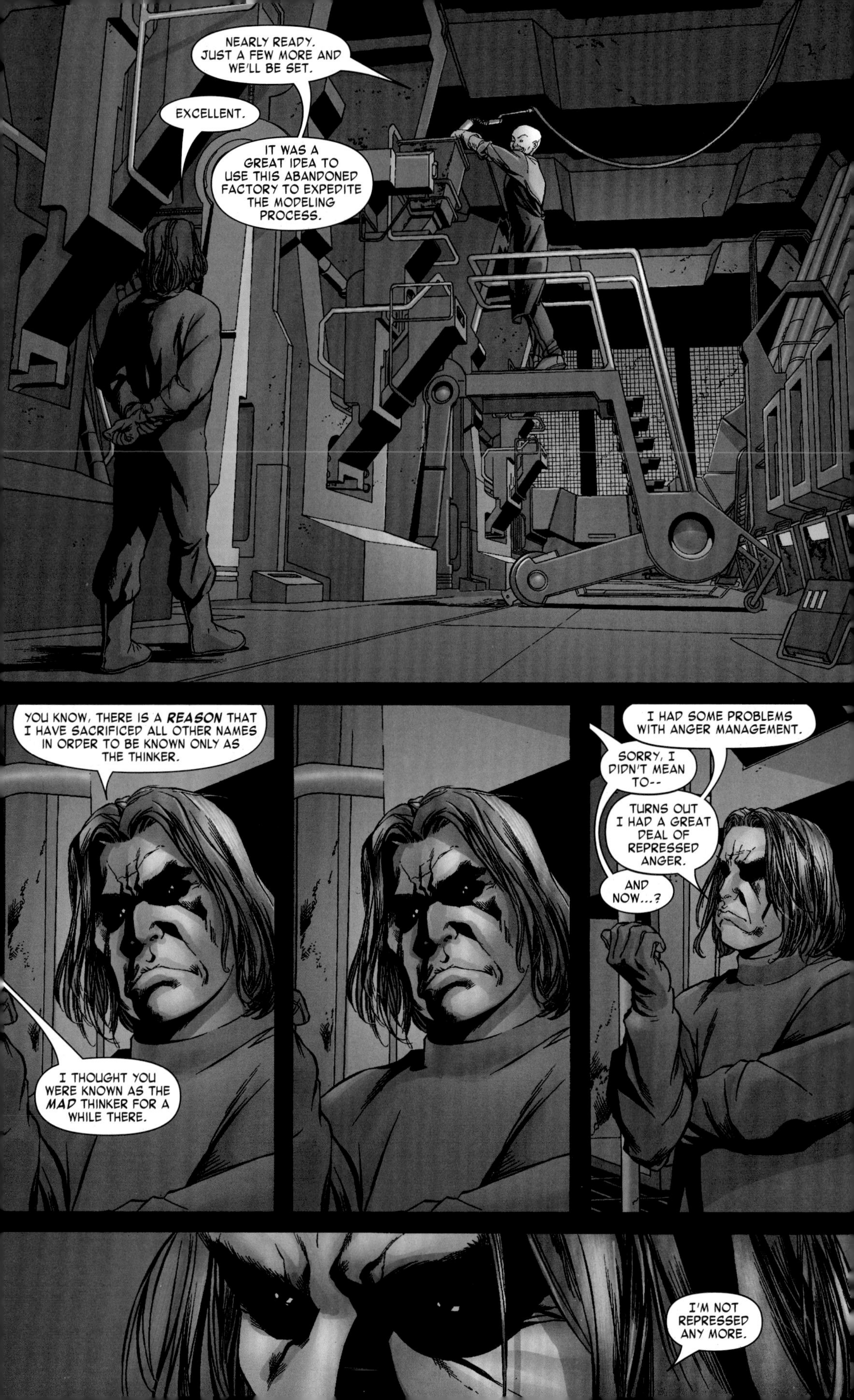
NEARLY READY. JUST A FEW MORE AND WE'LL BE SET.
EXCELLENT.
IT WAS A GREAT IDEA TO USE THIS ABANDONED FACTORY TO EXPEDITE THE MODELING PROCESS.
YOU KNOW, THERE IS A REASON THAT I HAVE SACRIFICED ALL OTHER NAMES IN ORDER TO BE KNOWN ONLY AS THE THINKER.
I THOUGHT YOU WERE KNOWN AS THE MAD THINKER FOR A WHILE THERE.
SORRY, I DIDN'T MEAN TO--
I HAD SOME PROBLEMS WITH ANGER MANAGEMENT.
TURNS OUT I HAD A GREAT DEAL OF REPRESSED ANGER.
AND NOW...?
I'M NOT REPRESSED ANY MORE.

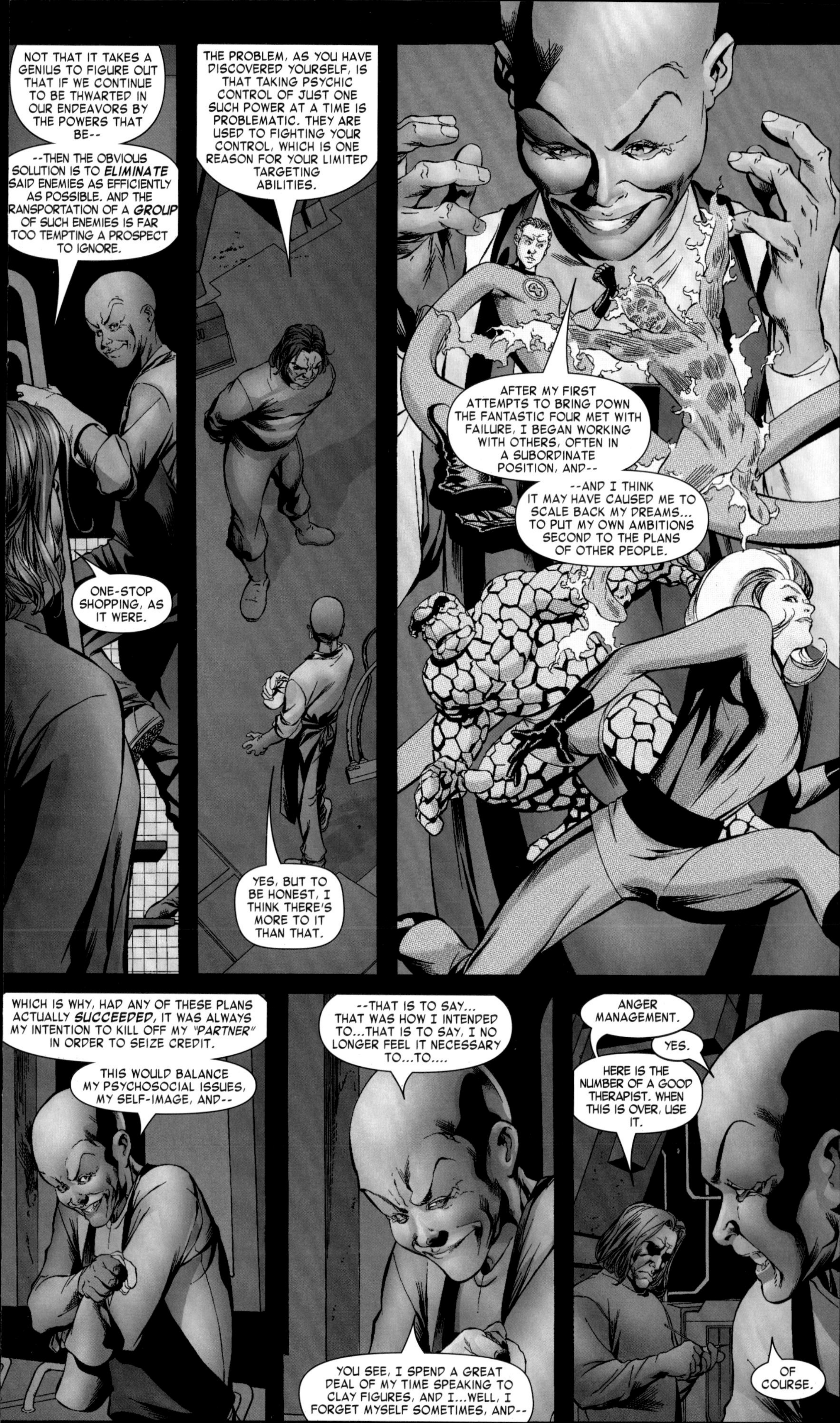
NOT THAT IT TAKES A GENIUS TO FIGURE OUT THAT IF WE CONTINUE TO BE THWARTED IN OUR ENDEAVORS BY THE POWERS THAT BE--
--THEN THE OBVIOUS SOLUTION IS TO *ELIMINATE* SAID ENEMIES AS EFFICIENTLY AS POSSIBLE. AND THE TRANSPORTATION OF A *GROUP* OF SUCH ENEMIES IS FAR TOO TEMPTING A PROSPECT TO IGNORE.
ONE-STOP SHOPPING, AS IT WERE.
THE PROBLEM, AS YOU HAVE DISCOVERED YOURSELF, IS THAT TAKING PSYCHIC CONTROL OF JUST ONE SUCH POWER AT A TIME IS PROBLEMATIC. THEY ARE USED TO FIGHTING YOUR CONTROL, WHICH IS ONE REASON FOR YOUR LIMITED TARGETING ABILITIES.
YES, BUT TO BE HONEST, I THINK THERE'S MORE TO IT THAN THAT.
AFTER MY FIRST ATTEMPTS TO BRING DOWN THE FANTASTIC FOUR MET WITH FAILURE, I BEGAN WORKING WITH OTHERS, OFTEN IN A SUBORDINATE POSITION, AND--
--AND I THINK IT MAY HAVE CAUSED ME TO SCALE BACK MY DREAMS... TO PUT MY OWN AMBITIONS SECOND TO THE PLANS OF OTHER PEOPLE.
WHICH IS WHY, HAD ANY OF THESE PLANS ACTUALLY *SUCCEEDED*, IT WAS ALWAYS MY INTENTION TO KILL OFF MY "*PARTNER*" IN ORDER TO SEIZE CREDIT.
THIS WOULD BALANCE MY PSYCHOSOCIAL ISSUES, MY SELF-IMAGE, AND--
--THAT IS TO SAY... THAT WAS HOW I INTENDED TO...THAT IS TO SAY, I NO LONGER FEEL IT NECESSARY TO...TO....
YOU SEE, I SPEND A GREAT DEAL OF MY TIME SPEAKING TO CLAY FIGURES, AND I...WELL, I FORGET MYSELF SOMETIMES, AND--
ANGER MANAGEMENT.
YES.
HERE IS THE NUMBER OF A GOOD THERAPIST. WHEN THIS IS OVER, USE IT.
OF COURSE.

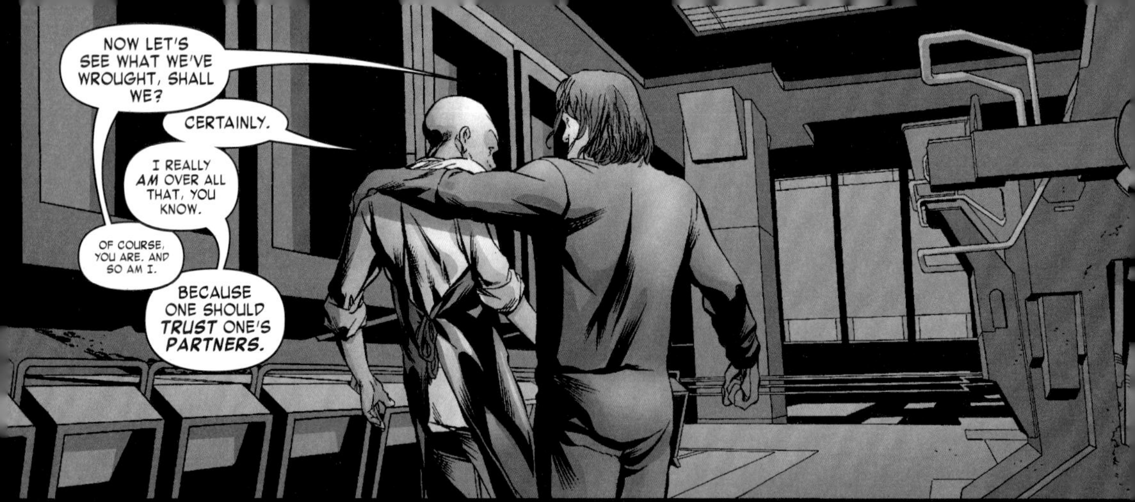
NOW LET'S SEE WHAT WE'VE WROUGHT, SHALL WE?
CERTAINLY.
I REALLY AM OVER ALL THAT, YOU KNOW.
OF COURSE, YOU ARE. AND SO AM I.
BECAUSE ONE SHOULD TRUST ONE'S PARTNERS.

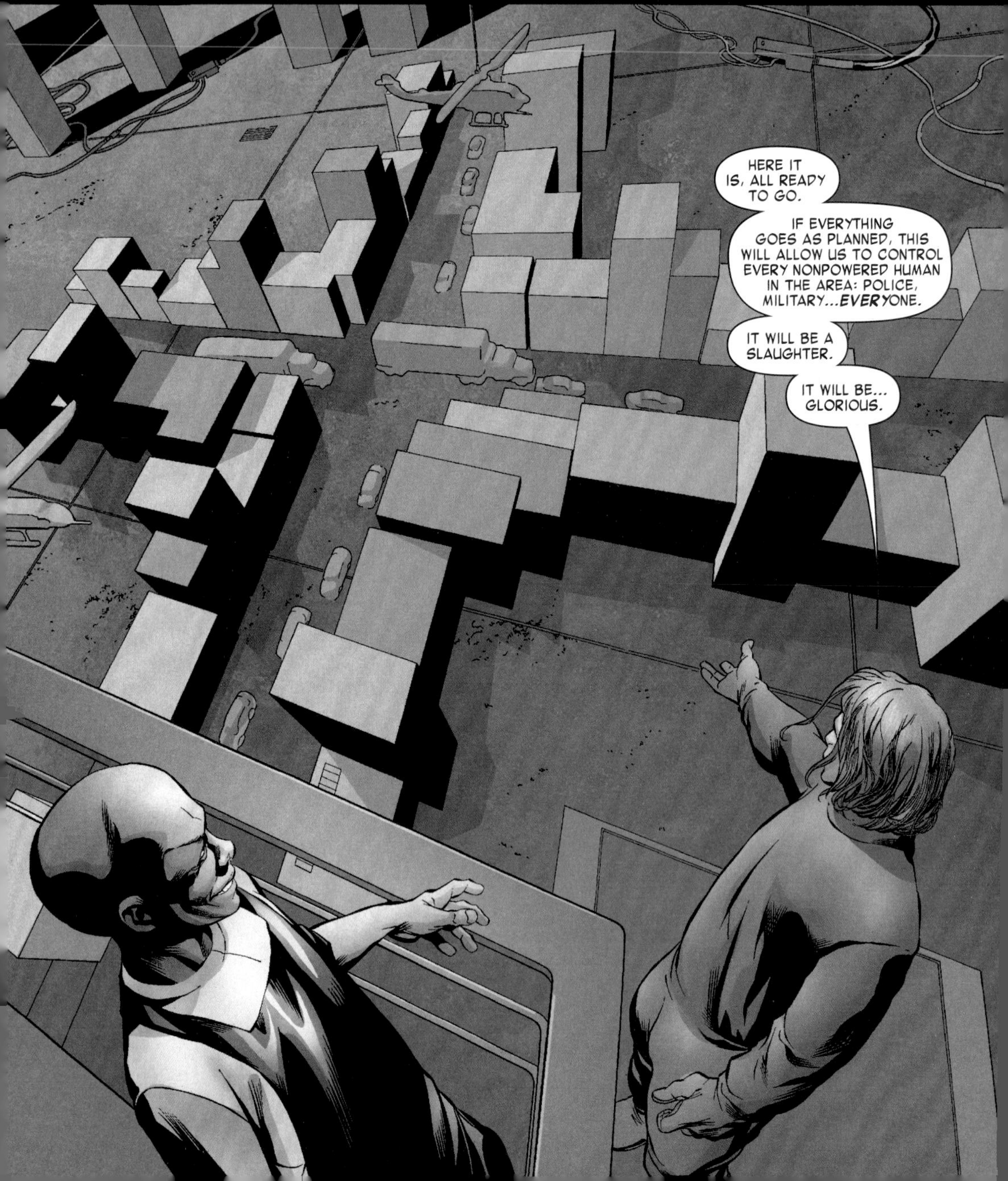
HERE IT IS, ALL READY TO GO.
IF EVERYTHING GOES AS PLANNED, THIS WILL ALLOW US TO CONTROL EVERY NONPOWERED HUMAN IN THE AREA: POLICE, MILITARY...EVERYONE.
IT WILL BE A SLAUGHTER.
IT WILL BE... GLORIOUS.

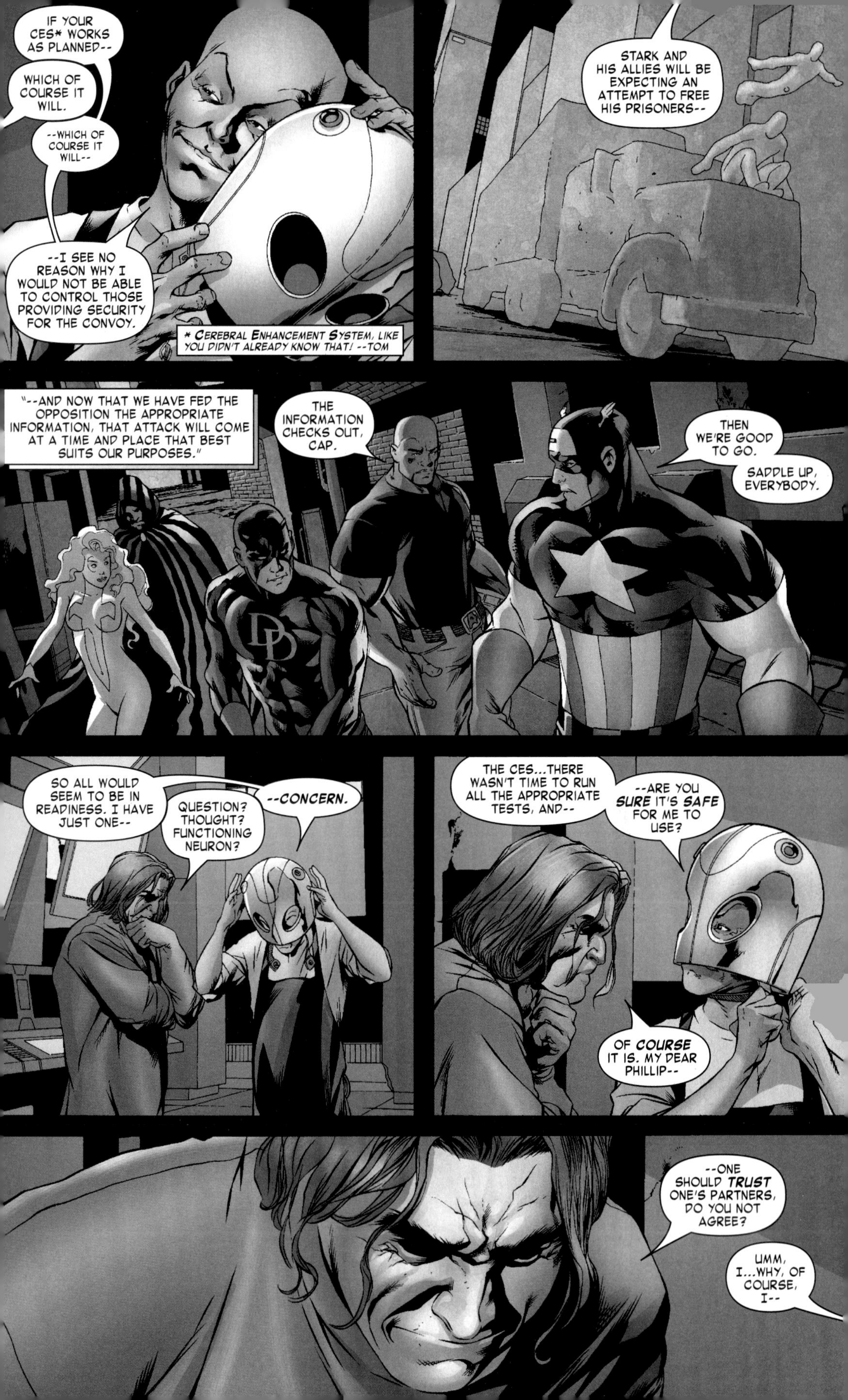
IF YOUR CES* WORKS AS PLANNED--
WHICH OF COURSE IT WILL.
--WHICH OF COURSE IT WILL--
--I SEE NO REASON WHY I WOULD NOT BE ABLE TO CONTROL THOSE PROVIDING SECURITY FOR THE CONVOY.
* CEREBRAL ENHANCEMENT SYSTEM, LIKE YOU DIDN'T ALREADY KNOW THAT! --TOM
STARK AND HIS ALLIES WILL BE EXPECTING AN ATTEMPT TO FREE HIS PRISONERS--
"--AND NOW THAT WE HAVE FED THE OPPOSITION THE APPROPRIATE INFORMATION, THAT ATTACK WILL COME AT A TIME AND PLACE THAT BEST SUITS OUR PURPOSES."
THE INFORMATION CHECKS OUT, CAP.
THEN WE'RE GOOD TO GO.
SADDLE UP, EVERYBODY.
SO ALL WOULD SEEM TO BE IN READINESS. I HAVE JUST ONE--
QUESTION? THOUGHT? FUNCTIONING NEURON?
--CONCERN.
THE CES...THERE WASN'T TIME TO RUN ALL THE APPROPRIATE TESTS, AND--
--ARE YOU SURE IT'S SAFE FOR ME TO USE?
OF COURSE IT IS. MY DEAR PHILLIP--
--ONE SHOULD TRUST ONE'S PARTNERS, DO YOU NOT AGREE?
UMM, I...WHY, OF COURSE, I--

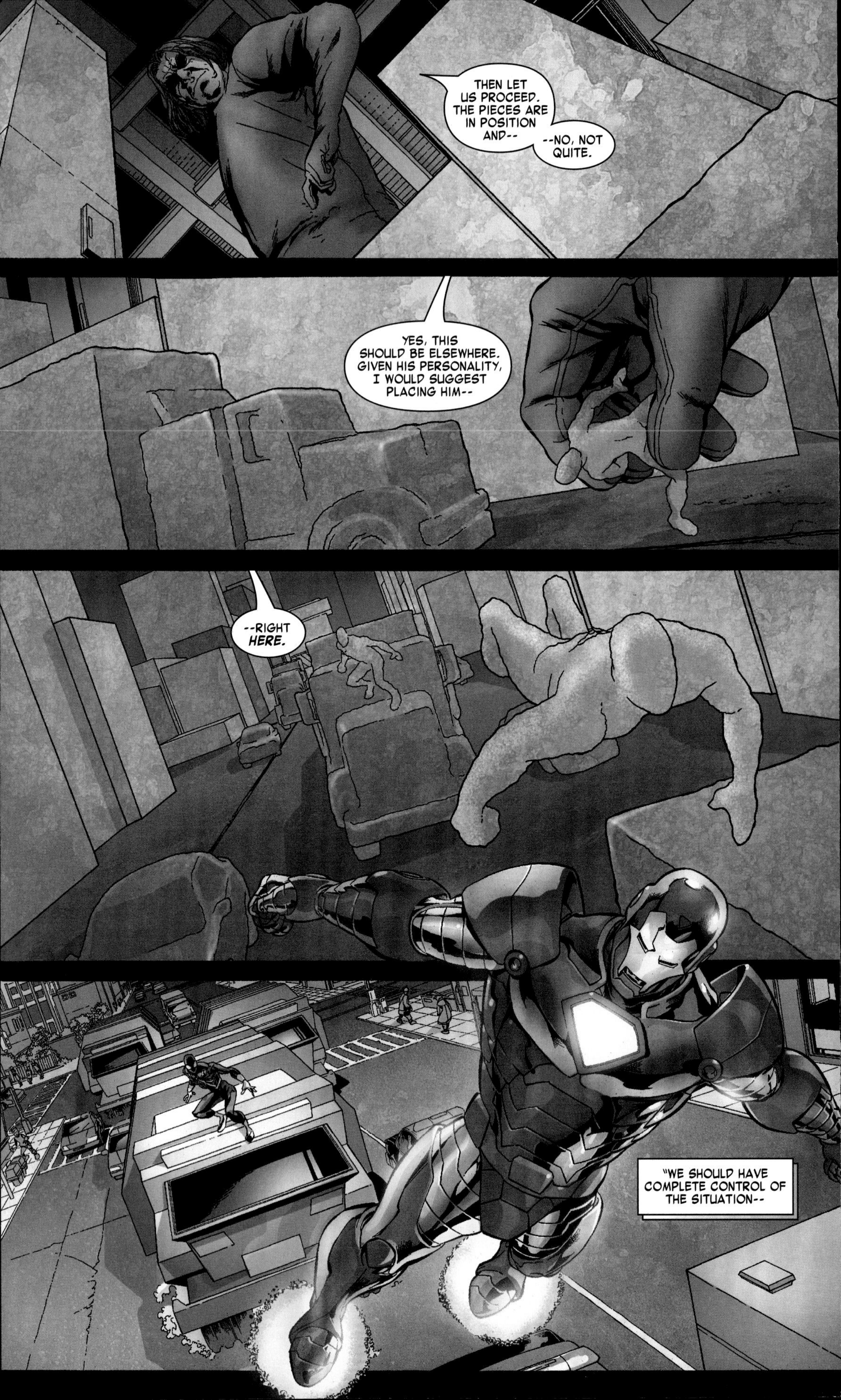
THEN LET US PROCEED. THE PIECES ARE IN POSITION AND--
--NO, NOT QUITE.
YES, THIS SHOULD BE ELSEWHERE. GIVEN HIS PERSONALITY, I WOULD SUGGEST PLACING HIM--
--RIGHT *HERE.*
"WE SHOULD HAVE COMPLETE CONTROL OF THE SITUATION--

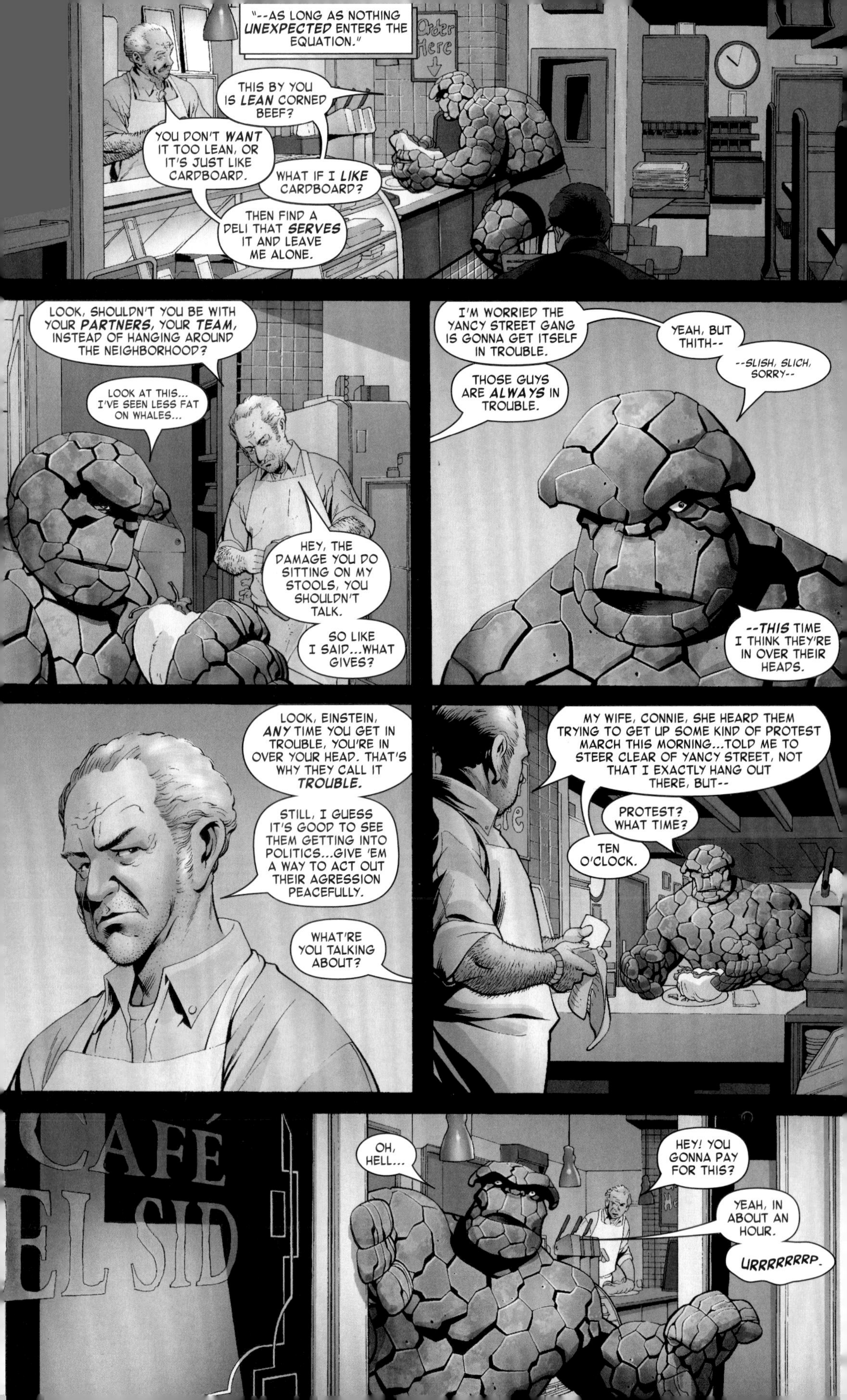

"--AS LONG AS NOTHING UNEXPECTED ENTERS THE EQUATION."
Order Here
THIS BY YOU IS LEAN CORNED BEEF?
YOU DON'T WANT IT TOO LEAN, OR IT'S JUST LIKE CARDBOARD.
WHAT IF I LIKE CARDBOARD?
THEN FIND A DELI THAT SERVES IT AND LEAVE ME ALONE.
LOOK, SHOULDN'T YOU BE WITH YOUR PARTNERS, YOUR TEAM, INSTEAD OF HANGING AROUND THE NEIGHBORHOOD?
LOOK AT THIS... I'VE SEEN LESS FAT ON WHALES...
HEY, THE DAMAGE YOU DO SITTING ON MY STOOLS, YOU SHOULDN'T TALK.
SO LIKE I SAID...WHAT GIVES?
I'M WORRIED THE YANCY STREET GANG IS GONNA GET ITSELF IN TROUBLE.
YEAH, BUT THITH--
--SLISH, SLICH, SORRY--
THOSE GUYS ARE ALWAYS IN TROUBLE.
--THIS TIME I THINK THEY'RE IN OVER THEIR HEADS.
LOOK, EINSTEIN, ANY TIME YOU GET IN TROUBLE, YOU'RE IN OVER YOUR HEAD. THAT'S WHY THEY CALL IT TROUBLE.
STILL, I GUESS IT'S GOOD TO SEE THEM GETTING INTO POLITICS...GIVE 'EM A WAY TO ACT OUT THEIR AGRESSION PEACEFULLY.
WHAT'RE YOU TALKING ABOUT?
MY WIFE, CONNIE, SHE HEARD THEM TRYING TO GET UP SOME KIND OF PROTEST MARCH THIS MORNING...TOLD ME TO STEER CLEAR OF YANCY STREET, NOT THAT I EXACTLY HANG OUT THERE, BUT--
PROTEST? WHAT TIME?
TEN O'CLOCK.
CAFÉ EL SID
OH, HELL...
HEY! YOU GONNA PAY FOR THIS?
YEAH, IN ABOUT AN HOUR.
URRRRRRRP.

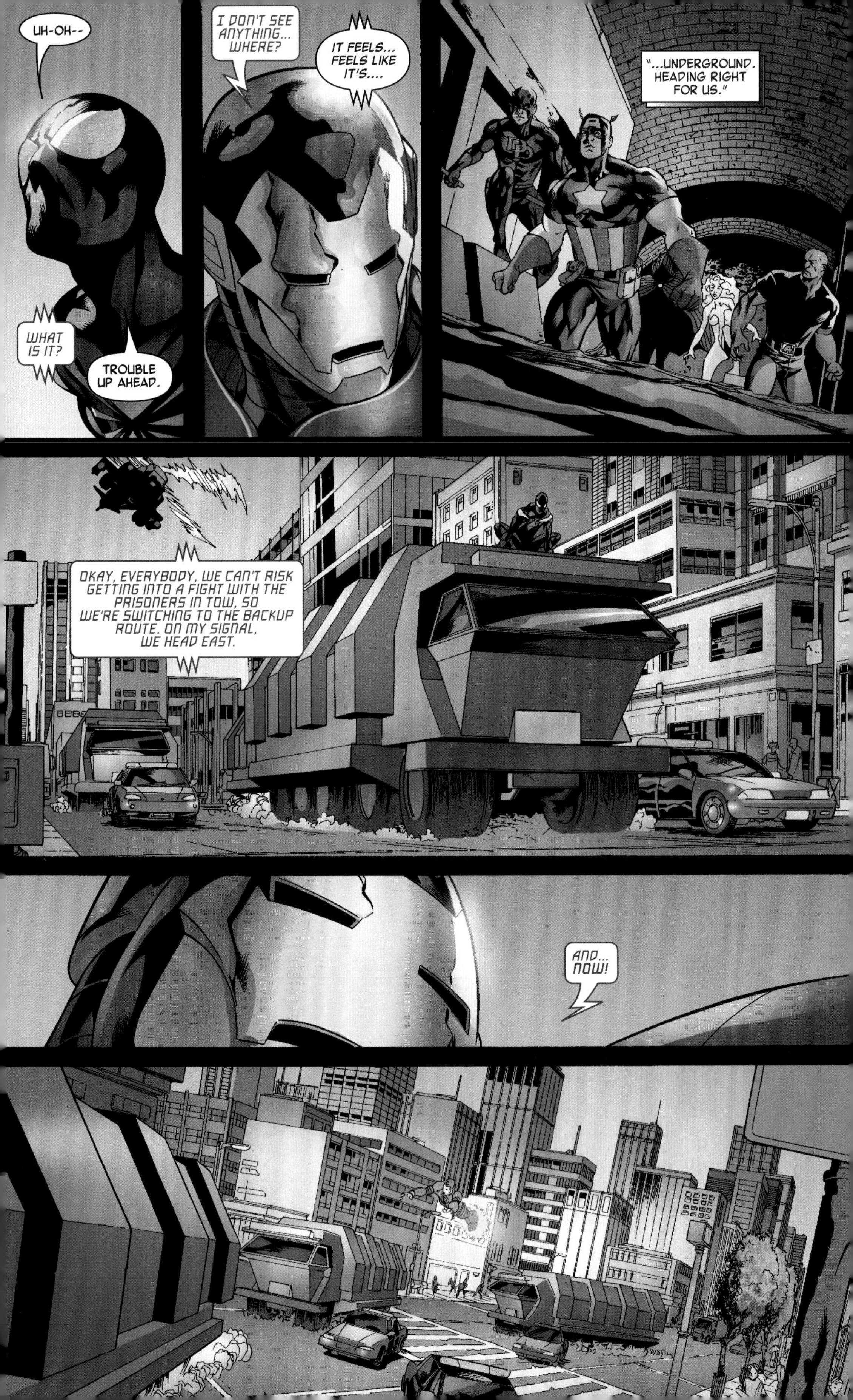
UH-OH--
WHAT IS IT?
TROUBLE UP AHEAD.
I DON'T SEE ANYTHING... WHERE?
IT FEELS... FEELS LIKE IT'S....
"...UNDERGROUND. HEADING RIGHT FOR US."
OKAY, EVERYBODY, WE CAN'T RISK GETTING INTO A FIGHT WITH THE PRISONERS IN TOW, SO WE'RE SWITCHING TO THE BACKUP ROUTE. ON MY SIGNAL, WE HEAD EAST.
AND... NOW!

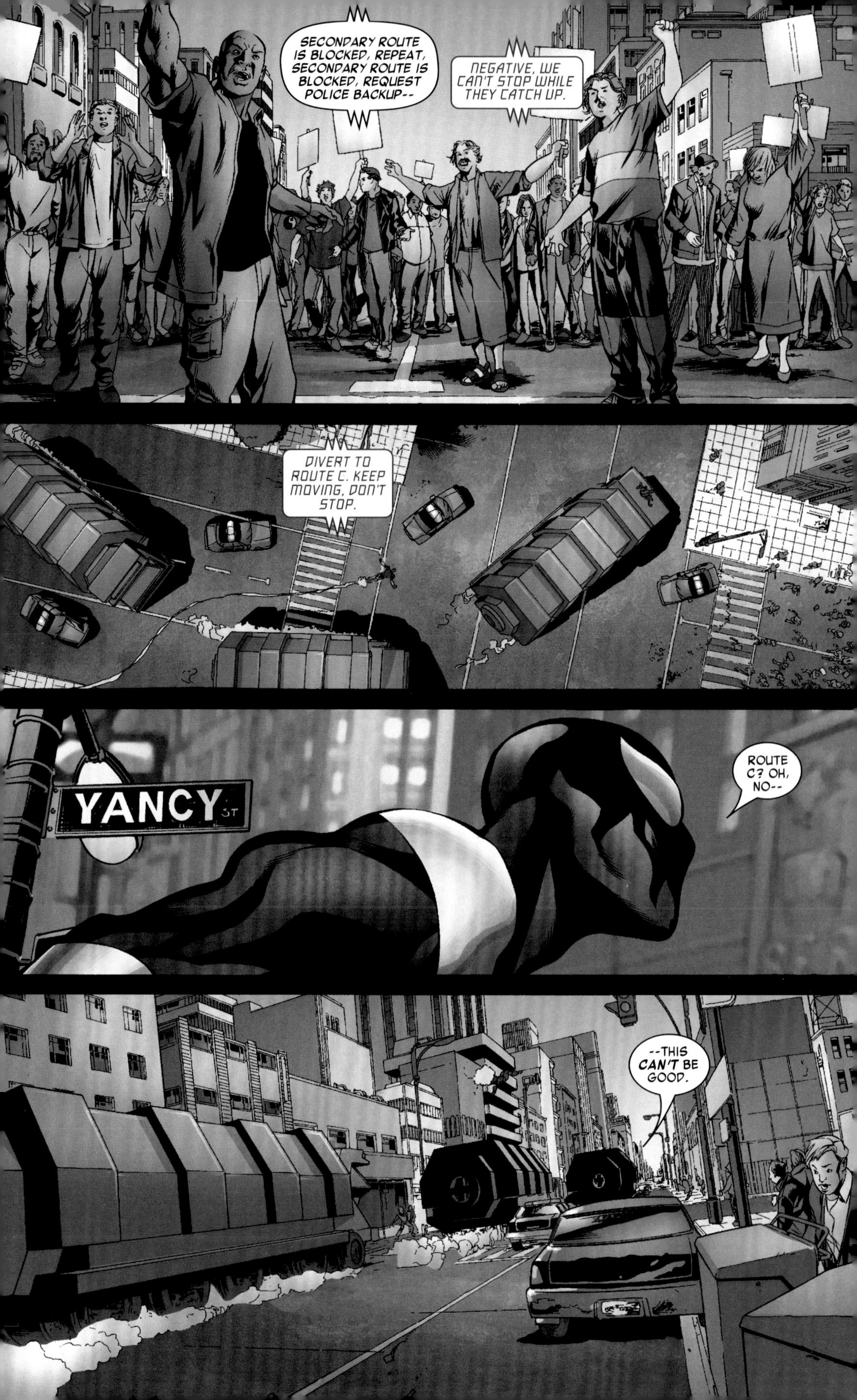
SECONDARY ROUTE IS BLOCKED, REPEAT, SECONDARY ROUTE IS BLOCKED, REQUEST POLICE BACKUP--
NEGATIVE, WE CAN'T STOP WHILE THEY CATCH UP.
DIVERT TO ROUTE C. KEEP MOVING, DON'T STOP.
YANCY ST
ROUTE C? OH, NO--
--THIS CAN'T BE GOOD.

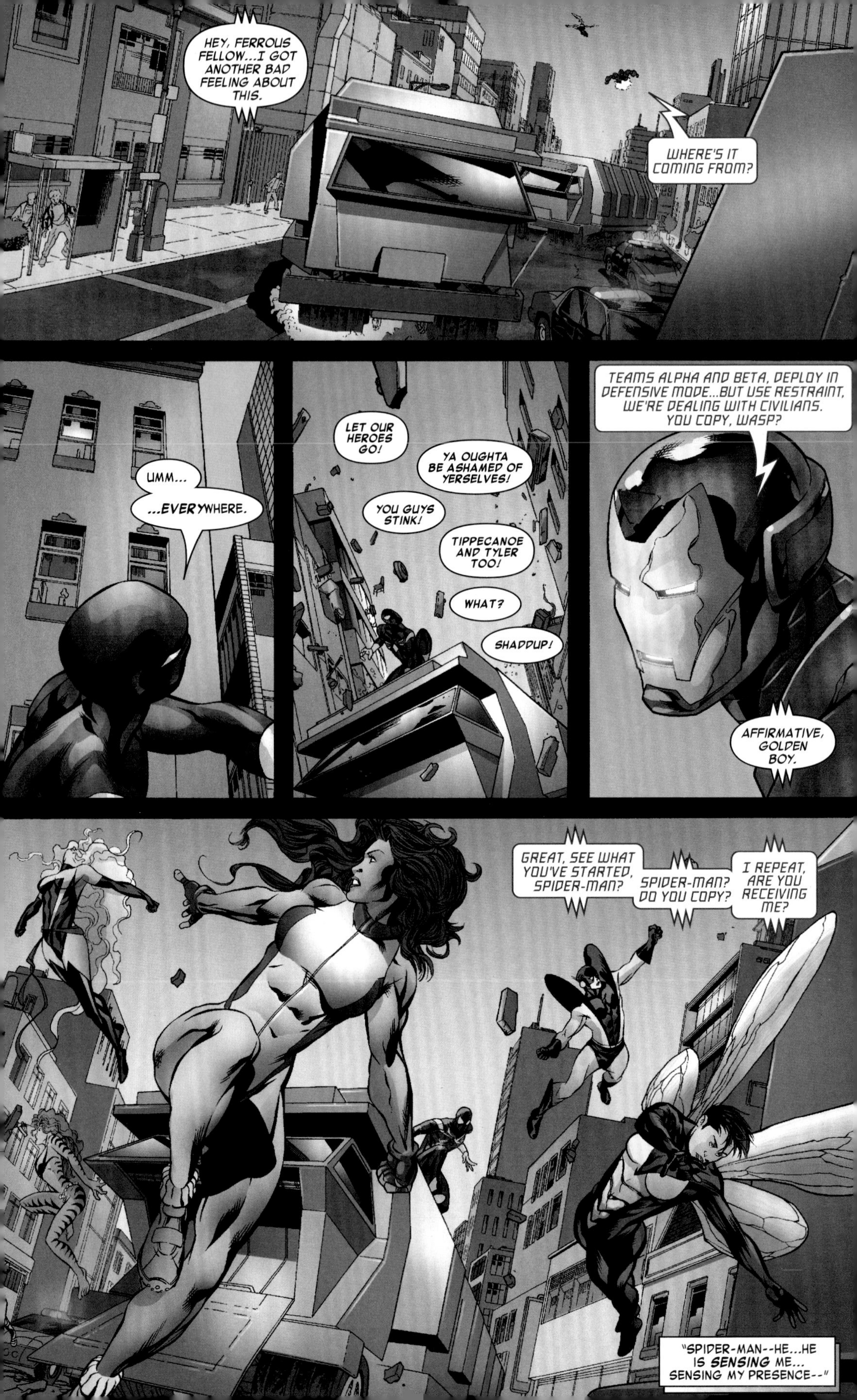
HEY, FERROUS FELLOW...I GOT ANOTHER BAD FEELING ABOUT THIS.
WHERE'S IT COMING FROM?
UMM...
...EVERYWHERE.
LET OUR HEROES GO!
YA OUGHTA BE ASHAMED OF YERSELVES!
YOU GUYS STINK!
TIPPECANOE AND TYLER TOO!
WHAT?
SHADDUP!
TEAMS ALPHA AND BETA, DEPLOY IN DEFENSIVE MODE...BUT USE RESTRAINT, WE'RE DEALING WITH CIVILIANS. YOU COPY, WASP?
AFFIRMATIVE, GOLDEN BOY.
GREAT, SEE WHAT YOU'VE STARTED, SPIDER-MAN?
SPIDER-MAN? DO YOU COPY?
I REPEAT, ARE YOU RECEIVING ME?
"SPIDER-MAN--HE...HE IS SENSING ME... SENSING MY PRESENCE--"

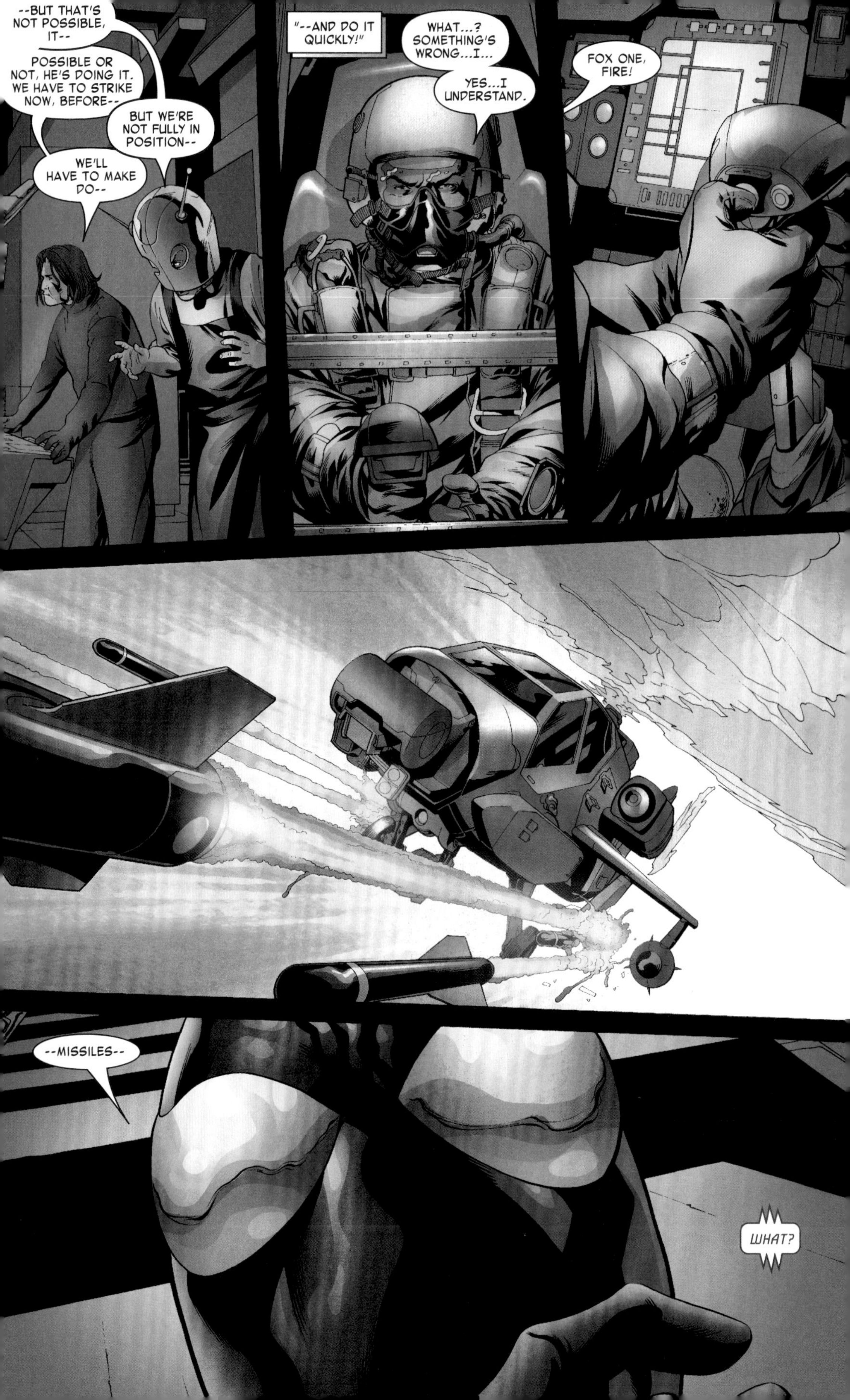
--BUT THAT'S NOT POSSIBLE, IT--
POSSIBLE OR NOT, HE'S DOING IT. WE HAVE TO STRIKE NOW, BEFORE--
BUT WE'RE NOT FULLY IN POSITION--
WE'LL HAVE TO MAKE DO--
"--AND DO IT QUICKLY!"
WHAT...? SOMETHING'S WRONG...I...
YES...I UNDERSTAND.
FOX ONE, FIRE!
--MISSILES--
WHAT?

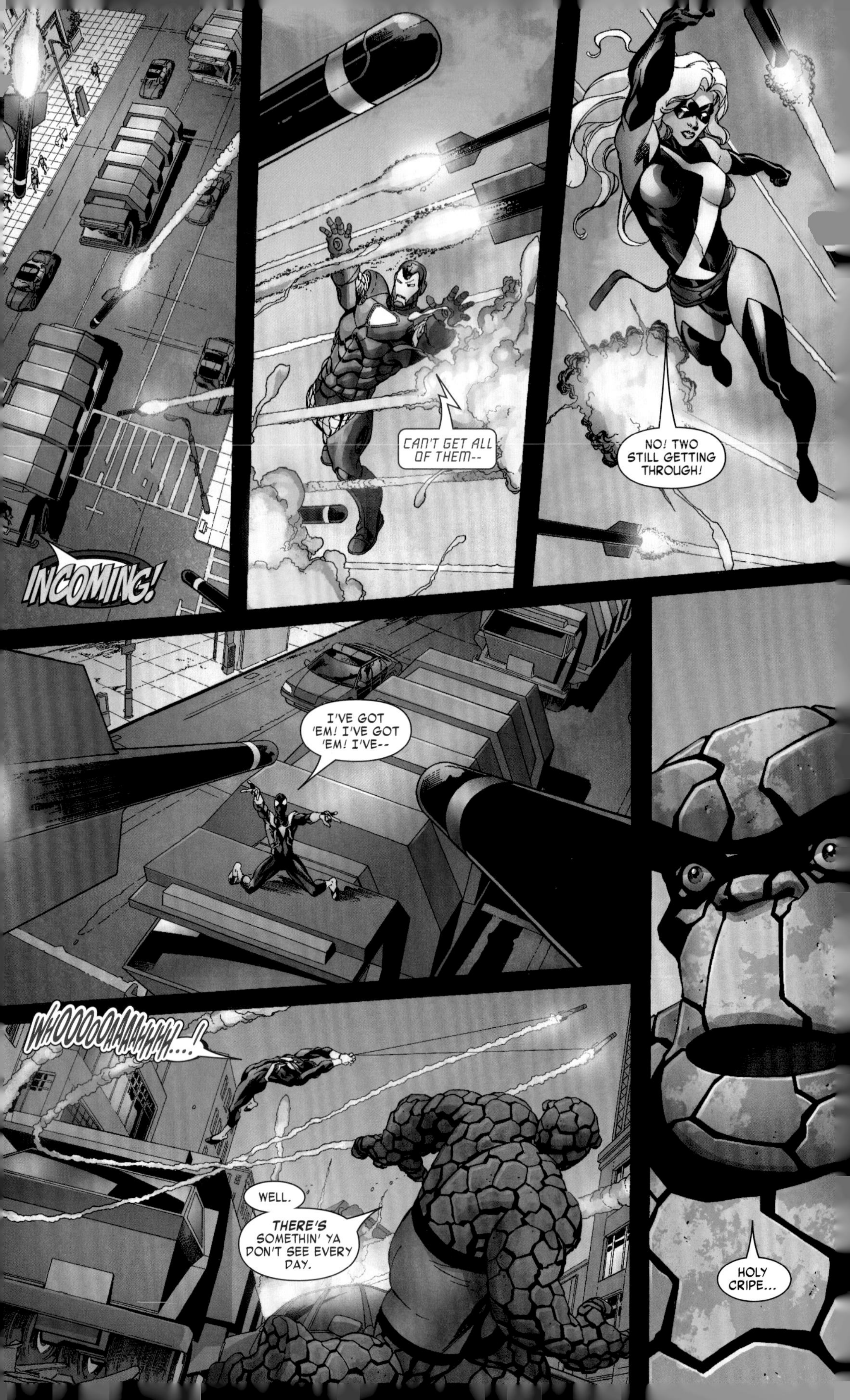
INCOMING!
CAN'T GET ALL OF THEM--
NO! TWO STILL GETTING THROUGH!
I'VE GOT 'EM! I'VE GOT 'EM! I'VE--
WHOOOOOAAAAHHHH...!
WELL.
THERE'S SOMETHIN' YA DON'T SEE EVERY DAY.
HOLY CRIPE...

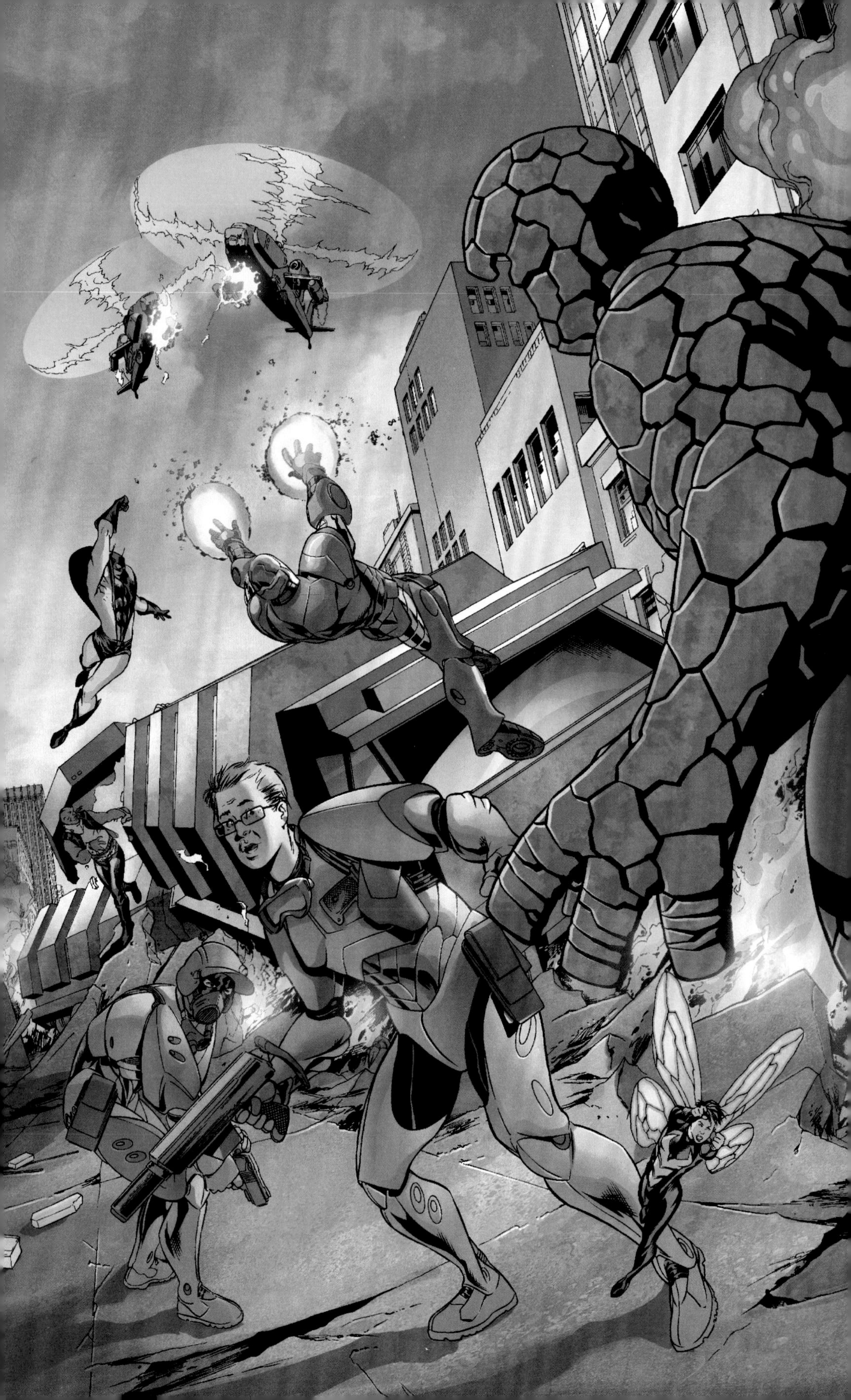

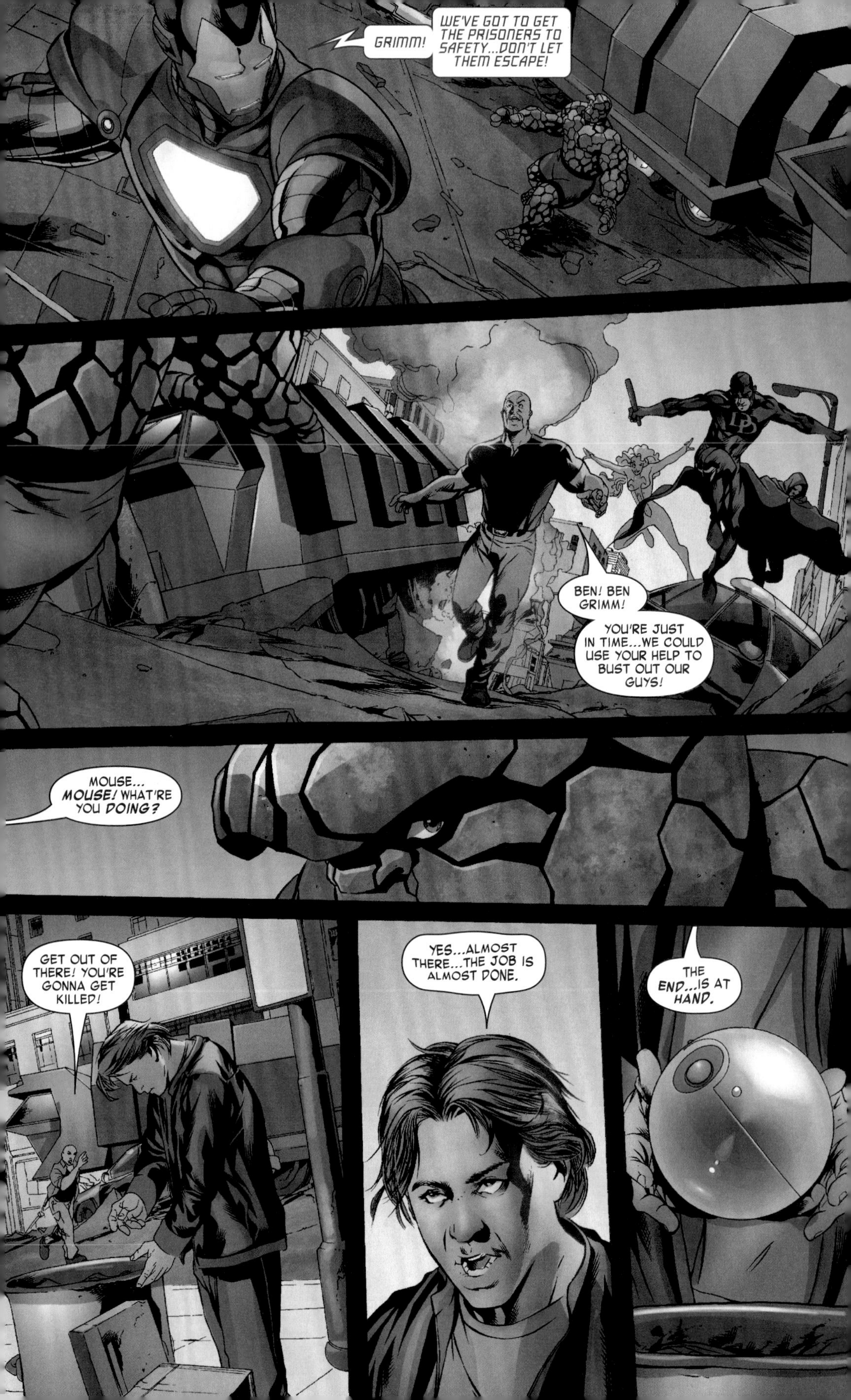
GRIMM!
WE'VE GOT TO GET THE PRISONERS TO SAFETY...DON'T LET THEM ESCAPE!
BEN! BEN GRIMM!
YOU'RE JUST IN TIME...WE COULD USE YOUR HELP TO BUST OUT OUR GUYS!
MOUSE... MOUSE! WHAT'RE YOU DOING?
GET OUT OF THERE! YOU'RE GONNA GET KILLED!
YES...ALMOST THERE...THE JOB IS ALMOST DONE.
THE END...IS AT HAND.

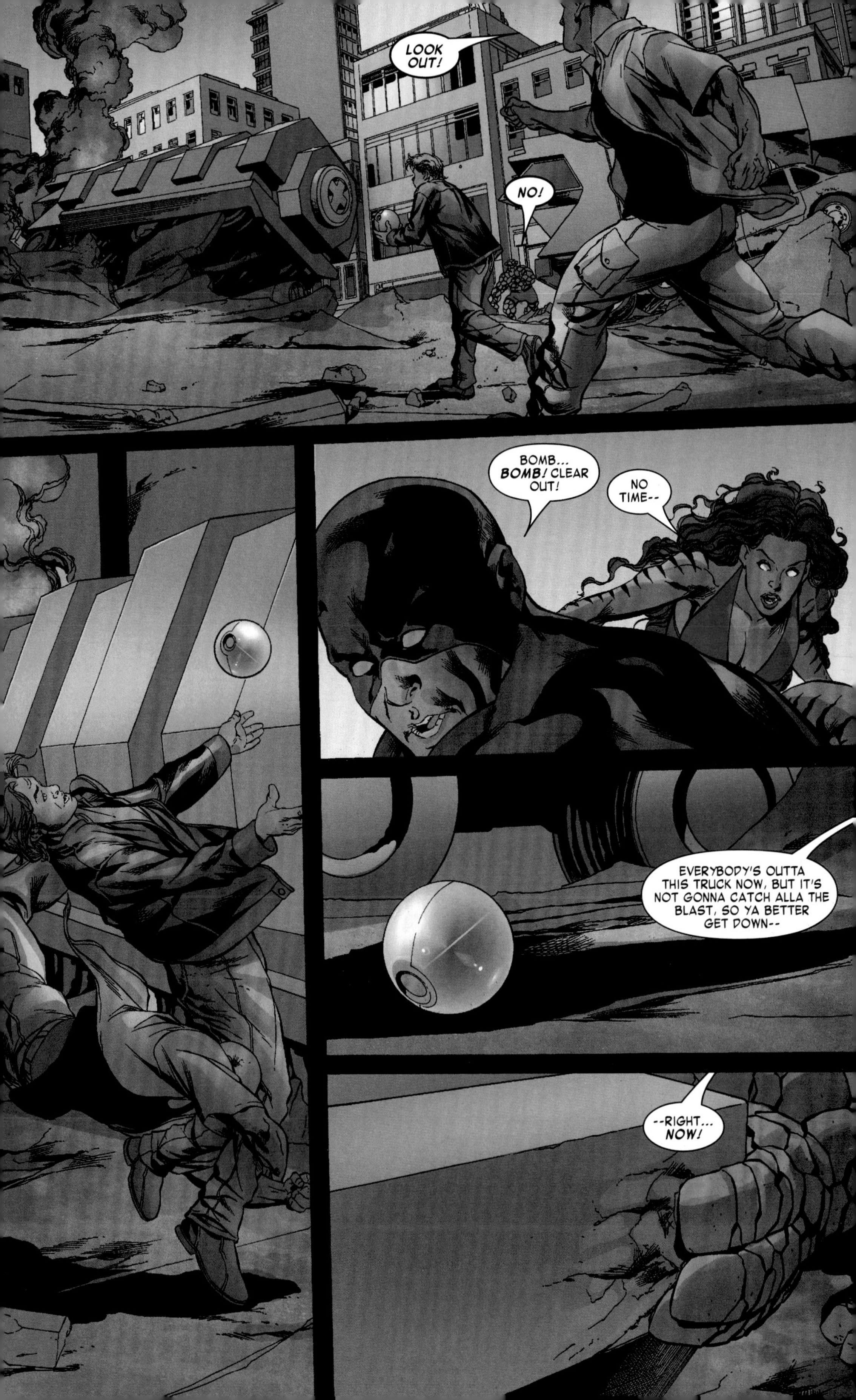
LOOK OUT!
NO!
BOMB... BOMB! CLEAR OUT!
NO TIME--
EVERYBODY'S OUTTA THIS TRUCK NOW, BUT IT'S NOT GONNA CATCH ALLA THE BLAST, SO YA BETTER GET DOWN--
--RIGHT... NOW!

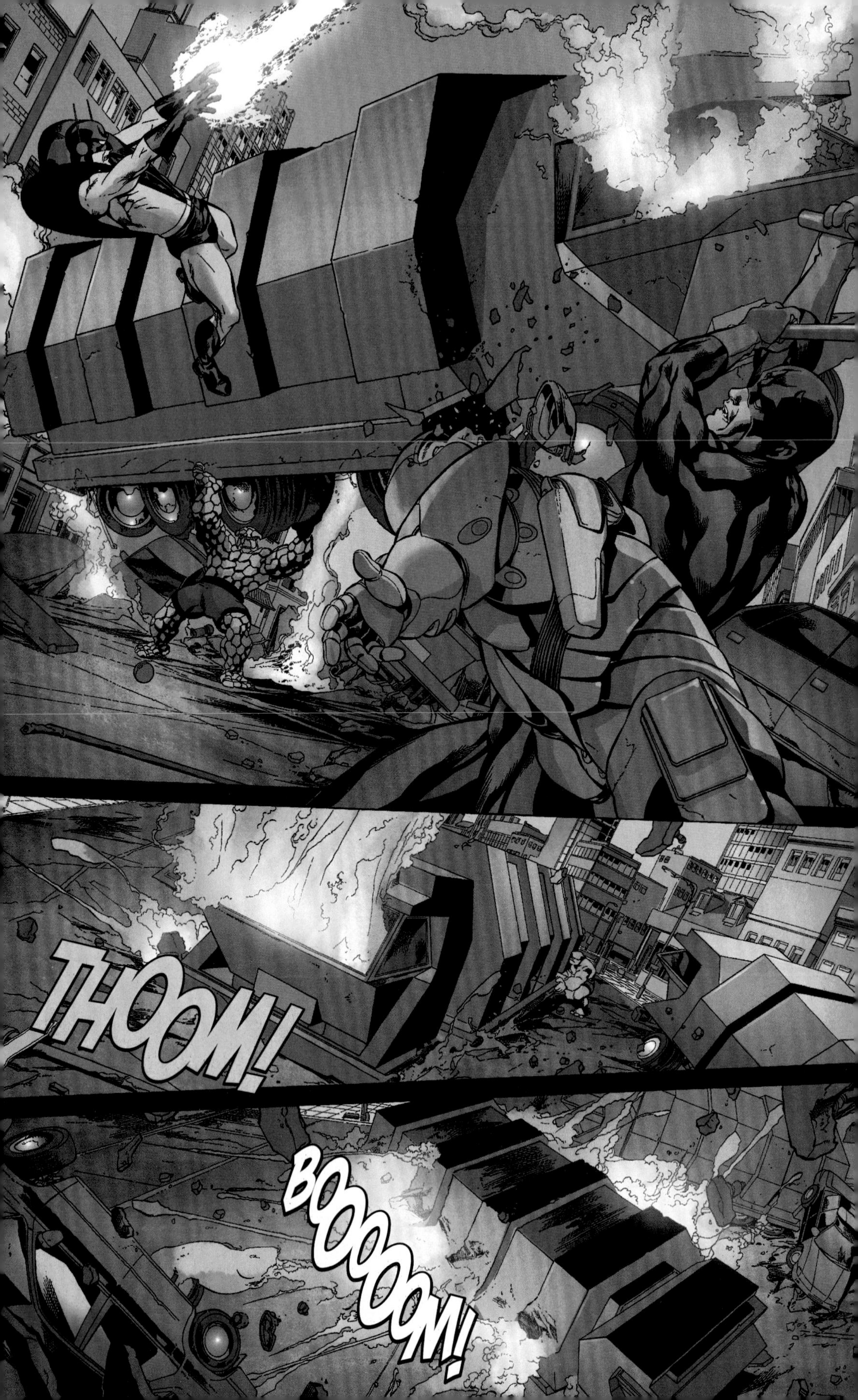
THOOM!
BOOOOOM!

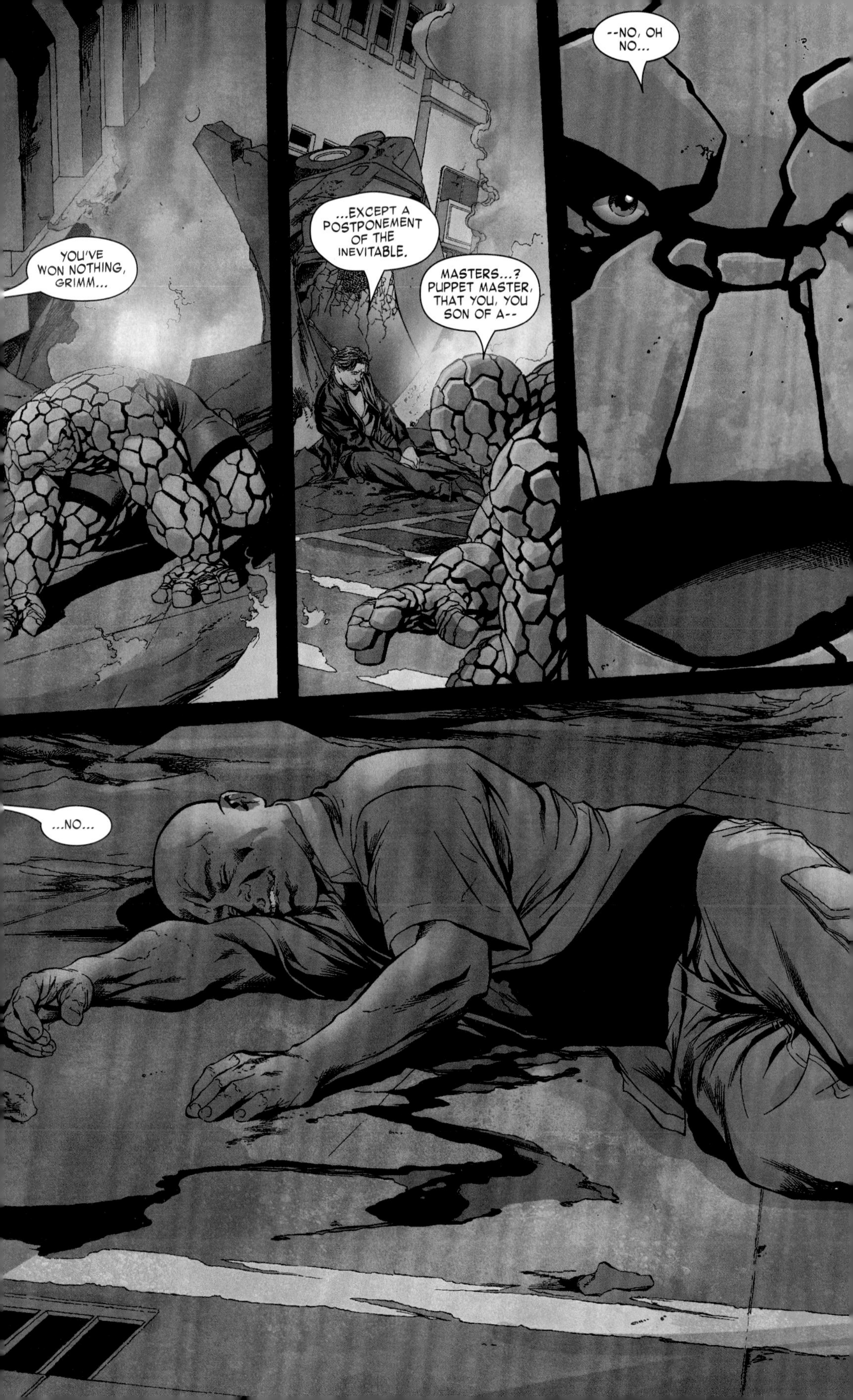
YOU'VE WON NOTHING, GRIMM...
...EXCEPT A POSTPONEMENT OF THE INEVITABLE.
MASTERS...? PUPPET MASTER, THAT YOU, YOU SON OF A--
--NO, OH NO...
...NO...

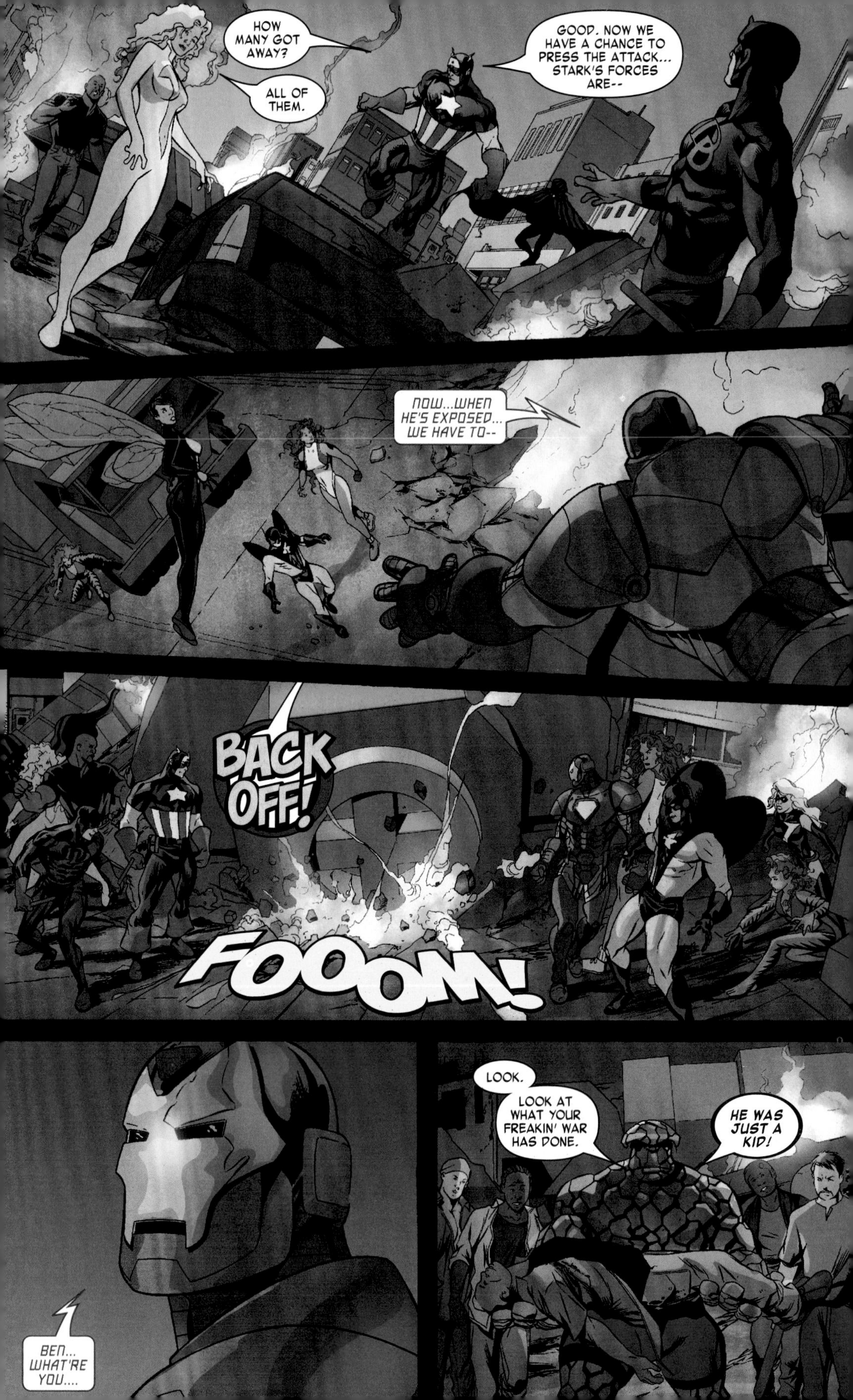
HOW MANY GOT AWAY?
ALL OF THEM.
GOOD. NOW WE HAVE A CHANCE TO PRESS THE ATTACK... STARK'S FORCES ARE--
NOW...WHEN HE'S EXPOSED... WE HAVE TO--
BACK OFF!
FOOOM!
BEN... WHAT'RE YOU....
LOOK.
LOOK AT WHAT YOUR FREAKIN' WAR HAS DONE.
HE WAS JUST A KID!

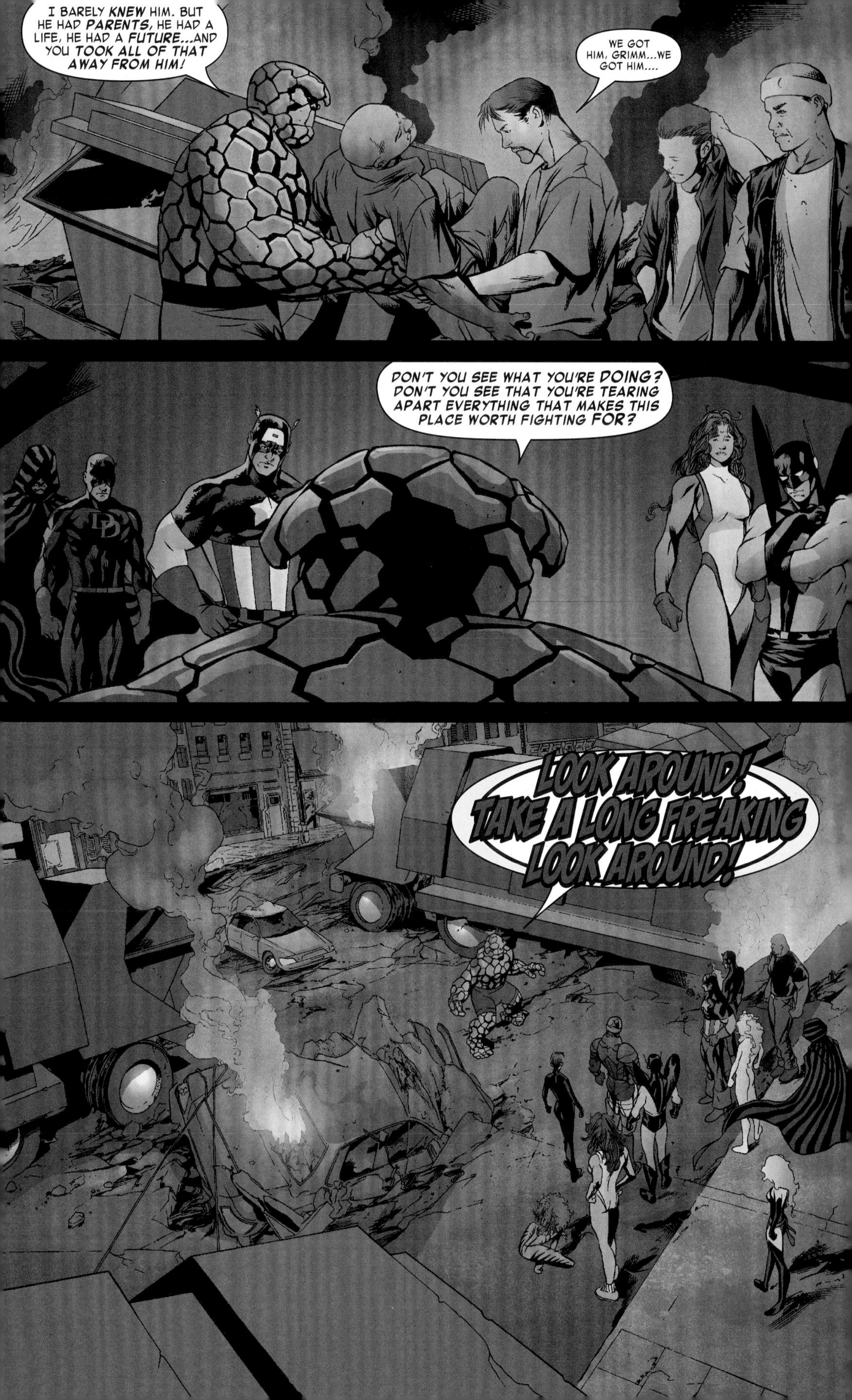
I BARELY KNEW HIM. BUT HE HAD PARENTS, HE HAD A LIFE, HE HAD A FUTURE...AND YOU TOOK ALL OF THAT AWAY FROM HIM!
WE GOT HIM, GRIMM...WE GOT HIM....
DON'T YOU SEE WHAT YOU'RE DOING? DON'T YOU SEE THAT YOU'RE TEARING APART EVERYTHING THAT MAKES THIS PLACE WORTH FIGHTING FOR?
LOOK AROUND! TAKE A LONG FREAKING LOOK AROUND!

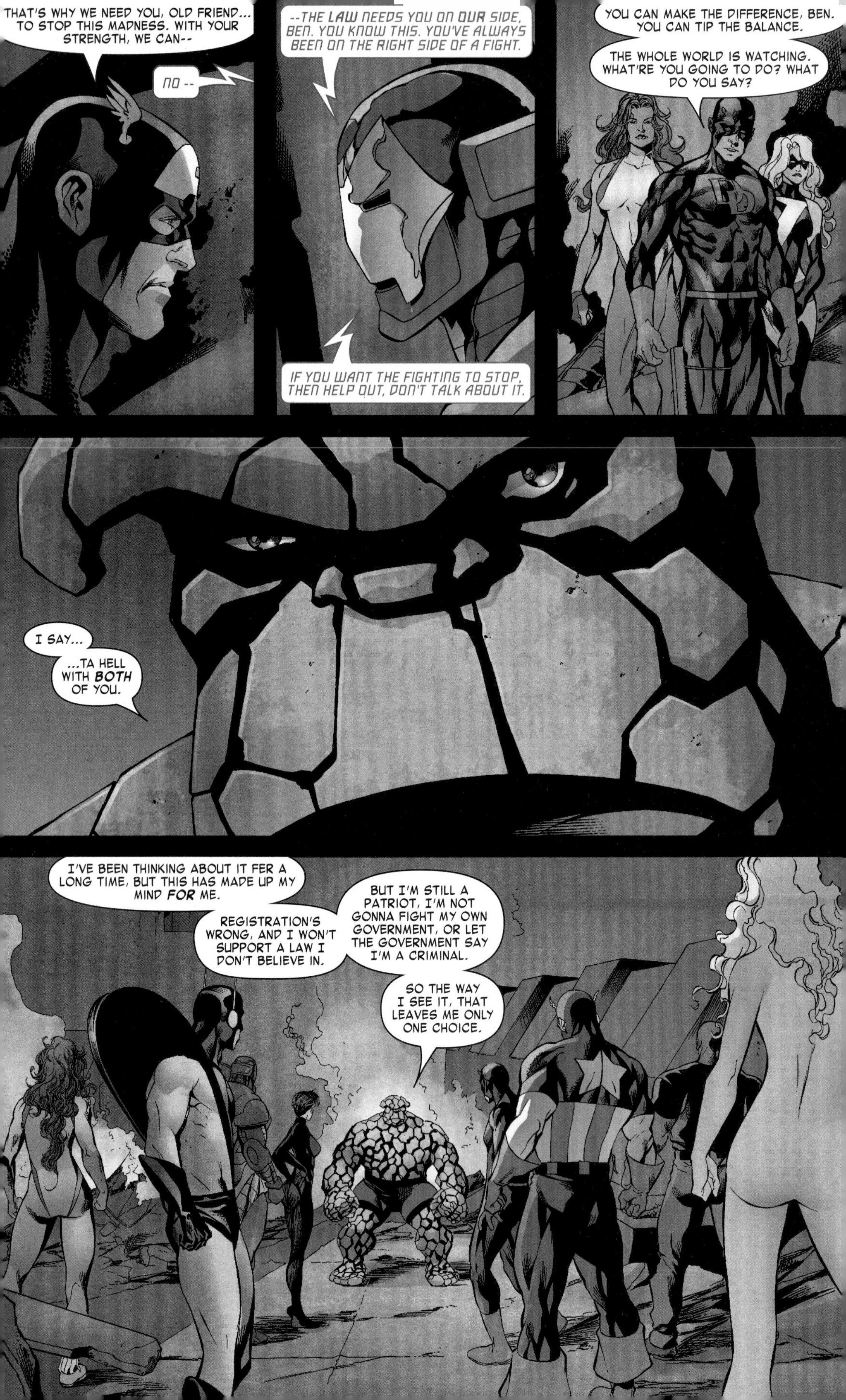

THAT'S WHY WE NEED YOU, OLD FRIEND... TO STOP THIS MADNESS. WITH YOUR STRENGTH, WE CAN--
NO --
--THE LAW NEEDS YOU ON OUR SIDE, BEN. YOU KNOW THIS. YOU'VE ALWAYS BEEN ON THE RIGHT SIDE OF A FIGHT.
IF YOU WANT THE FIGHTING TO STOP, THEN HELP OUT, DON'T TALK ABOUT IT.
YOU CAN MAKE THE DIFFERENCE, BEN. YOU CAN TIP THE BALANCE.
THE WHOLE WORLD IS WATCHING. WHAT'RE YOU GOING TO DO? WHAT DO YOU SAY?
I SAY...
...TA HELL WITH BOTH OF YOU.
I'VE BEEN THINKING ABOUT IT FER A LONG TIME, BUT THIS HAS MADE UP MY MIND FOR ME.
REGISTRATION'S WRONG, AND I WON'T SUPPORT A LAW I DON'T BELIEVE IN.
BUT I'M STILL A PATRIOT, I'M NOT GONNA FIGHT MY OWN GOVERNMENT, OR LET THE GOVERNMENT SAY I'M A CRIMINAL.
SO THE WAY I SEE IT, THAT LEAVES ME ONLY ONE CHOICE.

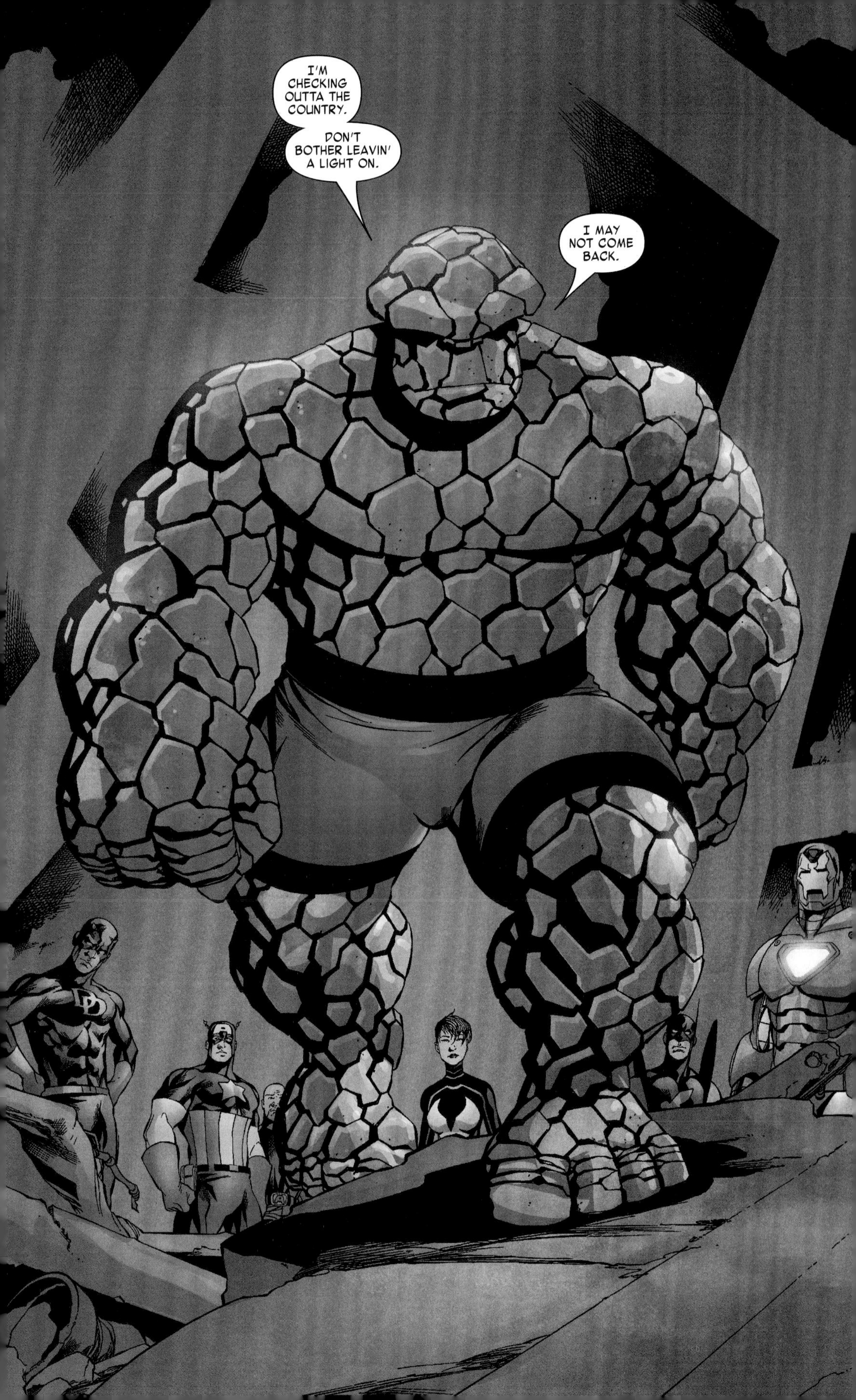
I'M CHECKING OUTTA THE COUNTRY.
DON'T BOTHER LEAVIN' A LIGHT ON.
I MAY NOT COME BACK.

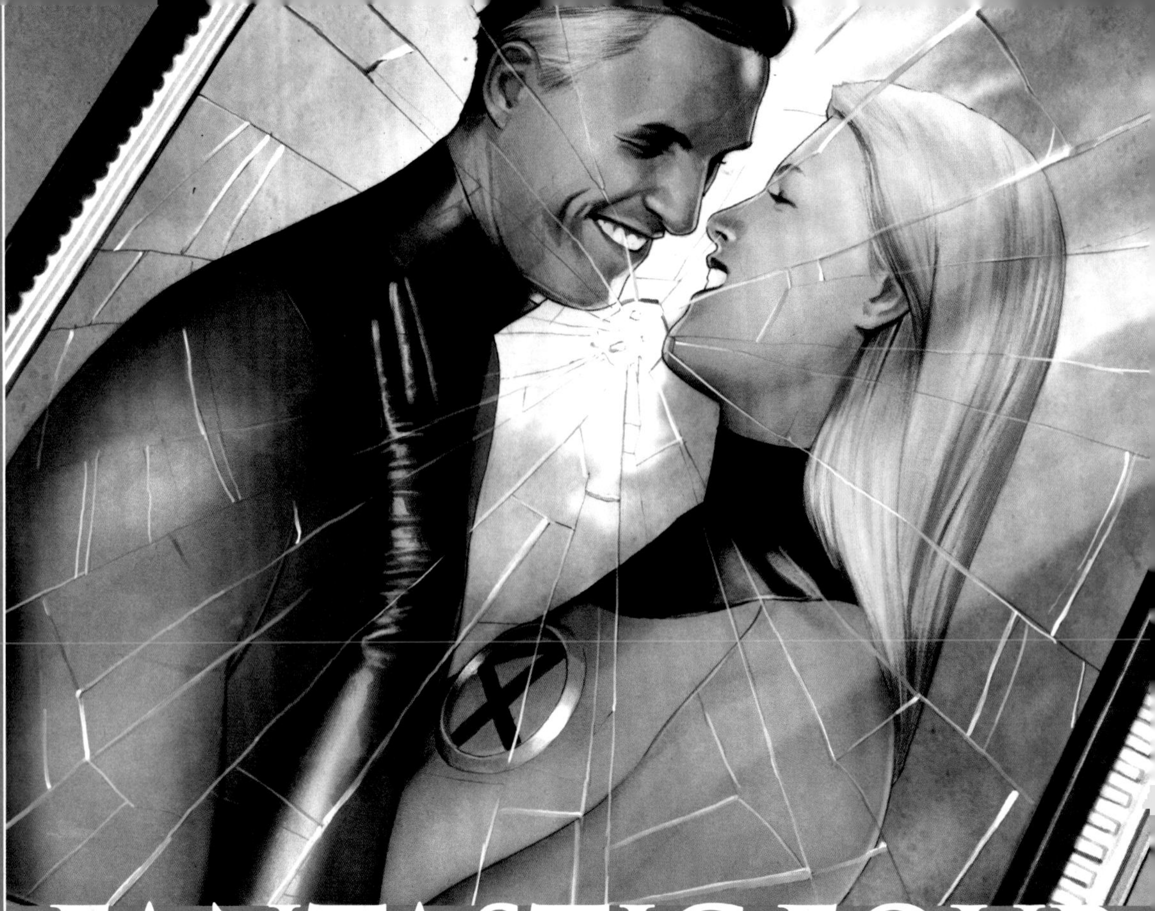

FANTASTIC FOUR

A MARVEL COMICS EVENT

CIVIL WAR

FANTASTIC FOUR #540

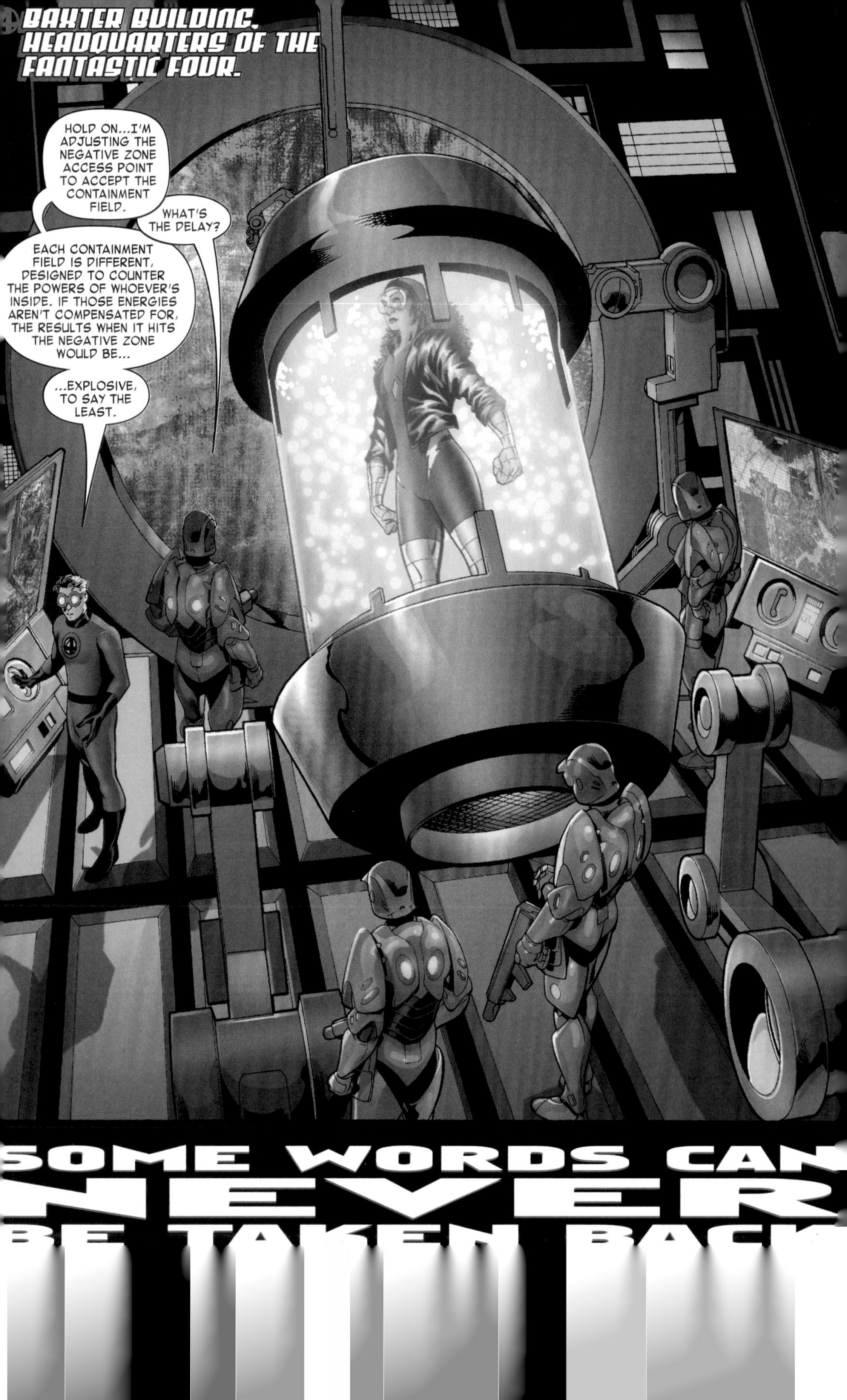
BAXTER BUILDING, HEADQUARTERS OF THE FANTASTIC FOUR.
HOLD ON...I'M ADJUSTING THE NEGATIVE ZONE ACCESS POINT TO ACCEPT THE CONTAINMENT FIELD.
WHAT'S THE DELAY?
EACH CONTAINMENT FIELD IS DIFFERENT, DESIGNED TO COUNTER THE POWERS OF WHOEVER'S INSIDE. IF THOSE ENERGIES AREN'T COMPENSATED FOR, THE RESULTS WHEN IT HITS THE NEGATIVE ZONE WOULD BE...
...EXPLOSIVE, TO SAY THE LEAST.
SOME WORDS CAN NEVER BE TAKEN BACK

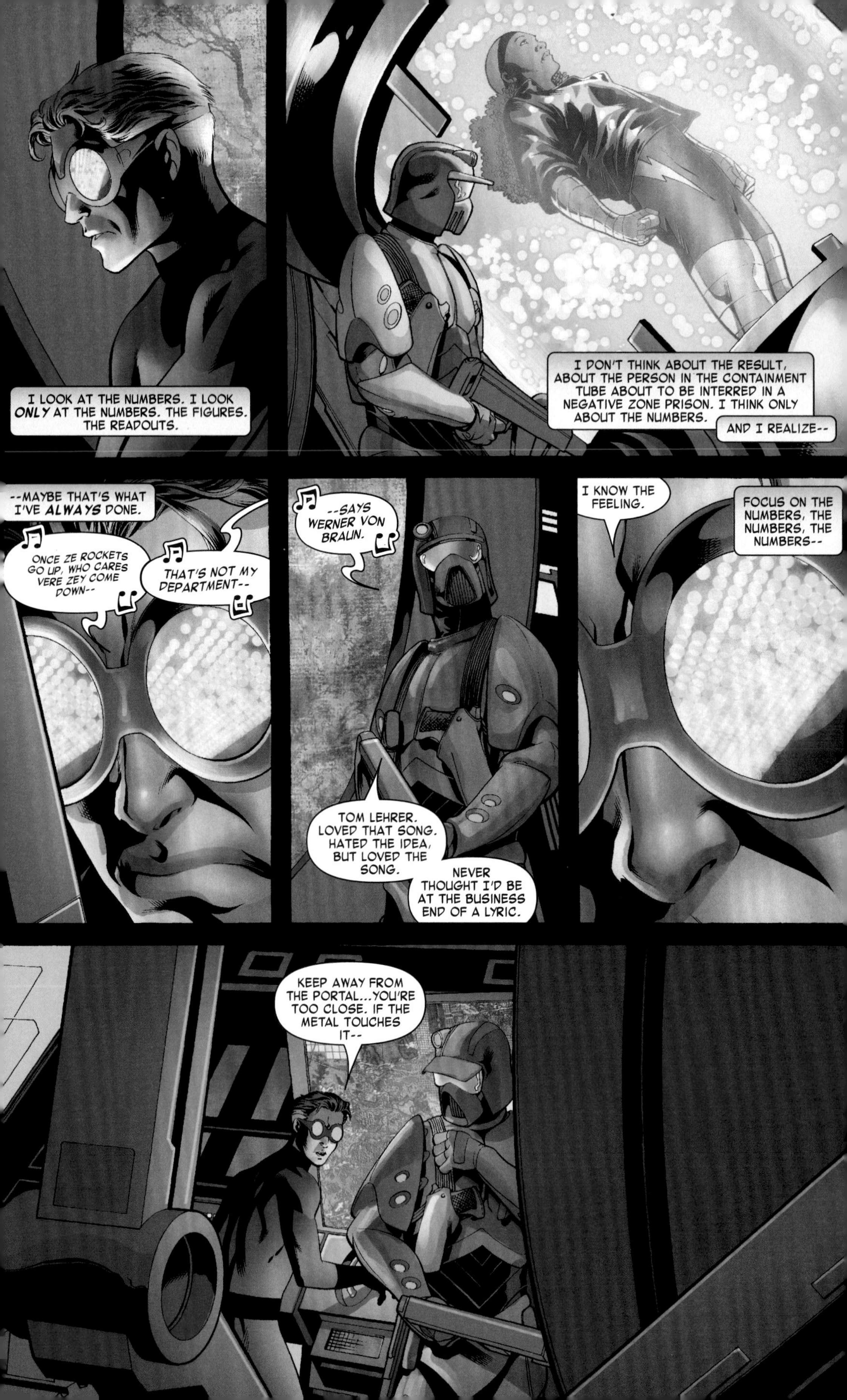
I LOOK AT THE NUMBERS. I LOOK ONLY AT THE NUMBERS. THE FIGURES. THE READOUTS.
I DON'T THINK ABOUT THE RESULT, ABOUT THE PERSON IN THE CONTAINMENT TUBE ABOUT TO BE INTERRED IN A NEGATIVE ZONE PRISON. I THINK ONLY ABOUT THE NUMBERS.
AND I REALIZE--
--MAYBE THAT'S WHAT I'VE ALWAYS DONE.
ONCE ZE ROCKETS GO UP, WHO CARES VERE ZEY COME DOWN--
THAT'S NOT MY DEPARTMENT--
--SAYS WERNER VON BRAUN.
TOM LEHRER. LOVED THAT SONG. HATED THE IDEA, BUT LOVED THE SONG.
NEVER THOUGHT I'D BE AT THE BUSINESS END OF A LYRIC.
I KNOW THE FEELING.
FOCUS ON THE NUMBERS, THE NUMBERS, THE NUMBERS--
KEEP AWAY FROM THE PORTAL... YOU'RE TOO CLOSE. IF THE METAL TOUCHES IT--

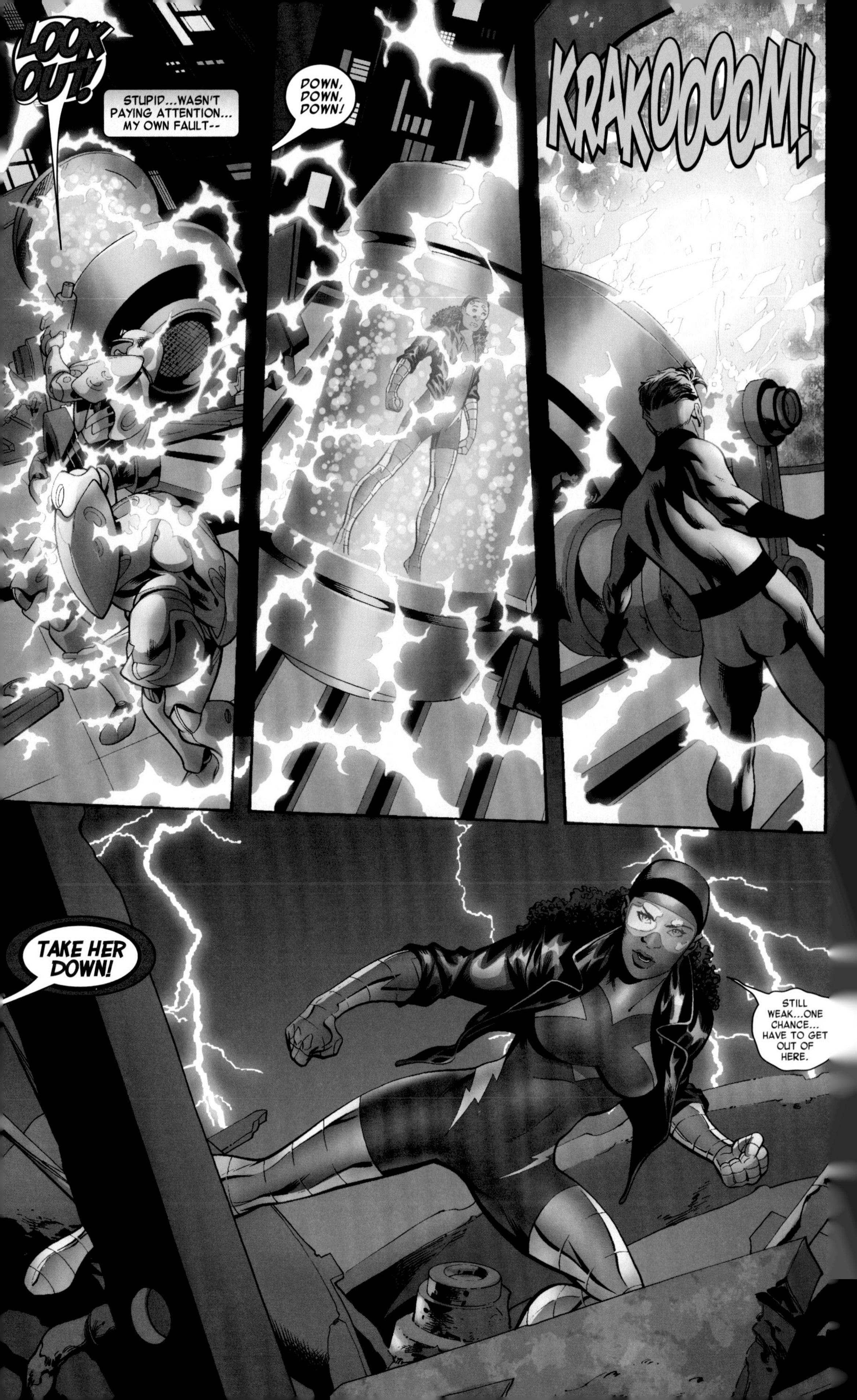
LOOK OUT!
STUPID...WASN'T PAYING ATTENTION... MY OWN FAULT--
DOWN, DOWN, DOWN!
KRAKOOOOM!
TAKE HER DOWN!
STILL WEAK...ONE CHANCE... HAVE TO GET OUT OF HERE.

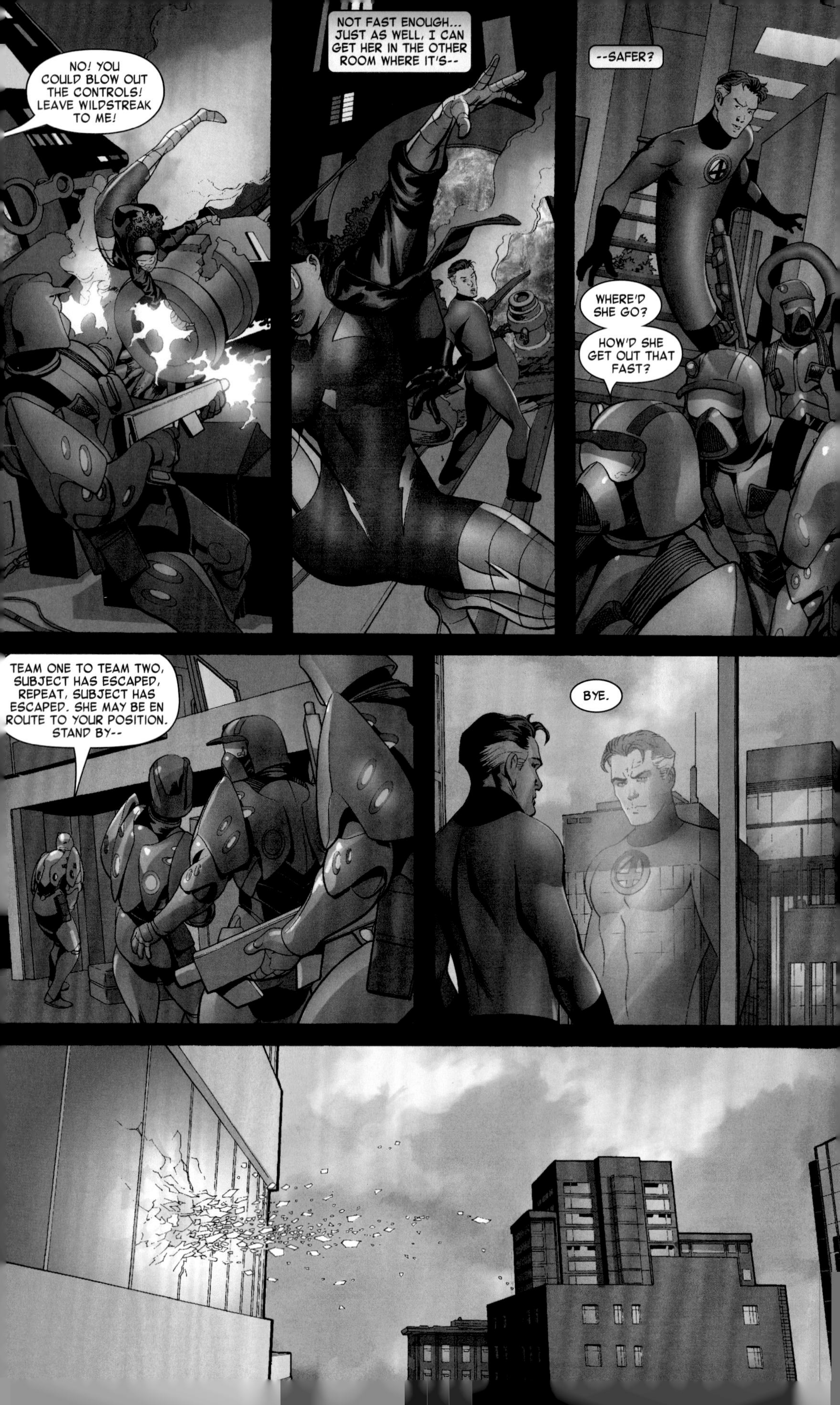

NO! YOU COULD BLOW OUT THE CONTROLS! LEAVE WILDSTREAK TO ME!
NOT FAST ENOUGH... JUST AS WELL, I CAN GET HER IN THE OTHER ROOM WHERE IT'S--
--SAFER?
WHERE'D SHE GO?
HOW'D SHE GET OUT THAT FAST?
TEAM ONE TO TEAM TWO, SUBJECT HAS ESCAPED, REPEAT, SUBJECT HAS ESCAPED. SHE MAY BE EN ROUTE TO YOUR POSITION. STAND BY--
BYE.

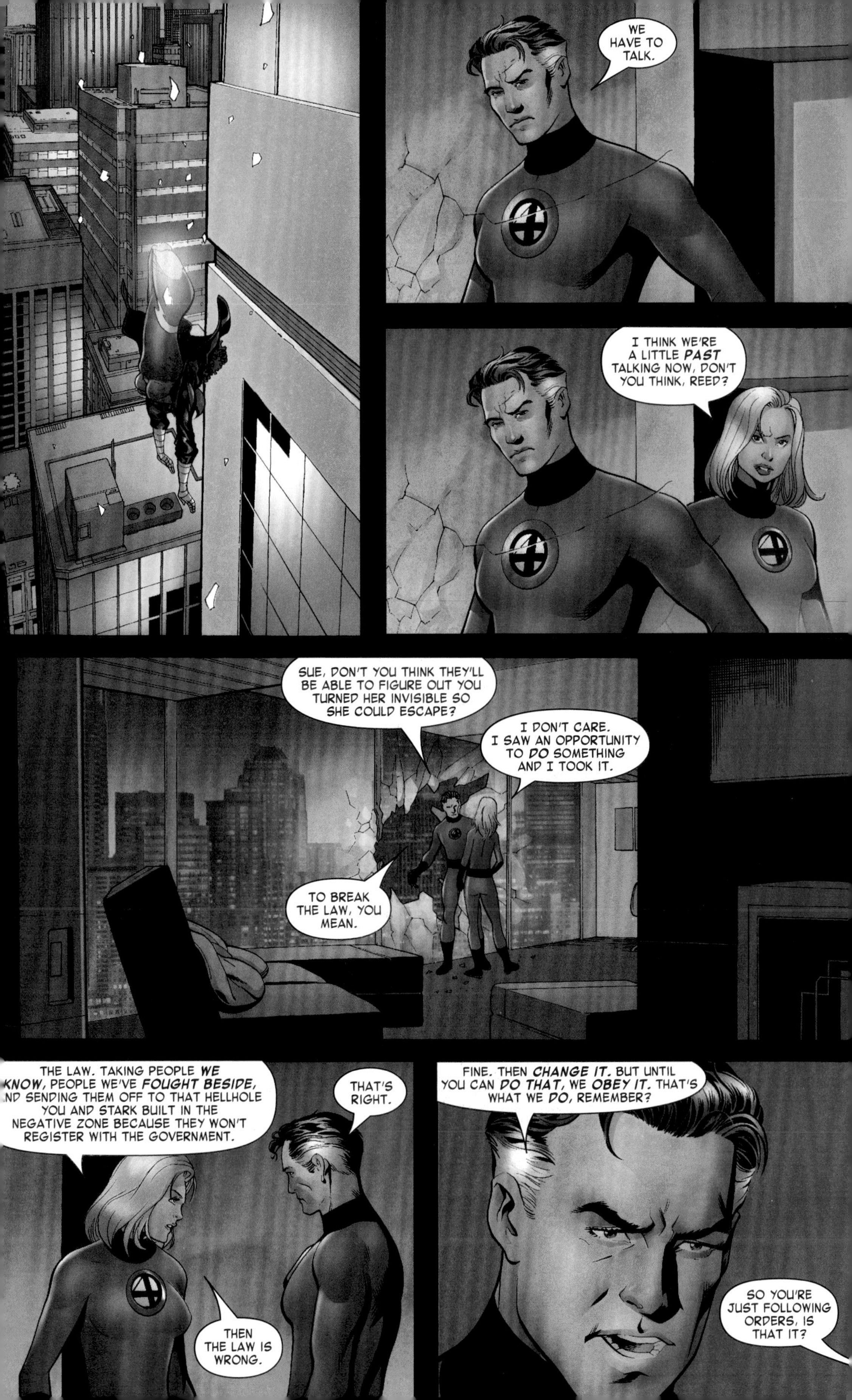
WE HAVE TO TALK.
I THINK WE'RE A LITTLE PAST TALKING NOW, DON'T YOU THINK, REED?
SUE, DON'T YOU THINK THEY'LL BE ABLE TO FIGURE OUT YOU TURNED HER INVISIBLE SO SHE COULD ESCAPE?
I DON'T CARE. I SAW AN OPPORTUNITY TO DO SOMETHING AND I TOOK IT.
TO BREAK THE LAW, YOU MEAN.
THE LAW. TAKING PEOPLE WE KNOW, PEOPLE WE'VE FOUGHT BESIDE, ND SENDING THEM OFF TO THAT HELLHOLE YOU AND STARK BUILT IN THE NEGATIVE ZONE BECAUSE THEY WON'T REGISTER WITH THE GOVERNMENT.
THAT'S RIGHT.
THEN THE LAW IS WRONG.
FINE. THEN CHANGE IT. BUT UNTIL YOU CAN DO THAT, WE OBEY IT. THAT'S WHAT WE DO, REMEMBER?
SO YOU'RE JUST FOLLOWING ORDERS, IS THAT IT?

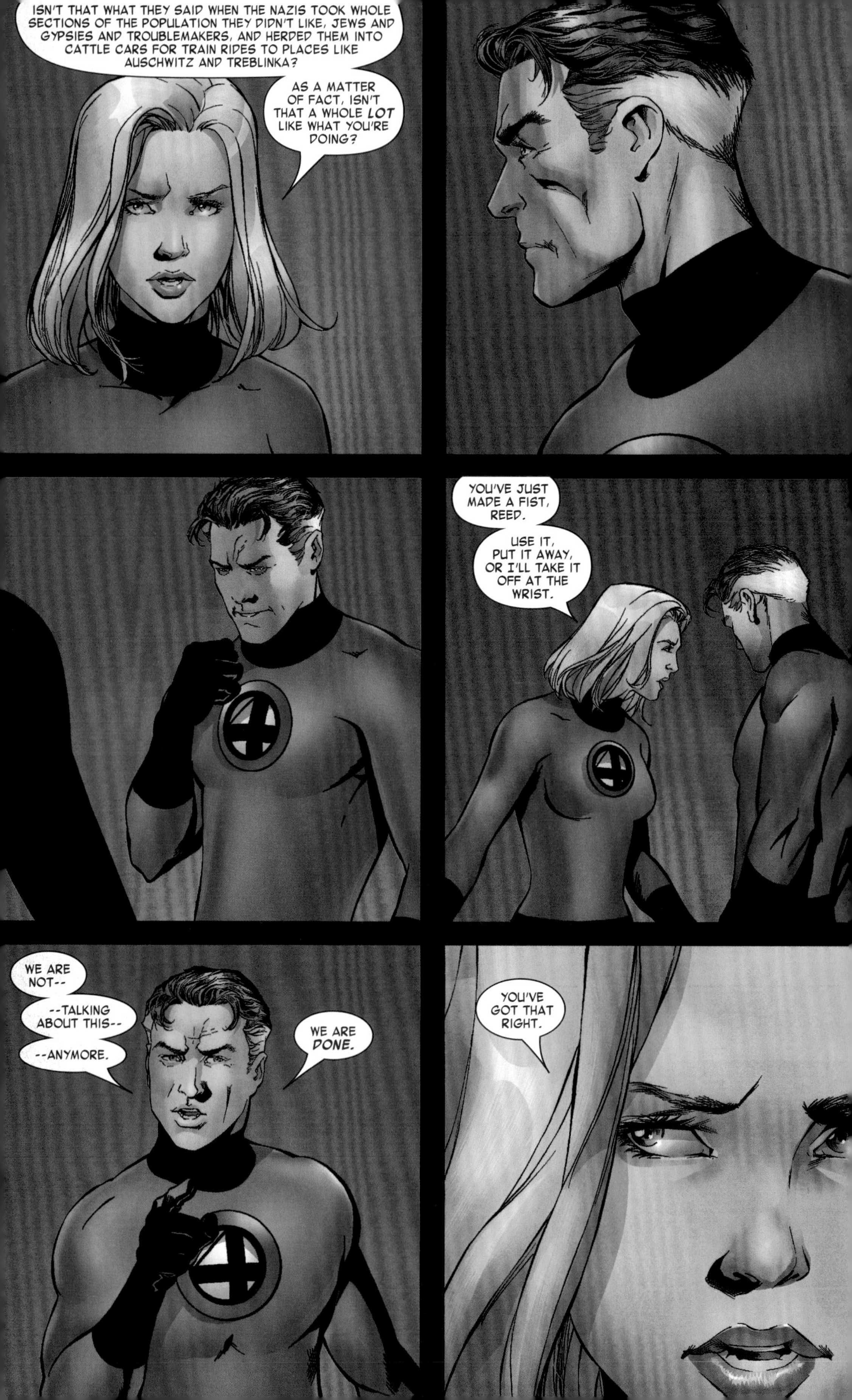
ISN'T THAT WHAT THEY SAID WHEN THE NAZIS TOOK WHOLE SECTIONS OF THE POPULATION THEY DIDN'T LIKE, JEWS AND GYPSIES AND TROUBLEMAKERS, AND HERDED THEM INTO CATTLE CARS FOR TRAIN RIDES TO PLACES LIKE AUSCHWITZ AND TREBLINKA?
AS A MATTER OF FACT, ISN'T THAT A WHOLE *LOT* LIKE WHAT YOU'RE DOING?
YOU'VE JUST MADE A FIST, REED.
USE IT, PUT IT AWAY, OR I'LL TAKE IT OFF AT THE WRIST.
WE ARE NOT--
--TALKING ABOUT THIS--
--ANYMORE.
WE ARE *DONE.*
YOU'VE GOT THAT RIGHT.

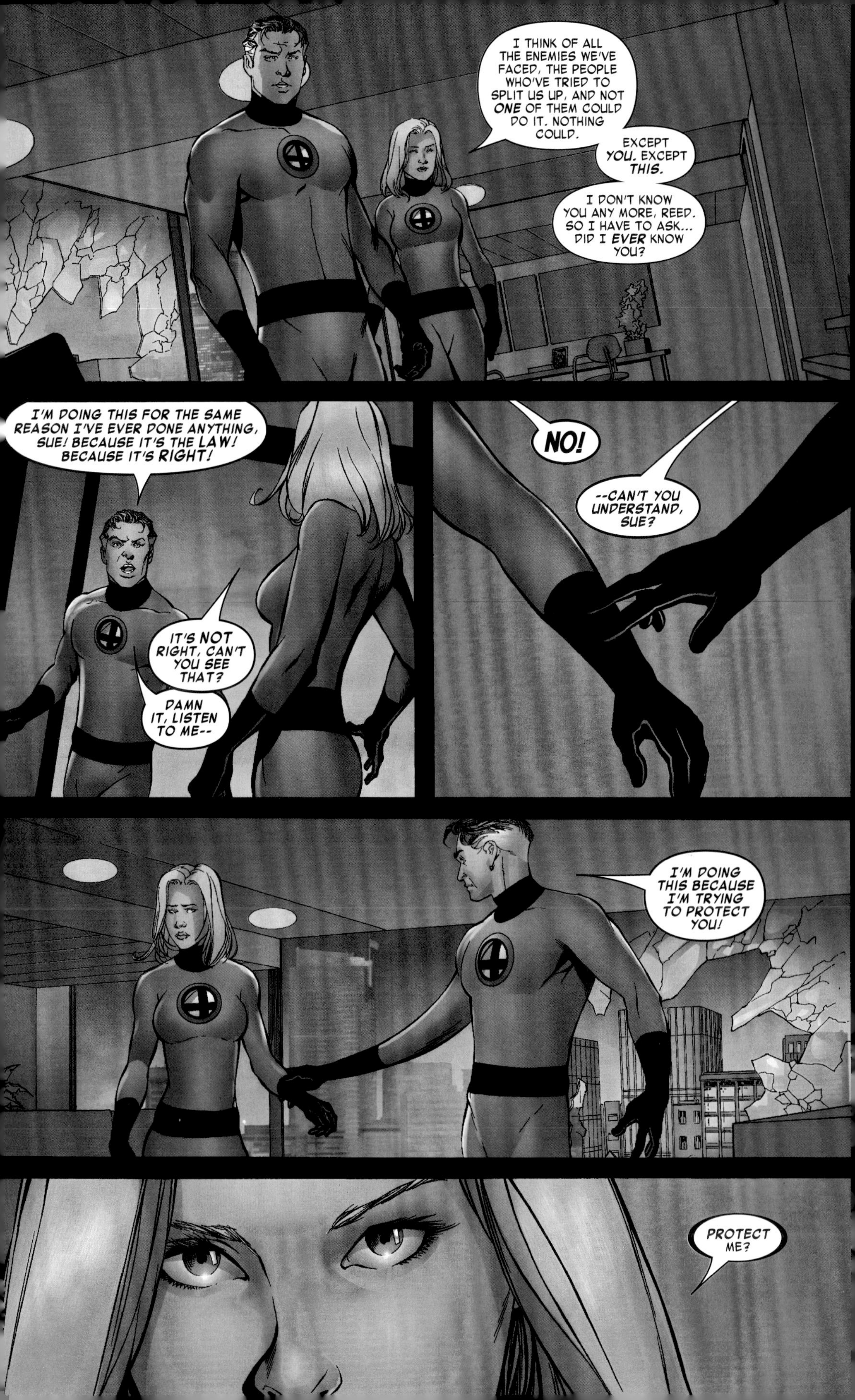
I THINK OF ALL THE ENEMIES WE'VE FACED, THE PEOPLE WHO'VE TRIED TO SPLIT US UP, AND NOT ONE OF THEM COULD DO IT. NOTHING COULD.
EXCEPT YOU. EXCEPT THIS.
I DON'T KNOW YOU ANY MORE, REED. SO I HAVE TO ASK... DID I EVER KNOW YOU?
I'M DOING THIS FOR THE SAME REASON I'VE EVER DONE ANYTHING, SUE! BECAUSE IT'S THE LAW! BECAUSE IT'S RIGHT!
IT'S NOT RIGHT, CAN'T YOU SEE THAT?
DAMN IT, LISTEN TO ME--
NO!
--CAN'T YOU UNDERSTAND, SUE?
I'M DOING THIS BECAUSE I'M TRYING TO PROTECT YOU!
PROTECT ME?

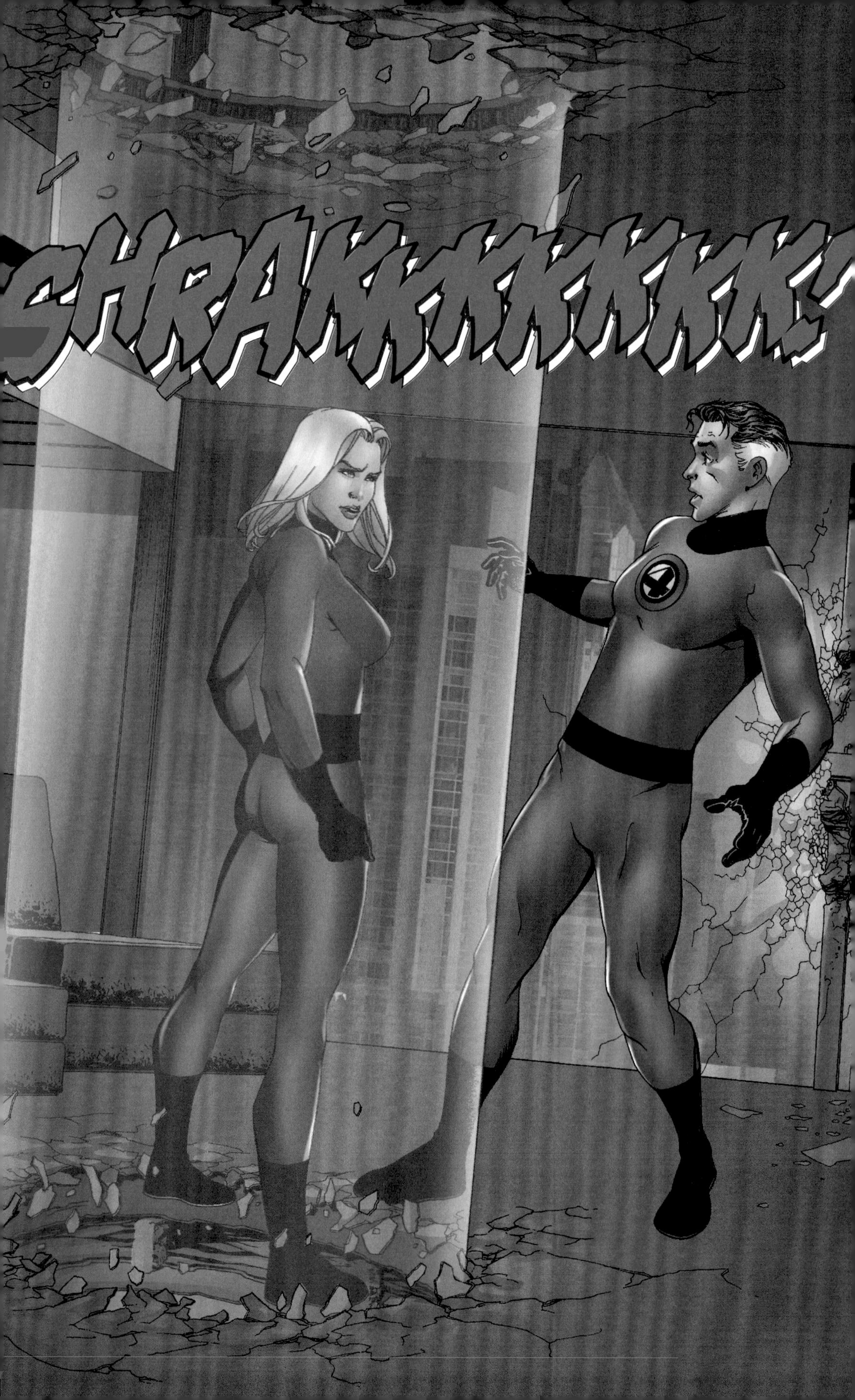
SHRAKKKKKK!

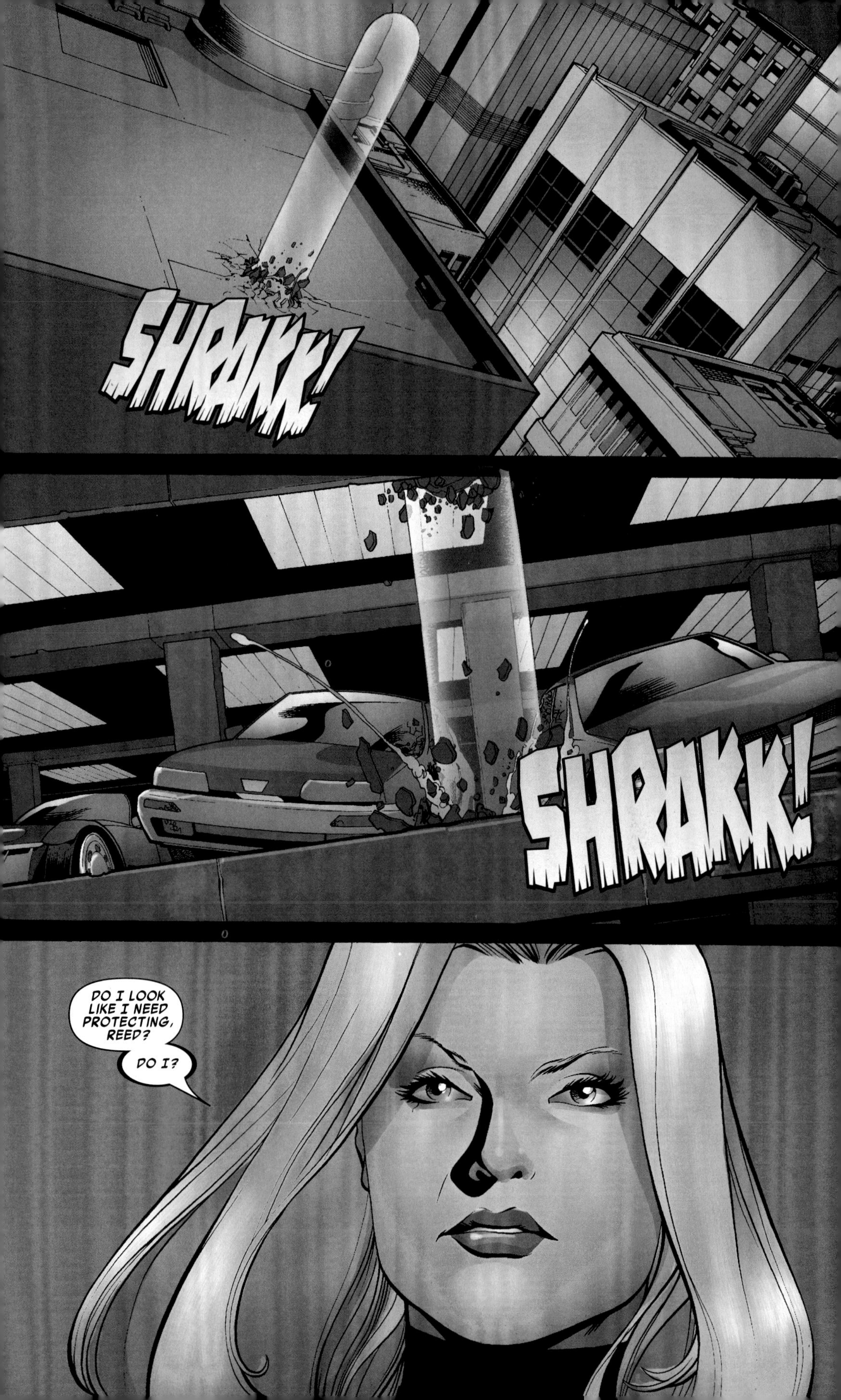
SHRAKK!
SHRAKK!
DO I LOOK LIKE I NEED PROTECTING, REED?
DO I?

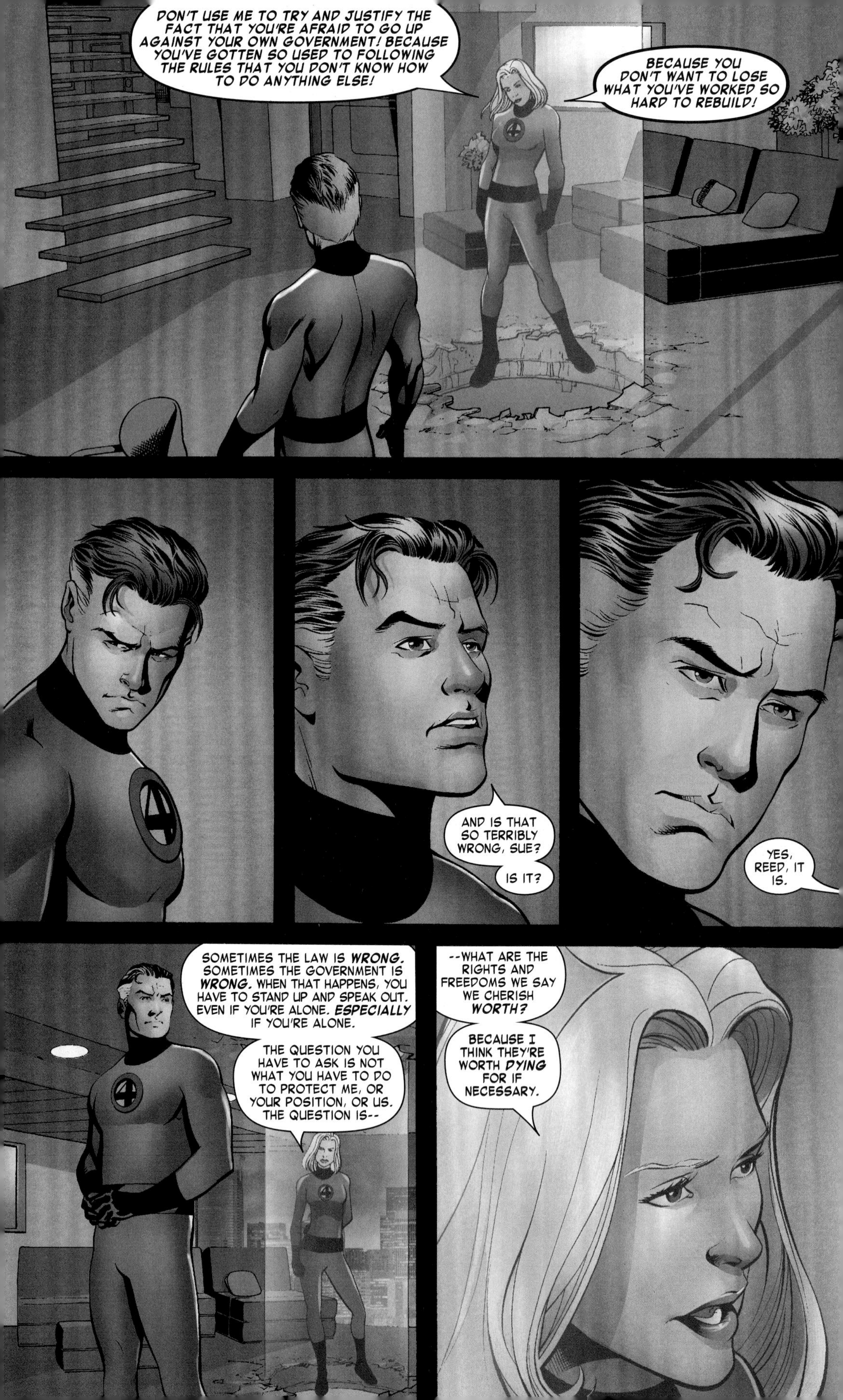
DON'T USE ME TO TRY AND JUSTIFY THE FACT THAT YOU'RE AFRAID TO GO UP AGAINST YOUR OWN GOVERNMENT! BECAUSE YOU'VE GOTTEN SO USED TO FOLLOWING THE RULES THAT YOU DON'T KNOW HOW TO DO ANYTHING ELSE!
BECAUSE YOU DON'T WANT TO LOSE WHAT YOU'VE WORKED SO HARD TO REBUILD!
AND IS THAT SO TERRIBLY WRONG, SUE?
IS IT?
YES, REED, IT IS.
SOMETIMES THE LAW IS WRONG. SOMETIMES THE GOVERNMENT IS WRONG. WHEN THAT HAPPENS, YOU HAVE TO STAND UP AND SPEAK OUT. EVEN IF YOU'RE ALONE. ESPECIALLY IF YOU'RE ALONE.
THE QUESTION YOU HAVE TO ASK IS NOT WHAT YOU HAVE TO DO TO PROTECT ME, OR YOUR POSITION, OR US. THE QUESTION IS--
--WHAT ARE THE RIGHTS AND FREEDOMS WE SAY WE CHERISH WORTH?
BECAUSE I THINK THEY'RE WORTH DYING FOR IF NECESSARY.

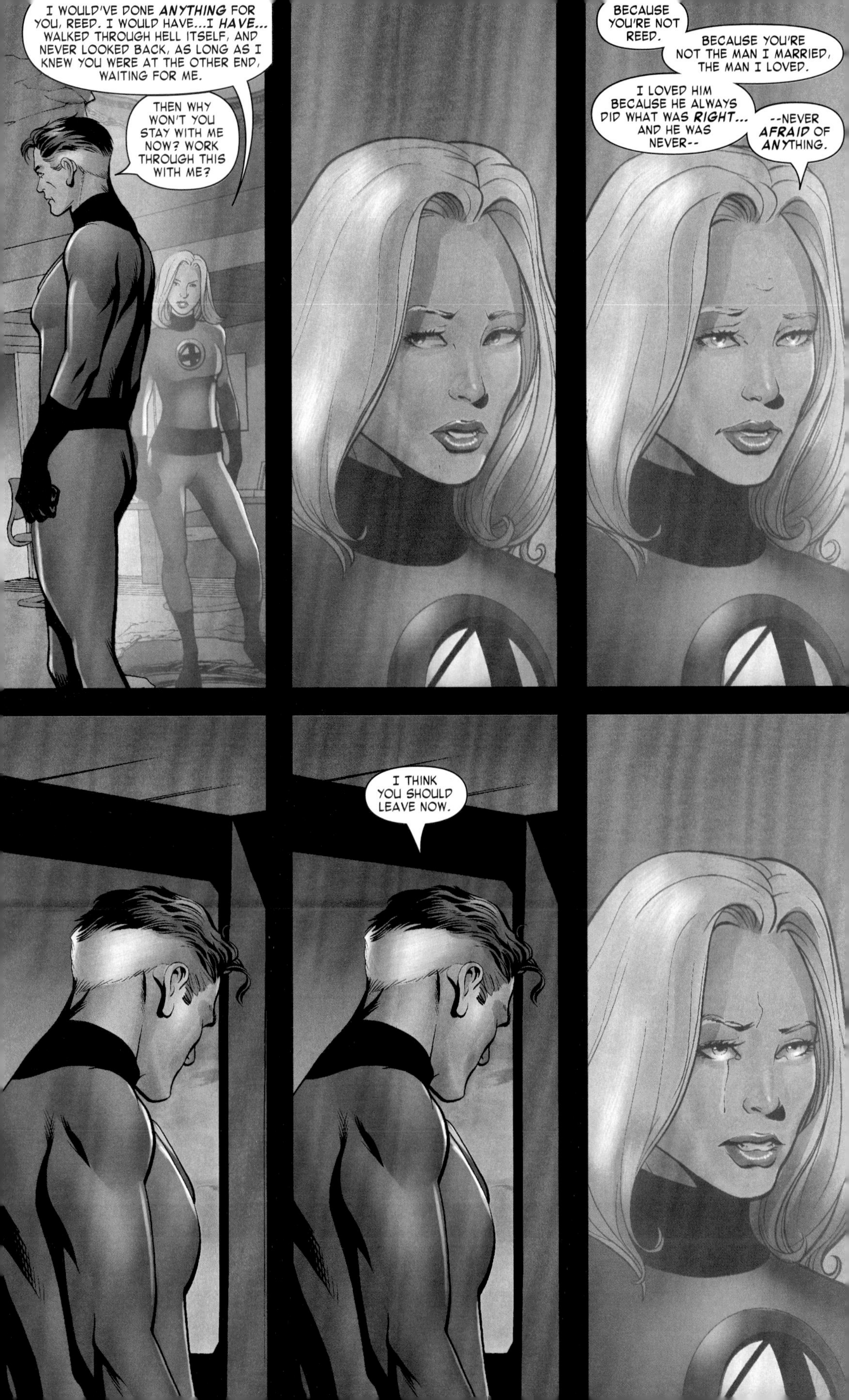
I WOULD'VE DONE ANYTHING FOR YOU, REED. I WOULD HAVE...I HAVE... WALKED THROUGH HELL ITSELF, AND NEVER LOOKED BACK, AS LONG AS I KNEW YOU WERE AT THE OTHER END, WAITING FOR ME.
THEN WHY WON'T YOU STAY WITH ME NOW? WORK THROUGH THIS WITH ME?
BECAUSE YOU'RE NOT REED.
BECAUSE YOU'RE NOT THE MAN I MARRIED, THE MAN I LOVED.
I LOVED HIM BECAUSE HE ALWAYS DID WHAT WAS RIGHT... AND HE WAS NEVER--
--NEVER AFRAID OF ANYTHING.
I THINK YOU SHOULD LEAVE NOW.

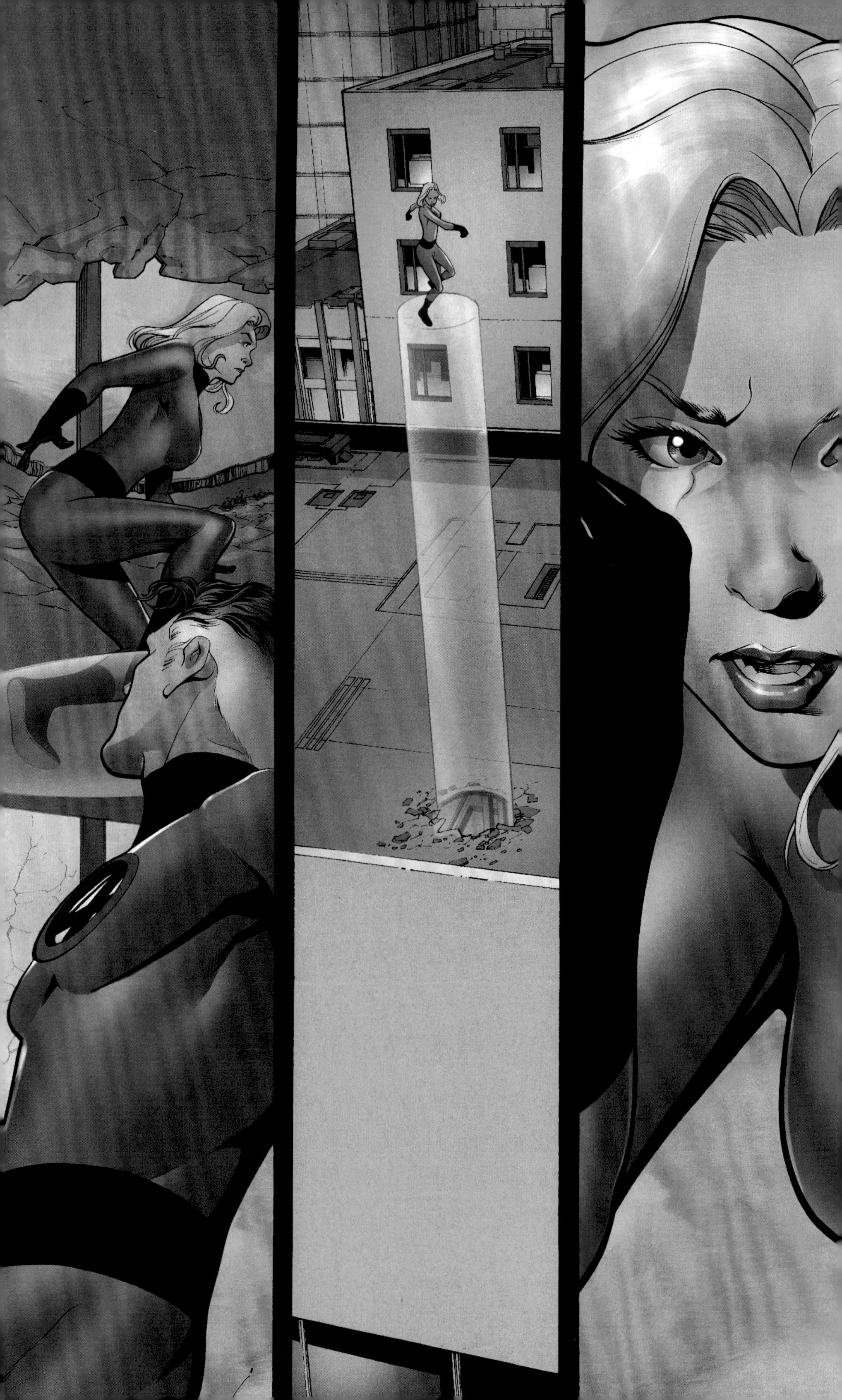

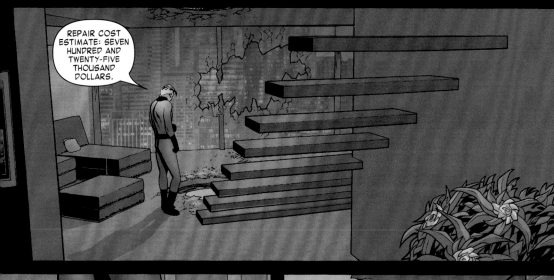

REPAIR COST ESTIMATE: SEVEN HUNDRED AND TWENTY-FIVE THOUSAND DOLLARS.

PLEASE LET HER COME BACK.

JUST THINK ABOUT THE NUMBERS. DON'T THINK ABOUT THE REST. YOU CAN'T. YOU CAN'T. YOU CAN'T.

SHE'S WRONG. SHE'LL SEE THAT. SHE'LL UNDERSTAND. SHE ALWAYS DOES.

SHE'LL COME BACK.

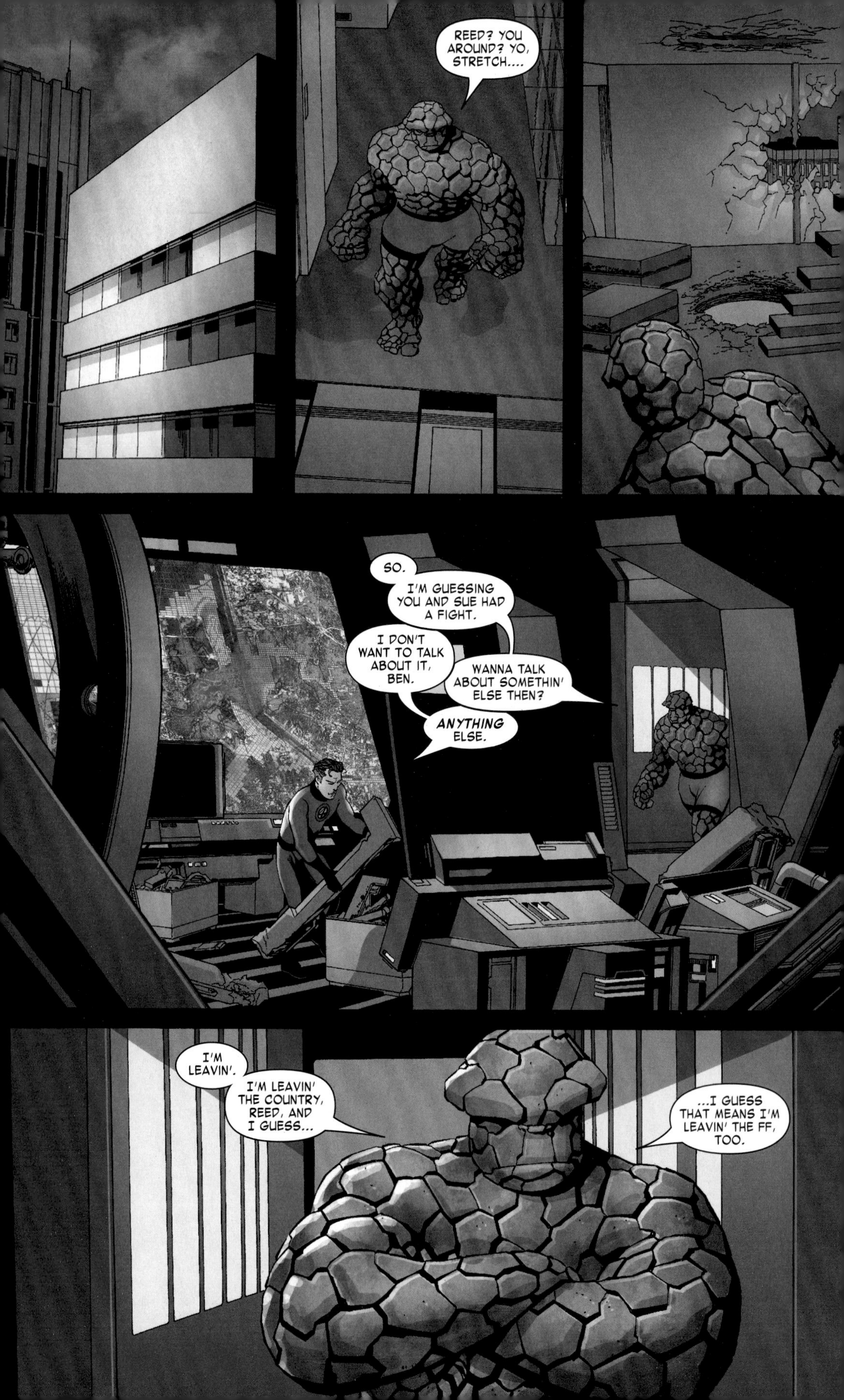
REED? YOU AROUND? YO, STRETCH....
SO.
I'M GUESSING YOU AND SUE HAD A FIGHT.
I DON'T WANT TO TALK ABOUT IT, BEN.
WANNA TALK ABOUT SOMETHIN' ELSE THEN?
ANYTHING ELSE.
I'M LEAVIN'.
I'M LEAVIN' THE COUNTRY, REED, AND I GUESS...
...I GUESS THAT MEANS I'M LEAVIN' THE FF, TOO.

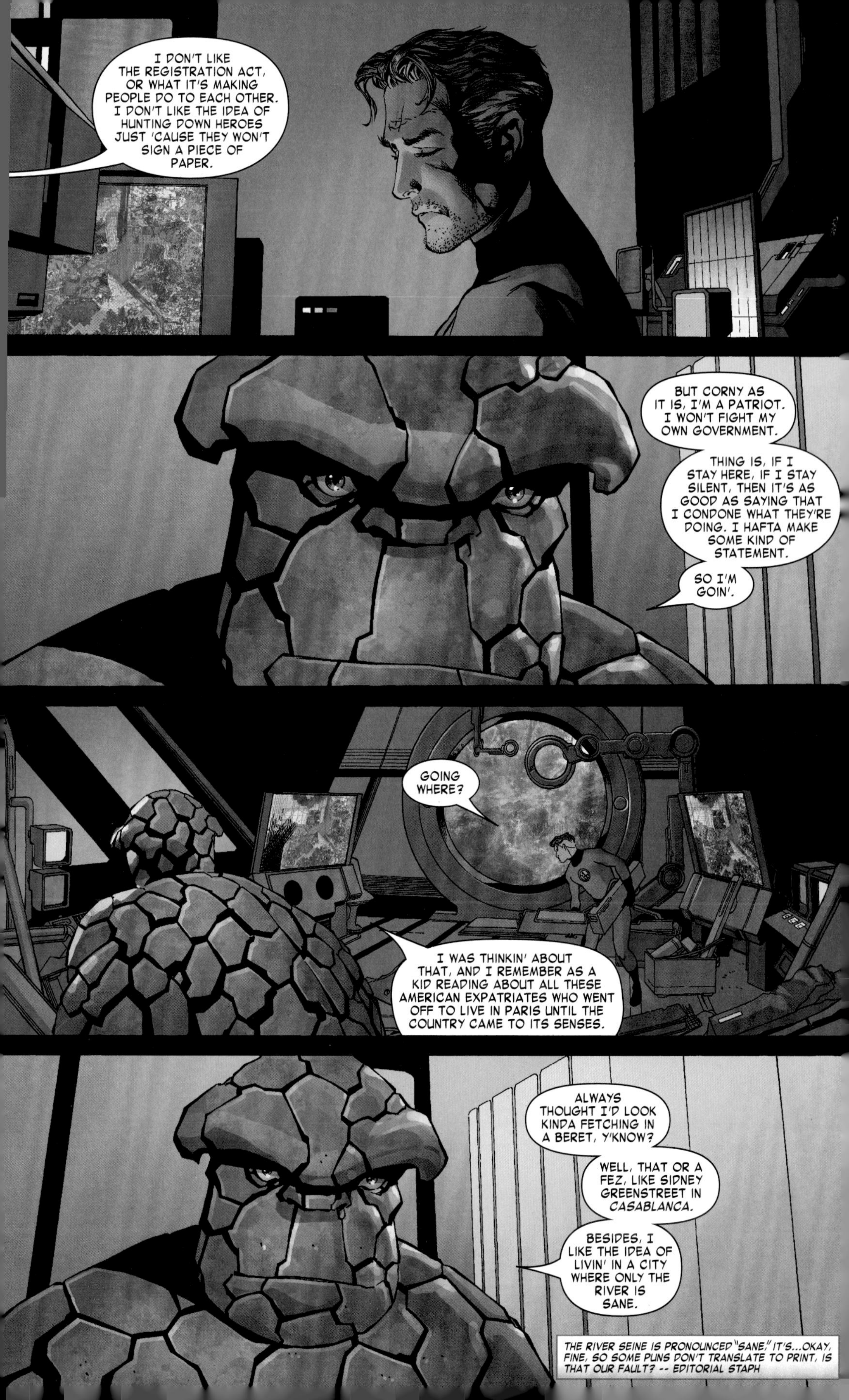
I DON'T LIKE THE REGISTRATION ACT, OR WHAT IT'S MAKING PEOPLE DO TO EACH OTHER. I DON'T LIKE THE IDEA OF HUNTING DOWN HEROES JUST 'CAUSE THEY WON'T SIGN A PIECE OF PAPER.
BUT CORNY AS IT IS, I'M A PATRIOT. I WON'T FIGHT MY OWN GOVERNMENT.
THING IS, IF I STAY HERE, IF I STAY SILENT, THEN IT'S AS GOOD AS SAYING THAT I CONDONE WHAT THEY'RE DOING. I HAFTA MAKE SOME KIND OF STATEMENT.
SO I'M GOIN'.
GOING WHERE?
I WAS THINKIN' ABOUT THAT, AND I REMEMBER AS A KID READING ABOUT ALL THESE AMERICAN EXPATRIATES WHO WENT OFF TO LIVE IN PARIS UNTIL THE COUNTRY CAME TO ITS SENSES.
ALWAYS THOUGHT I'D LOOK KINDA FETCHING IN A BERET, Y'KNOW?
WELL, THAT OR A FEZ, LIKE SIDNEY GREENSTREET IN *CASABLANCA.*
BESIDES, I LIKE THE IDEA OF LIVIN' IN A CITY WHERE ONLY THE RIVER IS SANE.
THE RIVER SEINE IS PRONOUNCED "SANE." IT'S...OKAY, FINE, SO SOME PUNS DON'T TRANSLATE TO PRINT, IS THAT OUR FAULT? -- EDITORIAL STAPH

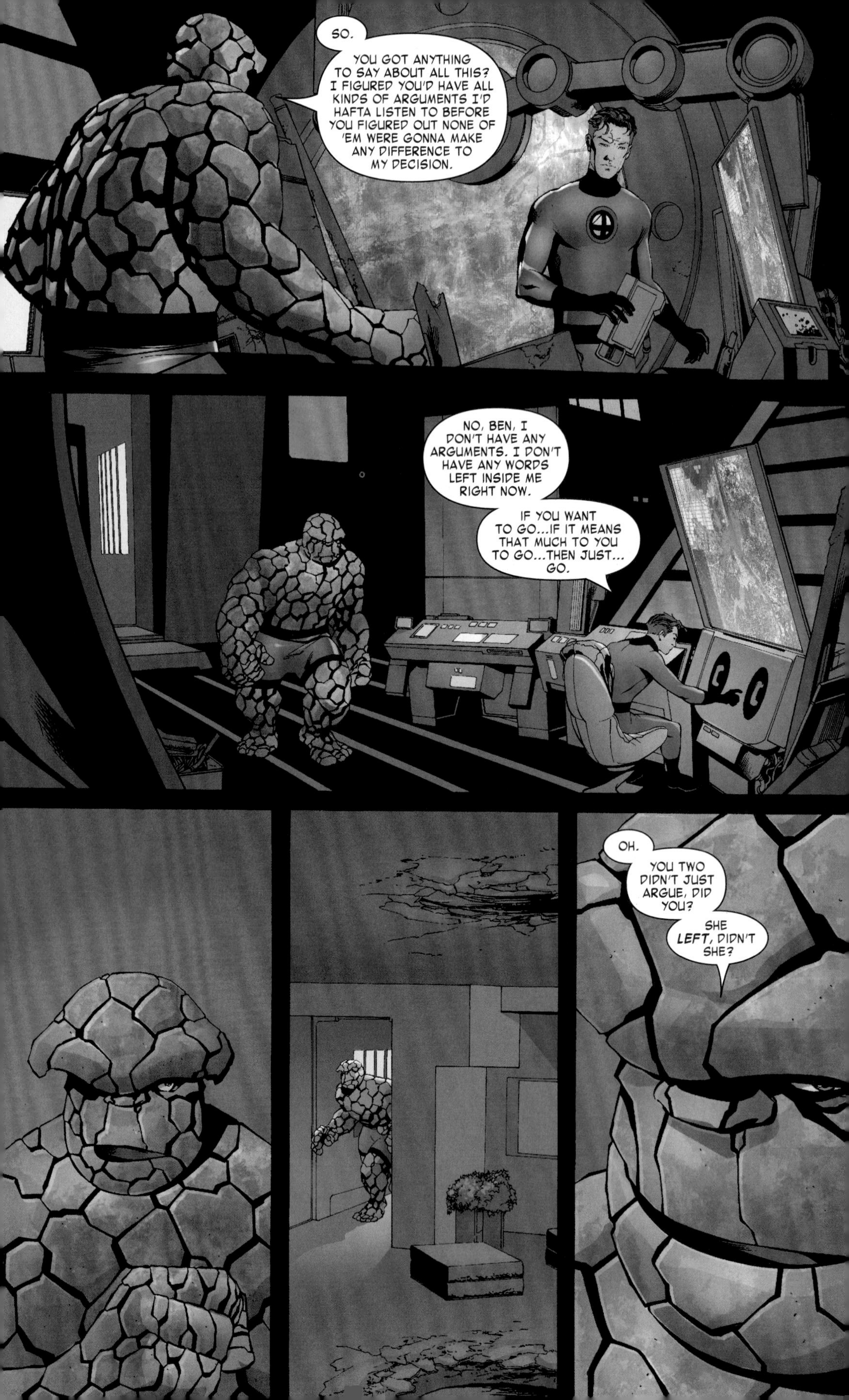
SO.
YOU GOT ANYTHING TO SAY ABOUT ALL THIS? I FIGURED YOU'D HAVE ALL KINDS OF ARGUMENTS I'D HAFTA LISTEN TO BEFORE YOU FIGURED OUT NONE OF 'EM WERE GONNA MAKE ANY DIFFERENCE TO MY DECISION.
NO, BEN, I DON'T HAVE ANY ARGUMENTS. I DON'T HAVE ANY WORDS LEFT INSIDE ME RIGHT NOW.
IF YOU WANT TO GO...IF IT MEANS THAT MUCH TO YOU TO GO...THEN JUST... GO.
OH.
YOU TWO DIDN'T JUST ARGUE, DID YOU?
SHE *LEFT*, DIDN'T SHE?

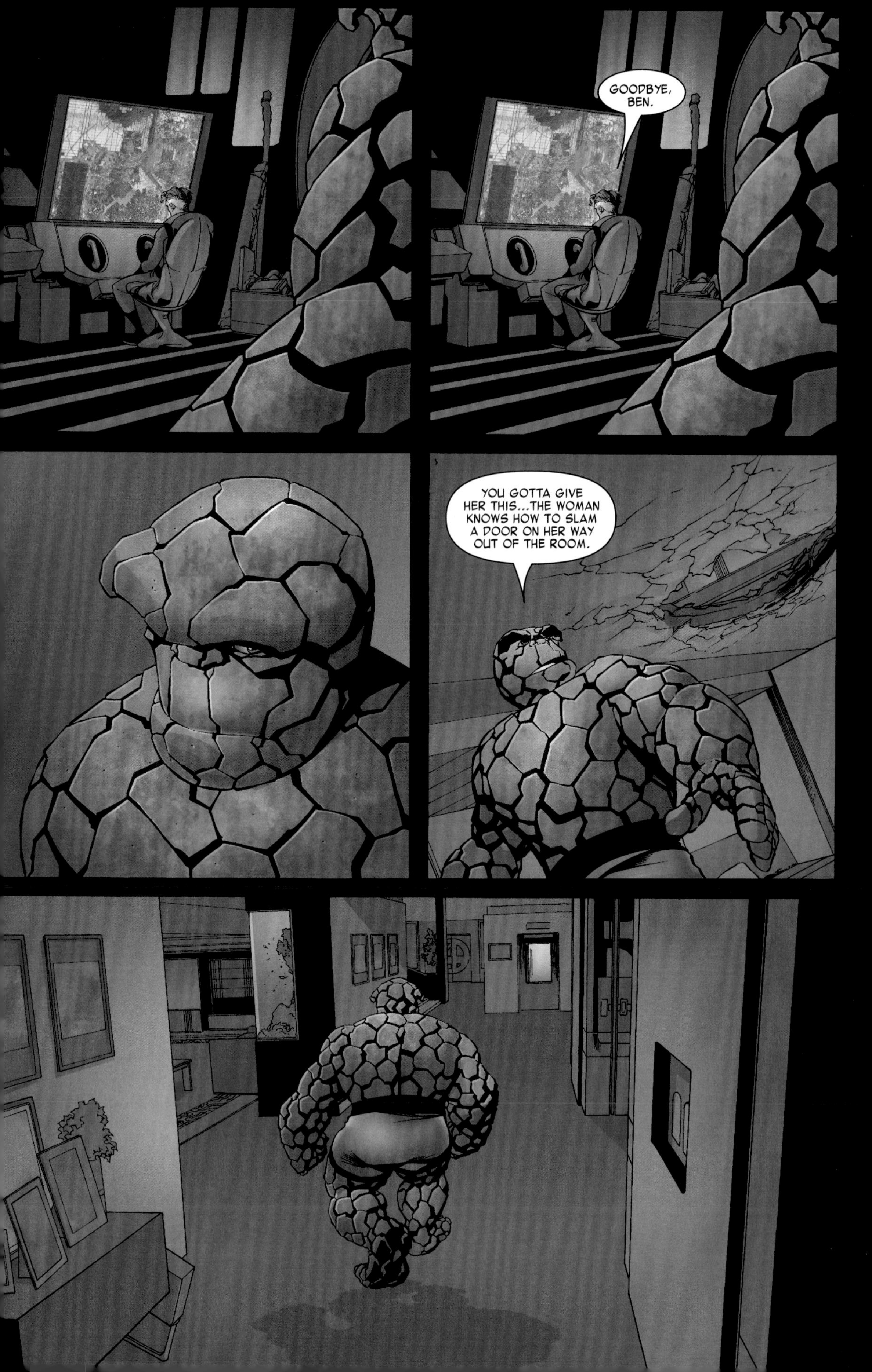
GOODBYE, BEN.
YOU GOTTA GIVE HER THIS...THE WOMAN KNOWS HOW TO SLAM A DOOR ON HER WAY OUT OF THE ROOM.

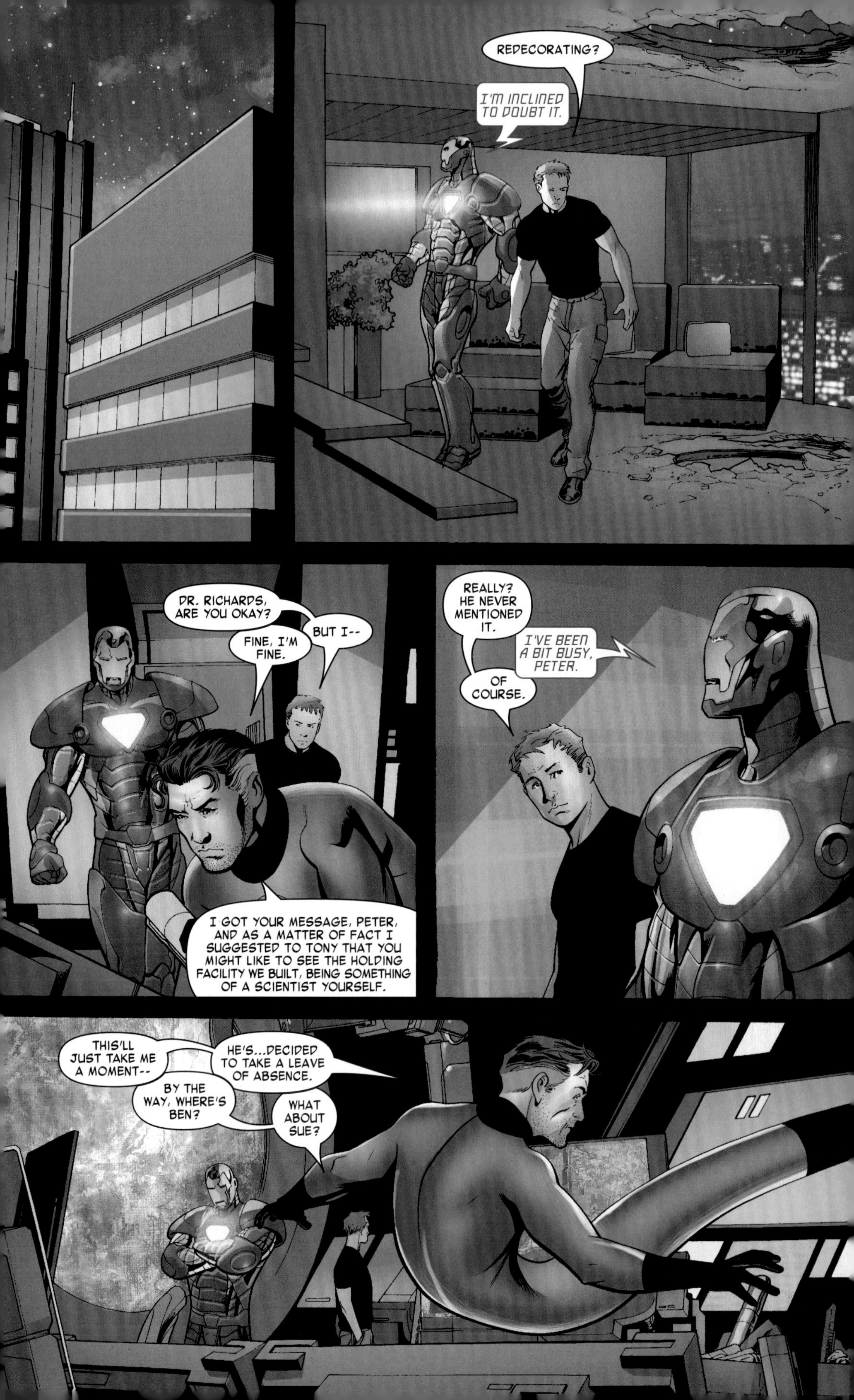

REDECORATING?
I'M INCLINED TO DOUBT IT.
DR. RICHARDS, ARE YOU OKAY?
FINE, I'M FINE.
BUT I--
I GOT YOUR MESSAGE, PETER, AND AS A MATTER OF FACT I SUGGESTED TO TONY THAT YOU MIGHT LIKE TO SEE THE HOLDING FACILITY WE BUILT, BEING SOMETHING OF A SCIENTIST YOURSELF.
REALLY? HE NEVER MENTIONED IT.
I'VE BEEN A BIT BUSY, PETER.
OF COURSE.
THIS'LL JUST TAKE ME A MOMENT--
BY THE WAY, WHERE'S BEN?
HE'S...DECIDED TO TAKE A LEAVE OF ABSENCE.
WHAT ABOUT SUE?

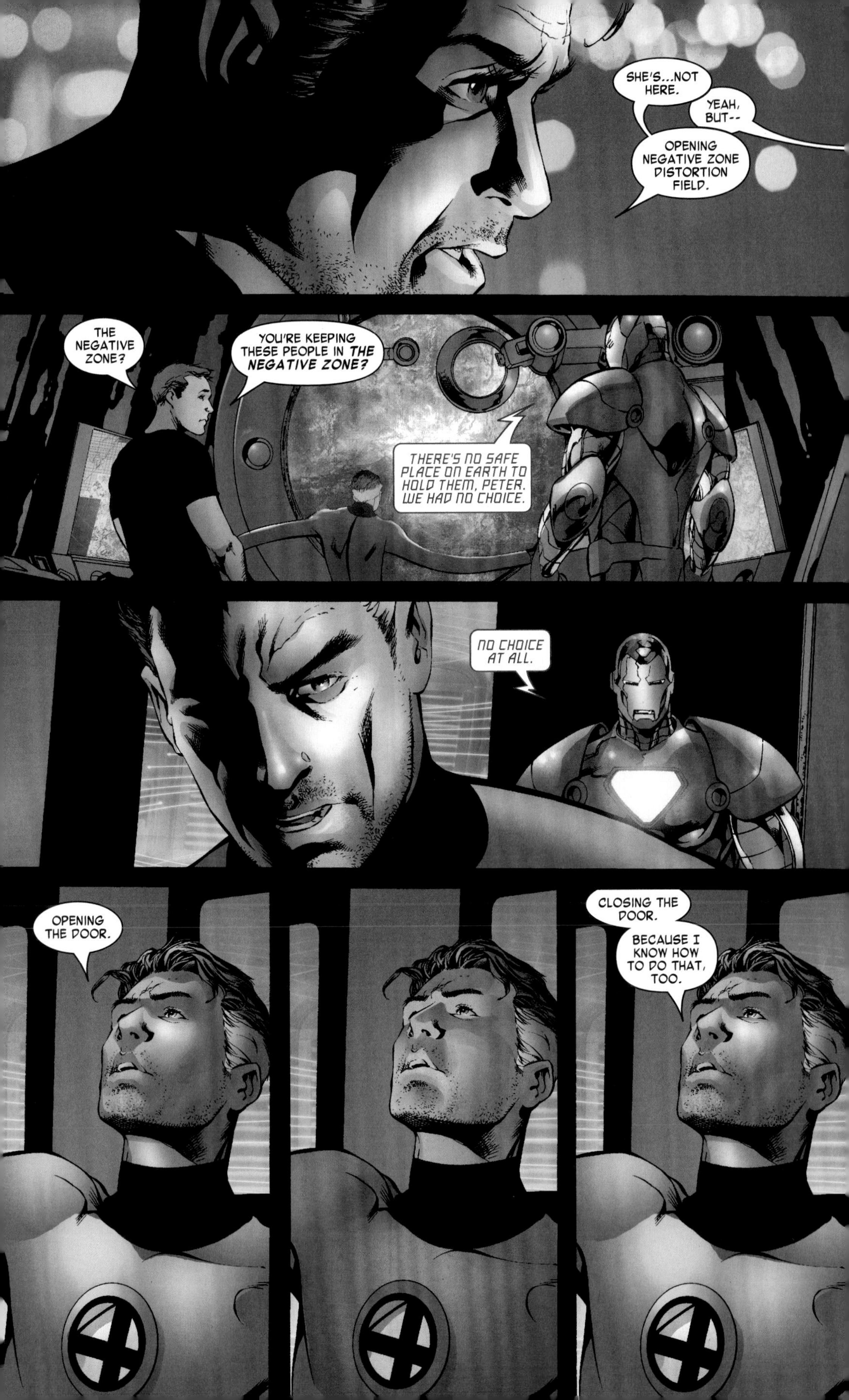
SHE'S...NOT HERE.
YEAH, BUT--
OPENING NEGATIVE ZONE DISTORTION FIELD.
THE NEGATIVE ZONE?
YOU'RE KEEPING THESE PEOPLE IN *THE NEGATIVE ZONE?*
THERE'S NO SAFE PLACE ON EARTH TO HOLD THEM, PETER. WE HAD NO CHOICE.
NO CHOICE AT ALL.
OPENING THE DOOR.
CLOSING THE DOOR.
BECAUSE I KNOW HOW TO DO THAT, TOO.

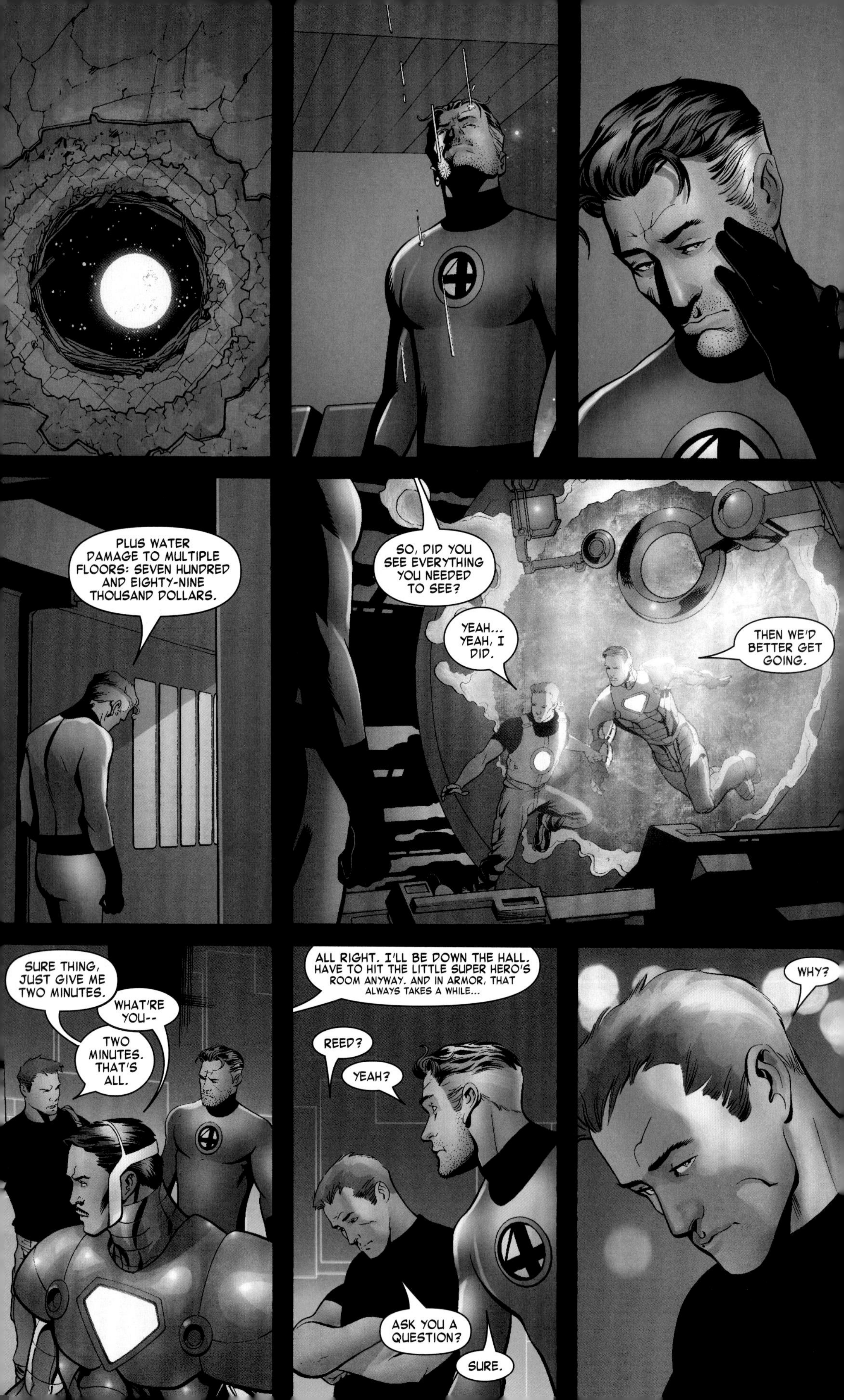
PLUS WATER DAMAGE TO MULTIPLE FLOORS: SEVEN HUNDRED AND EIGHTY-NINE THOUSAND DOLLARS.
SO, DID YOU SEE EVERYTHING YOU NEEDED TO SEE?
YEAH... YEAH, I DID.
THEN WE'D BETTER GET GOING.
SURE THING, JUST GIVE ME TWO MINUTES.
WHAT'RE YOU--
TWO MINUTES. THAT'S ALL.
ALL RIGHT. I'LL BE DOWN THE HALL. HAVE TO HIT THE LITTLE SUPER HERO'S ROOM ANYWAY. AND IN ARMOR, THAT ALWAYS TAKES A WHILE...
REED?
YEAH?
ASK YOU A QUESTION?
SURE.
WHY?

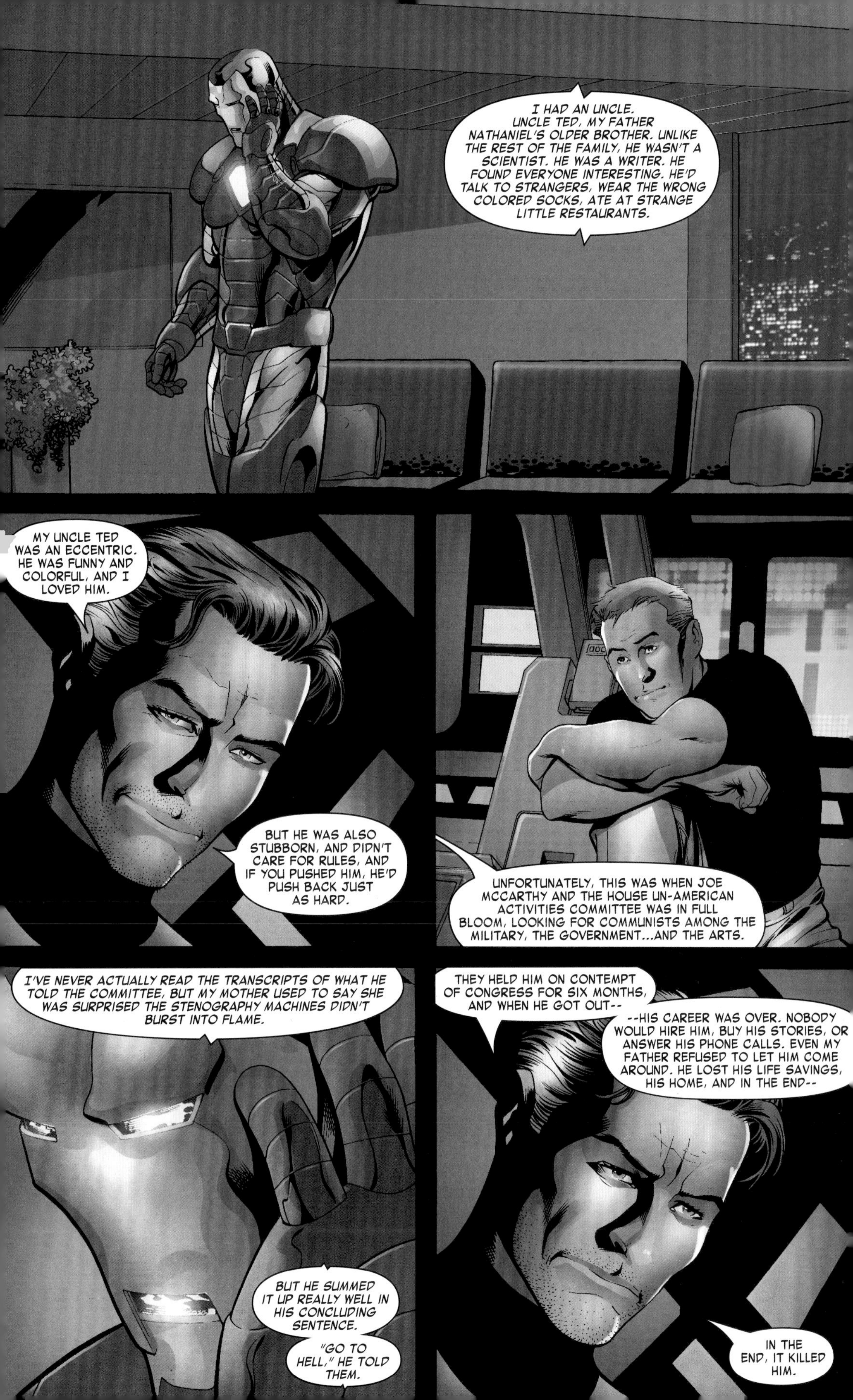
I HAD AN UNCLE. UNCLE TED, MY FATHER NATHANIEL'S OLDER BROTHER. UNLIKE THE REST OF THE FAMILY, HE WASN'T A SCIENTIST. HE WAS A WRITER. HE FOUND EVERYONE INTERESTING. HE'D TALK TO STRANGERS, WEAR THE WRONG COLORED SOCKS, ATE AT STRANGE LITTLE RESTAURANTS.
MY UNCLE TED WAS AN ECCENTRIC. HE WAS FUNNY AND COLORFUL, AND I LOVED HIM.
BUT HE WAS ALSO STUBBORN, AND DIDN'T CARE FOR RULES, AND IF YOU PUSHED HIM, HE'D PUSH BACK JUST AS HARD.
UNFORTUNATELY, THIS WAS WHEN JOE MCCARTHY AND THE HOUSE UN-AMERICAN ACTIVITIES COMMITTEE WAS IN FULL BLOOM, LOOKING FOR COMMUNISTS AMONG THE MILITARY, THE GOVERNMENT...AND THE ARTS.
I'VE NEVER ACTUALLY READ THE TRANSCRIPTS OF WHAT HE TOLD THE COMMITTEE, BUT MY MOTHER USED TO SAY SHE WAS SURPRISED THE STENOGRAPHY MACHINES DIDN'T BURST INTO FLAME.
BUT HE SUMMED IT UP REALLY WELL IN HIS CONCLUDING SENTENCE.
"GO TO HELL," HE TOLD THEM.
THEY HELD HIM ON CONTEMPT OF CONGRESS FOR SIX MONTHS, AND WHEN HE GOT OUT--
--HIS CAREER WAS OVER. NOBODY WOULD HIRE HIM, BUY HIS STORIES, OR ANSWER HIS PHONE CALLS. EVEN MY FATHER REFUSED TO LET HIM COME AROUND. HE LOST HIS LIFE SAVINGS, HIS HOME, AND IN THE END--
IN THE END, IT KILLED HIM.

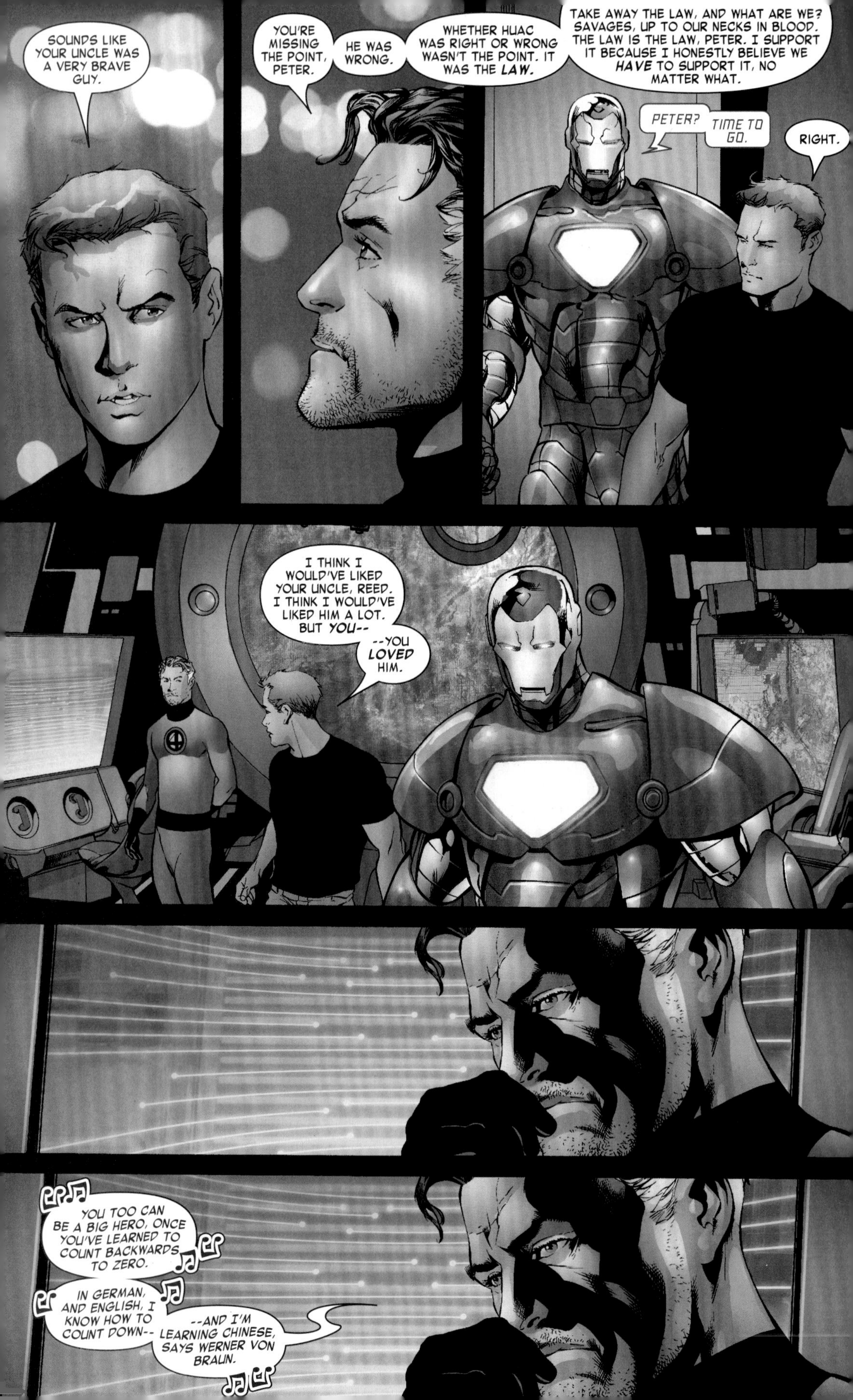
SOUNDS LIKE YOUR UNCLE WAS A VERY BRAVE GUY.
YOU'RE MISSING THE POINT, PETER.
HE WAS WRONG.
WHETHER HUAC WAS RIGHT OR WRONG WASN'T THE POINT. IT WAS THE LAW.
TAKE AWAY THE LAW, AND WHAT ARE WE? SAVAGES, UP TO OUR NECKS IN BLOOD. THE LAW IS THE LAW, PETER. I SUPPORT IT BECAUSE I HONESTLY BELIEVE WE HAVE TO SUPPORT IT, NO MATTER WHAT.
PETER?
TIME TO GO.
RIGHT.
I THINK I WOULD'VE LIKED YOUR UNCLE, REED. I THINK I WOULD'VE LIKED HIM A LOT. BUT YOU--
--YOU LOVED HIM.
YOU TOO CAN BE A BIG HERO, ONCE YOU'VE LEARNED TO COUNT BACKWARDS TO ZERO.
IN GERMAN, AND ENGLISH, I KNOW HOW TO COUNT DOWN--
--AND I'M LEARNING CHINESE, SAYS WERNER VON BRAUN.

FANTASTIC FOUR

A MARVEL COMICS EVENT

CIVIL WAR

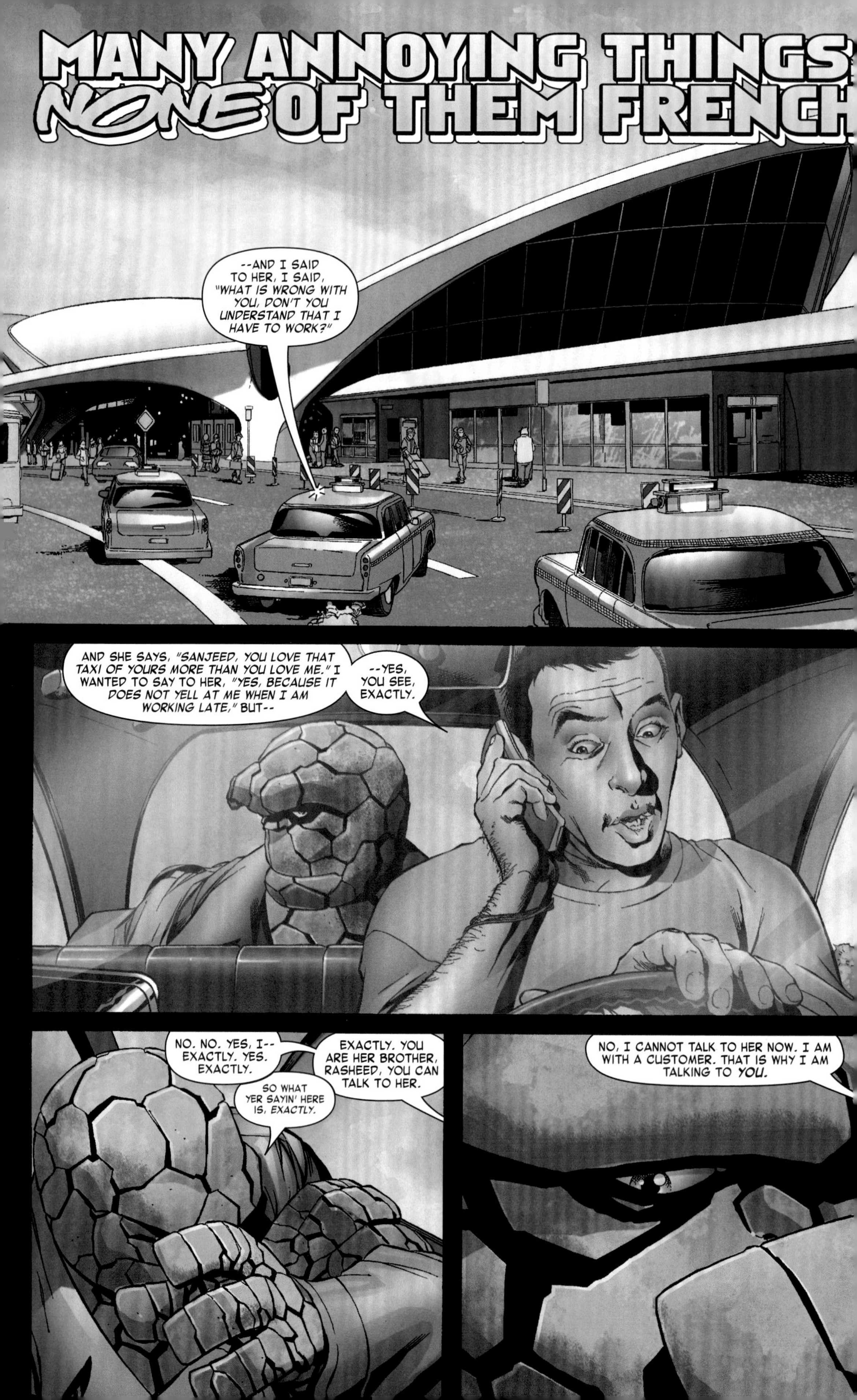
MANY ANNOYING THINGS: NONE OF THEM FRENCH
--AND I SAID TO HER, I SAID, "WHAT IS WRONG WITH YOU, DON'T YOU UNDERSTAND THAT I HAVE TO WORK?"
AND SHE SAYS, "SANJEED, YOU LOVE THAT TAXI OF YOURS MORE THAN YOU LOVE ME." I WANTED TO SAY TO HER, "YES, BECAUSE IT DOES NOT YELL AT ME WHEN I AM WORKING LATE," BUT--
--YES, YOU SEE, EXACTLY.
NO. NO. YES, I-- EXACTLY. YES. EXACTLY.
EXACTLY. YOU ARE HER BROTHER, RASHEED, YOU CAN TALK TO HER.
SO WHAT YER SAYIN' HERE IS, EXACTLY.
NO, I CANNOT TALK TO HER NOW. I AM WITH A CUSTOMER. THAT IS WHY I AM TALKING TO YOU.

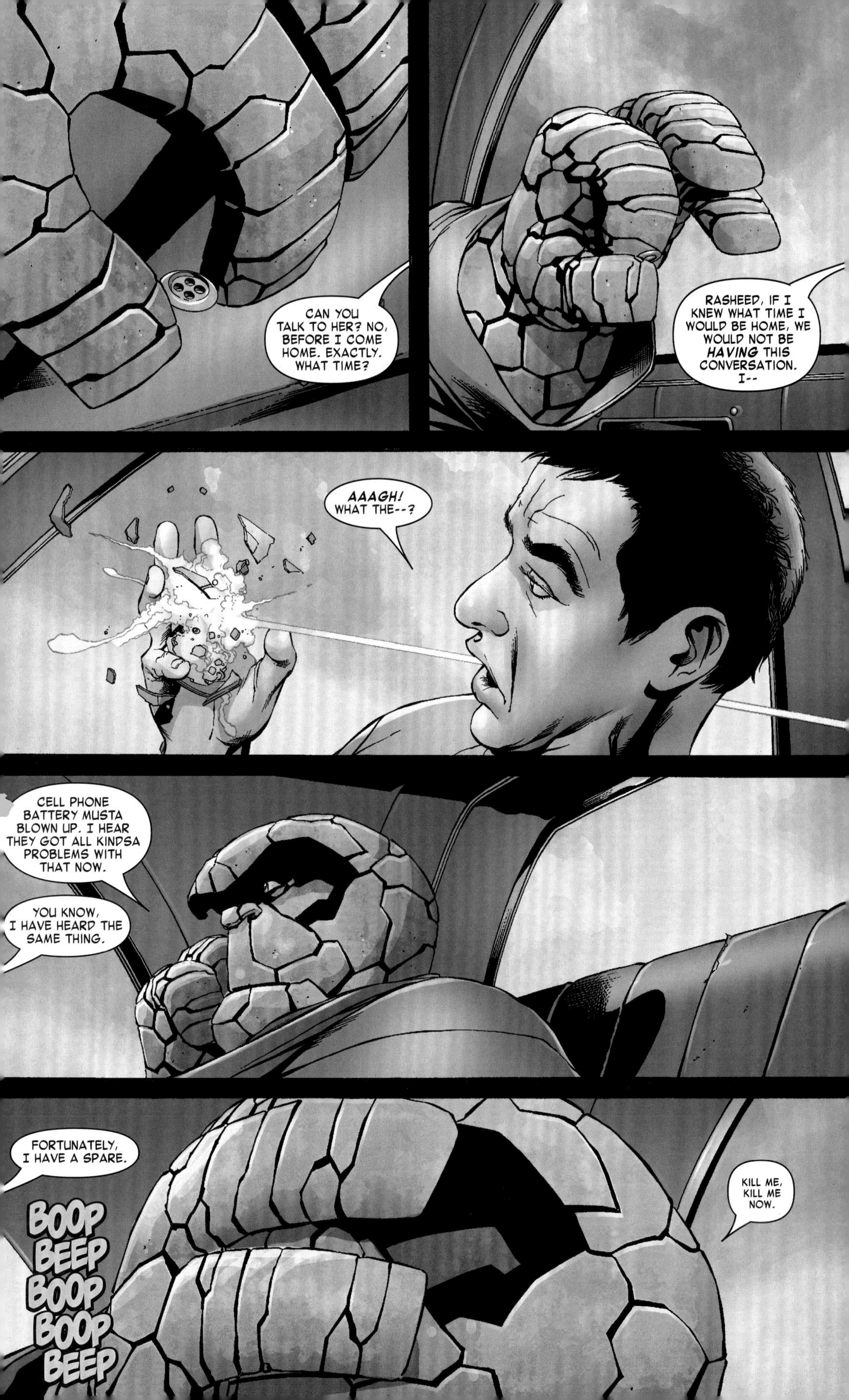
CAN YOU TALK TO HER? NO, BEFORE I COME HOME. EXACTLY. WHAT TIME?
RASHEED, IF I KNEW WHAT TIME I WOULD BE HOME, WE WOULD NOT BE HAVING THIS CONVERSATION. I--
AAAGH! WHAT THE--?
CELL PHONE BATTERY MUSTA BLOWN UP. I HEAR THEY GOT ALL KINDSA PROBLEMS WITH THAT NOW.
YOU KNOW, I HAVE HEARD THE SAME THING.
FORTUNATELY, I HAVE A SPARE.
KILL ME, KILL ME NOW.
BOOP BEEP BOOP BOOP BEEP

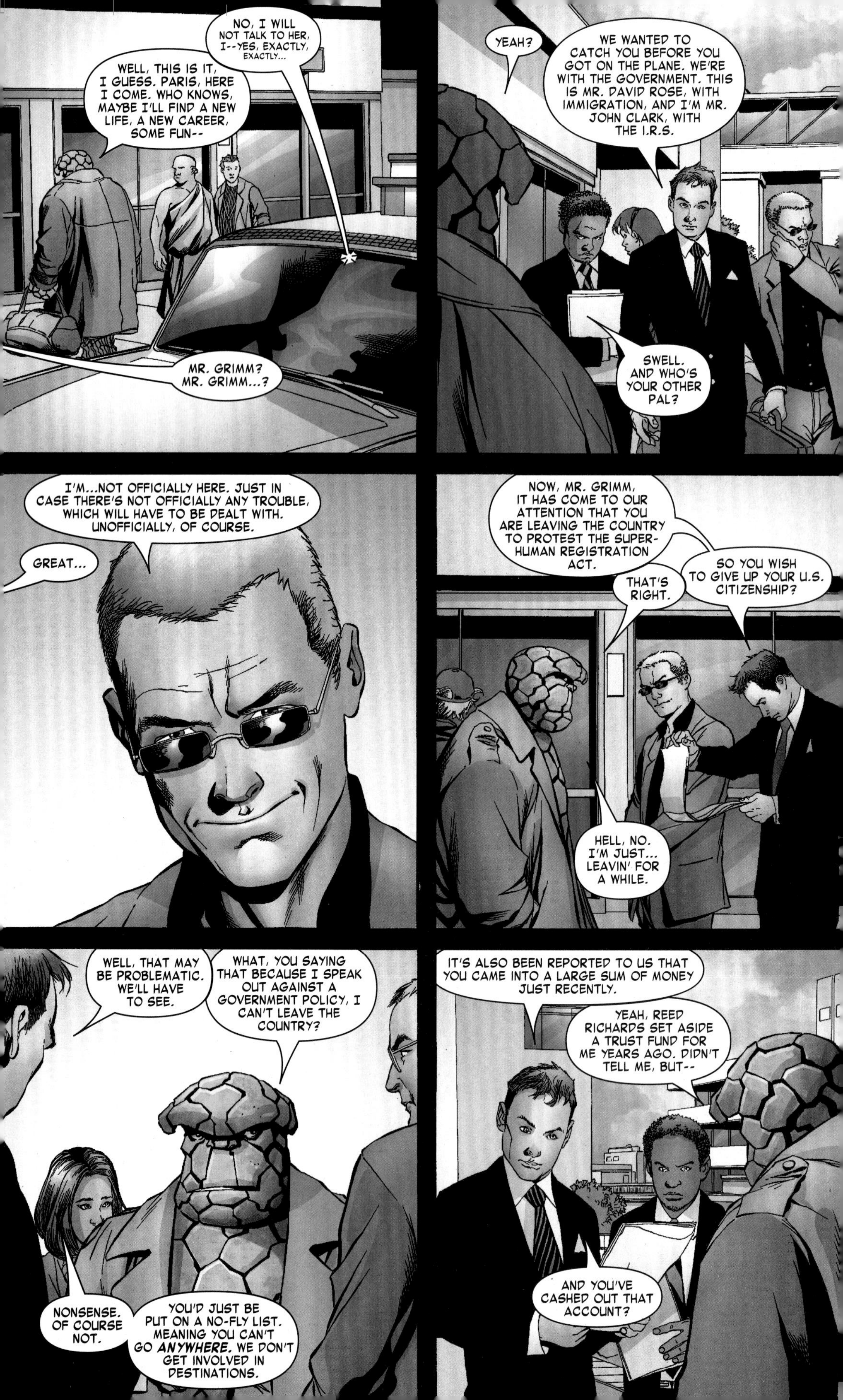
WELL, THIS IS IT, I GUESS. PARIS, HERE I COME. WHO KNOWS, MAYBE I'LL FIND A NEW LIFE, A NEW CAREER, SOME FUN--
NO, I WILL NOT TALK TO HER, I--YES, EXACTLY, EXACTLY...
MR. GRIMM? MR. GRIMM...?
YEAH?
WE WANTED TO CATCH YOU BEFORE YOU GOT ON THE PLANE. WE'RE WITH THE GOVERNMENT. THIS IS MR. DAVID ROSE, WITH IMMIGRATION, AND I'M MR. JOHN CLARK, WITH THE I.R.S.
SWELL. AND WHO'S YOUR OTHER PAL?
I'M...NOT OFFICIALLY HERE. JUST IN CASE THERE'S NOT OFFICIALLY ANY TROUBLE, WHICH WILL HAVE TO BE DEALT WITH. UNOFFICIALLY, OF COURSE.
GREAT...
NOW, MR. GRIMM, IT HAS COME TO OUR ATTENTION THAT YOU ARE LEAVING THE COUNTRY TO PROTEST THE SUPER-HUMAN REGISTRATION ACT.
THAT'S RIGHT.
SO YOU WISH TO GIVE UP YOUR U.S. CITIZENSHIP?
HELL, NO. I'M JUST... LEAVIN' FOR A WHILE.
WELL, THAT MAY BE PROBLEMATIC. WE'LL HAVE TO SEE.
WHAT, YOU SAYING THAT BECAUSE I SPEAK OUT AGAINST A GOVERNMENT POLICY, I CAN'T LEAVE THE COUNTRY?
NONSENSE. OF COURSE NOT.
YOU'D JUST BE PUT ON A NO-FLY LIST. MEANING YOU CAN'T GO ANYWHERE. WE DON'T GET INVOLVED IN DESTINATIONS.
IT'S ALSO BEEN REPORTED TO US THAT YOU CAME INTO A LARGE SUM OF MONEY JUST RECENTLY.
YEAH, REED RICHARDS SET ASIDE A TRUST FUND FOR ME YEARS AGO. DIDN'T TELL ME, BUT--
AND YOU'VE CASHED OUT THAT ACCOUNT?

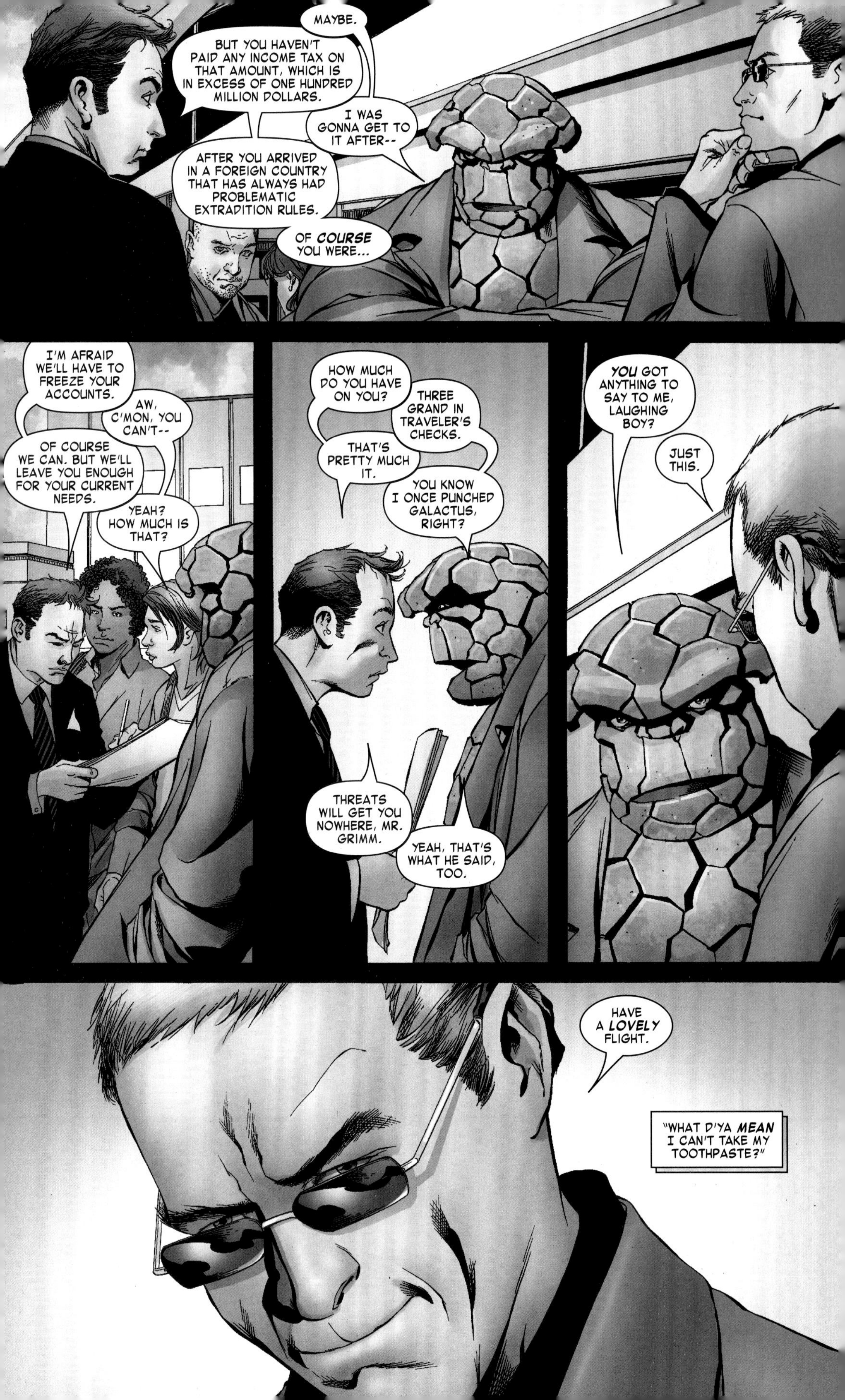
MAYBE.
BUT YOU HAVEN'T PAID ANY INCOME TAX ON THAT AMOUNT, WHICH IS IN EXCESS OF ONE HUNDRED MILLION DOLLARS.
I WAS GONNA GET TO IT AFTER--
AFTER YOU ARRIVED IN A FOREIGN COUNTRY THAT HAS ALWAYS HAD PROBLEMATIC EXTRADITION RULES.
OF COURSE YOU WERE...
I'M AFRAID WE'LL HAVE TO FREEZE YOUR ACCOUNTS.
AW, C'MON, YOU CAN'T--
OF COURSE WE CAN. BUT WE'LL LEAVE YOU ENOUGH FOR YOUR CURRENT NEEDS.
YEAH? HOW MUCH IS THAT?
HOW MUCH DO YOU HAVE ON YOU?
THREE GRAND IN TRAVELER'S CHECKS.
THAT'S PRETTY MUCH IT.
YOU KNOW I ONCE PUNCHED GALACTUS, RIGHT?
THREATS WILL GET YOU NOWHERE, MR. GRIMM.
YEAH, THAT'S WHAT HE SAID, TOO.
YOU GOT ANYTHING TO SAY TO ME, LAUGHING BOY?
JUST THIS.
HAVE A LOVELY FLIGHT.
"WHAT D'YA MEAN I CAN'T TAKE MY TOOTHPASTE?"

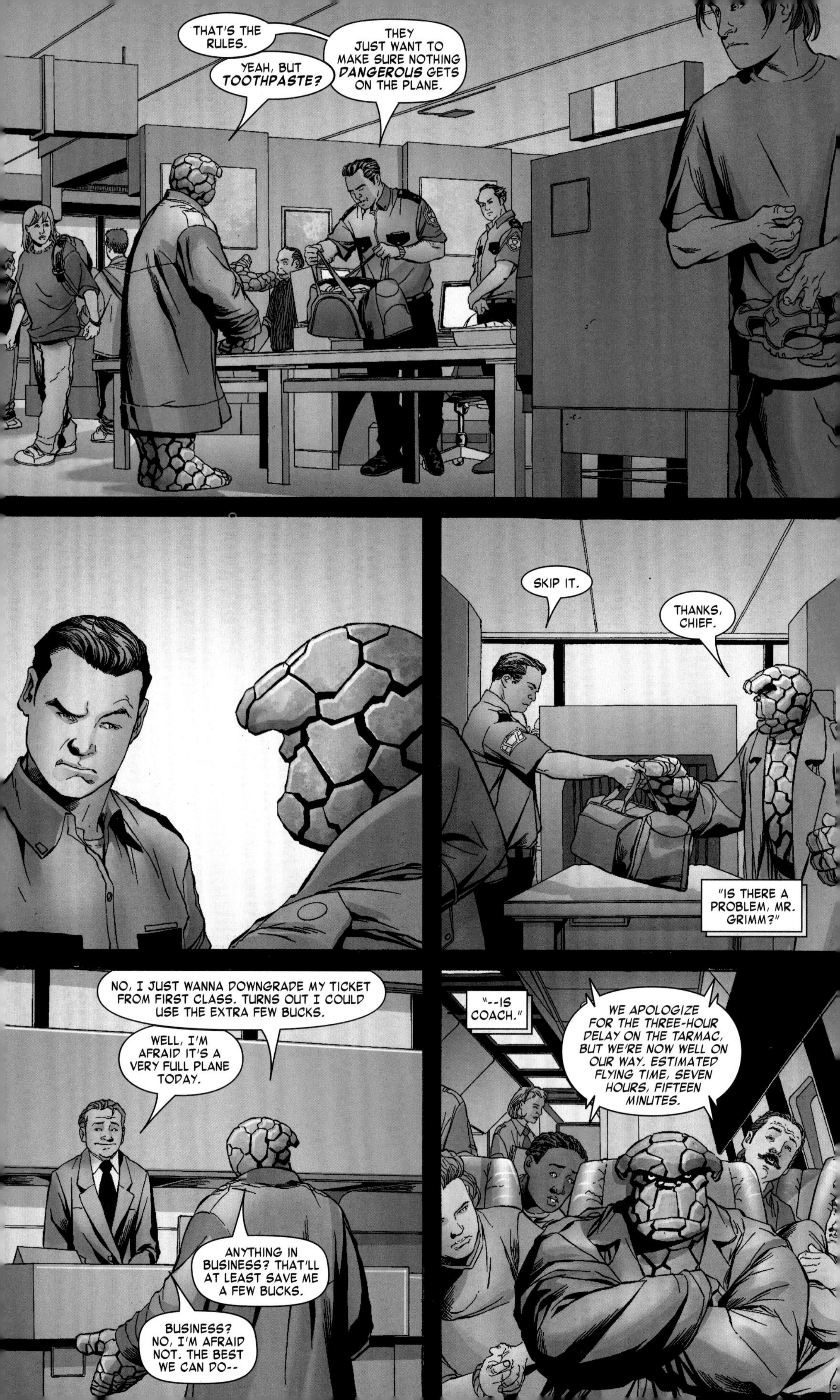
THAT'S THE RULES.
YEAH, BUT TOOTHPASTE?
THEY JUST WANT TO MAKE SURE NOTHING DANGEROUS GETS ON THE PLANE.
SKIP IT.
THANKS, CHIEF.
"IS THERE A PROBLEM, MR. GRIMM?"
NO, I JUST WANNA DOWNGRADE MY TICKET FROM FIRST CLASS. TURNS OUT I COULD USE THE EXTRA FEW BUCKS.
WELL, I'M AFRAID IT'S A VERY FULL PLANE TODAY.
ANYTHING IN BUSINESS? THAT'LL AT LEAST SAVE ME A FEW BUCKS.
BUSINESS? NO, I'M AFRAID NOT. THE BEST WE CAN DO--
"--IS COACH."
WE APOLOGIZE FOR THE THREE-HOUR DELAY ON THE TARMAC, BUT WE'RE NOW WELL ON OUR WAY. ESTIMATED FLYING TIME, SEVEN HOURS, FIFTEEN MINUTES.

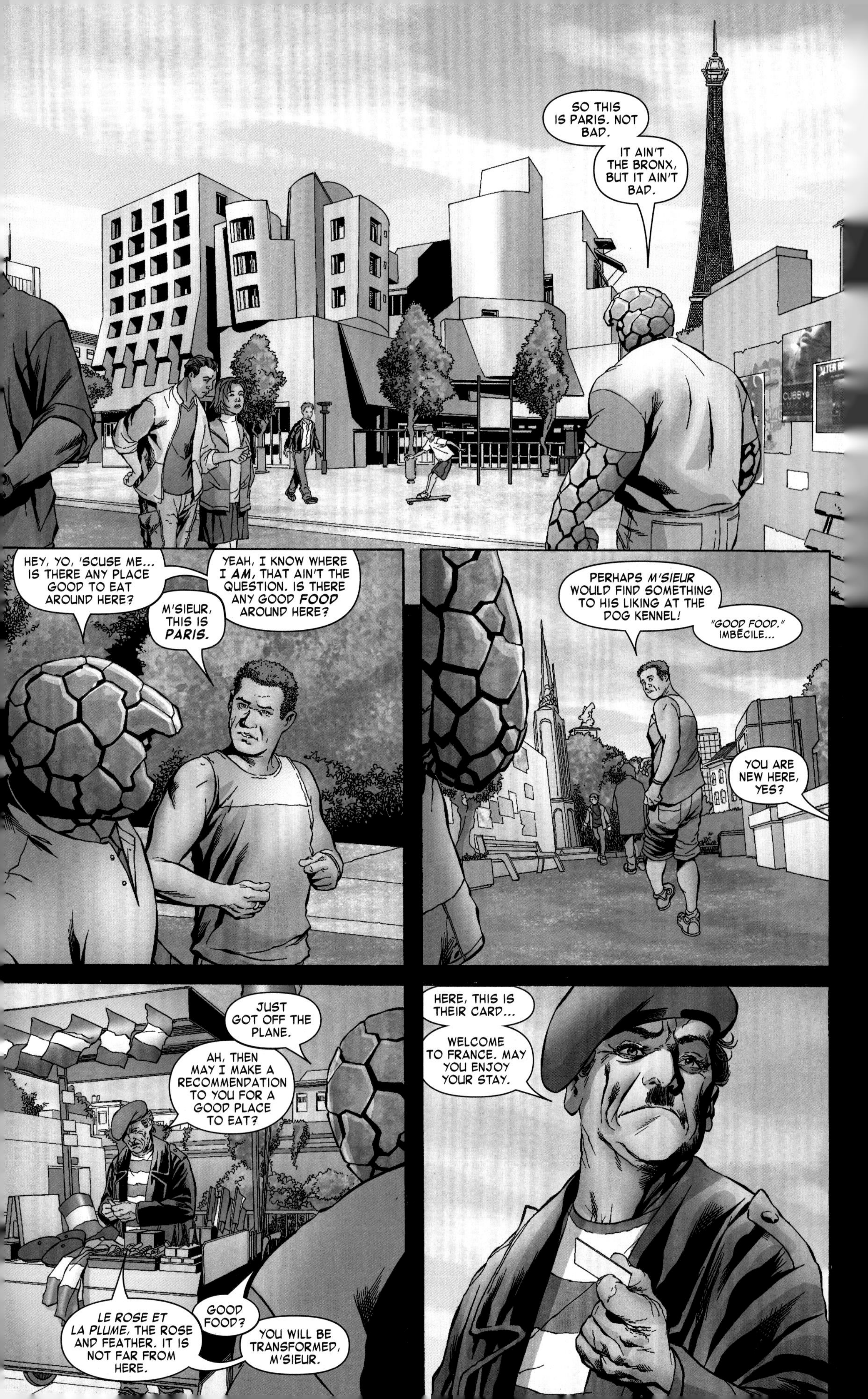
SO THIS IS PARIS. NOT BAD.
IT AIN'T THE BRONX, BUT IT AIN'T BAD.
HEY, YO, 'SCUSE ME... IS THERE ANY PLACE GOOD TO EAT AROUND HERE?
M'SIEUR, THIS IS *PARIS.*
YEAH, I KNOW WHERE I *AM,* THAT AIN'T THE QUESTION. IS THERE ANY GOOD *FOOD* AROUND HERE?
PERHAPS *M'SIEUR* WOULD FIND SOMETHING TO HIS LIKING AT THE DOG KENNEL!
"GOOD FOOD." IMBÉCILE...
YOU ARE NEW HERE, YES?
JUST GOT OFF THE PLANE.
AH, THEN MAY I MAKE A RECOMMENDATION TO YOU FOR A GOOD PLACE TO EAT?
LE ROSE ET LA PLUME, THE ROSE AND FEATHER. IT IS NOT FAR FROM HERE.
GOOD FOOD?
YOU WILL BE TRANSFORMED, M'SIEUR.
HERE, THIS IS THEIR CARD...
WELCOME TO FRANCE. MAY YOU ENJOY YOUR STAY.

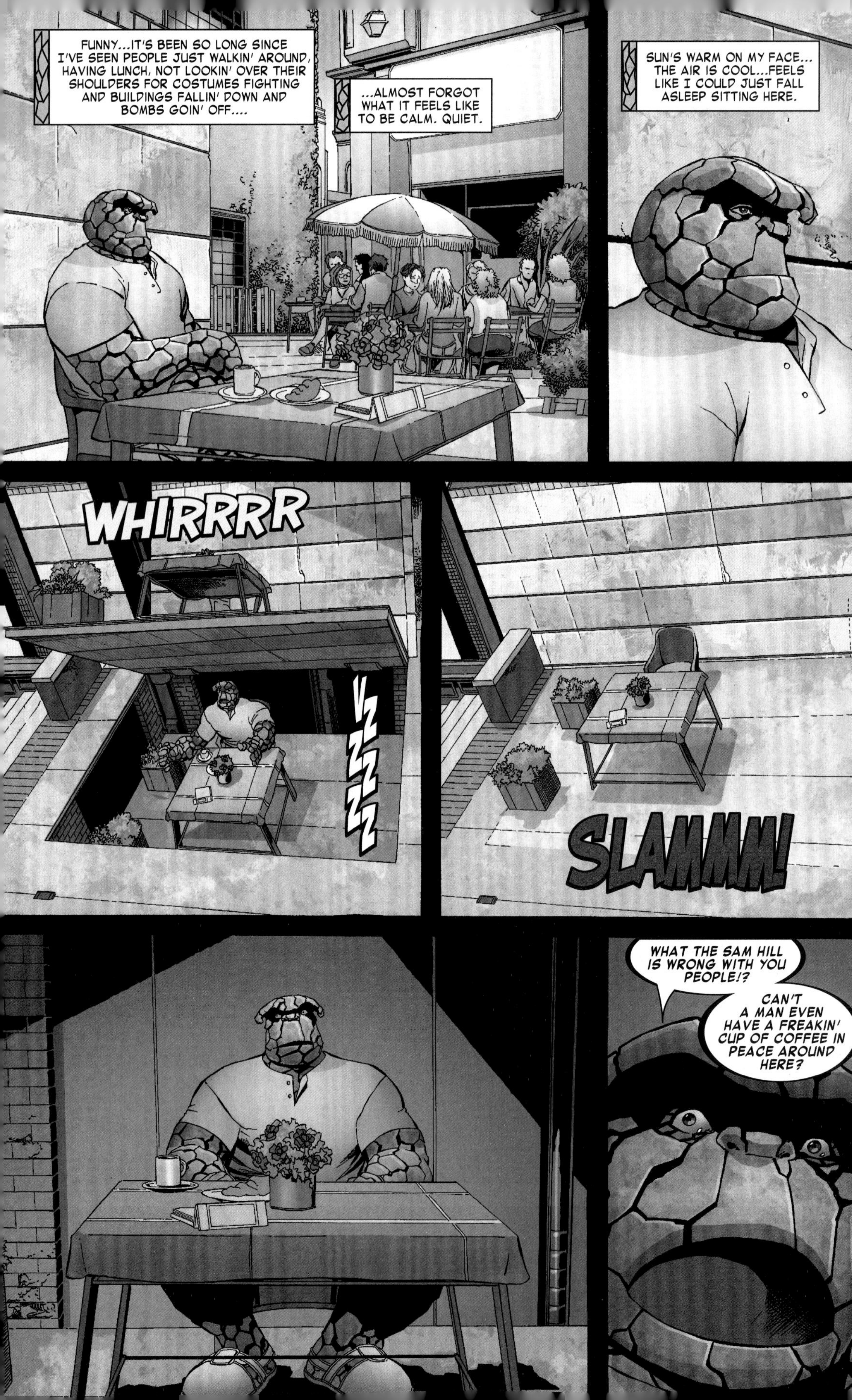
FUNNY...IT'S BEEN SO LONG SINCE I'VE SEEN PEOPLE JUST WALKIN' AROUND, HAVING LUNCH, NOT LOOKIN' OVER THEIR SHOULDERS FOR COSTUMES FIGHTING AND BUILDINGS FALLIN' DOWN AND BOMBS GOIN' OFF....
...ALMOST FORGOT WHAT IT FEELS LIKE TO BE CALM. QUIET.
SUN'S WARM ON MY FACE... THE AIR IS COOL...FEELS LIKE I COULD JUST FALL ASLEEP SITTING HERE.
WHIRRRR
ZZZZZ
SLAMMM!
WHAT THE SAM HILL IS WRONG WITH YOU PEOPLE!?
CAN'T A MAN EVEN HAVE A FREAKIN' CUP OF COFFEE IN PEACE AROUND HERE?

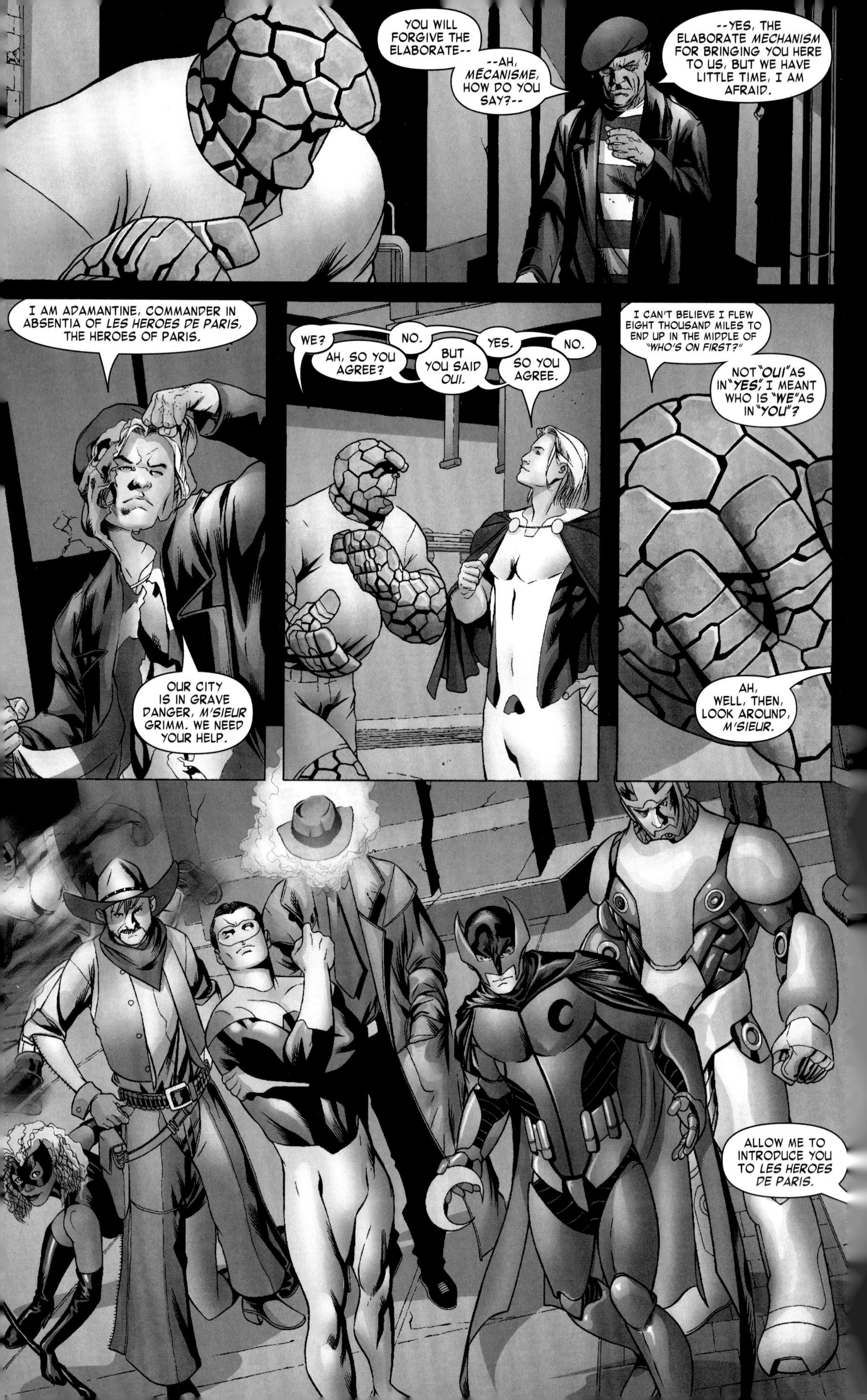
YOU WILL FORGIVE THE ELABORATE--
--AH, MÉCANISME, HOW DO YOU SAY?--
--YES, THE ELABORATE MECHANISM FOR BRINGING YOU HERE TO US, BUT WE HAVE LITTLE TIME, I AM AFRAID.
I AM ADAMANTINE, COMMANDER IN ABSENTIA OF LES HEROES DE PARIS, THE HEROES OF PARIS.
OUR CITY IS IN GRAVE DANGER, M'SIEUR GRIMM. WE NEED YOUR HELP.
WE?
AH, SO YOU AGREE?
NO.
BUT YOU SAID OUI.
YES.
SO YOU AGREE.
NO.
I CAN'T BELIEVE I FLEW EIGHT THOUSAND MILES TO END UP IN THE MIDDLE OF "WHO'S ON FIRST?"
NOT "OUI" AS IN "YES," I MEANT WHO IS "WE" AS IN "YOU"?
AH, WELL, THEN, LOOK AROUND, M'SIEUR.
ALLOW ME TO INTRODUCE YOU TO LES HEROES DE PARIS.

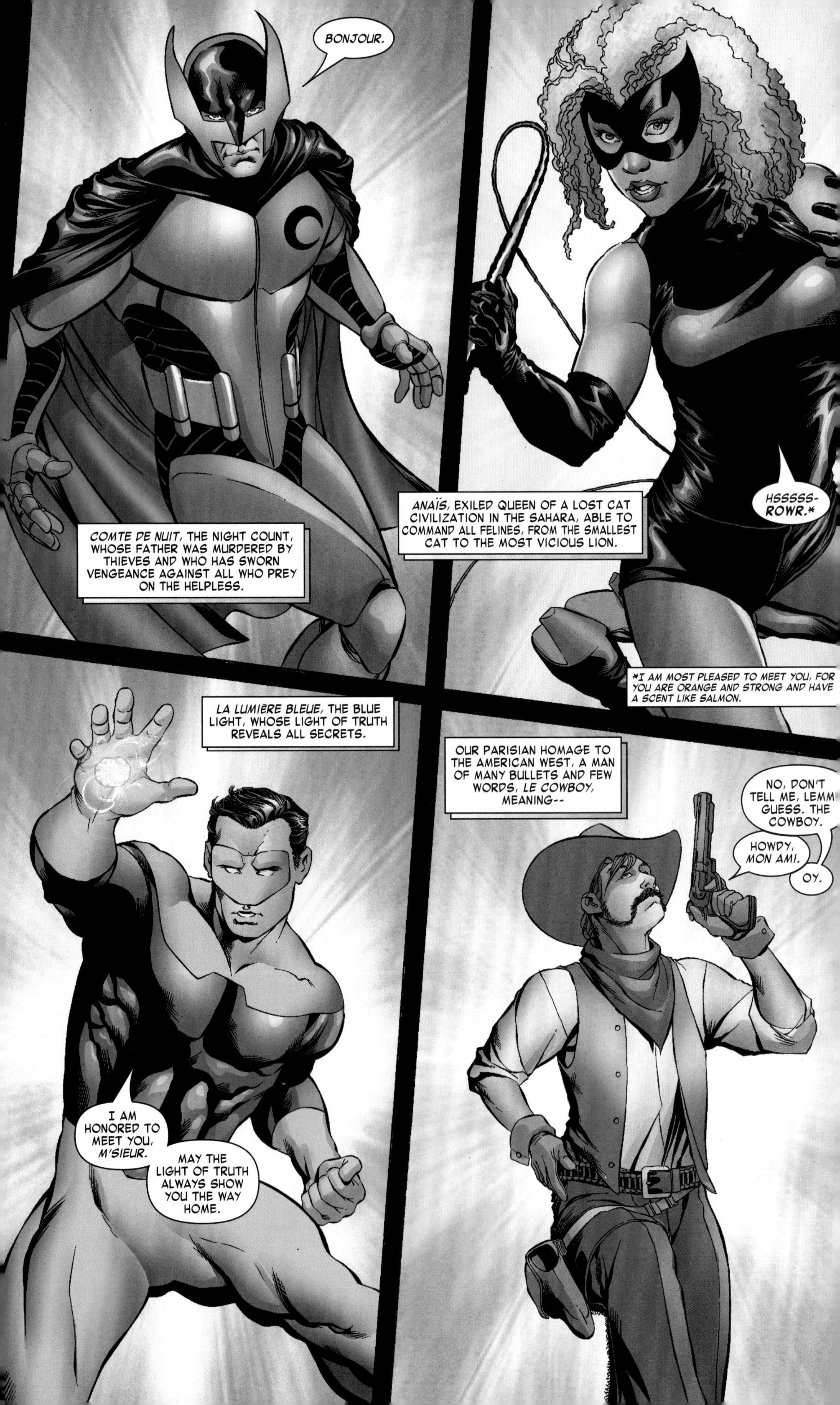

BONJOUR.
COMTE DE NUIT, THE NIGHT COUNT, WHOSE FATHER WAS MURDERED BY THIEVES AND WHO HAS SWORN VENGEANCE AGAINST ALL WHO PREY ON THE HELPLESS.
ANAÏS, EXILED QUEEN OF A LOST CAT CIVILIZATION IN THE SAHARA, ABLE TO COMMAND ALL FELINES, FROM THE SMALLEST CAT TO THE MOST VICIOUS LION.
HSSSSS-ROWR.*
*I AM MOST PLEASED TO MEET YOU, FOR YOU ARE ORANGE AND STRONG AND HAVE A SCENT LIKE SALMON.
LA LUMIÈRE BLEUE, THE BLUE LIGHT, WHOSE LIGHT OF TRUTH REVEALS ALL SECRETS.
I AM HONORED TO MEET YOU, M'SIEUR.
MAY THE LIGHT OF TRUTH ALWAYS SHOW YOU THE WAY HOME.
OUR PARISIAN HOMAGE TO THE AMERICAN WEST, A MAN OF MANY BULLETS AND FEW WORDS, LE COWBOY, MEANING--
NO, DON'T TELL ME, LEMM GUESS. THE COWBOY.
HOWDY, MON AMI.
OY.

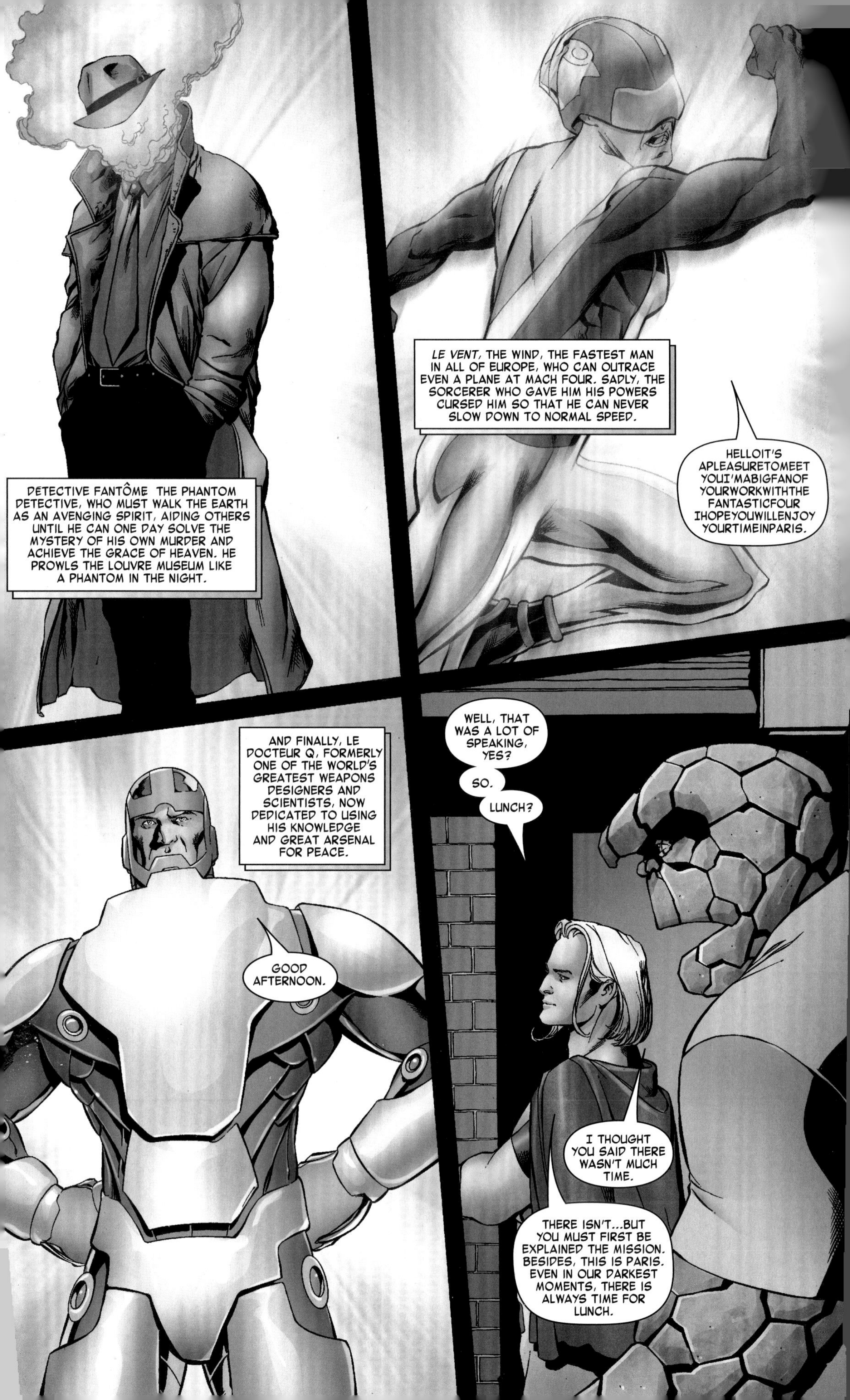
DETECTIVE FANTÔME THE PHANTOM DETECTIVE, WHO MUST WALK THE EARTH AS AN AVENGING SPIRIT, AIDING OTHERS UNTIL HE CAN ONE DAY SOLVE THE MYSTERY OF HIS OWN MURDER AND ACHIEVE THE GRACE OF HEAVEN. HE PROWLS THE LOUVRE MUSEUM LIKE A PHANTOM IN THE NIGHT.
LE VENT, THE WIND, THE FASTEST MAN IN ALL OF EUROPE, WHO CAN OUTRACE EVEN A PLANE AT MACH FOUR. SADLY, THE SORCERER WHO GAVE HIM HIS POWERS CURSED HIM SO THAT HE CAN NEVER SLOW DOWN TO NORMAL SPEED.
HELLOIT'S APLEASURETOMEET YOUI'MABIGFANOF YOURWORKWITHTHE FANTASTICFOUR IHOPEYOUWILLENJOY YOURTIMEINPARIS.
AND FINALLY, LE DOCTEUR Q, FORMERLY ONE OF THE WORLD'S GREATEST WEAPONS DESIGNERS AND SCIENTISTS, NOW DEDICATED TO USING HIS KNOWLEDGE AND GREAT ARSENAL FOR PEACE.
GOOD AFTERNOON.
WELL, THAT WAS A LOT OF SPEAKING, YES?
SO.
LUNCH?
I THOUGHT YOU SAID THERE WASN'T MUCH TIME.
THERE ISN'T...BUT YOU MUST FIRST BE EXPLAINED THE MISSION. BESIDES, THIS IS PARIS. EVEN IN OUR DARKEST MOMENTS, THERE IS ALWAYS TIME FOR LUNCH.

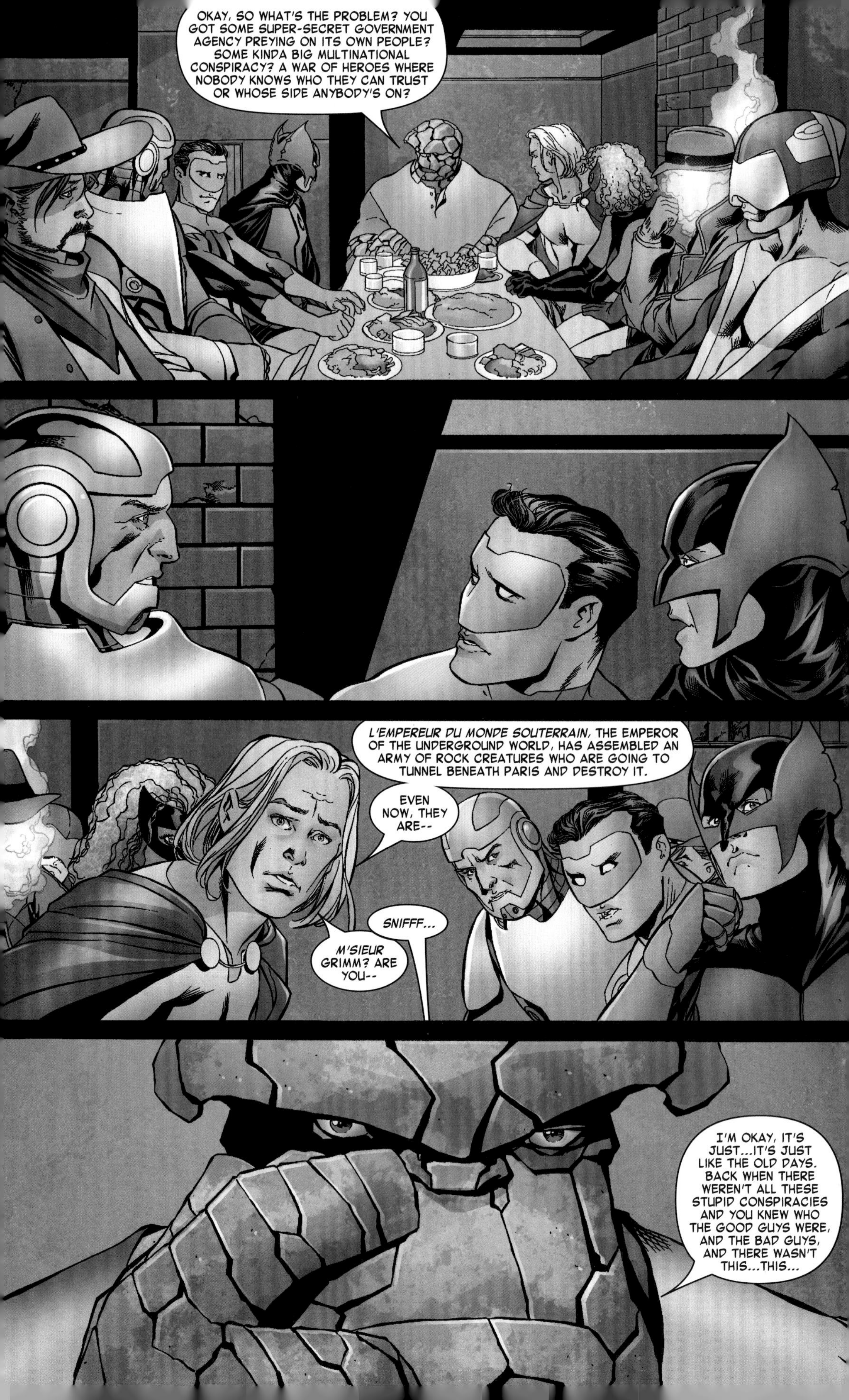
OKAY, SO WHAT'S THE PROBLEM? YOU GOT SOME SUPER-SECRET GOVERNMENT AGENCY PREYING ON ITS OWN PEOPLE? SOME KINDA BIG MULTINATIONAL CONSPIRACY? A WAR OF HEROES WHERE NOBODY KNOWS WHO THEY CAN TRUST OR WHOSE SIDE ANYBODY'S ON?
L'EMPEREUR DU MONDE SOUTERRAIN, THE EMPEROR OF THE UNDERGROUND WORLD, HAS ASSEMBLED AN ARMY OF ROCK CREATURES WHO ARE GOING TO TUNNEL BENEATH PARIS AND DESTROY IT.
EVEN NOW, THEY ARE--
SNIFFF...
M'SIEUR GRIMM? ARE YOU--
I'M OKAY, IT'S JUST...IT'S JUST LIKE THE OLD DAYS. BACK WHEN THERE WEREN'T ALL THESE STUPID CONSPIRACIES AND YOU KNEW WHO THE GOOD GUYS WERE, AND THE BAD GUYS, AND THERE WASN'T THIS...THIS...

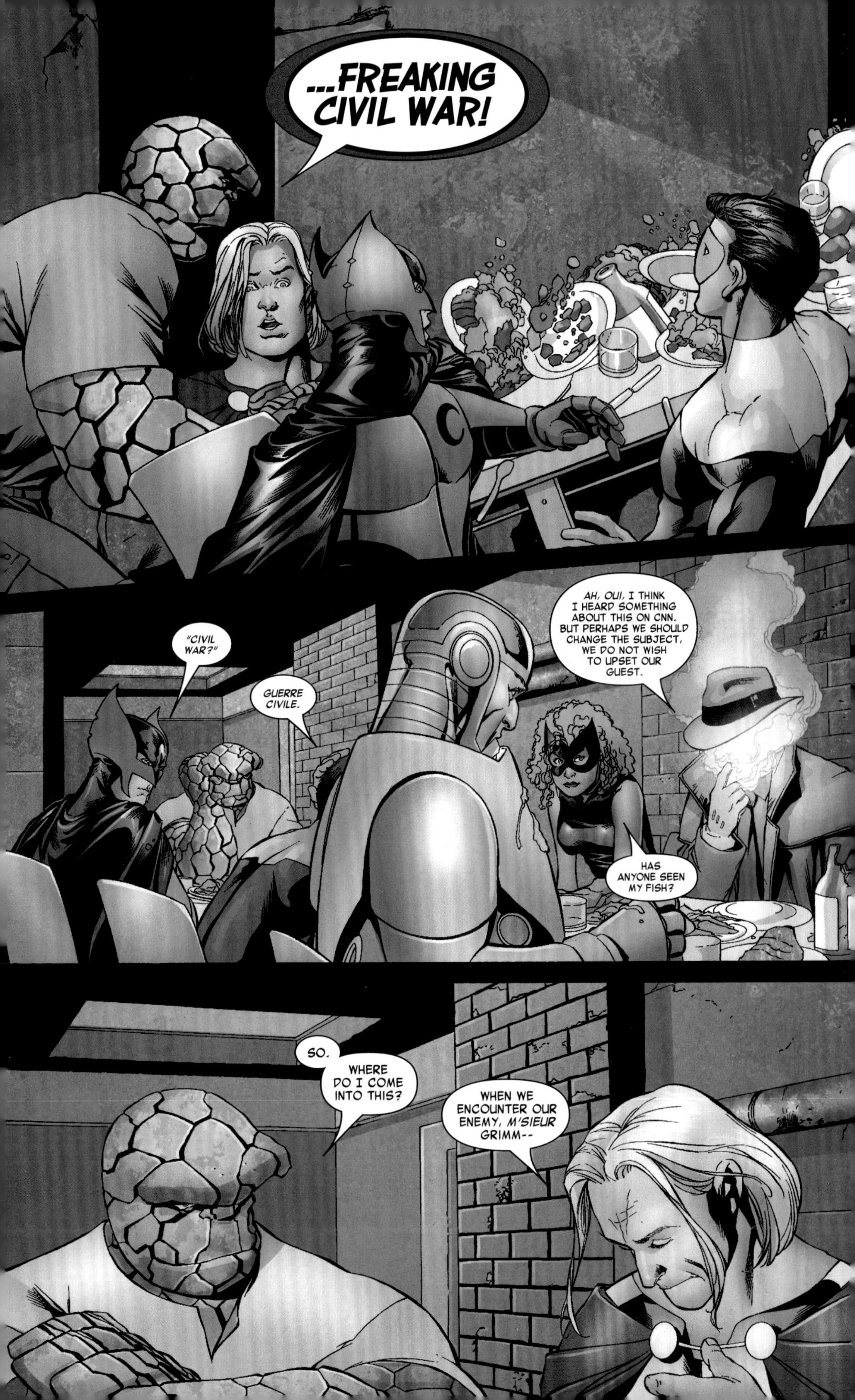
...FREAKING CIVIL WAR!
"CIVIL WAR?"
GUERRE CIVILE.
AH, OUI, I THINK I HEARD SOMETHING ABOUT THIS ON CNN. BUT PERHAPS WE SHOULD CHANGE THE SUBJECT, WE DO NOT WISH TO UPSET OUR GUEST.
HAS ANYONE SEEN MY FISH?
SO.
WHERE DO I COME INTO THIS?
WHEN WE ENCOUNTER OUR ENEMY, M'SIEUR GRIMM--

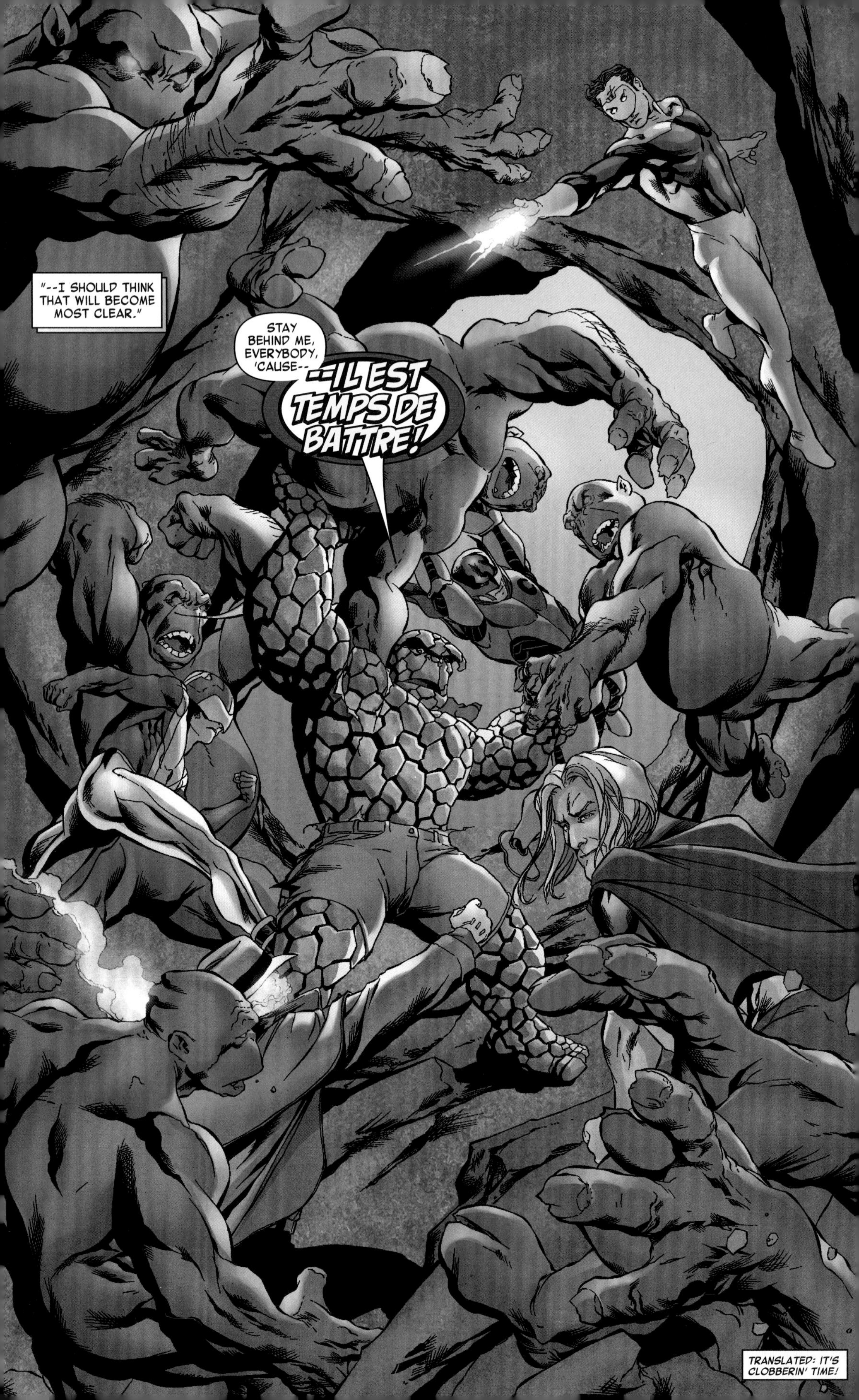
"--I SHOULD THINK THAT WILL BECOME MOST CLEAR."
STAY BEHIND ME, EVERYBODY, 'CAUSE--
--IL EST TEMPS DE BATTRE!
TRANSLATED: IT'S CLOBBERIN' TIME!

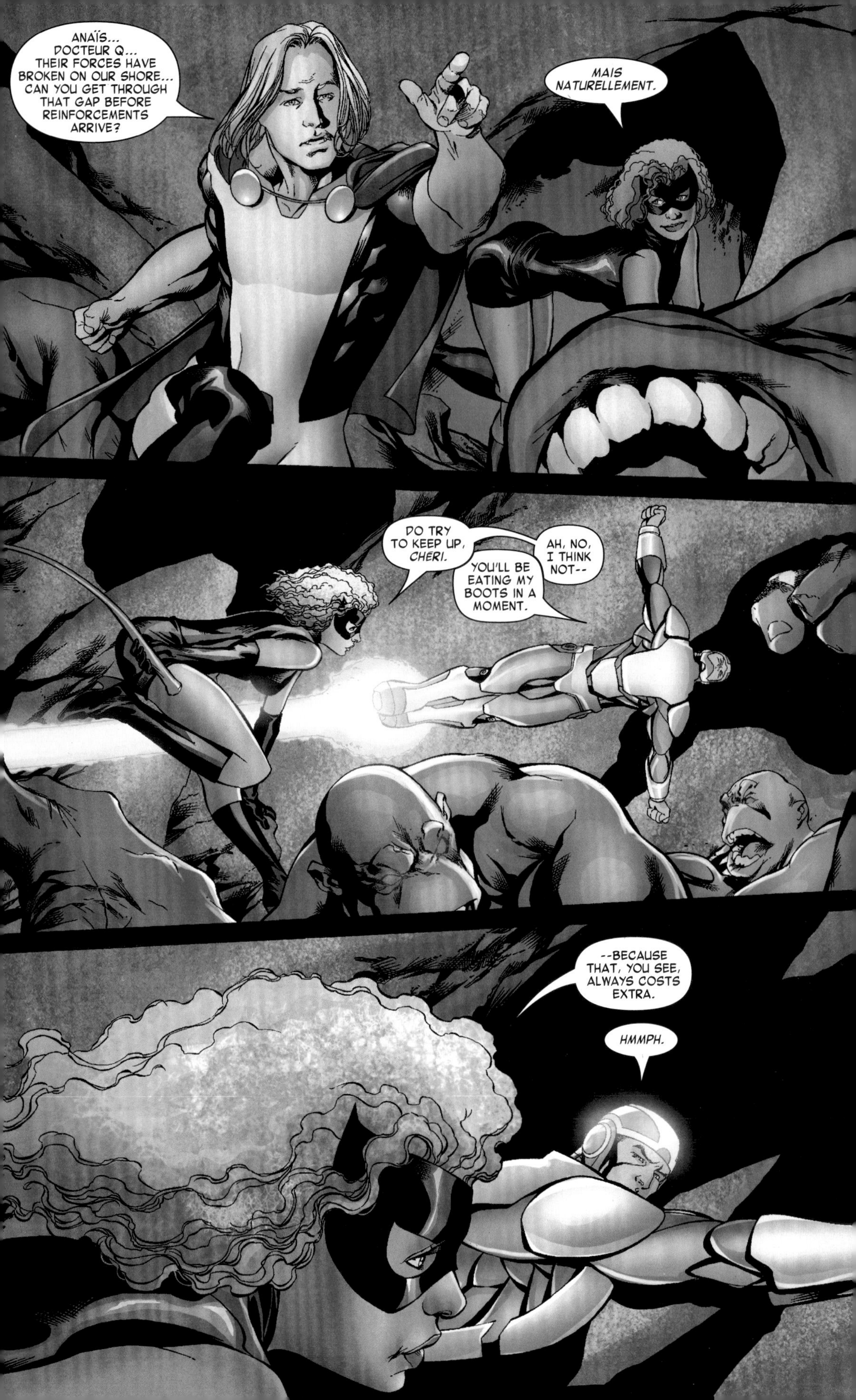
ANAÏS... DOCTEUR Q... THEIR FORCES HAVE BROKEN ON OUR SHORE... CAN YOU GET THROUGH THAT GAP BEFORE REINFORCEMENTS ARRIVE?
MAIS NATURELLEMENT.
DO TRY TO KEEP UP, CHERI.
YOU'LL BE EATING MY BOOTS IN A MOMENT.
AH, NO, I THINK NOT--
--BECAUSE THAT, YOU SEE, ALWAYS COSTS EXTRA.
HMMPH.

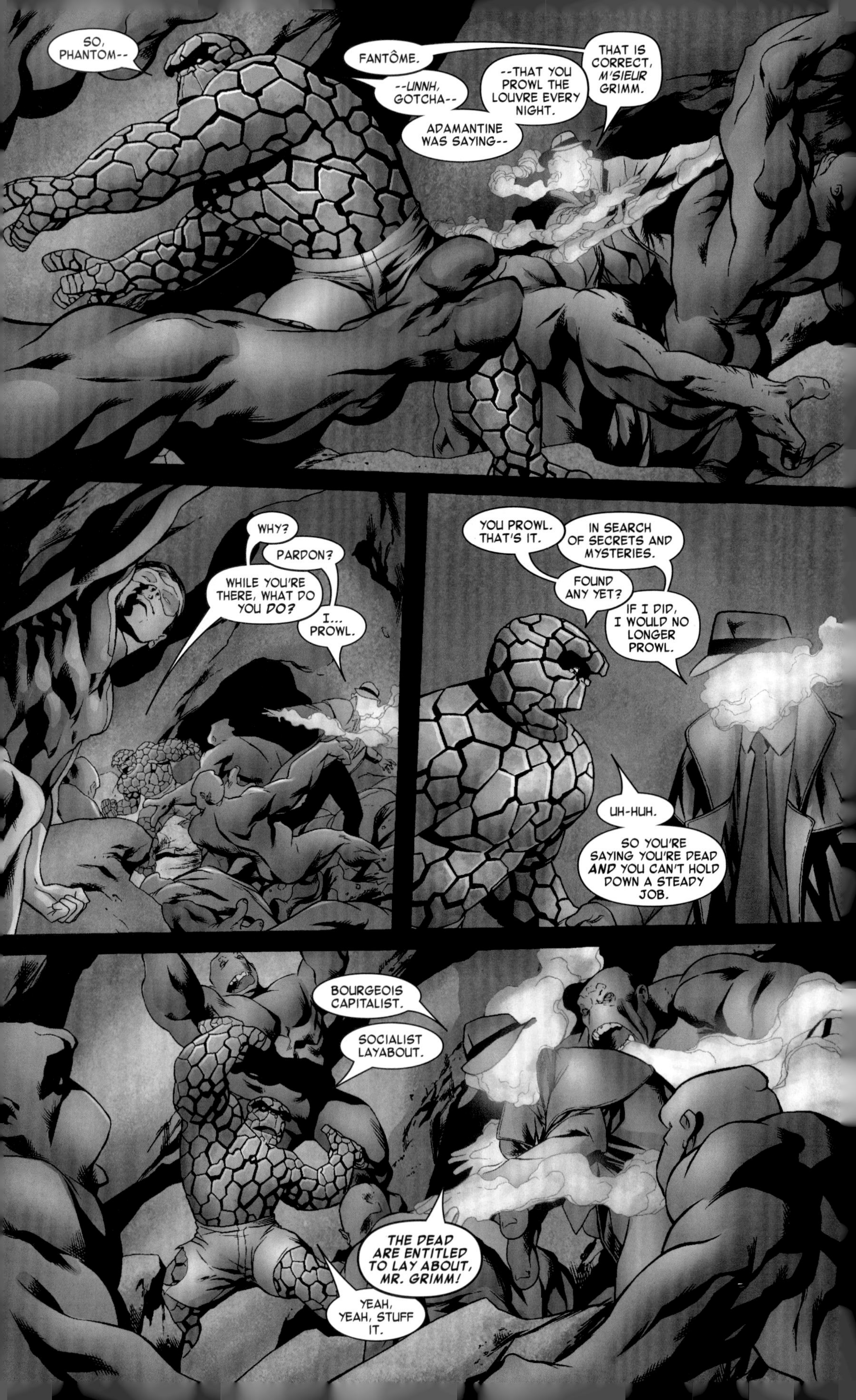
SO, PHANTOM--
FANTÔME.
--UNNH, GOTCHA--
ADAMANTINE WAS SAYING--
--THAT YOU PROWL THE LOUVRE EVERY NIGHT.
THAT IS CORRECT, M'SIEUR GRIMM.
WHY?
PARDON?
WHILE YOU'RE THERE, WHAT DO YOU DO?
I... PROWL.
YOU PROWL. THAT'S IT.
IN SEARCH OF SECRETS AND MYSTERIES.
FOUND ANY YET?
IF I DID, I WOULD NO LONGER PROWL.
UH-HUH.
SO YOU'RE SAYING YOU'RE DEAD AND YOU CAN'T HOLD DOWN A STEADY JOB.
BOURGEOIS CAPITALIST.
SOCIALIST LAYABOUT.
THE DEAD ARE ENTITLED TO LAY ABOUT, MR. GRIMM!
YEAH, YEAH, STUFF IT.

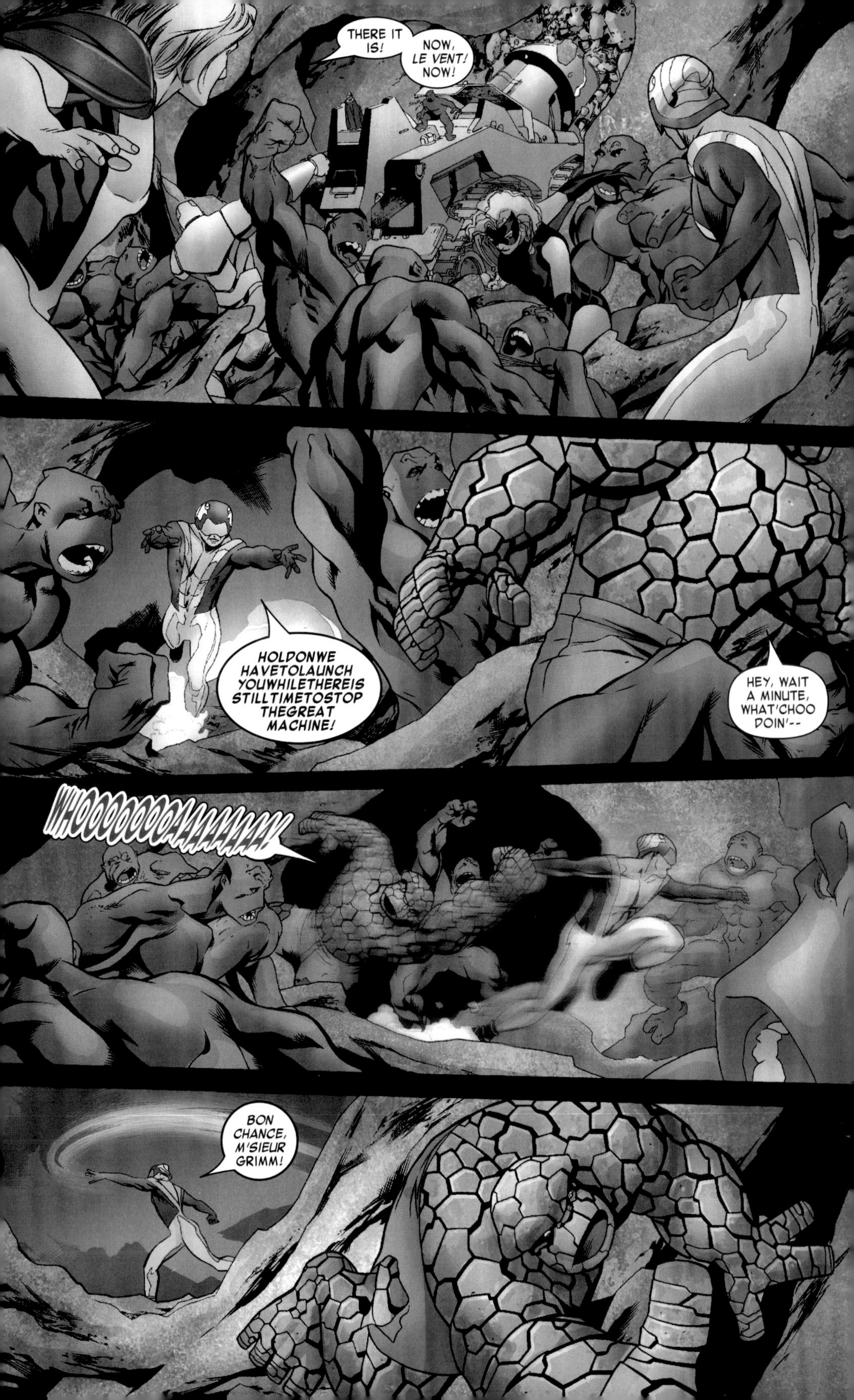
THERE IT IS!
NOW, LE VENT! NOW!
HOLDONWE HAVETOLAUNCH YOUWHILETHEREIS STILLTIMETOSTOP THEGREAT MACHINE!
HEY, WAIT A MINUTE, WHAT'CHOO DOIN'--
WHOOOOOOOAAAAAAAY!
BON CHANCE, M'SIEUR GRIMM!

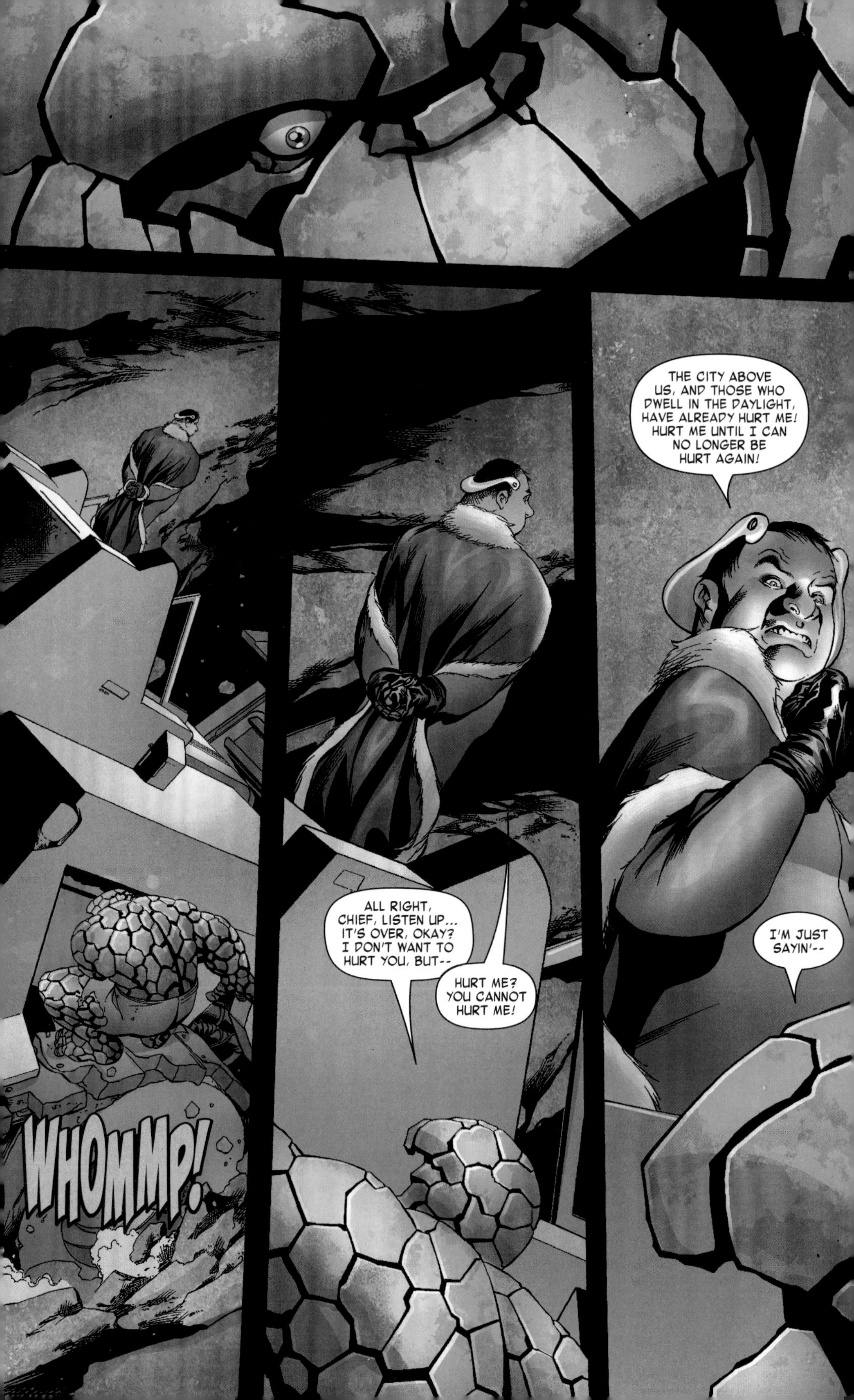
THE CITY ABOVE US, AND THOSE WHO DWELL IN THE DAYLIGHT, HAVE ALREADY HURT ME! HURT ME UNTIL I CAN NO LONGER BE HURT AGAIN!
ALL RIGHT, CHIEF, LISTEN UP... IT'S OVER, OKAY? I DON'T WANT TO HURT YOU, BUT--
HURT ME? YOU CANNOT HURT ME!
I'M JUST SAYIN'--
WHOMMP!

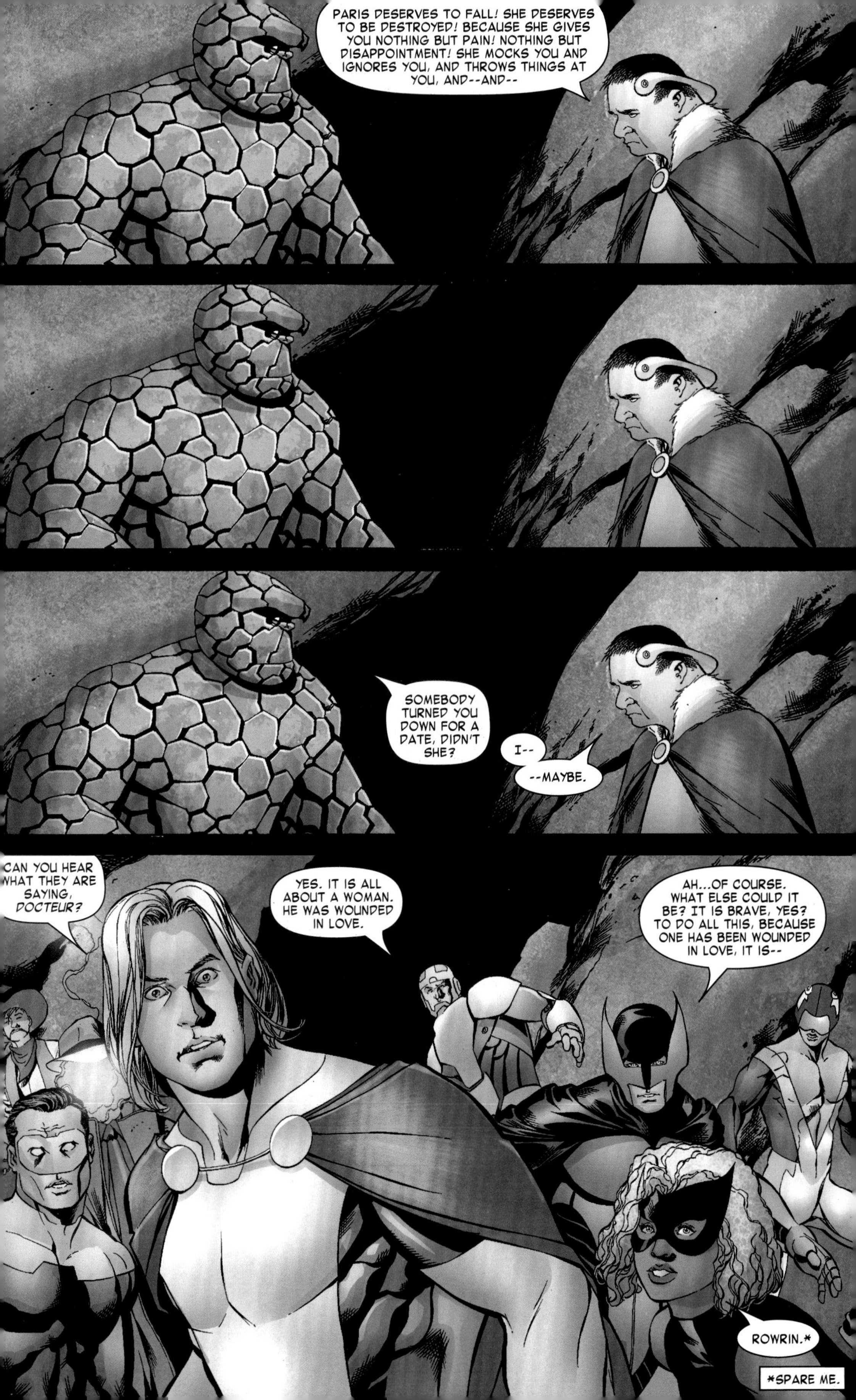
PARIS DESERVES TO FALL! SHE DESERVES TO BE DESTROYED! BECAUSE SHE GIVES YOU NOTHING BUT PAIN! NOTHING BUT DISAPPOINTMENT! SHE MOCKS YOU AND IGNORES YOU, AND THROWS THINGS AT YOU, AND--AND--
SOMEBODY TURNED YOU DOWN FOR A DATE, DIDN'T SHE?
I--
--MAYBE.
CAN YOU HEAR WHAT THEY ARE SAYING, DOCTEUR?
YES. IT IS ALL ABOUT A WOMAN. HE WAS WOUNDED IN LOVE.
AH...OF COURSE. WHAT ELSE COULD IT BE? IT IS BRAVE, YES? TO DO ALL THIS, BECAUSE ONE HAS BEEN WOUNDED IN LOVE, IT IS--
ROWRIN.*
*SPARE ME.

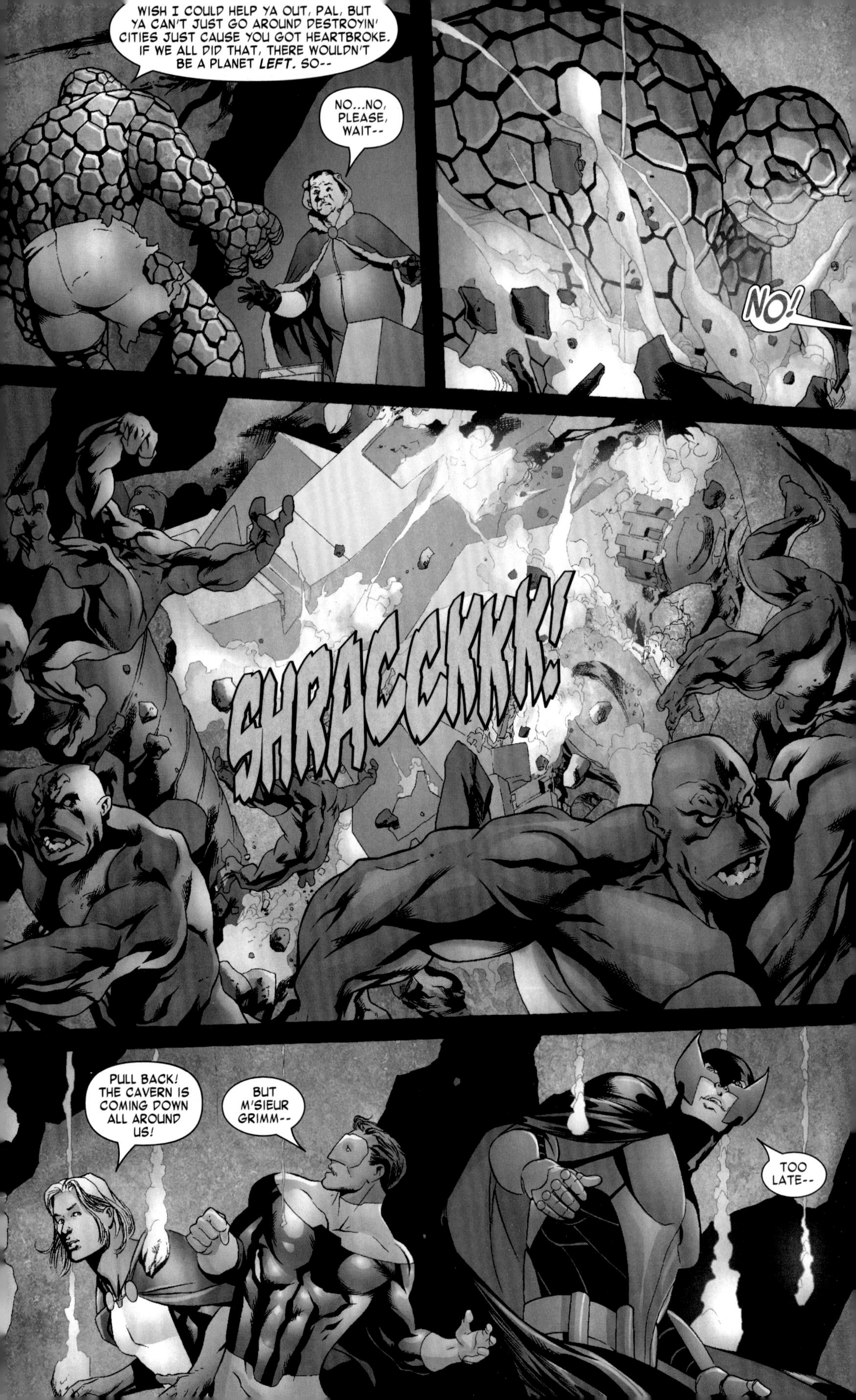
WISH I COULD HELP YA OUT, PAL, BUT YA CAN'T JUST GO AROUND DESTROYIN' CITIES JUST CAUSE YOU GOT HEARTBROKE. IF WE ALL DID THAT, THERE WOULDN'T BE A PLANET *LEFT.* SO--
NO...NO, PLEASE, WAIT--
NO!
SHRACCKKK!
PULL BACK! THE CAVERN IS COMING DOWN ALL AROUND US!
BUT M'SIEUR GRIMM--
TOO LATE--

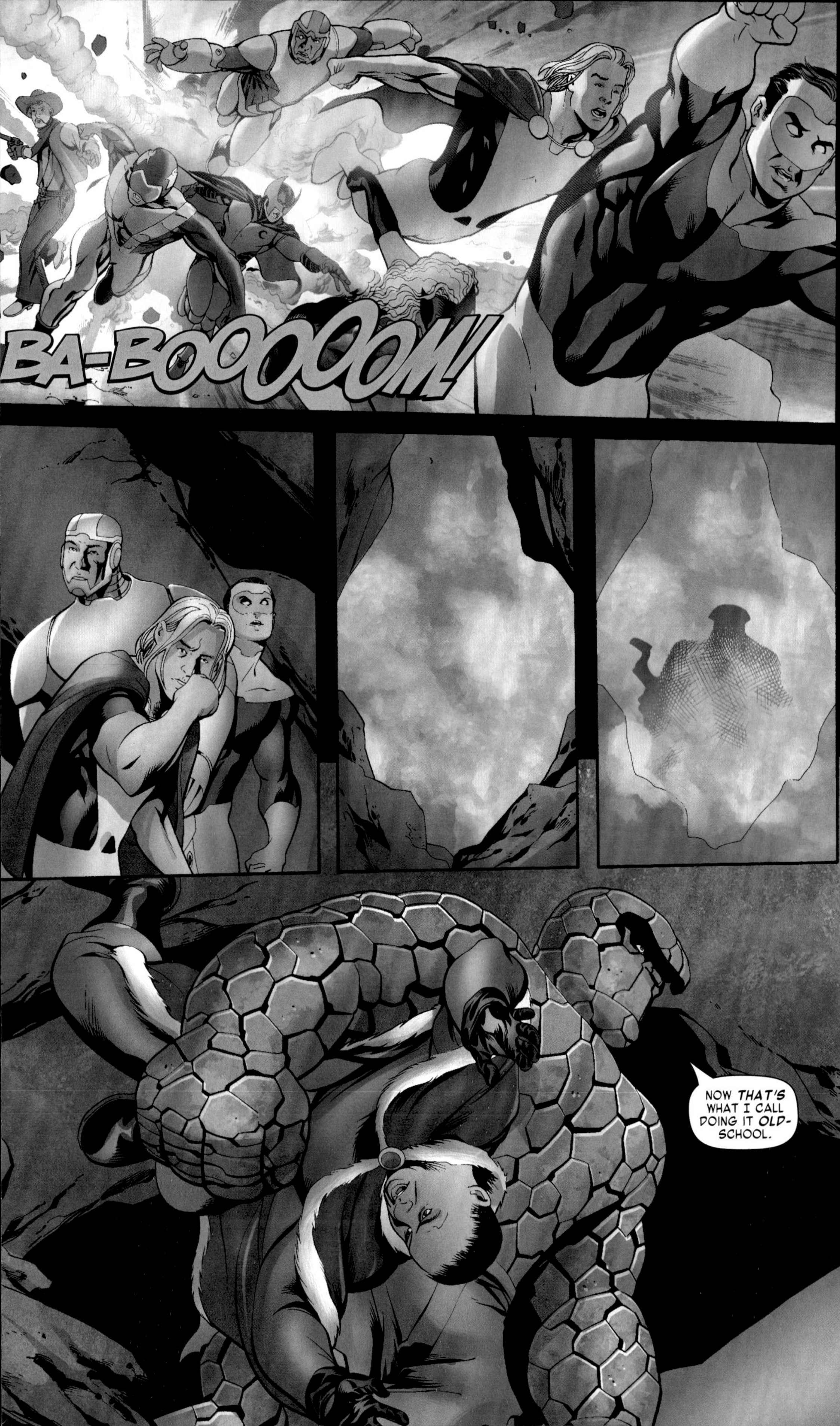
BA-BOOOOOM!
NOW THAT'S WHAT I CALL DOING IT OLD-SCHOOL.

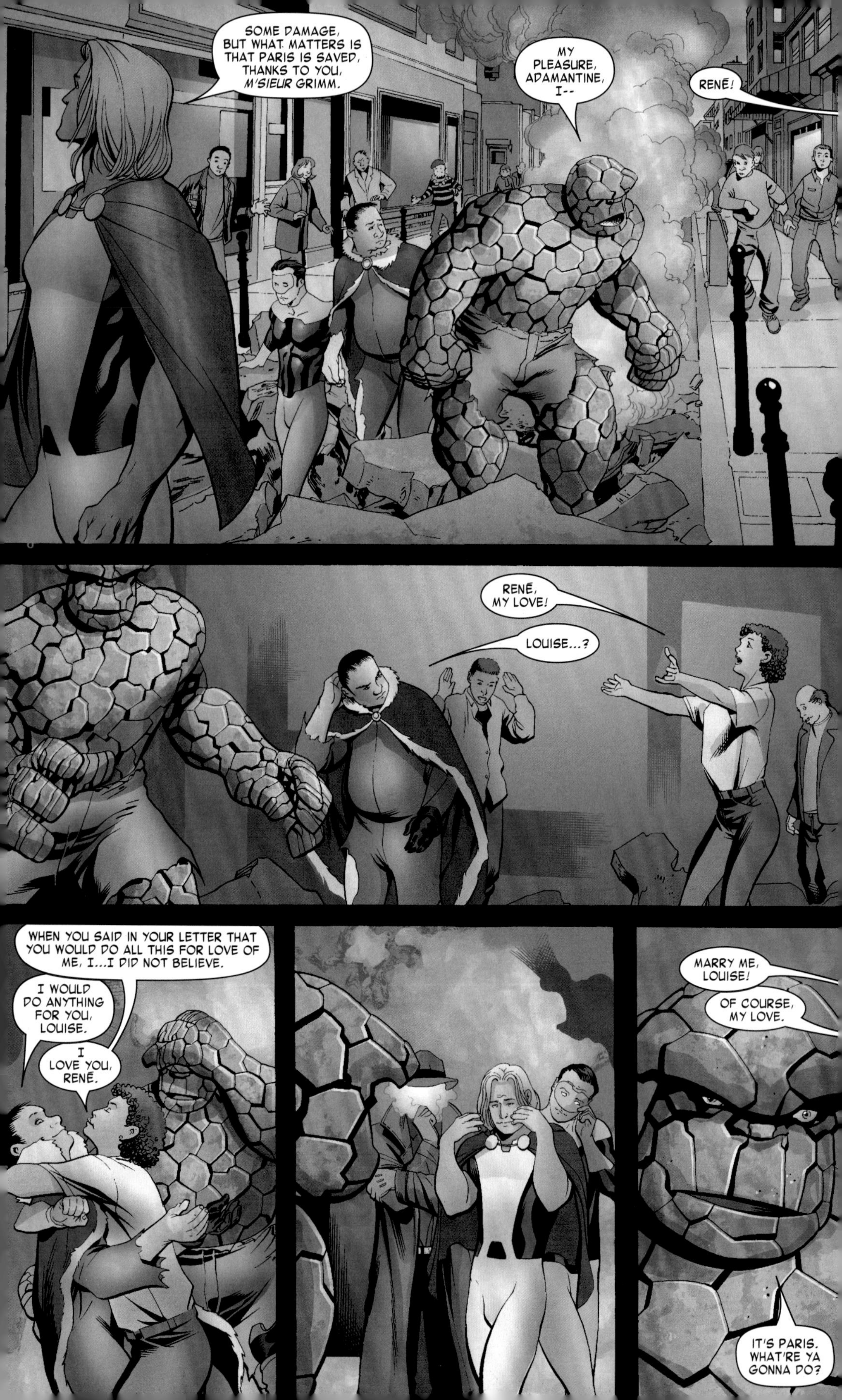
SOME DAMAGE, BUT WHAT MATTERS IS THAT PARIS IS SAVED, THANKS TO YOU, M'SIEUR GRIMM.
MY PLEASURE, ADAMANTINE, I--
RENÉ!
RENÉ, MY LOVE!
LOUISE...?
WHEN YOU SAID IN YOUR LETTER THAT YOU WOULD DO ALL THIS FOR LOVE OF ME, I...I DID NOT BELIEVE.
I WOULD DO ANYTHING FOR YOU, LOUISE.
I LOVE YOU, RENÉ.
MARRY ME, LOUISE!
OF COURSE, MY LOVE.
IT'S PARIS. WHAT'RE YA GONNA DO?

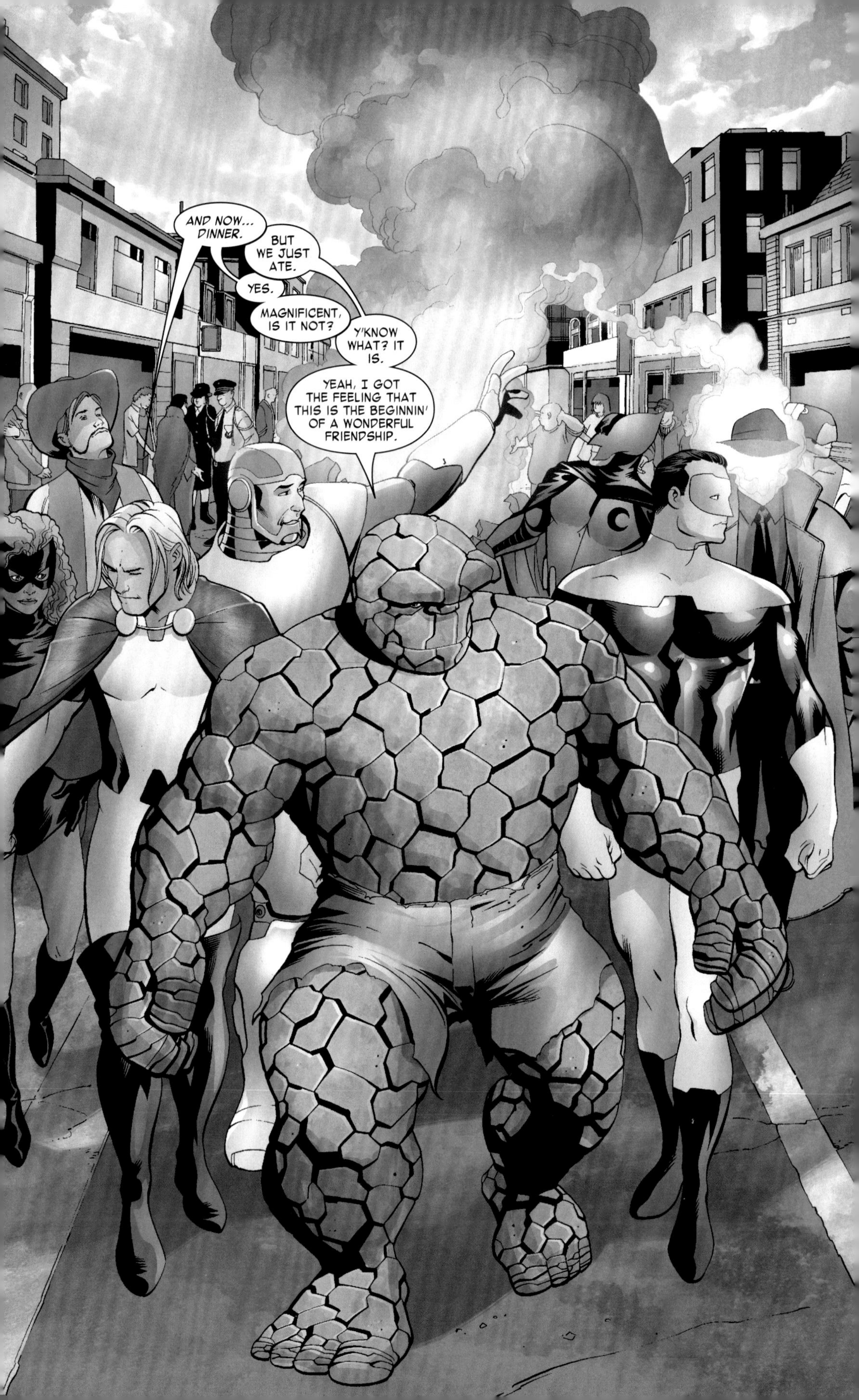
AND NOW... DINNER.
BUT WE JUST ATE.
YES.
MAGNIFICENT, IS IT NOT?
Y'KNOW WHAT? IT IS.
YEAH, I GOT THE FEELING THAT THIS IS THE BEGINNIN' OF A WONDERFUL FRIENDSHIP.

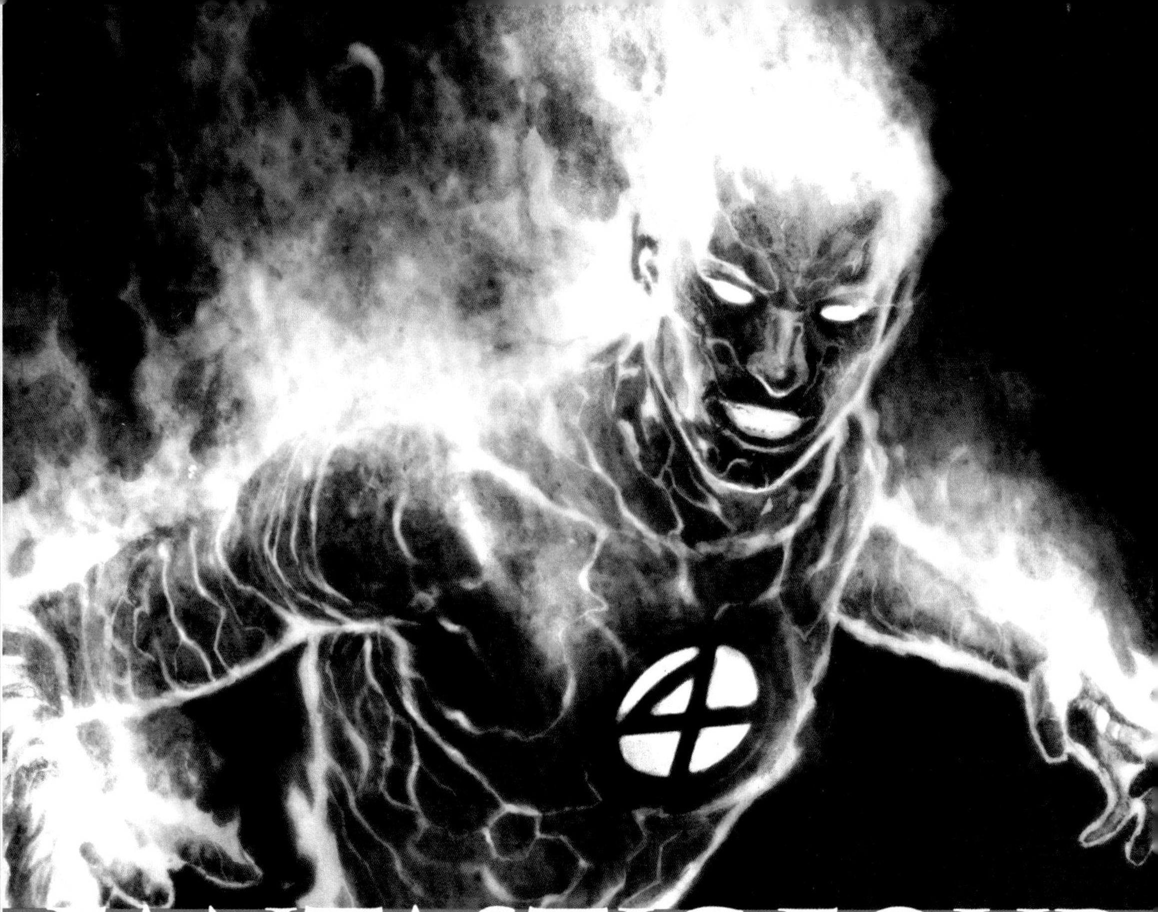

FANTASTIC FOUR

A MARVEL COMICS EVENT

CIVIL WAR

FANTASTIC FOUR #542

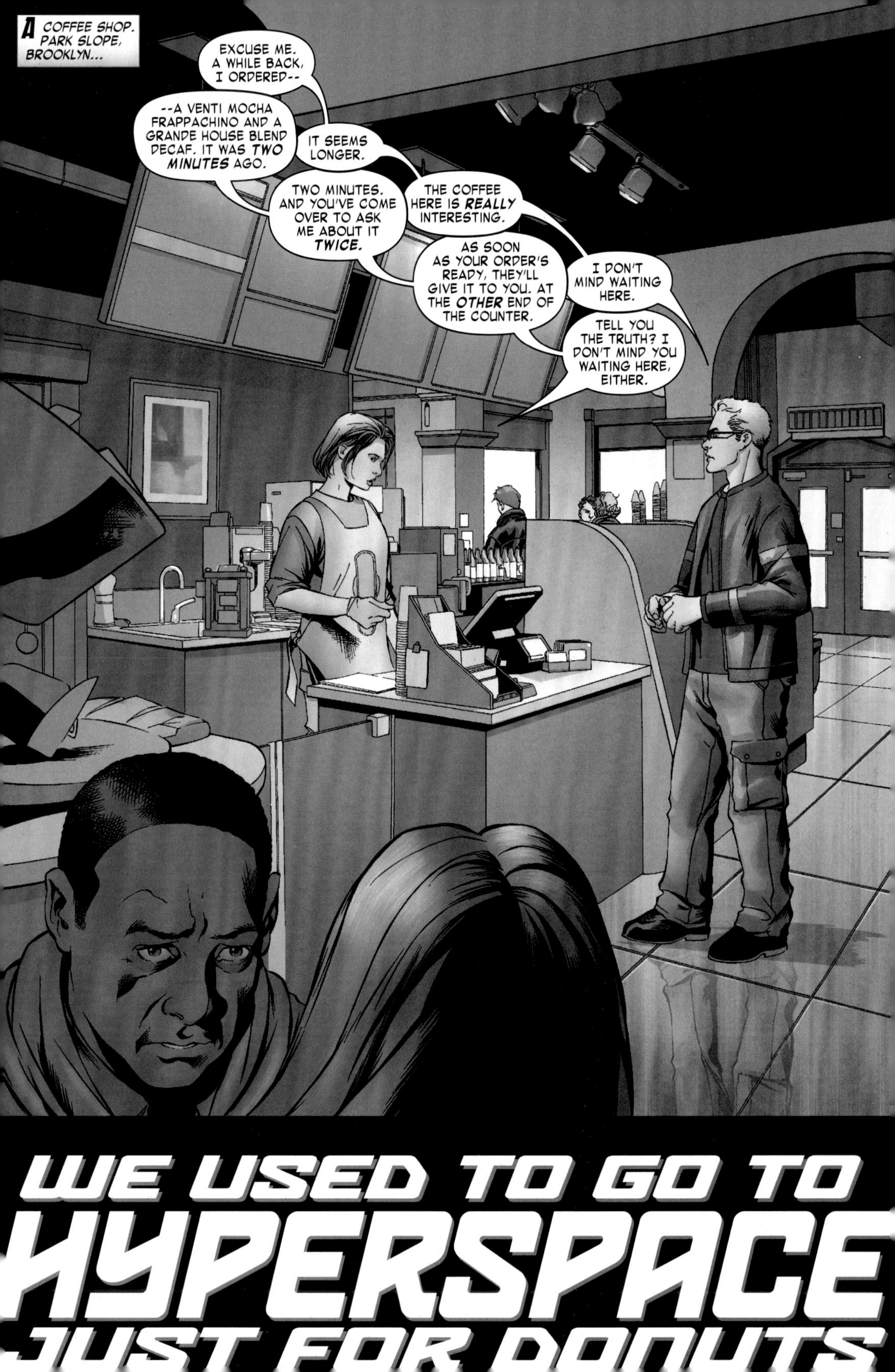
A COFFEE SHOP. PARK SLOPE, BROOKLYN...
EXCUSE ME. A WHILE BACK, I ORDERED--
--A VENTI MOCHA FRAPPACHINO AND A GRANDE HOUSE BLEND DECAF. IT WAS TWO MINUTES AGO.
IT SEEMS LONGER.
TWO MINUTES. AND YOU'VE COME OVER TO ASK ME ABOUT IT TWICE.
THE COFFEE HERE IS REALLY INTERESTING.
AS SOON AS YOUR ORDER'S READY, THEY'LL GIVE IT TO YOU. AT THE OTHER END OF THE COUNTER.
I DON'T MIND WAITING HERE.
TELL YOU THE TRUTH? I DON'T MIND YOU WAITING HERE, EITHER.
WE USED TO GO TO HYPERSPACE JUST FOR DONUTS

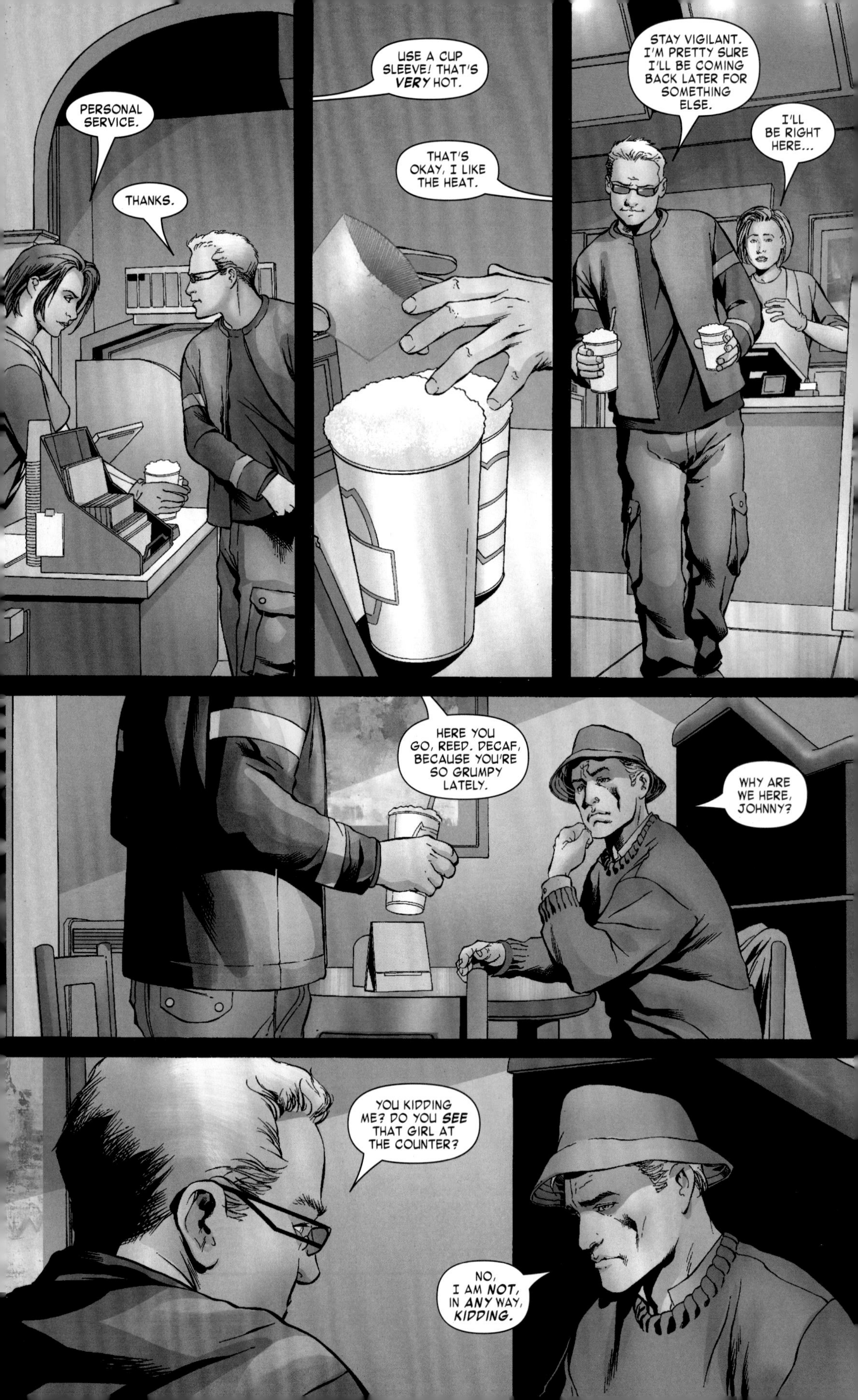
PERSONAL SERVICE.
THANKS.
USE A CUP SLEEVE! THAT'S *VERY* HOT.
THAT'S OKAY, I LIKE THE HEAT.
STAY VIGILANT. I'M PRETTY SURE I'LL BE COMING BACK LATER FOR SOMETHING ELSE.
I'LL BE RIGHT HERE...
HERE YOU GO, REED. DECAF, BECAUSE YOU'RE SO GRUMPY LATELY.
WHY ARE WE HERE, JOHNNY?
YOU KIDDING ME? DO YOU *SEE* THAT GIRL AT THE COUNTER?
NO, I AM *NOT*, IN *ANY* WAY, *KIDDING*.

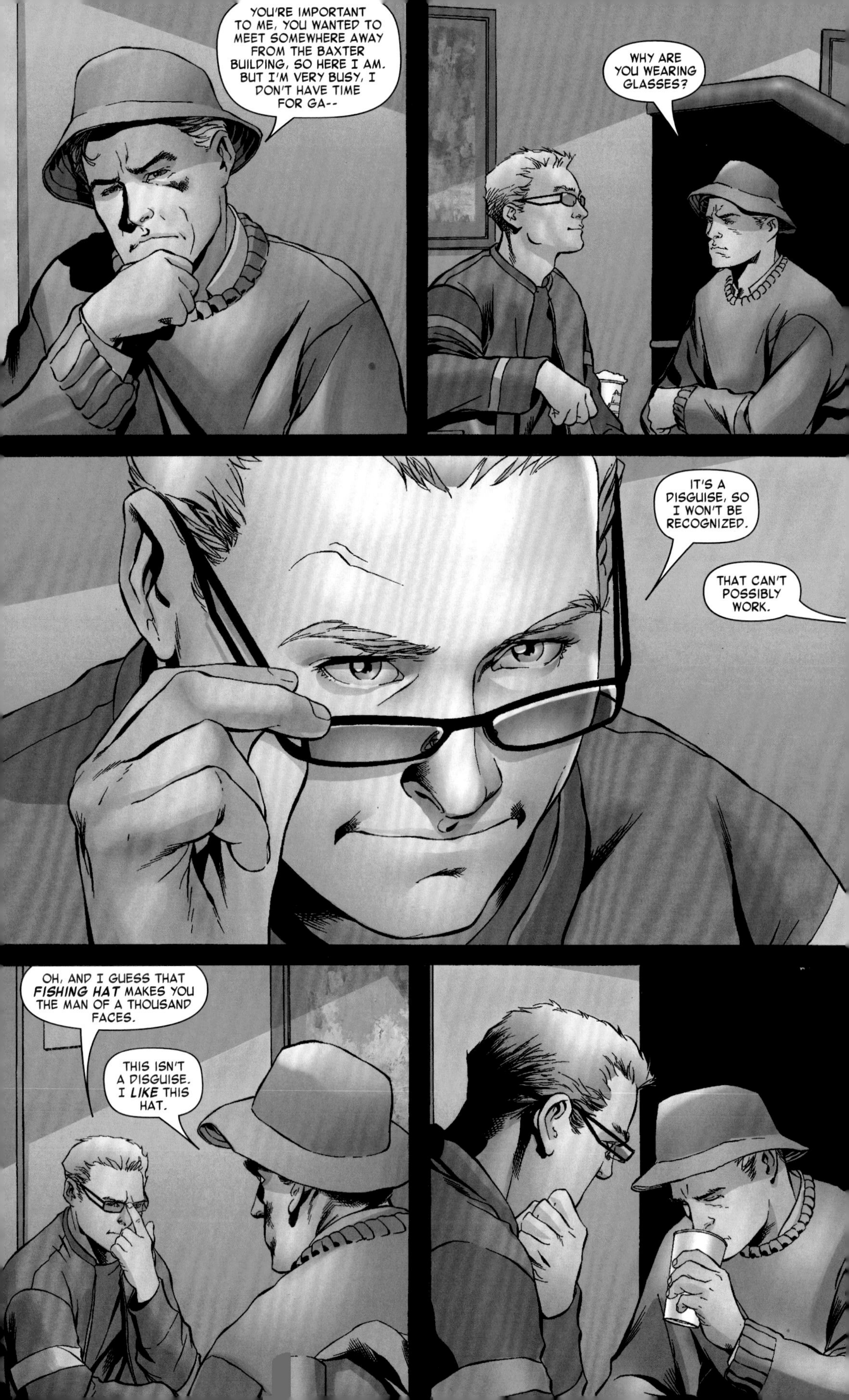
YOU'RE IMPORTANT TO ME, YOU WANTED TO MEET SOMEWHERE AWAY FROM THE BAXTER BUILDING, SO HERE I AM. BUT I'M VERY BUSY, I DON'T HAVE TIME FOR GA--
WHY ARE YOU WEARING GLASSES?
IT'S A DISGUISE, SO I WON'T BE RECOGNIZED.
THAT CAN'T POSSIBLY WORK.
OH, AND I GUESS THAT FISHING HAT MAKES YOU THE MAN OF A THOUSAND FACES.
THIS ISN'T A DISGUISE. I LIKE THIS HAT.

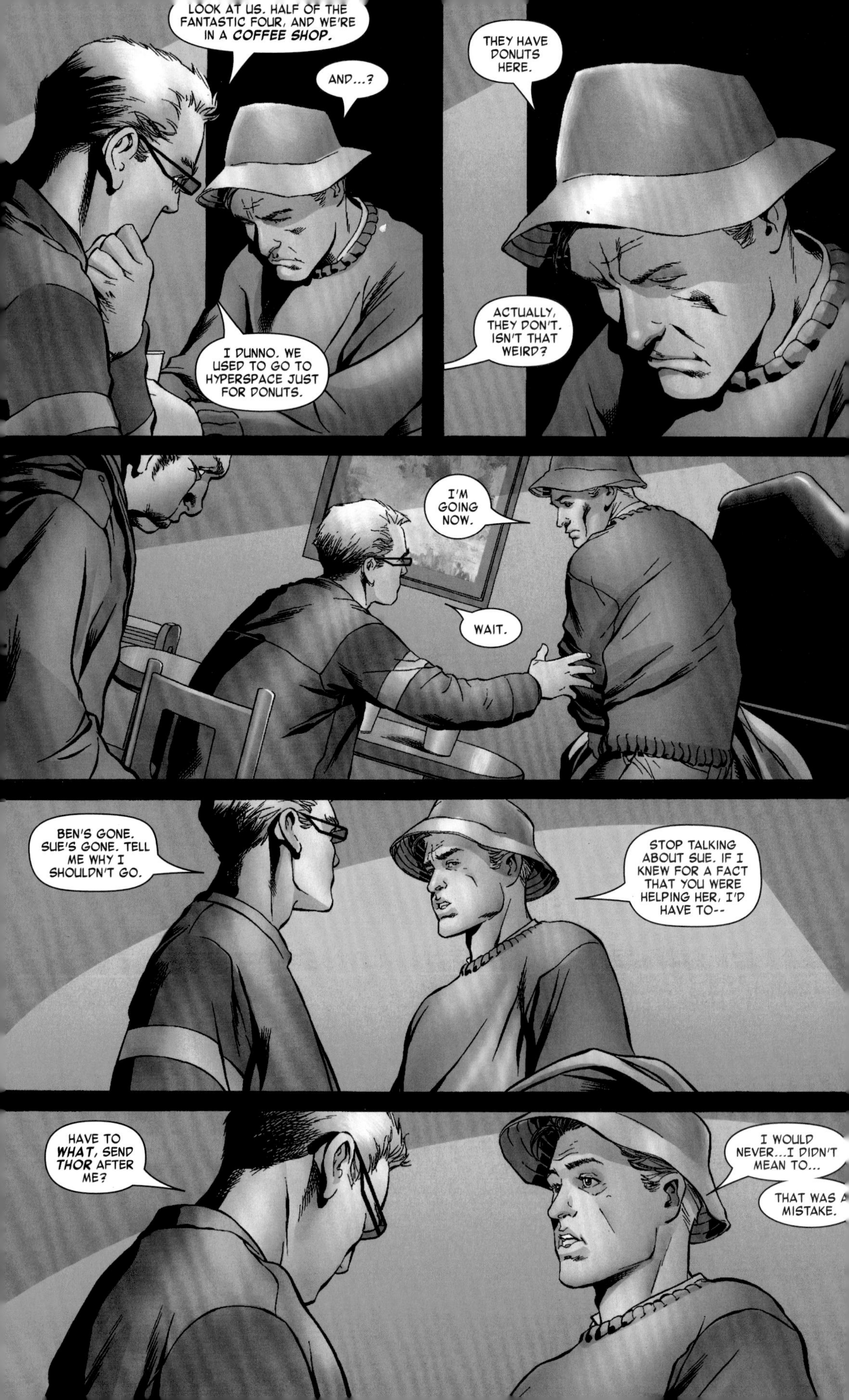
LOOK AT US. HALF OF THE FANTASTIC FOUR, AND WE'RE IN A COFFEE SHOP.
AND...?
I DUNNO. WE USED TO GO TO HYPERSPACE JUST FOR DONUTS.
THEY HAVE DONUTS HERE.
ACTUALLY, THEY DON'T. ISN'T THAT WEIRD?
I'M GOING NOW.
WAIT.
BEN'S GONE. SUE'S GONE. TELL ME WHY I SHOULDN'T GO.
STOP TALKING ABOUT SUE. IF I KNEW FOR A FACT THAT YOU WERE HELPING HER, I'D HAVE TO--
HAVE TO WHAT, SEND THOR AFTER ME?
I WOULD NEVER...I DIDN'T MEAN TO...
THAT WAS A MISTAKE.

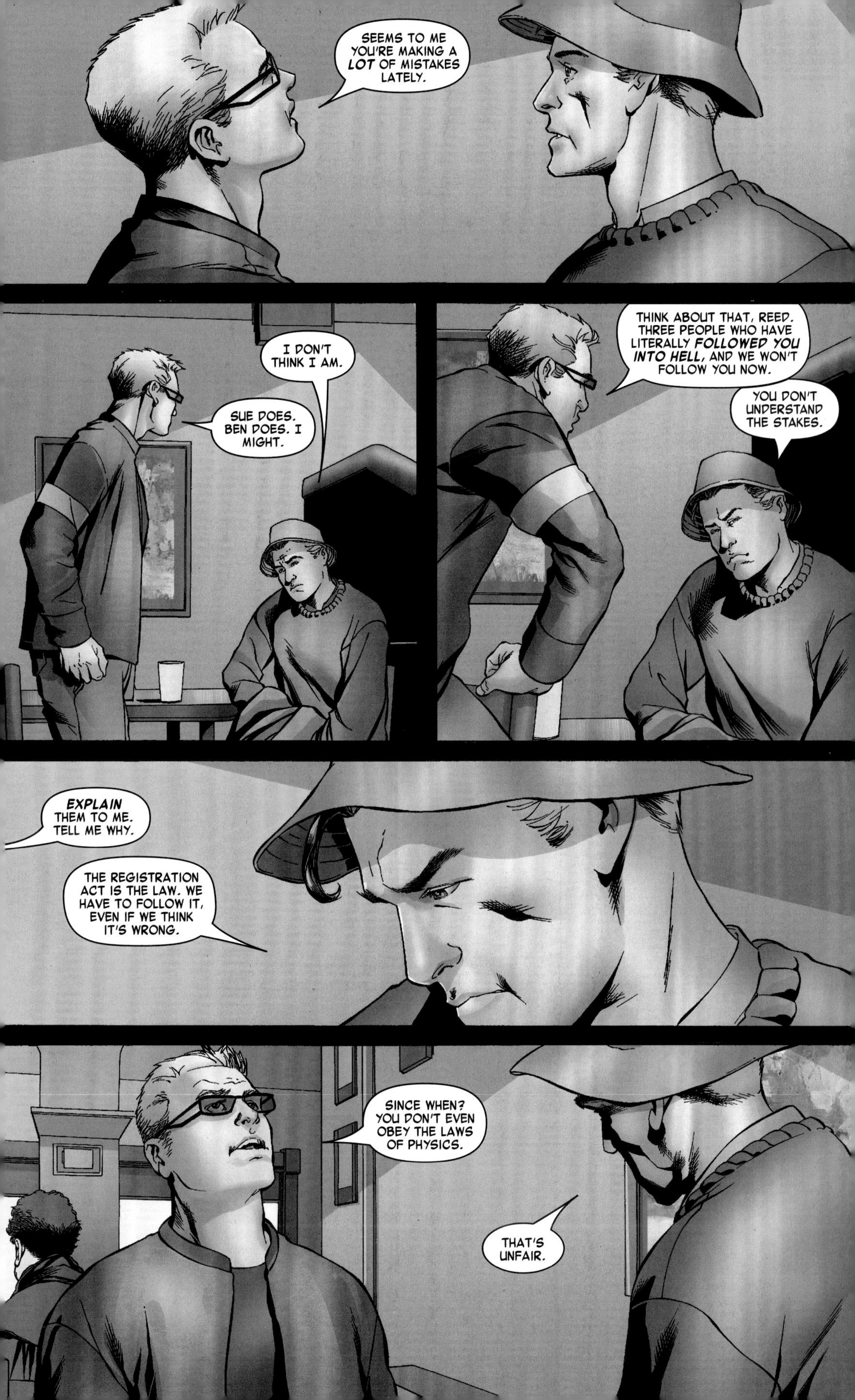
SEEMS TO ME YOU'RE MAKING A LOT OF MISTAKES LATELY.
I DON'T THINK I AM.
SUE DOES. BEN DOES. I MIGHT.
THINK ABOUT THAT, REED. THREE PEOPLE WHO HAVE LITERALLY FOLLOWED YOU INTO HELL, AND WE WON'T FOLLOW YOU NOW.
YOU DON'T UNDERSTAND THE STAKES.
EXPLAIN THEM TO ME. TELL ME WHY.
THE REGISTRATION ACT IS THE LAW. WE HAVE TO FOLLOW IT, EVEN IF WE THINK IT'S WRONG.
SINCE WHEN? YOU DON'T EVEN OBEY THE LAWS OF PHYSICS.
THAT'S UNFAIR.

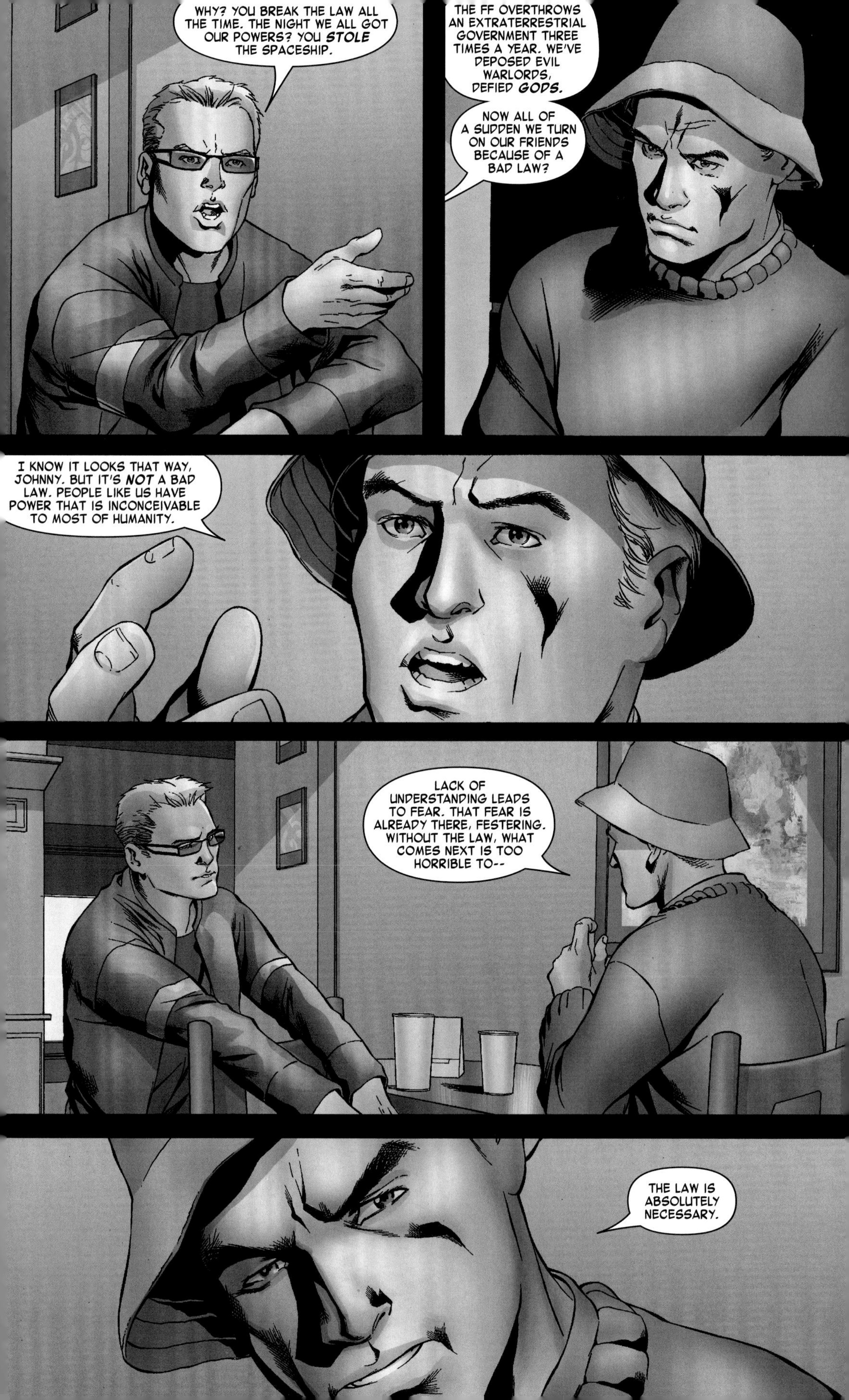
WHY? YOU BREAK THE LAW ALL THE TIME. THE NIGHT WE ALL GOT OUR POWERS? YOU STOLE THE SPACESHIP.
THE FF OVERTHROWS AN EXTRATERRESTRIAL GOVERNMENT THREE TIMES A YEAR. WE'VE DEPOSED EVIL WARLORDS, DEFIED GODS.
NOW ALL OF A SUDDEN WE TURN ON OUR FRIENDS BECAUSE OF A BAD LAW?
I KNOW IT LOOKS THAT WAY, JOHNNY. BUT IT'S NOT A BAD LAW. PEOPLE LIKE US HAVE POWER THAT IS INCONCEIVABLE TO MOST OF HUMANITY.
LACK OF UNDERSTANDING LEADS TO FEAR. THAT FEAR IS ALREADY THERE, FESTERING. WITHOUT THE LAW, WHAT COMES NEXT IS TOO HORRIBLE TO--
THE LAW IS ABSOLUTELY NECESSARY.

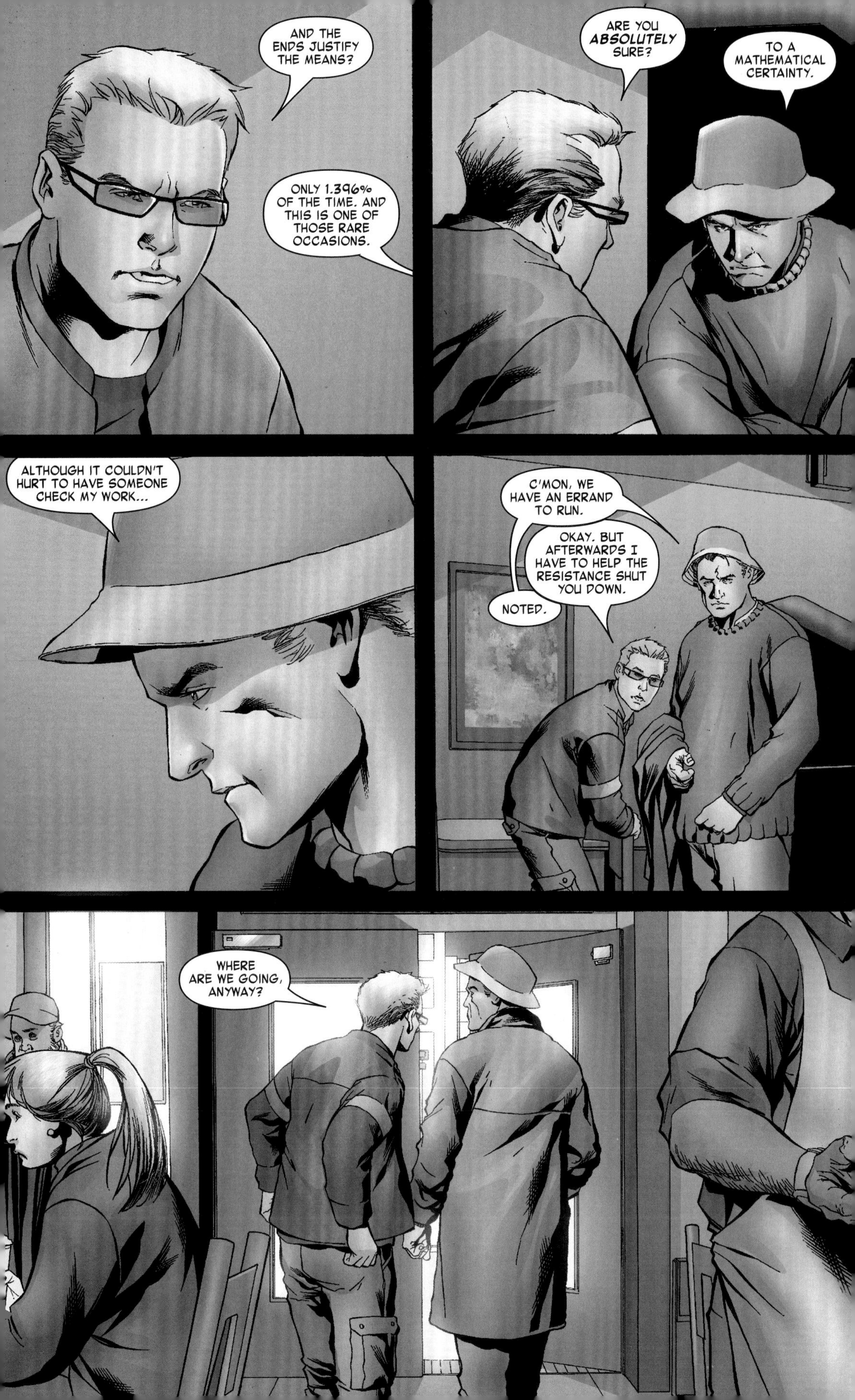
AND THE ENDS JUSTIFY THE MEANS?
ONLY 1.396% OF THE TIME. AND THIS IS ONE OF THOSE RARE OCCASIONS.
ARE YOU ABSOLUTELY SURE?
TO A MATHEMATICAL CERTAINTY.
ALTHOUGH IT COULDN'T HURT TO HAVE SOMEONE CHECK MY WORK...
C'MON, WE HAVE AN ERRAND TO RUN.
OKAY. BUT AFTERWARDS I HAVE TO HELP THE RESISTANCE SHUT YOU DOWN.
NOTED.
WHERE ARE WE GOING, ANYWAY?

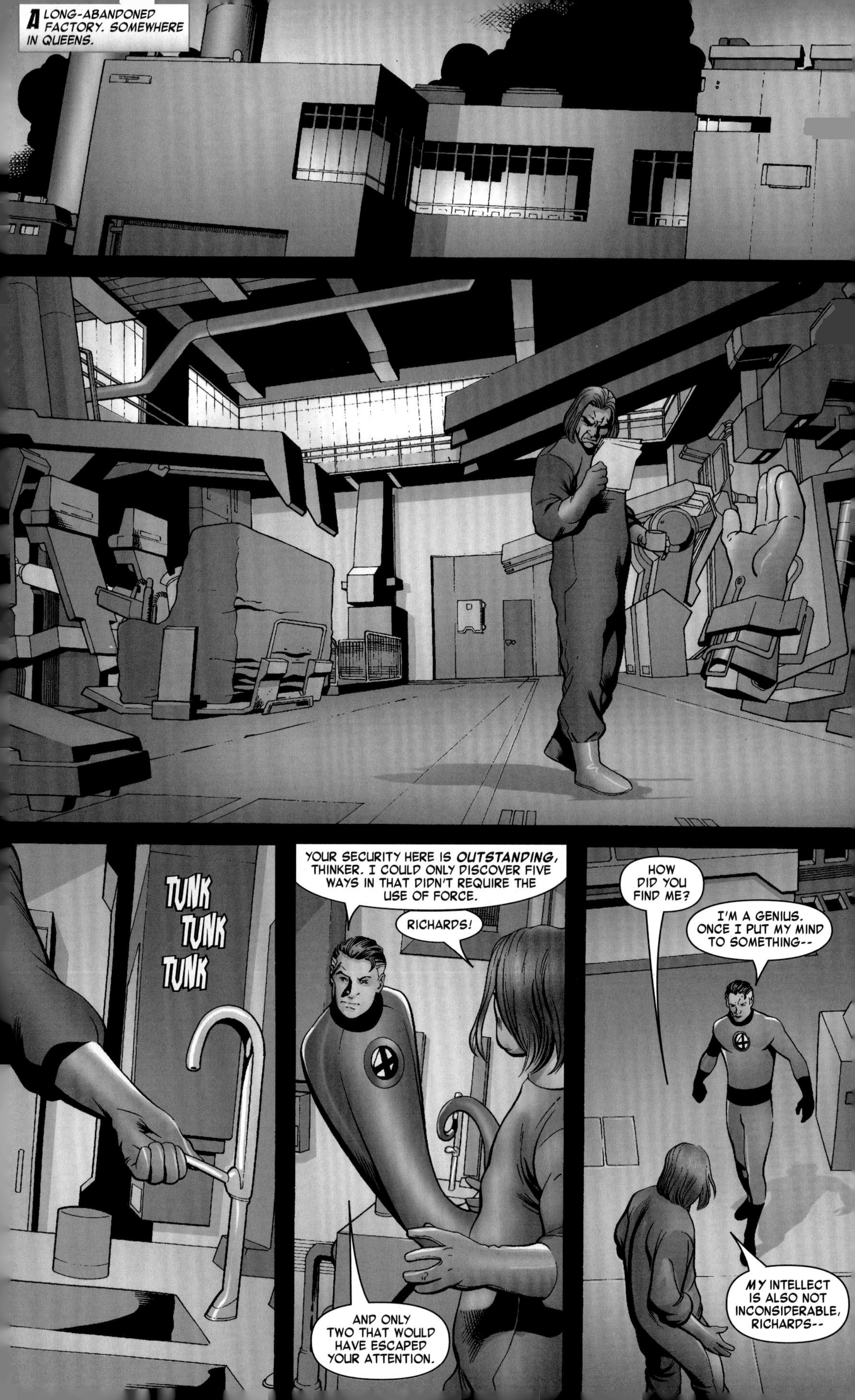
A LONG-ABANDONED FACTORY. SOMEWHERE IN QUEENS.
TUNK TUNK TUNK
YOUR SECURITY HERE IS OUTSTANDING, THINKER. I COULD ONLY DISCOVER FIVE WAYS IN THAT DIDN'T REQUIRE THE USE OF FORCE.
RICHARDS!
AND ONLY TWO THAT WOULD HAVE ESCAPED YOUR ATTENTION.
HOW DID YOU FIND ME?
I'M A GENIUS. ONCE I PUT MY MIND TO SOMETHING--
MY INTELLECT IS ALSO NOT INCONSIDERABLE, RICHARDS--

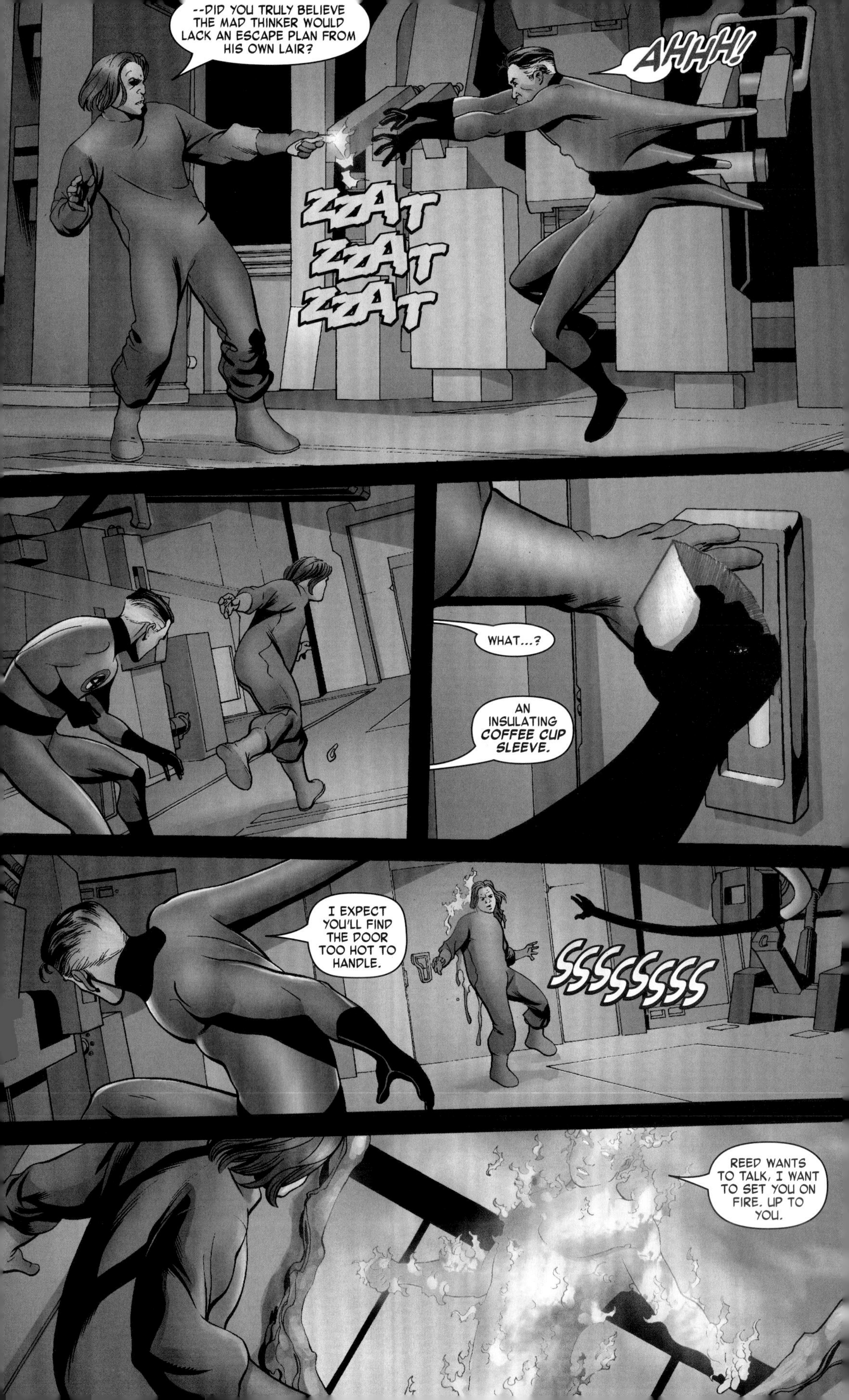
--DID YOU TRULY BELIEVE THE MAD THINKER WOULD LACK AN ESCAPE PLAN FROM HIS OWN LAIR?
AHHH!
ZZAT ZZAT ZZAT
WHAT...?
AN INSULATING COFFEE CUP SLEEVE.
I EXPECT YOU'LL FIND THE DOOR TOO HOT TO HANDLE.
SSSSSSSS
REED WANTS TO TALK, I WANT TO SET YOU ON FIRE. UP TO YOU.

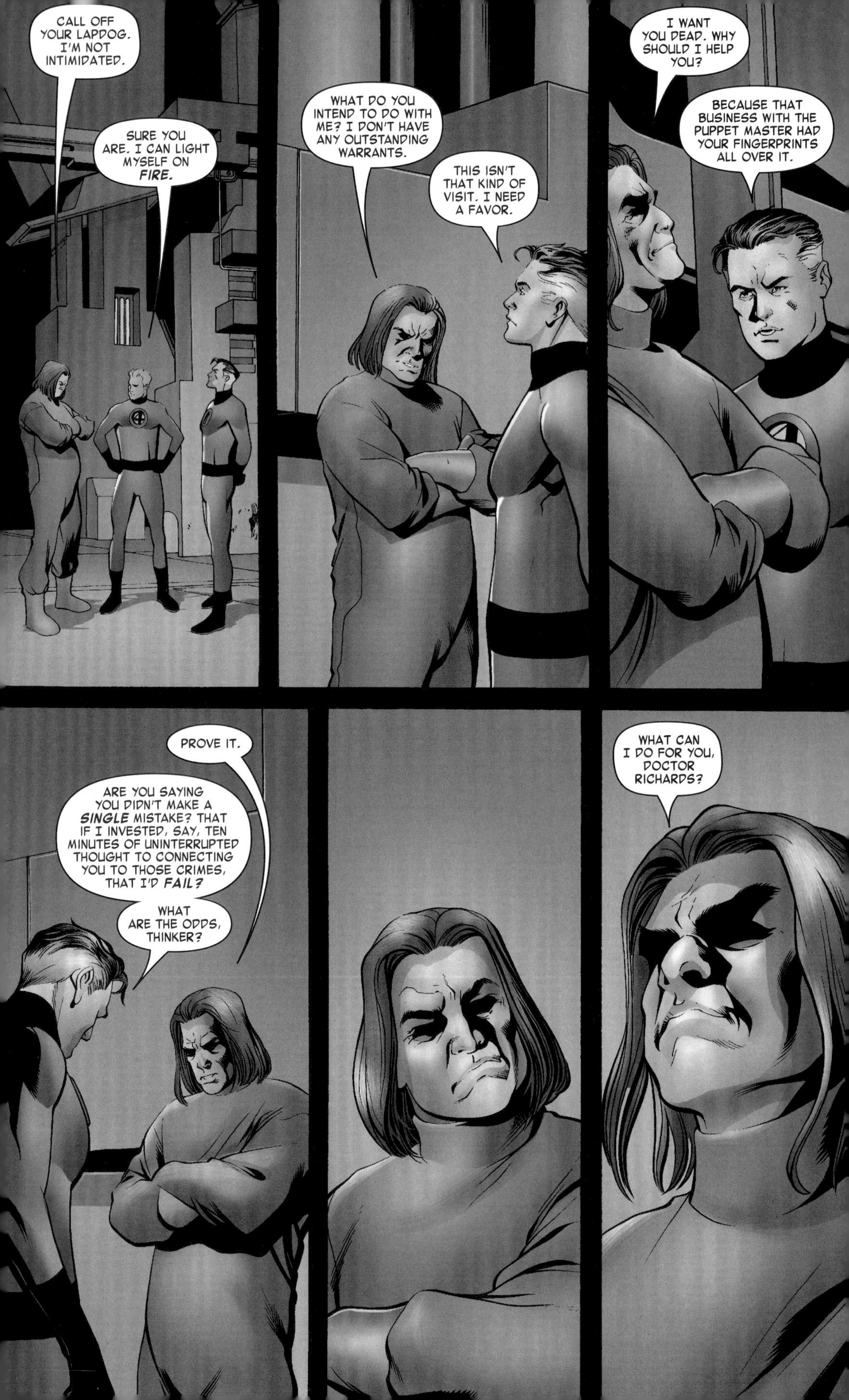
CALL OFF YOUR LAPDOG. I'M NOT INTIMIDATED.
SURE YOU ARE. I CAN LIGHT MYSELF ON FIRE.
WHAT DO YOU INTEND TO DO WITH ME? I DON'T HAVE ANY OUTSTANDING WARRANTS.
THIS ISN'T THAT KIND OF VISIT. I NEED A FAVOR.
I WANT YOU DEAD. WHY SHOULD I HELP YOU?
BECAUSE THAT BUSINESS WITH THE PUPPET MASTER HAD YOUR FINGERPRINTS ALL OVER IT.
PROVE IT.
ARE YOU SAYING YOU DIDN'T MAKE A SINGLE MISTAKE? THAT IF I INVESTED, SAY, TEN MINUTES OF UNINTERRUPTED THOUGHT TO CONNECTING YOU TO THOSE CRIMES, THAT I'D FAIL?
WHAT ARE THE ODDS, THINKER?
WHAT CAN I DO FOR YOU, DOCTOR RICHARDS?

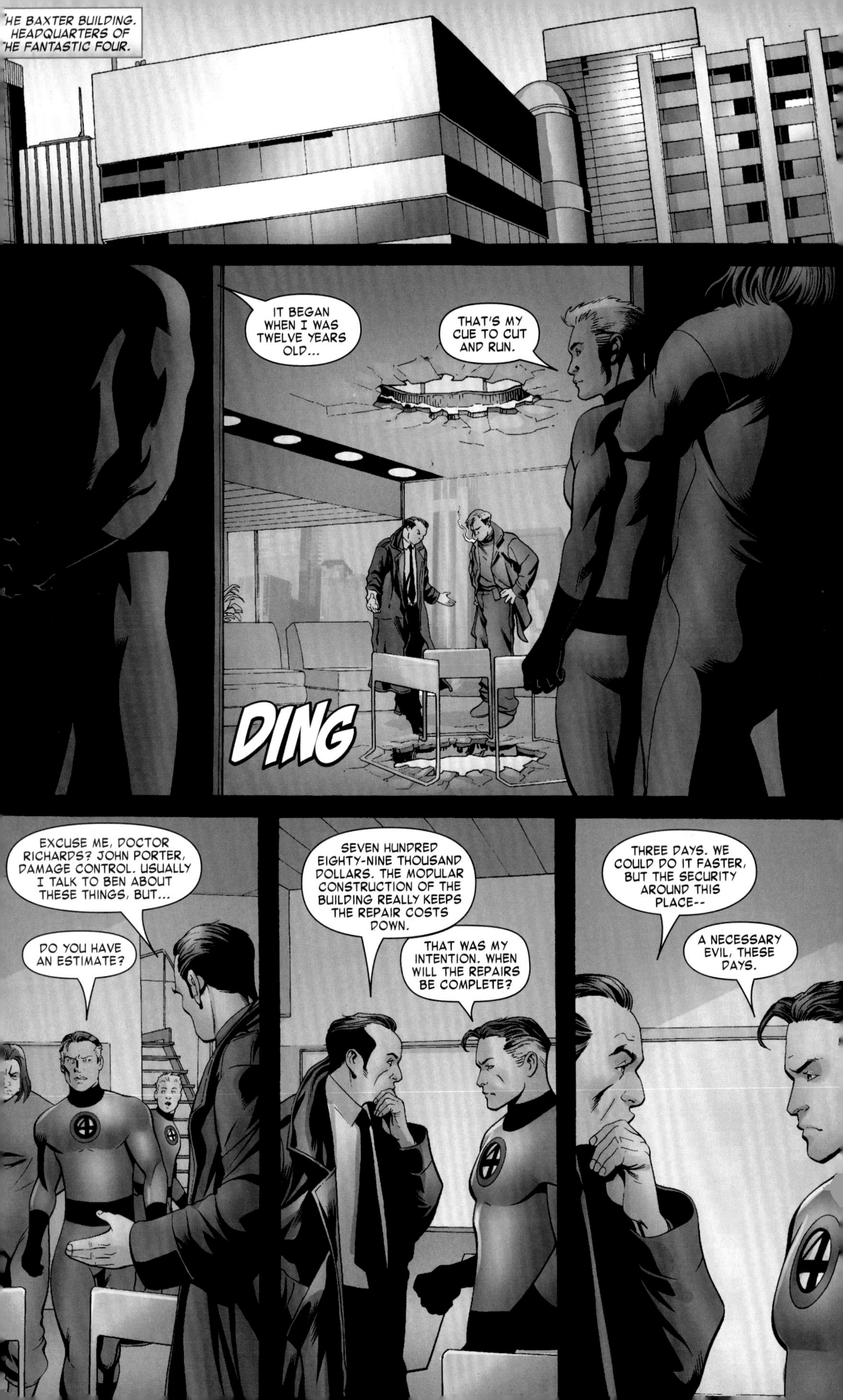
HE BAXTER BUILDING. HEADQUARTERS OF HE FANTASTIC FOUR.
IT BEGAN WHEN I WAS TWELVE YEARS OLD...
THAT'S MY CUE TO CUT AND RUN.
DING
EXCUSE ME, DOCTOR RICHARDS? JOHN PORTER, DAMAGE CONTROL. USUALLY I TALK TO BEN ABOUT THESE THINGS, BUT...
DO YOU HAVE AN ESTIMATE?
SEVEN HUNDRED EIGHTY-NINE THOUSAND DOLLARS. THE MODULAR CONSTRUCTION OF THE BUILDING REALLY KEEPS THE REPAIR COSTS DOWN.
THAT WAS MY INTENTION. WHEN WILL THE REPAIRS BE COMPLETE?
THREE DAYS. WE COULD DO IT FASTER, BUT THE SECURITY AROUND THIS PLACE--
A NECESSARY EVIL, THESE DAYS.

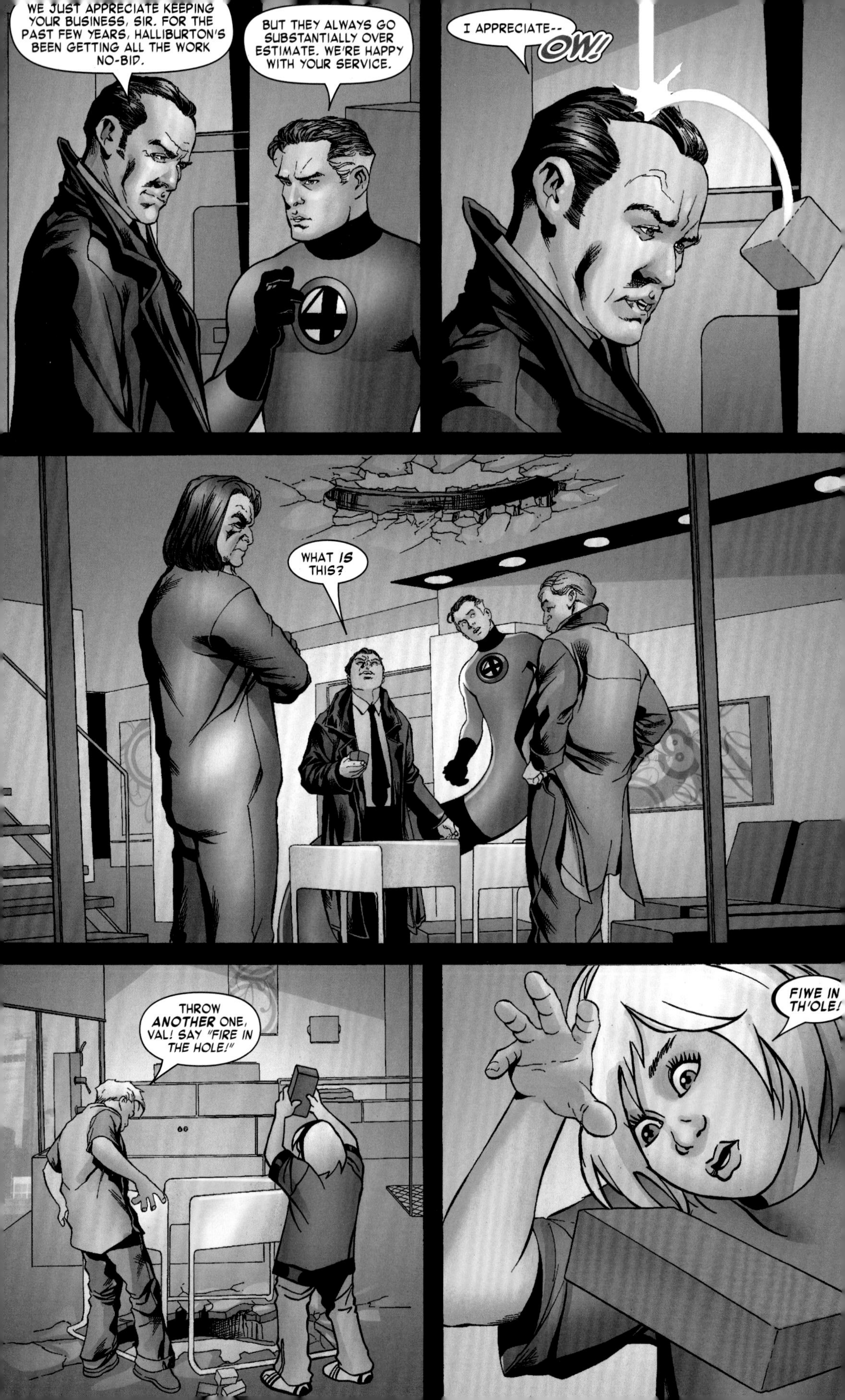
WE JUST APPRECIATE KEEPING YOUR BUSINESS, SIR. FOR THE PAST FEW YEARS, HALLIBURTON'S BEEN GETTING ALL THE WORK NO-BID.
BUT THEY ALWAYS GO SUBSTANTIALLY OVER ESTIMATE. WE'RE HAPPY WITH YOUR SERVICE.
I APPRECIATE--
OW!
WHAT IS THIS?
THROW ANOTHER ONE, VAL! SAY "FIRE IN THE HOLE!"
FIWE IN TH'OLE!

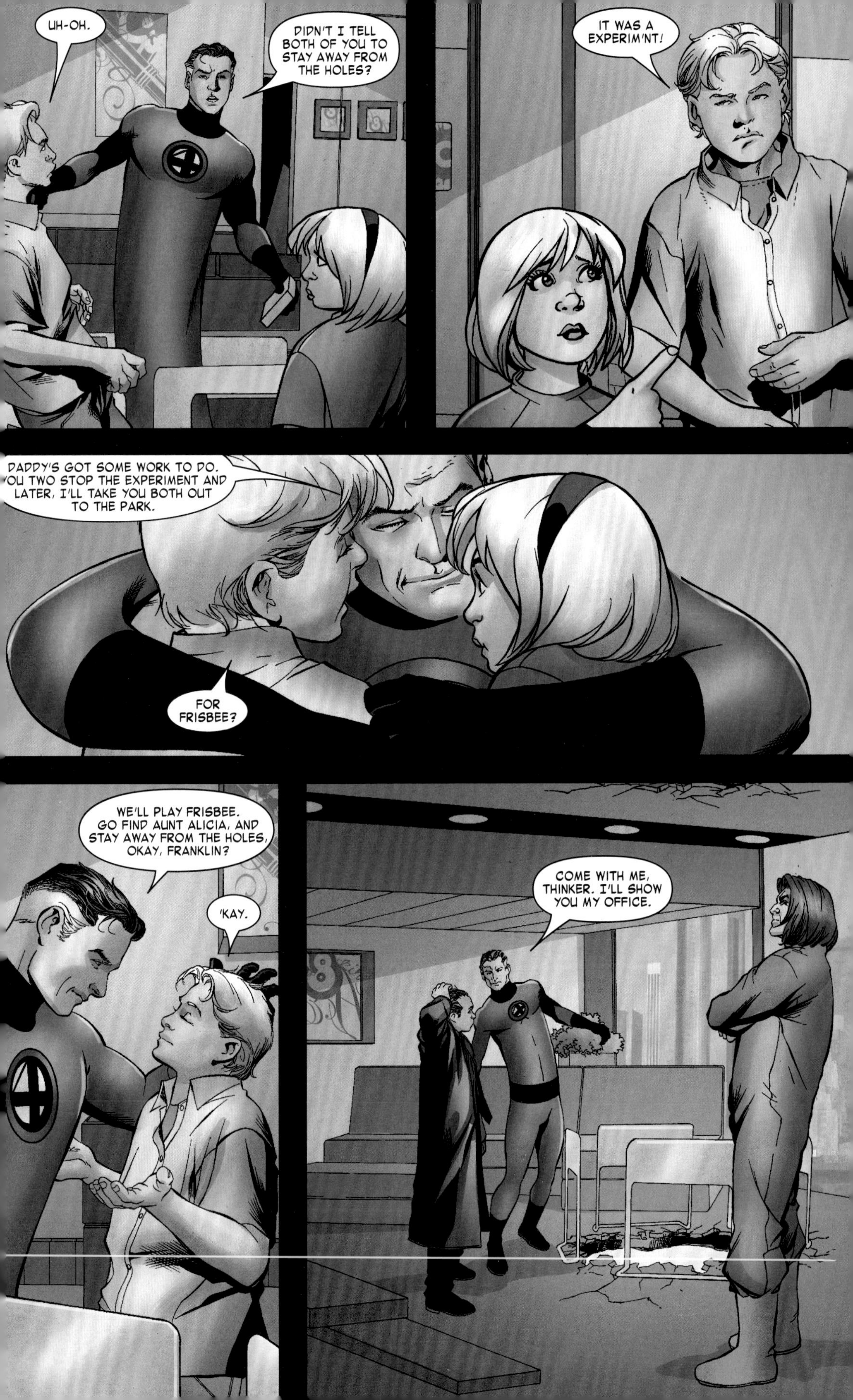
UH-OH.
DIDN'T I TELL BOTH OF YOU TO STAY AWAY FROM THE HOLES?
IT WAS A EXPERIM'NT!
DADDY'S GOT SOME WORK TO DO. OU TWO STOP THE EXPERIMENT AND LATER, I'LL TAKE YOU BOTH OUT TO THE PARK.
FOR FRISBEE?
WE'LL PLAY FRISBEE. GO FIND AUNT ALICIA, AND STAY AWAY FROM THE HOLES, OKAY, FRANKLIN?
'KAY.
COME WITH ME, THINKER. I'LL SHOW YOU MY OFFICE.

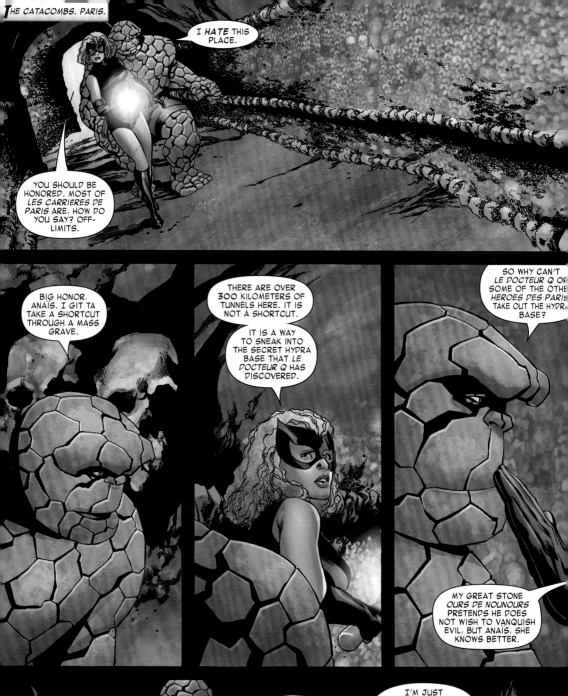

I *HATE* THIS PLACE.

YOU SHOULD BE HONORED. MOST OF *LES CARRIÈRES DE PARIS* ARE, HOW DO YOU SAY? OFF-LIMITS.

BIG HONOR, ANAÏS. I GIT TA TAKE A SHORTCUT THROUGH A MASS GRAVE.

THERE ARE OVER 300 KILOMETERS OF TUNNELS HERE. IT IS NOT A SHORTCUT.

IT IS A WAY TO SNEAK INTO THE SECRET HYDRA BASE THAT *LE DOCTEUR Q* HAS DISCOVERED.

SO WHY CAN'T *LE DOCTEUR Q* OR SOME OF THE OTHER *HEROES DES PARIS* TAKE OUT THE HYDRA BASE?

MY GREAT STONE *OURS DE NOUNOURS* PRETENDS HE DOES NOT WISH TO VANQUISH EVIL, BUT ANAÏS, SHE KNOWS BETTER.

I'M JUST WONDERIN' IF THERE ARE ANY SUPER-VILLAINS IN PARIS WHO DON'T LIVE UNNERGROUND.

COME, WE ARE VERY CLOSE. THEY WILL NEVER EXPECT US TO ATTACK FROM--

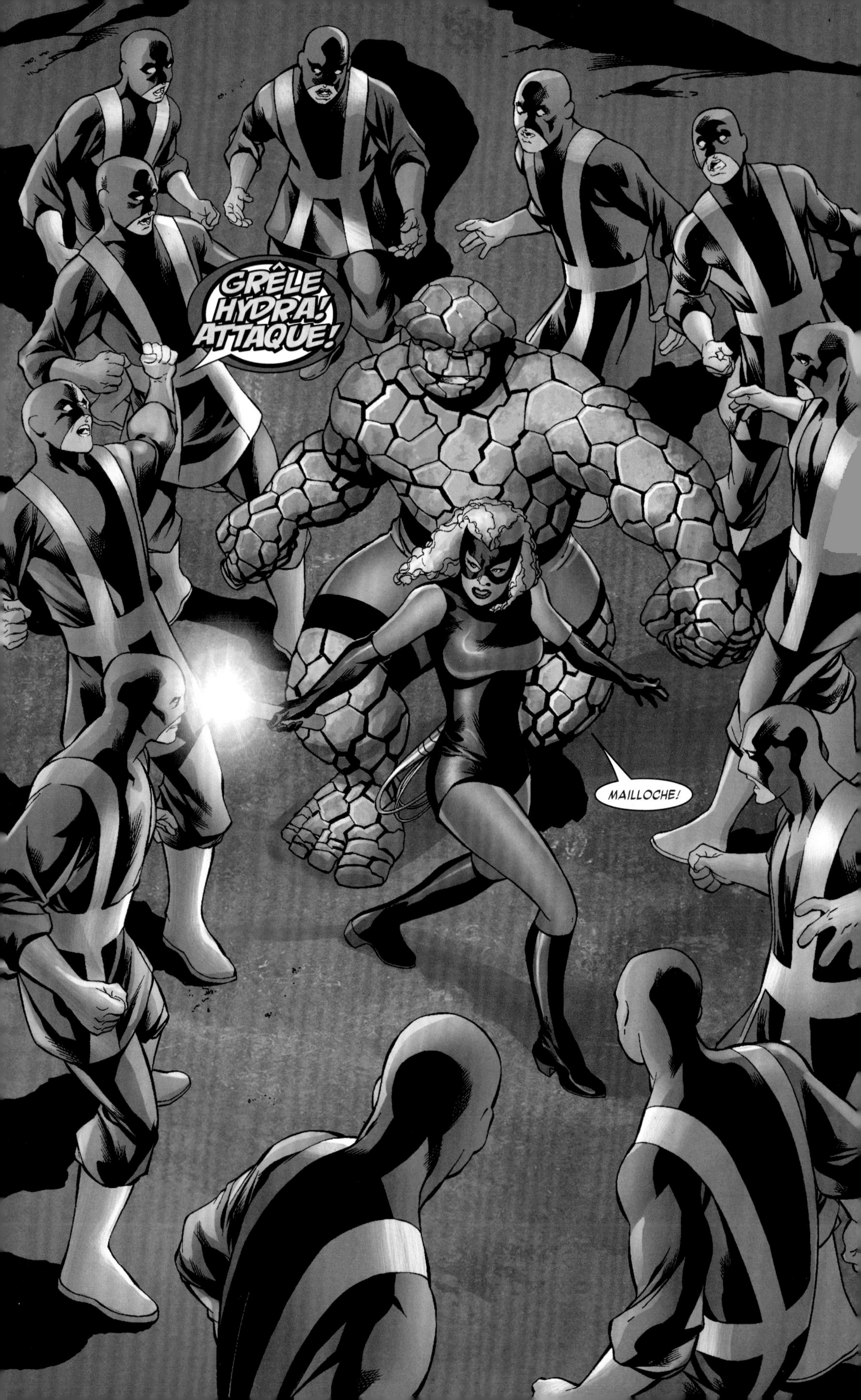
GRÊLE HYDRA! ATTAQUE!
MAILLOCHE!

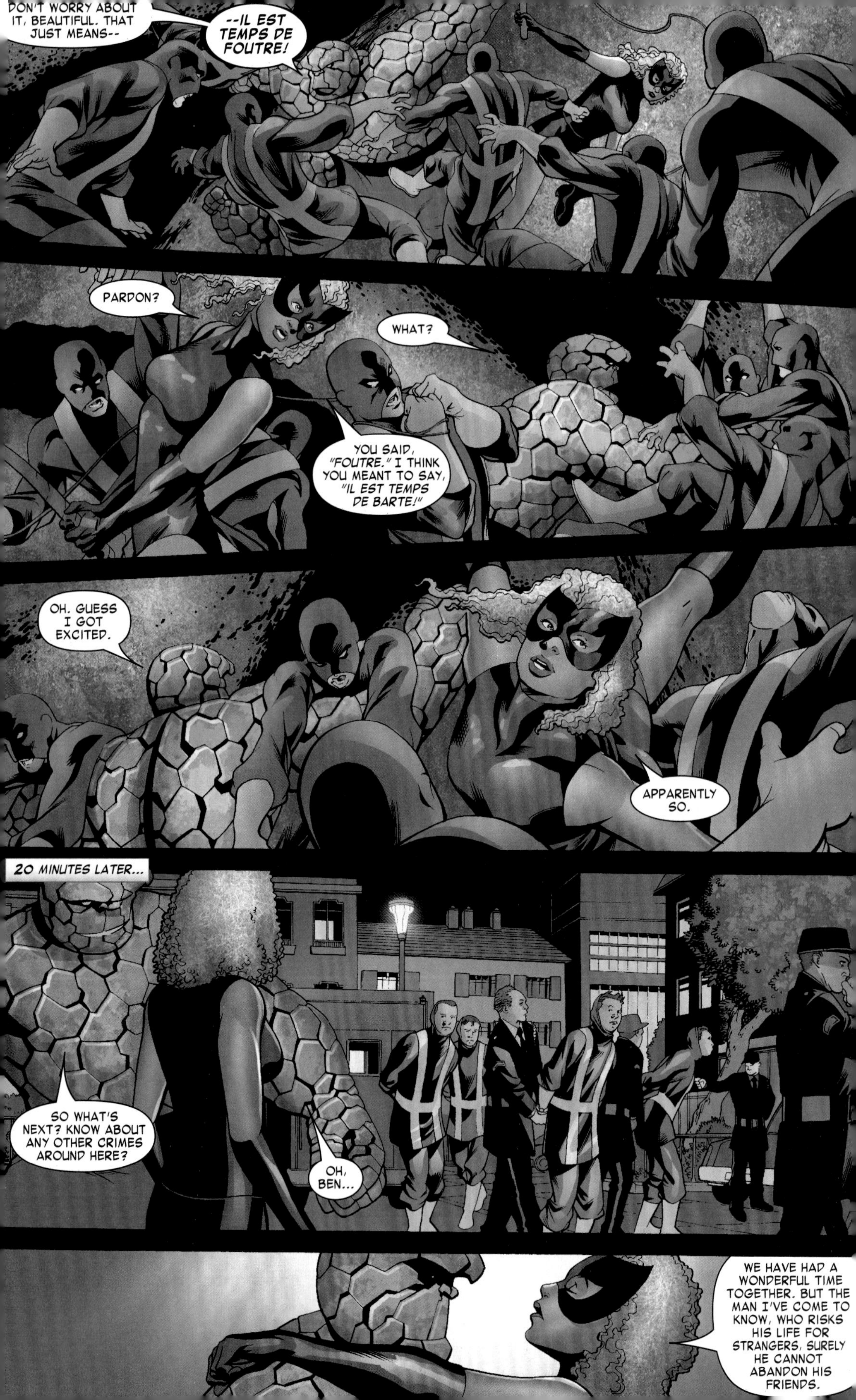
DON'T WORRY ABOUT IT, BEAUTIFUL. THAT JUST MEANS--
--IL EST TEMPS DE FOUTRE!
PARDON?
WHAT?
YOU SAID, "FOUTRE." I THINK YOU MEANT TO SAY, "IL EST TEMPS DE BARTE!"
OH. GUESS I GOT EXCITED.
APPARENTLY SO.
20 MINUTES LATER...
SO WHAT'S NEXT? KNOW ABOUT ANY OTHER CRIMES AROUND HERE?
OH, BEN...
WE HAVE HAD A WONDERFUL TIME TOGETHER. BUT THE MAN I'VE COME TO KNOW, WHO RISKS HIS LIFE FOR STRANGERS, SURELY HE CANNOT ABANDON HIS FRIENDS.

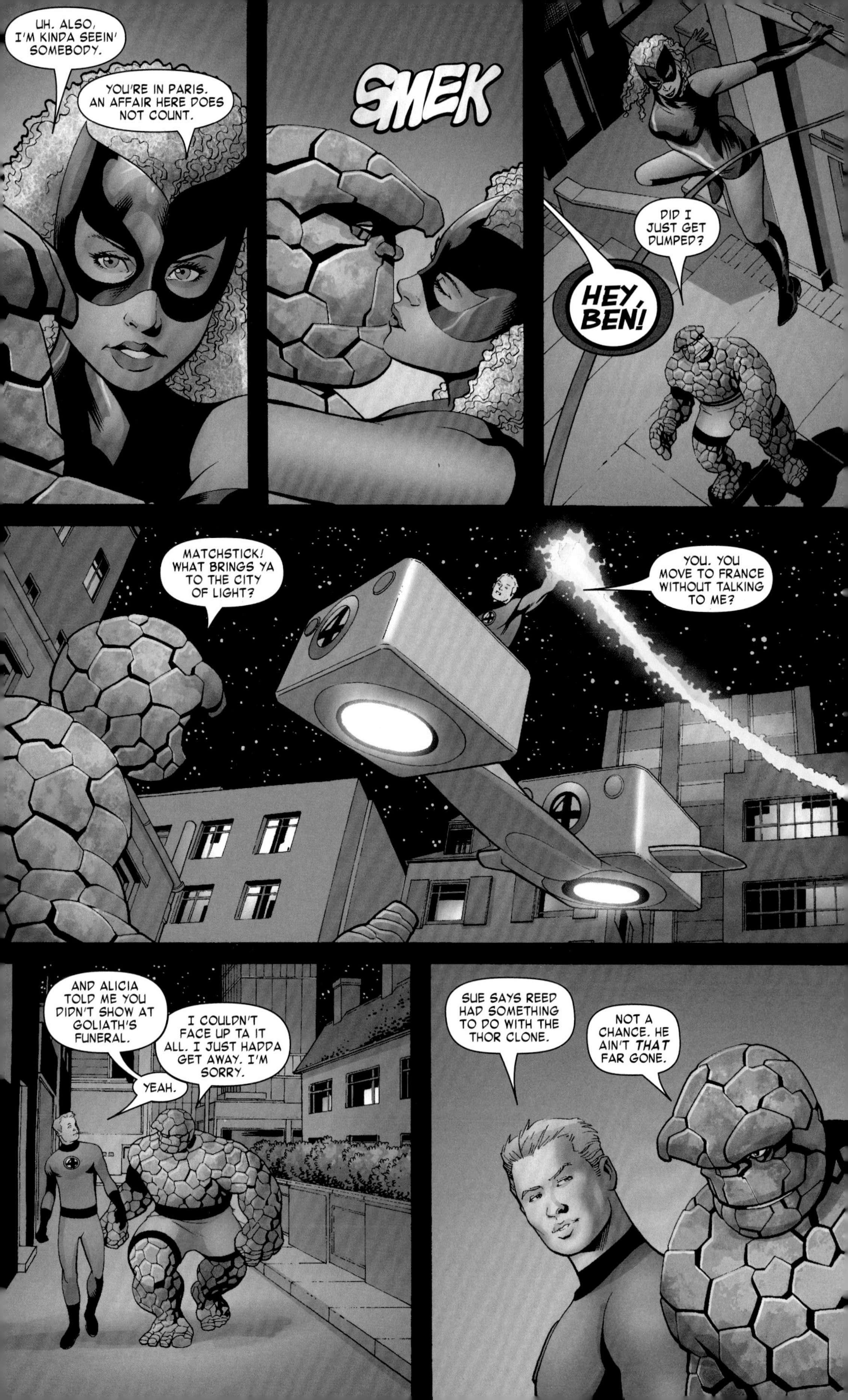
UH. ALSO, I'M KINDA SEEIN' SOMEBODY.
YOU'RE IN PARIS. AN AFFAIR HERE DOES NOT COUNT.
SMEK
HEY, BEN!
DID I JUST GET DUMPED?
MATCHSTICK! WHAT BRINGS YA TO THE CITY OF LIGHT?
YOU. YOU MOVE TO FRANCE WITHOUT TALKING TO ME?
AND ALICIA TOLD ME YOU DIDN'T SHOW AT GOLIATH'S FUNERAL.
YEAH.
I COULDN'T FACE UP TA IT ALL. I JUST HADDA GET AWAY. I'M SORRY.
SUE SAYS REED HAD SOMETHING TO DO WITH THE THOR CLONE.
NOT A CHANCE. HE AIN'T *THAT* FAR GONE.

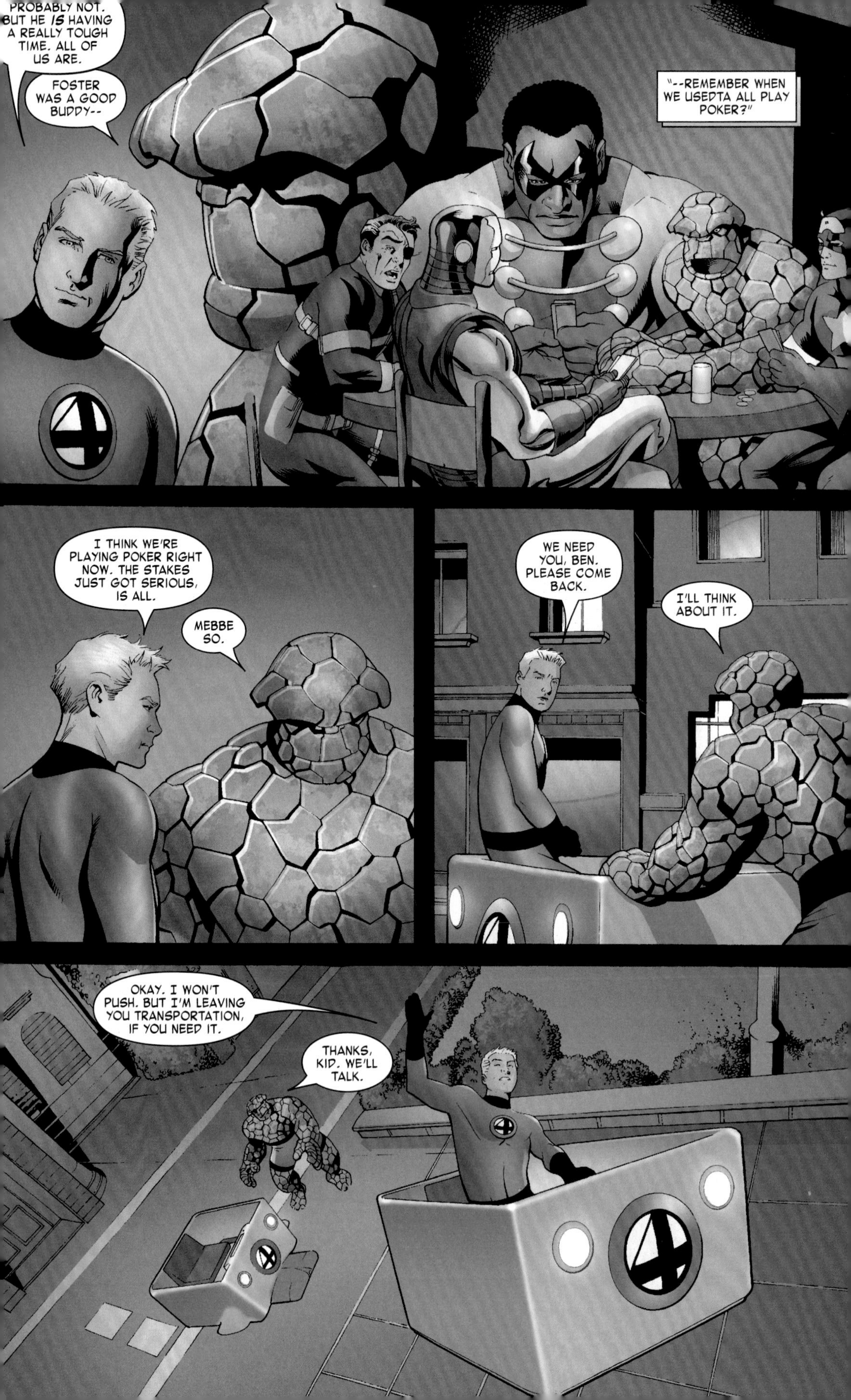
PROBABLY NOT. BUT HE *IS* HAVING A REALLY TOUGH TIME. ALL OF US ARE.
FOSTER WAS A GOOD BUDDY--
"--REMEMBER WHEN WE USEDTA ALL PLAY POKER?"
I THINK WE'RE PLAYING POKER RIGHT NOW. THE STAKES JUST GOT SERIOUS, IS ALL.
MEBBE SO.
WE NEED YOU, BEN. PLEASE COME BACK.
I'LL THINK ABOUT IT.
OKAY. I WON'T PUSH. BUT I'M LEAVING YOU TRANSPORTATION, IF YOU NEED IT.
THANKS, KID. WE'LL TALK.

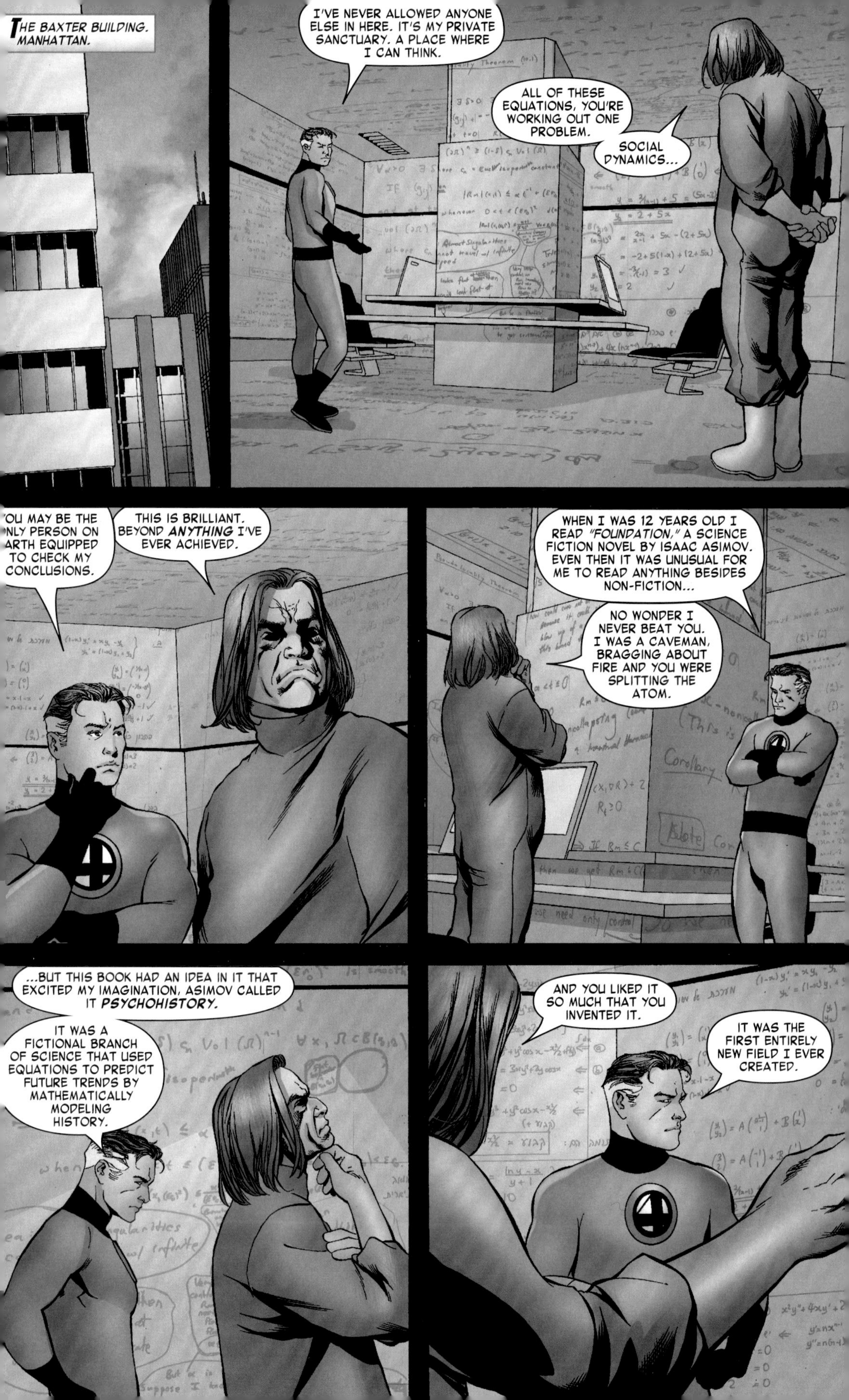
THE BAXTER BUILDING. MANHATTAN.
I'VE NEVER ALLOWED ANYONE ELSE IN HERE. IT'S MY PRIVATE SANCTUARY. A PLACE WHERE I CAN THINK.
ALL OF THESE EQUATIONS, YOU'RE WORKING OUT ONE PROBLEM.
SOCIAL DYNAMICS...
THIS IS BRILLIANT. BEYOND ANYTHING I'VE EVER ACHIEVED.
YOU MAY BE THE ONLY PERSON ON EARTH EQUIPPED TO CHECK MY CONCLUSIONS.
WHEN I WAS 12 YEARS OLD I READ "FOUNDATION," A SCIENCE FICTION NOVEL BY ISAAC ASIMOV. EVEN THEN IT WAS UNUSUAL FOR ME TO READ ANYTHING BESIDES NON-FICTION...
NO WONDER I NEVER BEAT YOU. I WAS A CAVEMAN, BRAGGING ABOUT FIRE AND YOU WERE SPLITTING THE ATOM.
...BUT THIS BOOK HAD AN IDEA IN IT THAT EXCITED MY IMAGINATION. ASIMOV CALLED IT PSYCHOHISTORY.
IT WAS A FICTIONAL BRANCH OF SCIENCE THAT USED EQUATIONS TO PREDICT FUTURE TRENDS BY MATHEMATICALLY MODELING HISTORY.
AND YOU LIKED IT SO MUCH THAT YOU INVENTED IT.
IT WAS THE FIRST ENTIRELY NEW FIELD I EVER CREATED.

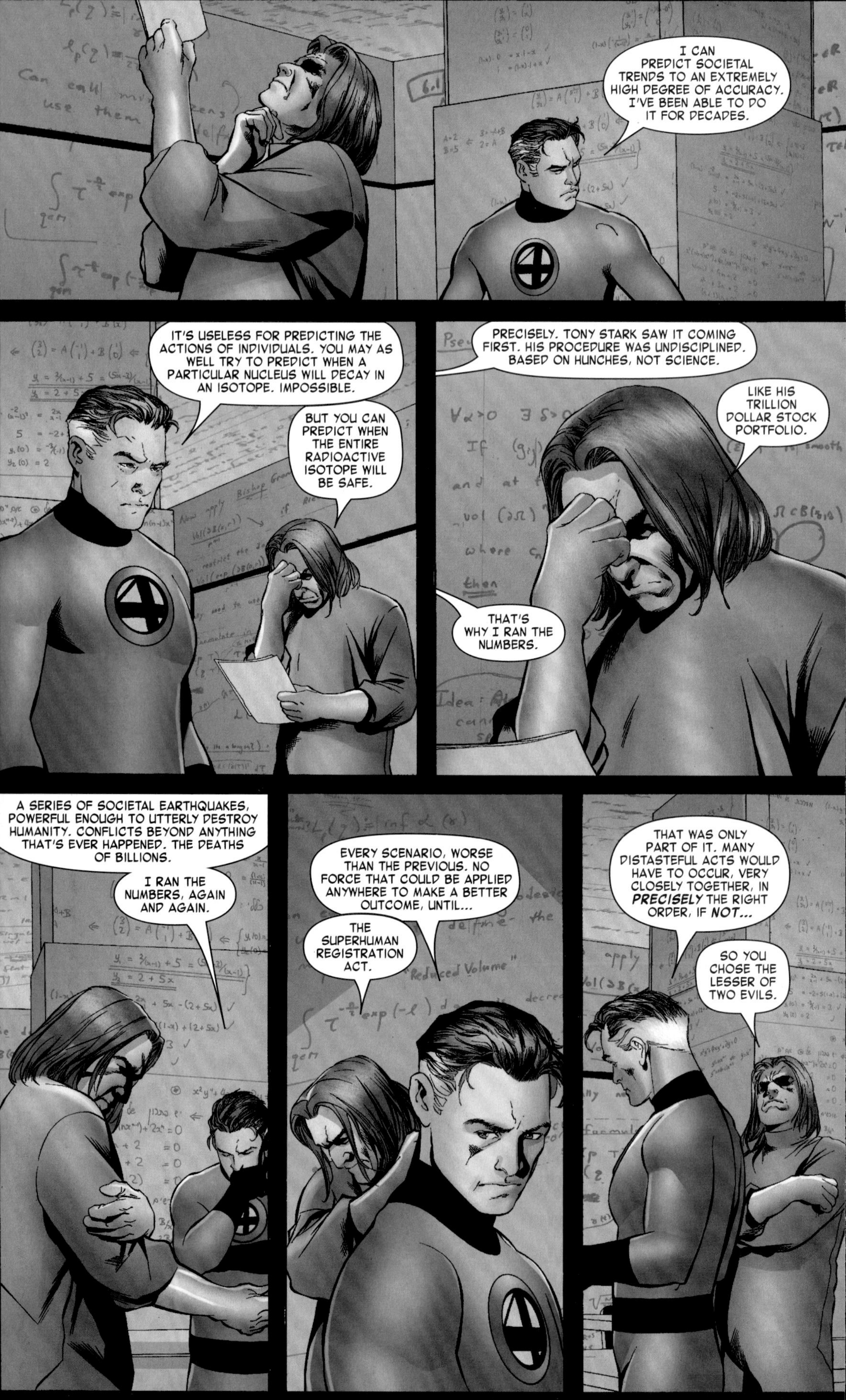

I CAN PREDICT SOCIETAL TRENDS TO AN EXTREMELY HIGH DEGREE OF ACCURACY. I'VE BEEN ABLE TO DO IT FOR DECADES.
IT'S USELESS FOR PREDICTING THE ACTIONS OF INDIVIDUALS. YOU MAY AS WELL TRY TO PREDICT WHEN A PARTICULAR NUCLEUS WILL DECAY IN AN ISOTOPE. IMPOSSIBLE.
BUT YOU CAN PREDICT WHEN THE ENTIRE RADIOACTIVE ISOTOPE WILL BE SAFE.
PRECISELY. TONY STARK SAW IT COMING FIRST. HIS PROCEDURE WAS UNDISCIPLINED. BASED ON HUNCHES, NOT SCIENCE.
LIKE HIS TRILLION DOLLAR STOCK PORTFOLIO.
THAT'S WHY I RAN THE NUMBERS.
A SERIES OF SOCIETAL EARTHQUAKES, POWERFUL ENOUGH TO UTTERLY DESTROY HUMANITY. CONFLICTS BEYOND ANYTHING THAT'S EVER HAPPENED. THE DEATHS OF BILLIONS.
I RAN THE NUMBERS, AGAIN AND AGAIN.
EVERY SCENARIO, WORSE THAN THE PREVIOUS. NO FORCE THAT COULD BE APPLIED ANYWHERE TO MAKE A BETTER OUTCOME, UNTIL...
THE SUPERHUMAN REGISTRATION ACT.
THAT WAS ONLY PART OF IT. MANY DISTASTEFUL ACTS WOULD HAVE TO OCCUR, VERY CLOSELY TOGETHER, IN ***PRECISELY*** THE RIGHT ORDER, IF ***NOT...***
SO YOU CHOSE THE LESSER OF TWO EVILS.

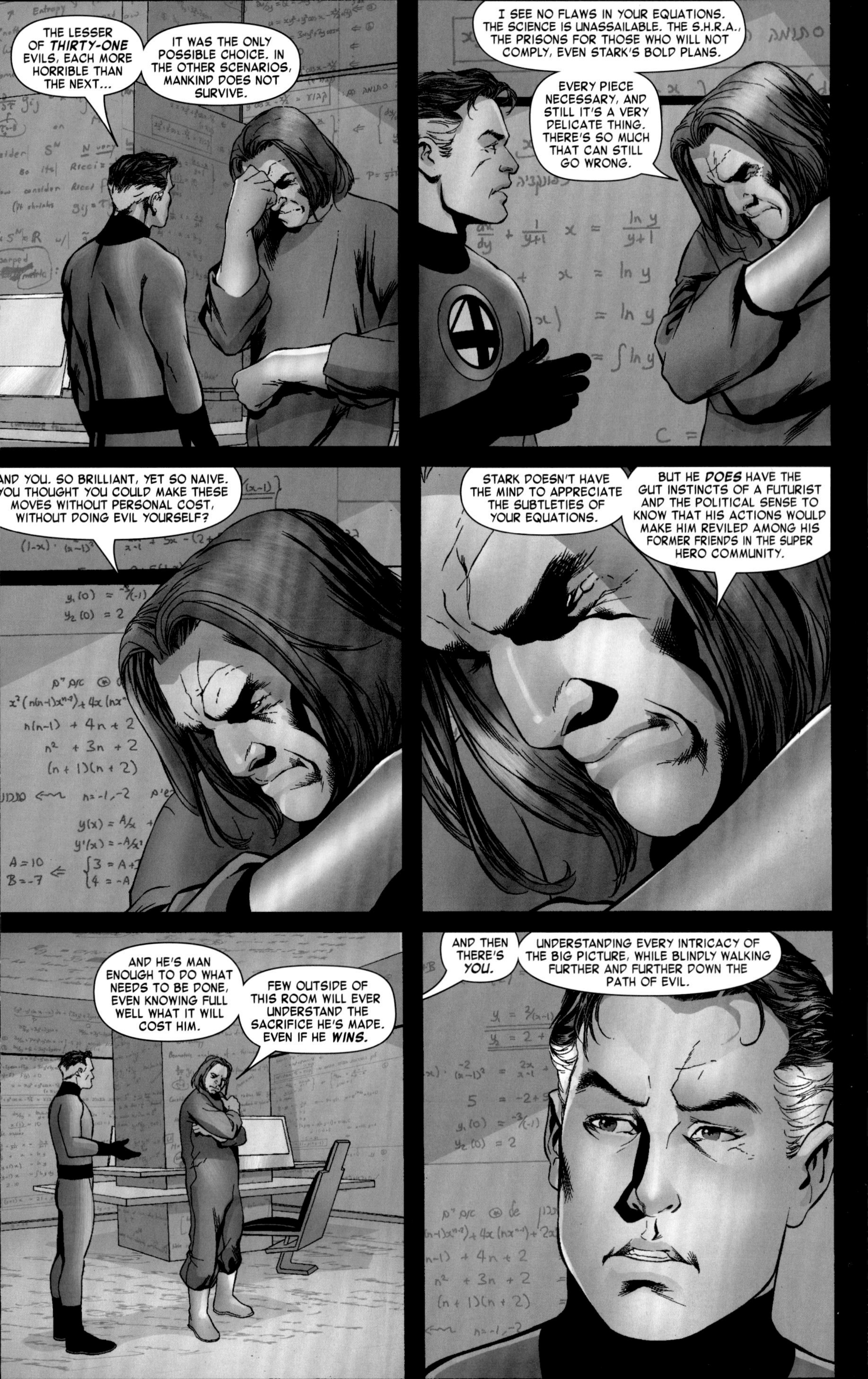

THE LESSER OF THIRTY-ONE EVILS, EACH MORE HORRIBLE THAN THE NEXT...
IT WAS THE ONLY POSSIBLE CHOICE. IN THE OTHER SCENARIOS, MANKIND DOES NOT SURVIVE.
I SEE NO FLAWS IN YOUR EQUATIONS. THE SCIENCE IS UNASSAILABLE. THE S.H.R.A., THE PRISONS FOR THOSE WHO WILL NOT COMPLY, EVEN STARK'S BOLD PLANS.
EVERY PIECE NECESSARY, AND STILL IT'S A VERY DELICATE THING. THERE'S SO MUCH THAT CAN STILL GO WRONG.
AND YOU. SO BRILLIANT, YET SO NAIVE. YOU THOUGHT YOU COULD MAKE THESE MOVES WITHOUT PERSONAL COST, WITHOUT DOING EVIL YOURSELF?
STARK DOESN'T HAVE THE MIND TO APPRECIATE THE SUBTLETIES OF YOUR EQUATIONS.
BUT HE DOES HAVE THE GUT INSTINCTS OF A FUTURIST AND THE POLITICAL SENSE TO KNOW THAT HIS ACTIONS WOULD MAKE HIM REVILED AMONG HIS FORMER FRIENDS IN THE SUPER HERO COMMUNITY.
AND HE'S MAN ENOUGH TO DO WHAT NEEDS TO BE DONE, EVEN KNOWING FULL WELL WHAT IT WILL COST HIM.
FEW OUTSIDE OF THIS ROOM WILL EVER UNDERSTAND THE SACRIFICE HE'S MADE. EVEN IF HE WINS.
AND THEN THERE'S YOU.
UNDERSTANDING EVERY INTRICACY OF THE BIG PICTURE, WHILE BLINDLY WALKING FURTHER AND FURTHER DOWN THE PATH OF EVIL.

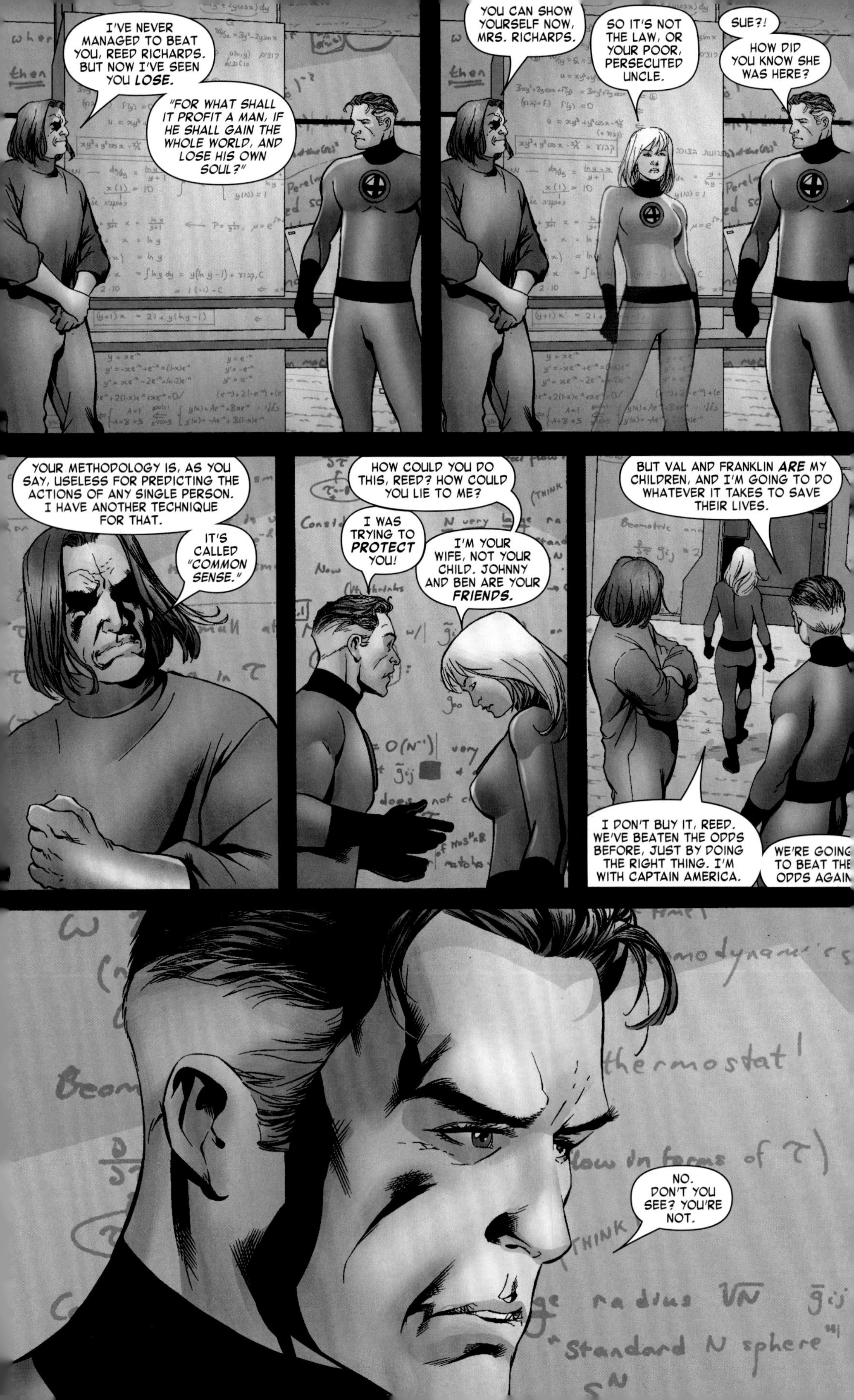

I'VE NEVER MANAGED TO BEAT YOU, REED RICHARDS. BUT NOW I'VE SEEN YOU *LOSE.*
"FOR WHAT SHALL IT PROFIT A MAN, IF HE SHALL GAIN THE WHOLE WORLD, AND LOSE HIS OWN SOUL?"
YOU CAN SHOW YOURSELF NOW, MRS. RICHARDS.
SO IT'S NOT THE LAW, OR YOUR POOR, PERSECUTED UNCLE.
SUE?!
HOW DID YOU KNOW SHE WAS HERE?
YOUR METHODOLOGY IS, AS YOU SAY, USELESS FOR PREDICTING THE ACTIONS OF ANY SINGLE PERSON. I HAVE ANOTHER TECHNIQUE FOR THAT.
IT'S CALLED "COMMON SENSE."
HOW COULD YOU DO THIS, REED? HOW COULD YOU LIE TO ME?
I WAS TRYING TO *PROTECT* YOU!
I'M YOUR WIFE, NOT YOUR CHILD. JOHNNY AND BEN ARE YOUR *FRIENDS.*
BUT VAL AND FRANKLIN *ARE* MY CHILDREN, AND I'M GOING TO DO WHATEVER IT TAKES TO SAVE THEIR LIVES.
I DON'T BUY IT, REED. WE'VE BEATEN THE ODDS BEFORE, JUST BY DOING THE RIGHT THING. I'M WITH CAPTAIN AMERICA.
WE'RE GOING TO BEAT THE ODDS AGAIN
NO. DON'T YOU SEE? YOU'RE NOT.

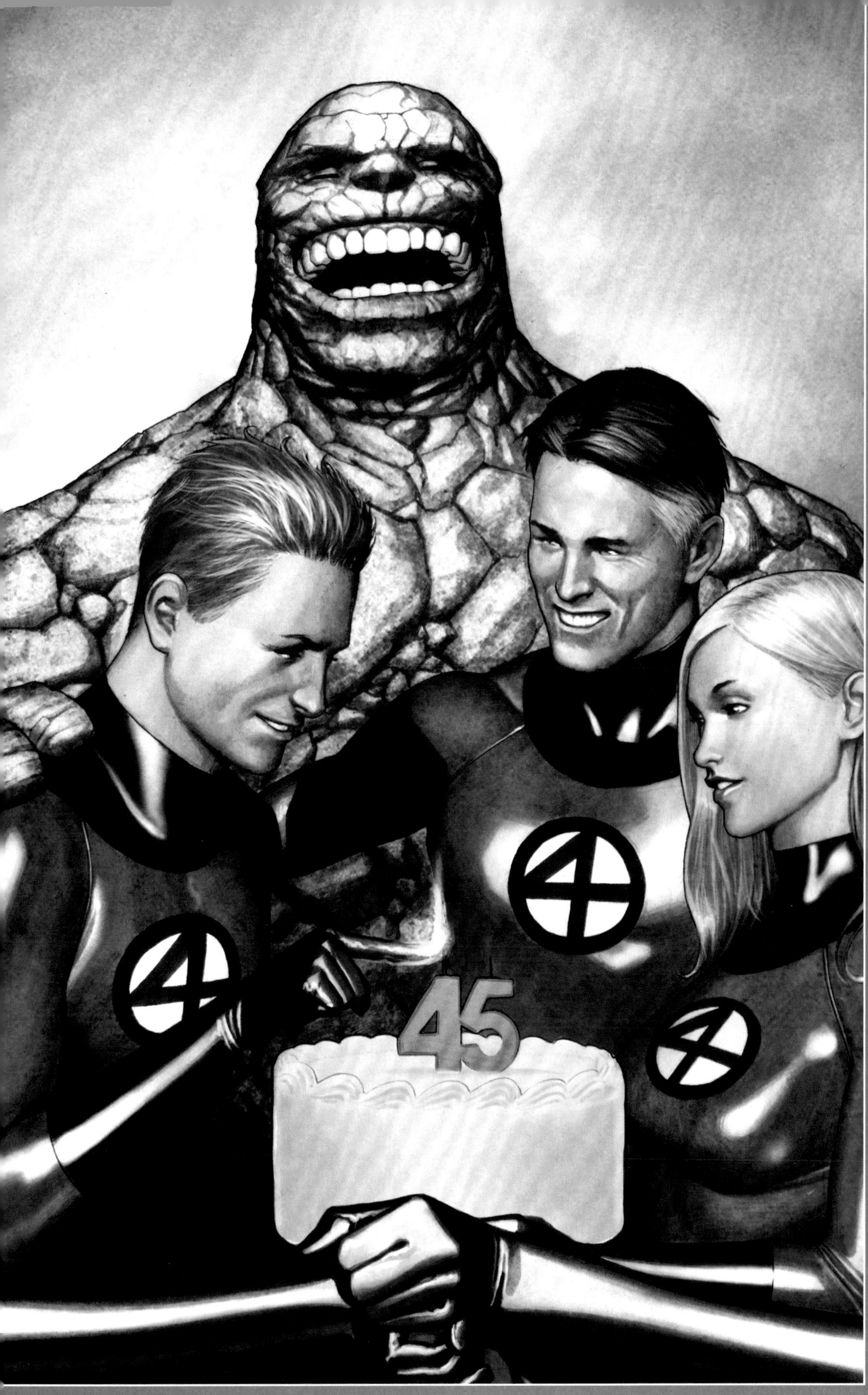
45

FANTASTIC FOUR #543

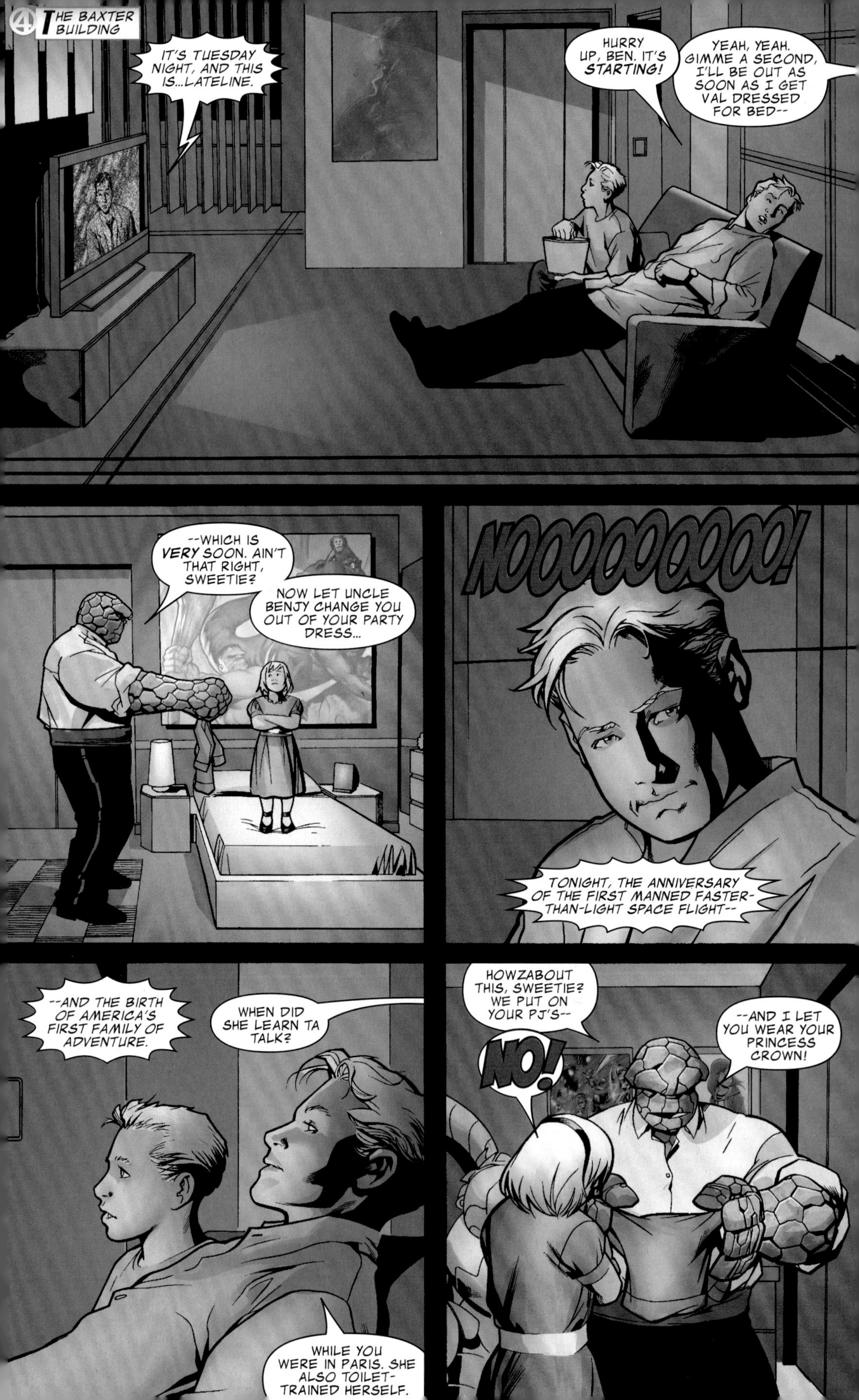
THE BAXTER BUILDING
IT'S TUESDAY NIGHT, AND THIS IS...LATELINE.
HURRY UP, BEN. IT'S STARTING!
YEAH, YEAH. GIMME A SECOND, I'LL BE OUT AS SOON AS I GET VAL DRESSED FOR BED--
--WHICH IS VERY SOON. AIN'T THAT RIGHT, SWEETIE?
NOW LET UNCLE BENJY CHANGE YOU OUT OF YOUR PARTY DRESS...
NOOOOOOOOOO!
TONIGHT, THE ANNIVERSARY OF THE FIRST MANNED FASTER-THAN-LIGHT SPACE FLIGHT--
--AND THE BIRTH OF AMERICA'S FIRST FAMILY OF ADVENTURE.
WHEN DID SHE LEARN TA TALK?
WHILE YOU WERE IN PARIS. SHE ALSO TOILET-TRAINED HERSELF.
HOWZABOUT THIS, SWEETIE? WE PUT ON YOUR PJ'S--
NO!
--AND I LET YOU WEAR YOUR PRINCESS CROWN!

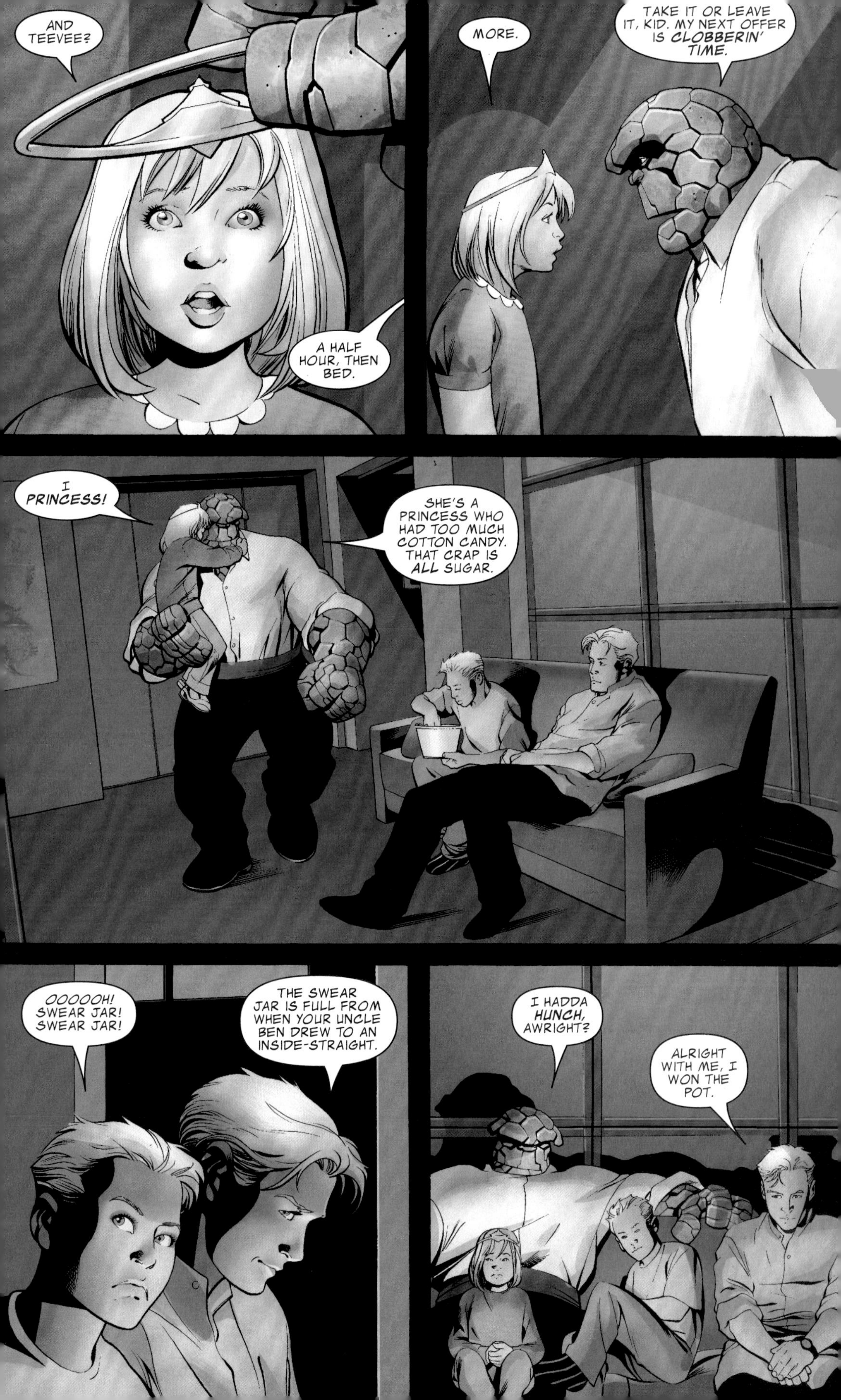

AND TEEVEE?
A HALF HOUR, THEN BED.
MORE.
TAKE IT OR LEAVE IT, KID. MY NEXT OFFER IS *CLOBBERIN'* *TIME*.
I *PRINCESS!*
SHE'S A PRINCESS WHO HAD TOO MUCH COTTON CANDY. THAT CRAP IS *ALL* SUGAR.
OOOOOH! SWEAR JAR! SWEAR JAR!
THE SWEAR JAR IS FULL FROM WHEN YOUR UNCLE BEN DREW TO AN INSIDE-STRAIGHT.
I HADDA *HUNCH*, AWRIGHT?
ALRIGHT WITH ME, I WON THE POT.

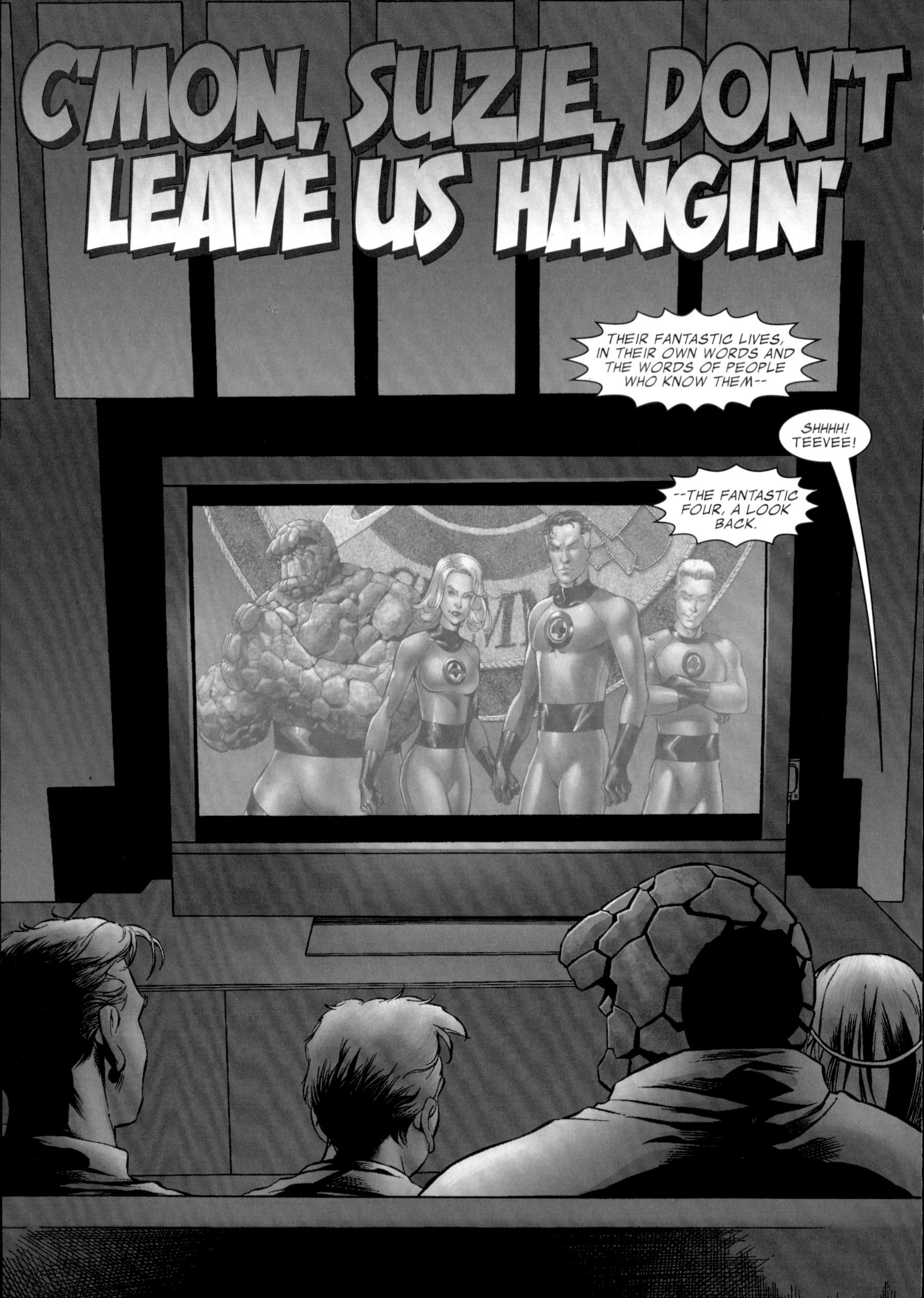
C'MON, SUZIE, DON'T LEAVE US HANGIN'
THEIR FANTASTIC LIVES, IN THEIR OWN WORDS AND THE WORDS OF PEOPLE WHO KNOW THEM--
SHHHH! TEEVEE!
--THE FANTASTIC FOUR, A LOOK BACK.

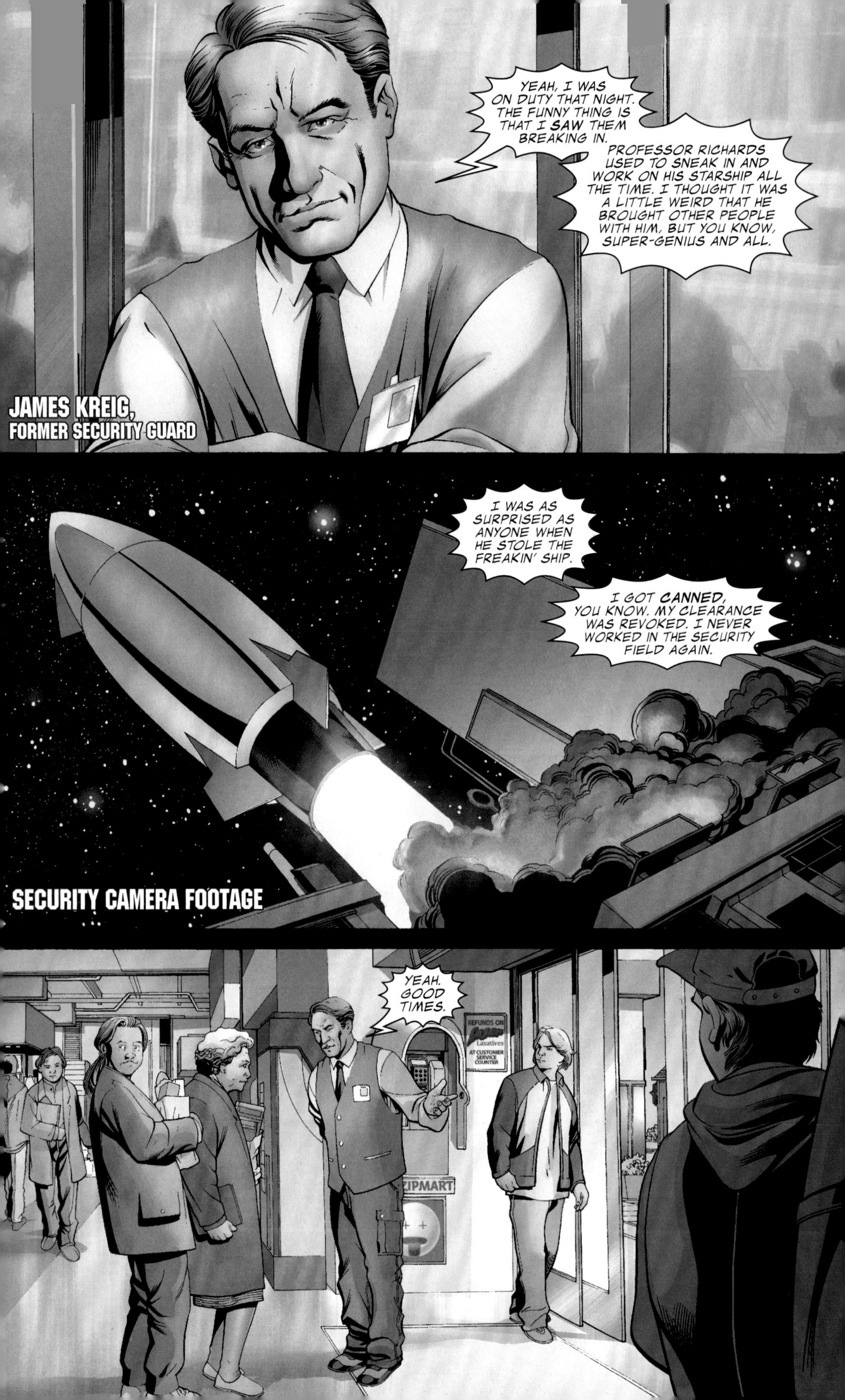
YEAH, I WAS ON DUTY THAT NIGHT. THE FUNNY THING IS THAT I SAW THEM BREAKING IN.
PROFESSOR RICHARDS USED TO SNEAK IN AND WORK ON HIS STARSHIP ALL THE TIME. I THOUGHT IT WAS A LITTLE WEIRD THAT HE BROUGHT OTHER PEOPLE WITH HIM, BUT YOU KNOW, SUPER-GENIUS AND ALL.
JAMES KREIG,
FORMER SECURITY GUARD
I WAS AS SURPRISED AS ANYONE WHEN HE STOLE THE FREAKIN' SHIP.
I GOT CANNED, YOU KNOW. MY CLEARANCE WAS REVOKED. I NEVER WORKED IN THE SECURITY FIELD AGAIN.
SECURITY CAMERA FOOTAGE
YEAH. GOOD TIMES.
REFUNDS ON
Laxatives
AT CUSTOMER SERVICE COUNTER
ZIPMART

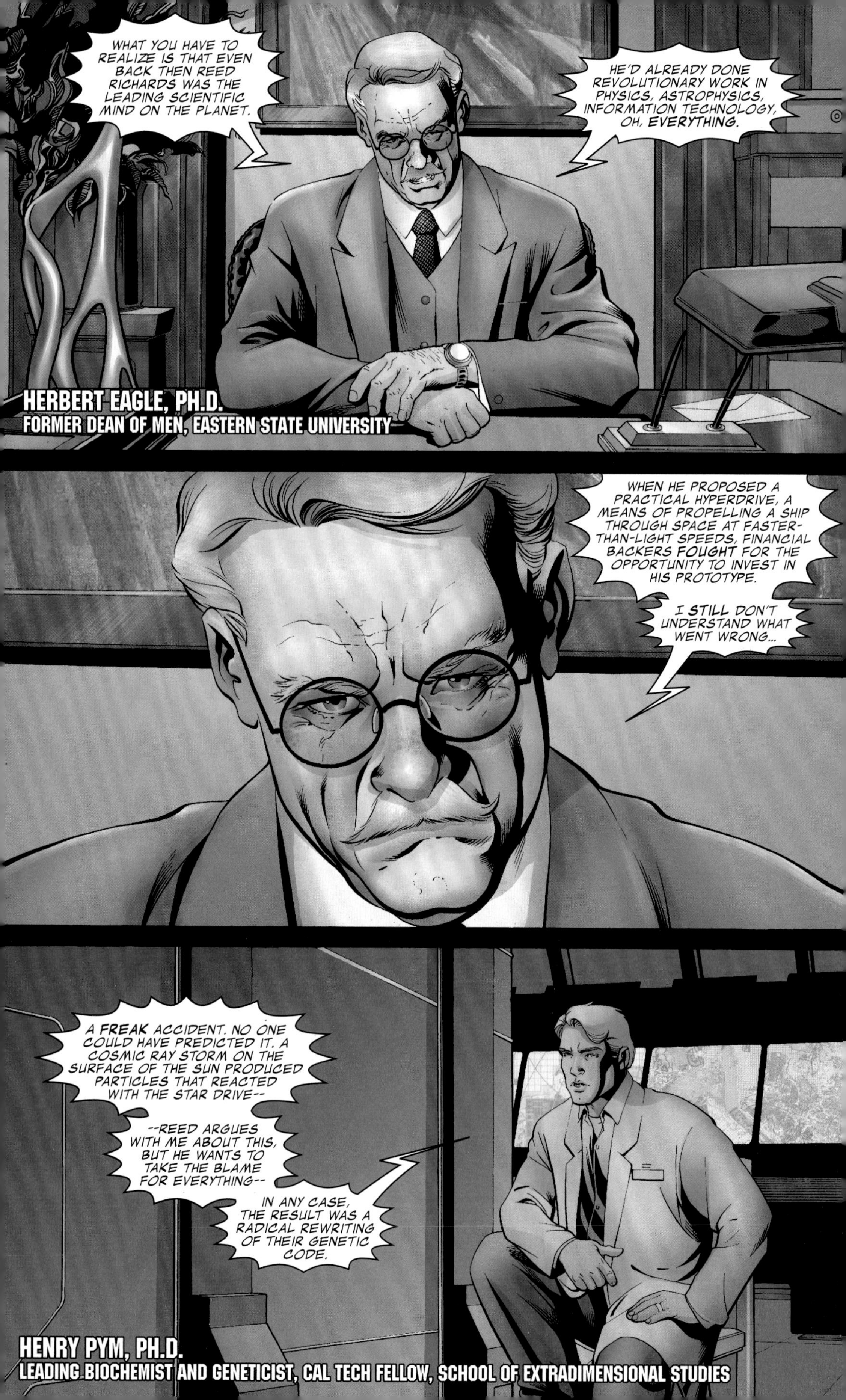
WHAT YOU HAVE TO REALIZE IS THAT EVEN BACK THEN REED RICHARDS WAS THE LEADING SCIENTIFIC MIND ON THE PLANET.
HE'D ALREADY DONE REVOLUTIONARY WORK IN PHYSICS, ASTROPHYSICS, INFORMATION TECHNOLOGY, OH, EVERYTHING.
HERBERT EAGLE, PH.D.
FORMER DEAN OF MEN, EASTERN STATE UNIVERSITY
WHEN HE PROPOSED A PRACTICAL HYPERDRIVE, A MEANS OF PROPELLING A SHIP THROUGH SPACE AT FASTER-THAN-LIGHT SPEEDS, FINANCIAL BACKERS FOUGHT FOR THE OPPORTUNITY TO INVEST IN HIS PROTOTYPE.
I STILL DON'T UNDERSTAND WHAT WENT WRONG...
A FREAK ACCIDENT. NO ONE COULD HAVE PREDICTED IT. A COSMIC RAY STORM ON THE SURFACE OF THE SUN PRODUCED PARTICLES THAT REACTED WITH THE STAR DRIVE--
--REED ARGUES WITH ME ABOUT THIS, BUT HE WANTS TO TAKE THE BLAME FOR EVERYTHING--
IN ANY CASE, THE RESULT WAS A RADICAL REWRITING OF THEIR GENETIC CODE.
HENRY PYM, PH.D.
LEADING BIOCHEMIST AND GENETICIST, CAL TECH FELLOW, SCHOOL OF EXTRADIMENSIONAL STUDIES

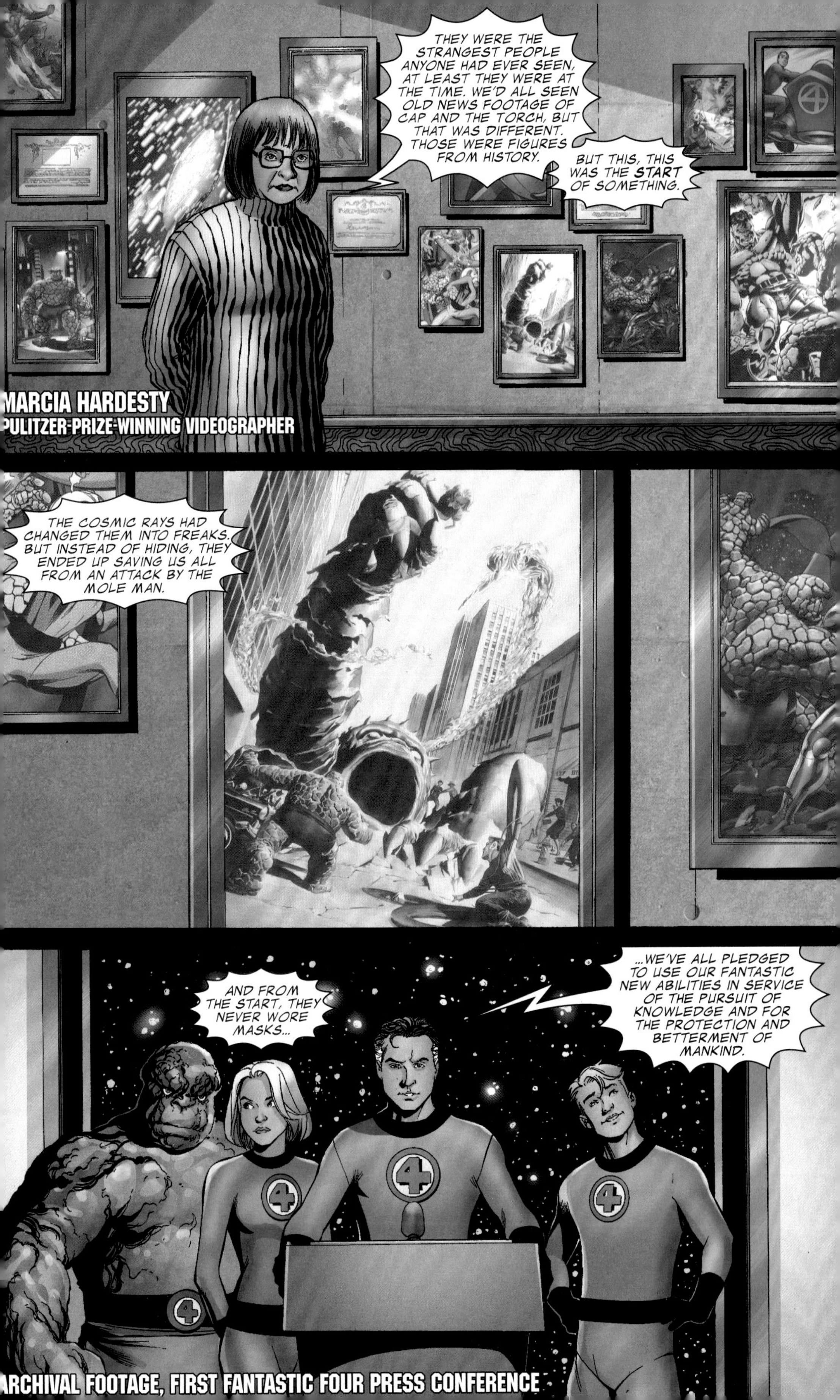
THEY WERE THE STRANGEST PEOPLE ANYONE HAD EVER SEEN, AT LEAST THEY WERE AT THE TIME. WE'D ALL SEEN OLD NEWS FOOTAGE OF CAP AND THE TORCH, BUT THAT WAS DIFFERENT. THOSE WERE FIGURES FROM HISTORY.
BUT THIS, THIS WAS THE **START** OF SOMETHING.
MARCIA HARDESTY
PULITZER-PRIZE-WINNING VIDEOGRAPHER
THE COSMIC RAYS HAD CHANGED THEM INTO FREAKS. BUT INSTEAD OF HIDING, THEY ENDED UP SAVING US ALL FROM AN ATTACK BY THE MOLE MAN.
AND FROM THE START, THEY NEVER WORE MASKS...
...WE'VE ALL PLEDGED TO USE OUR FANTASTIC NEW ABILITIES IN SERVICE OF THE PURSUIT OF KNOWLEDGE AND FOR THE PROTECTION AND BETTERMENT OF MANKIND.
ARCHIVAL FOOTAGE, FIRST FANTASTIC FOUR PRESS CONFERENCE

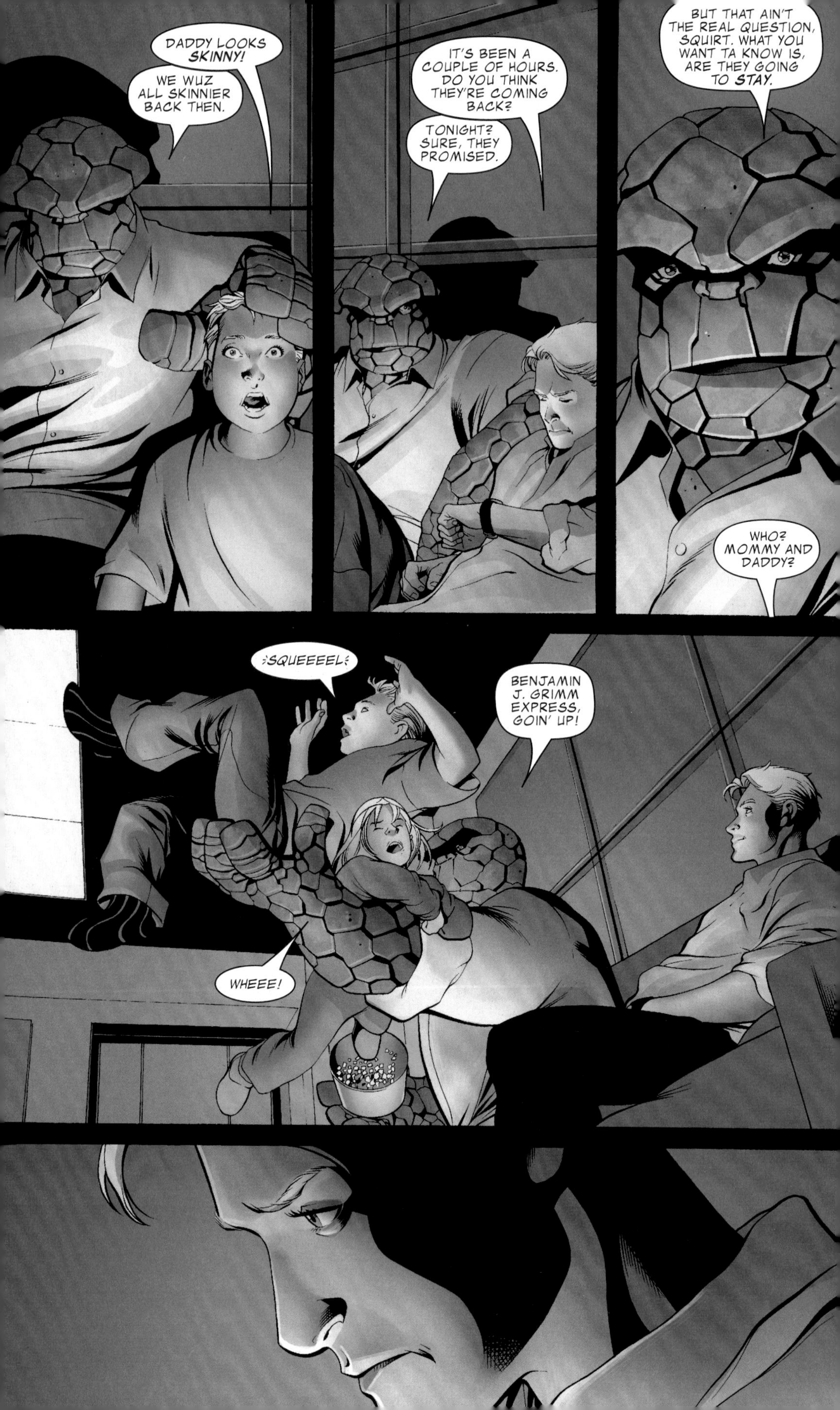
DADDY LOOKS SKINNY!
WE WUZ ALL SKINNIER BACK THEN.
IT'S BEEN A COUPLE OF HOURS. DO YOU THINK THEY'RE COMING BACK?
TONIGHT? SURE, THEY PROMISED.
BUT THAT AIN'T THE REAL QUESTION, SQUIRT. WHAT YOU WANT TA KNOW IS, ARE THEY GOING TO STAY.
WHO? MOMMY AND DADDY?
SQUEEEEL
BENJAMIN J. GRIMM EXPRESS, GOIN' UP!
WHEEE!

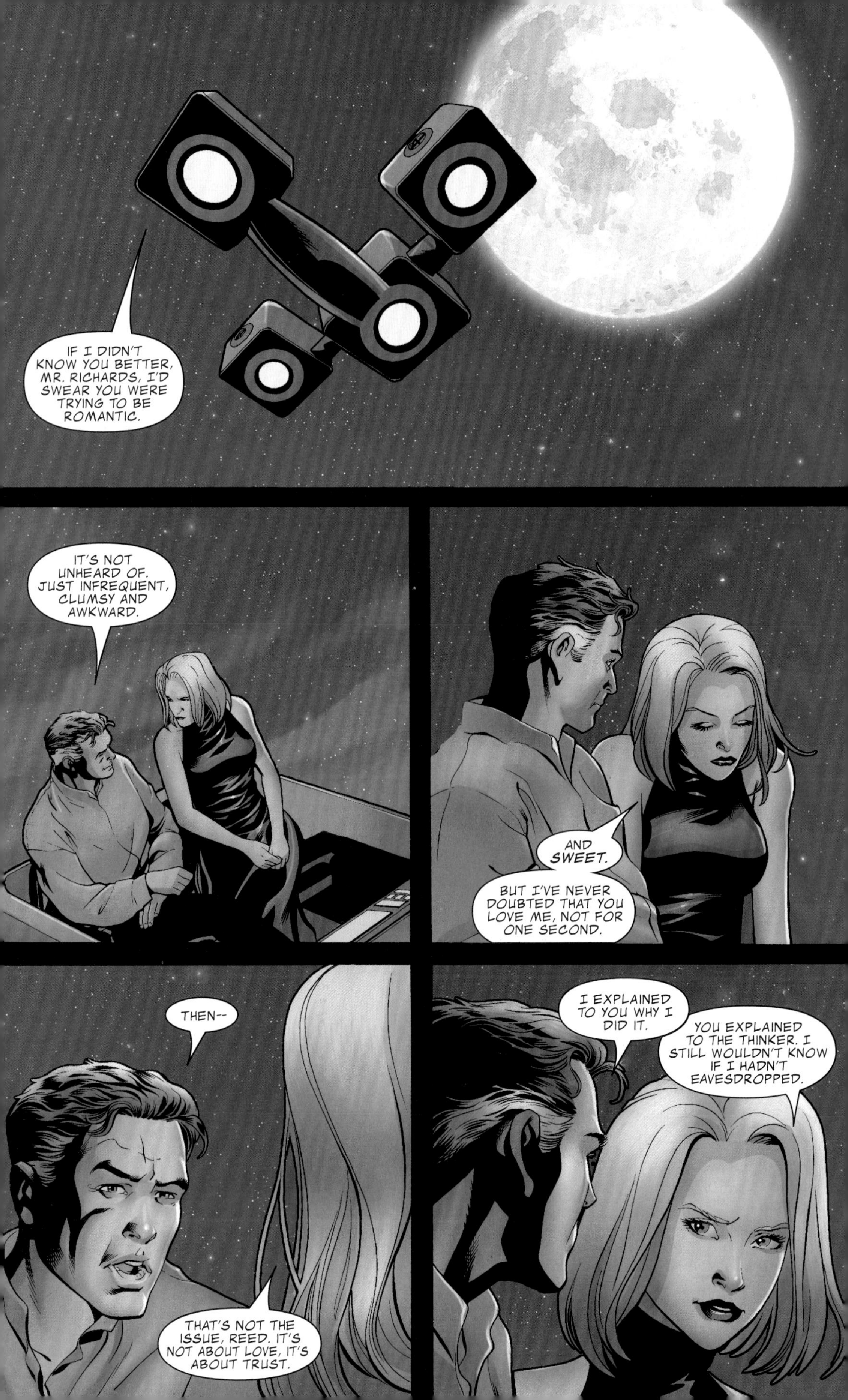
IF I DIDN'T KNOW YOU BETTER, MR. RICHARDS, I'D SWEAR YOU WERE TRYING TO BE ROMANTIC.
IT'S NOT UNHEARD OF. JUST INFREQUENT, CLUMSY AND AWKWARD.
AND SWEET.
BUT I'VE NEVER DOUBTED THAT YOU LOVE ME, NOT FOR ONE SECOND.
THEN--
THAT'S NOT THE ISSUE, REED. IT'S NOT ABOUT LOVE, IT'S ABOUT TRUST.
I EXPLAINED TO YOU WHY I DID IT.
YOU EXPLAINED TO THE THINKER. I STILL WOULDN'T KNOW IF I HADN'T EAVESDROPPED.

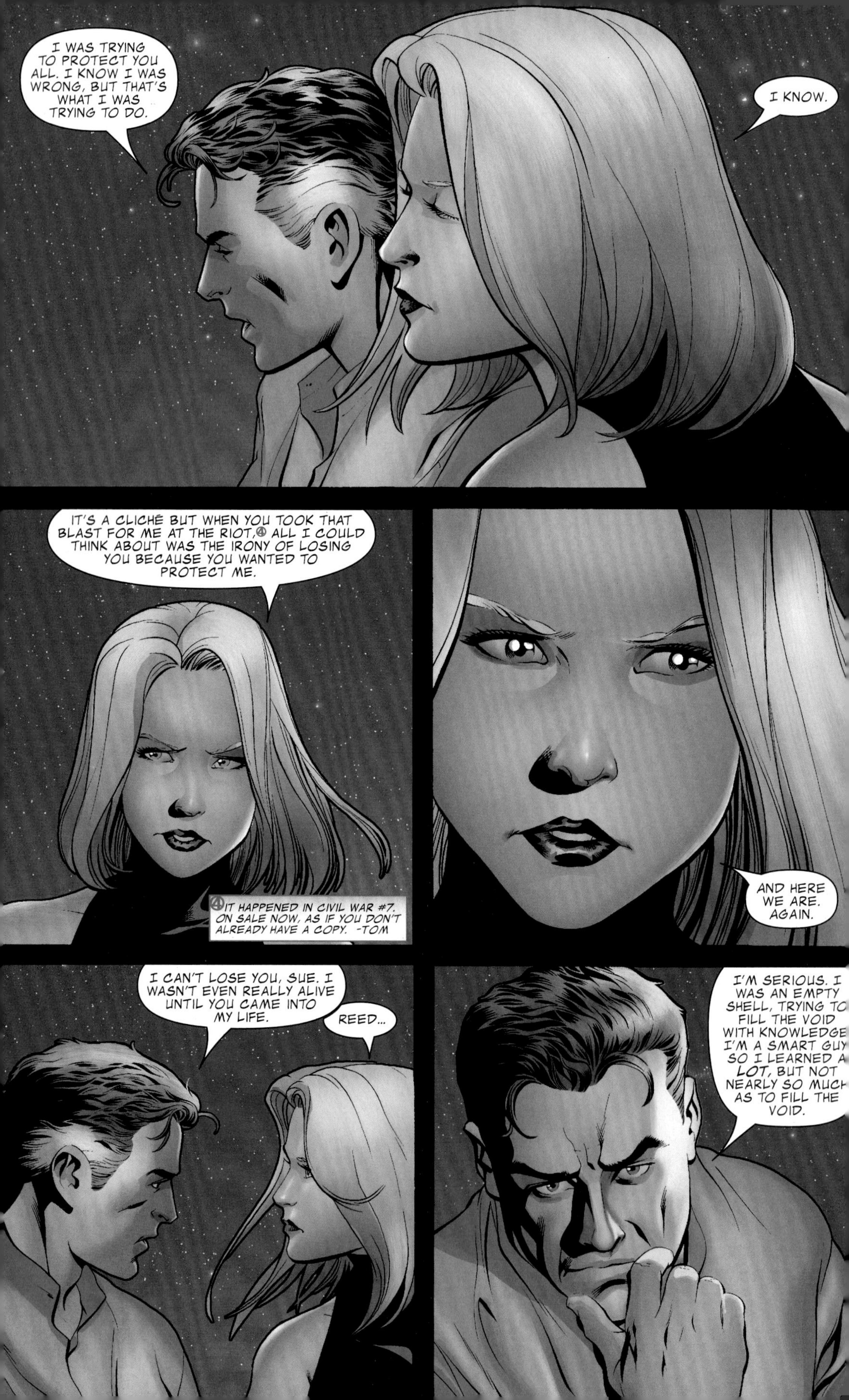
I WAS TRYING TO PROTECT YOU ALL. I KNOW I WAS WRONG, BUT THAT'S WHAT I WAS TRYING TO DO.
I KNOW.
IT'S A CLICHÉ BUT WHEN YOU TOOK THAT BLAST FOR ME AT THE RIOT, ALL I COULD THINK ABOUT WAS THE IRONY OF LOSING YOU BECAUSE YOU WANTED TO PROTECT ME.
IT HAPPENED IN CIVIL WAR #7. ON SALE NOW, AS IF YOU DON'T ALREADY HAVE A COPY. -TOM
AND HERE WE ARE. AGAIN.
I CAN'T LOSE YOU, SUE. I WASN'T EVEN REALLY ALIVE UNTIL YOU CAME INTO MY LIFE.
REED...
I'M SERIOUS. I WAS AN EMPTY SHELL, TRYING TO FILL THE VOID WITH KNOWLEDGE. I'M A SMART GUY SO I LEARNED A LOT, BUT NOT NEARLY SO MUCH AS TO FILL THE VOID.

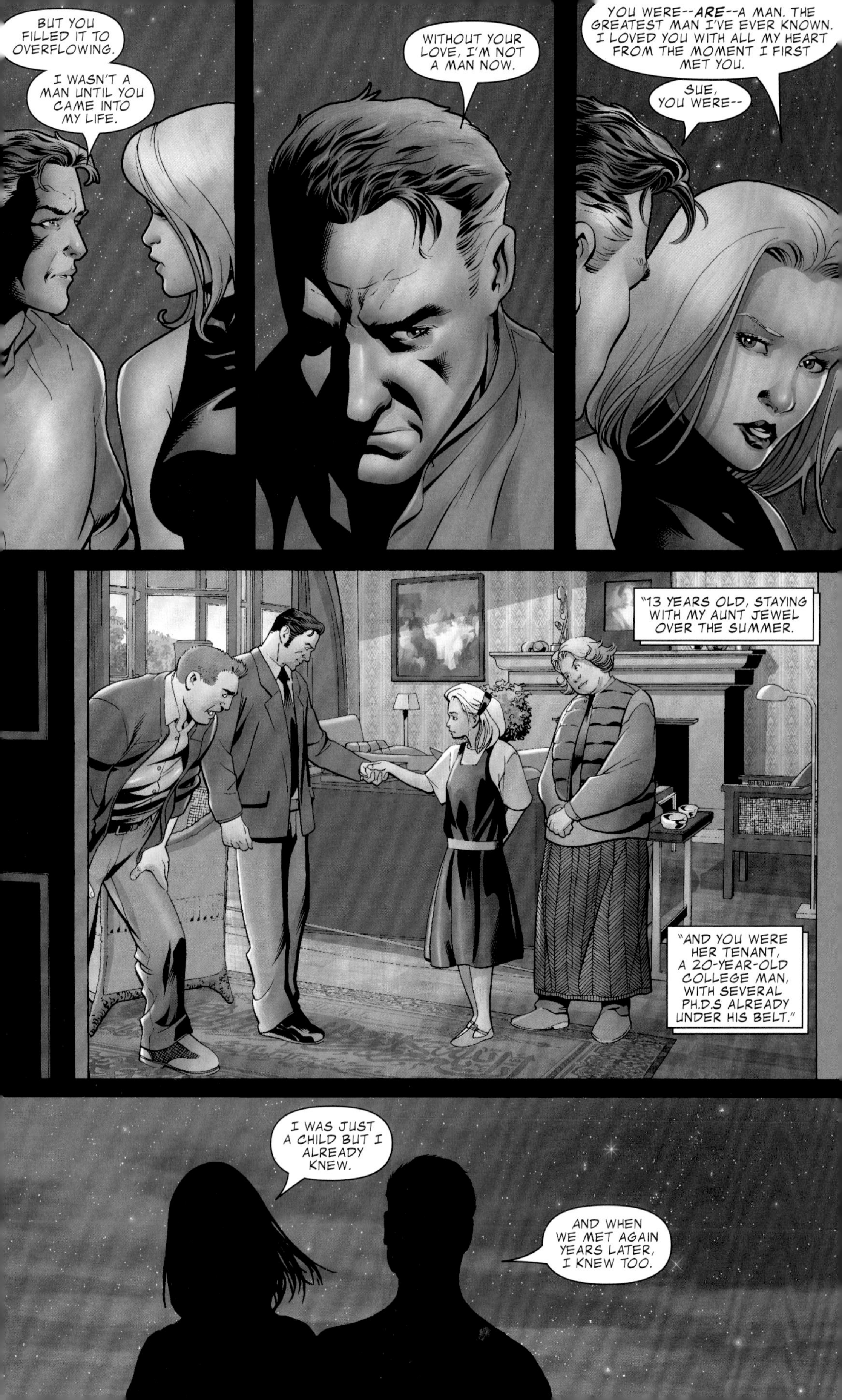

BUT YOU FILLED IT TO OVERFLOWING.
I WASN'T A MAN UNTIL YOU CAME INTO MY LIFE.
WITHOUT YOUR LOVE, I'M NOT A MAN NOW.
SUE, YOU WERE--
YOU WERE--ARE--A MAN. THE GREATEST MAN I'VE EVER KNOWN. I LOVED YOU WITH ALL MY HEART FROM THE MOMENT I FIRST MET YOU.
"13 YEARS OLD, STAYING WITH MY AUNT JEWEL OVER THE SUMMER.
"AND YOU WERE HER TENANT, A 20-YEAR-OLD COLLEGE MAN, WITH SEVERAL PH.D.S ALREADY UNDER HIS BELT."
I WAS JUST A CHILD BUT I ALREADY KNEW.
AND WHEN WE MET AGAIN YEARS LATER, I KNEW TOO.

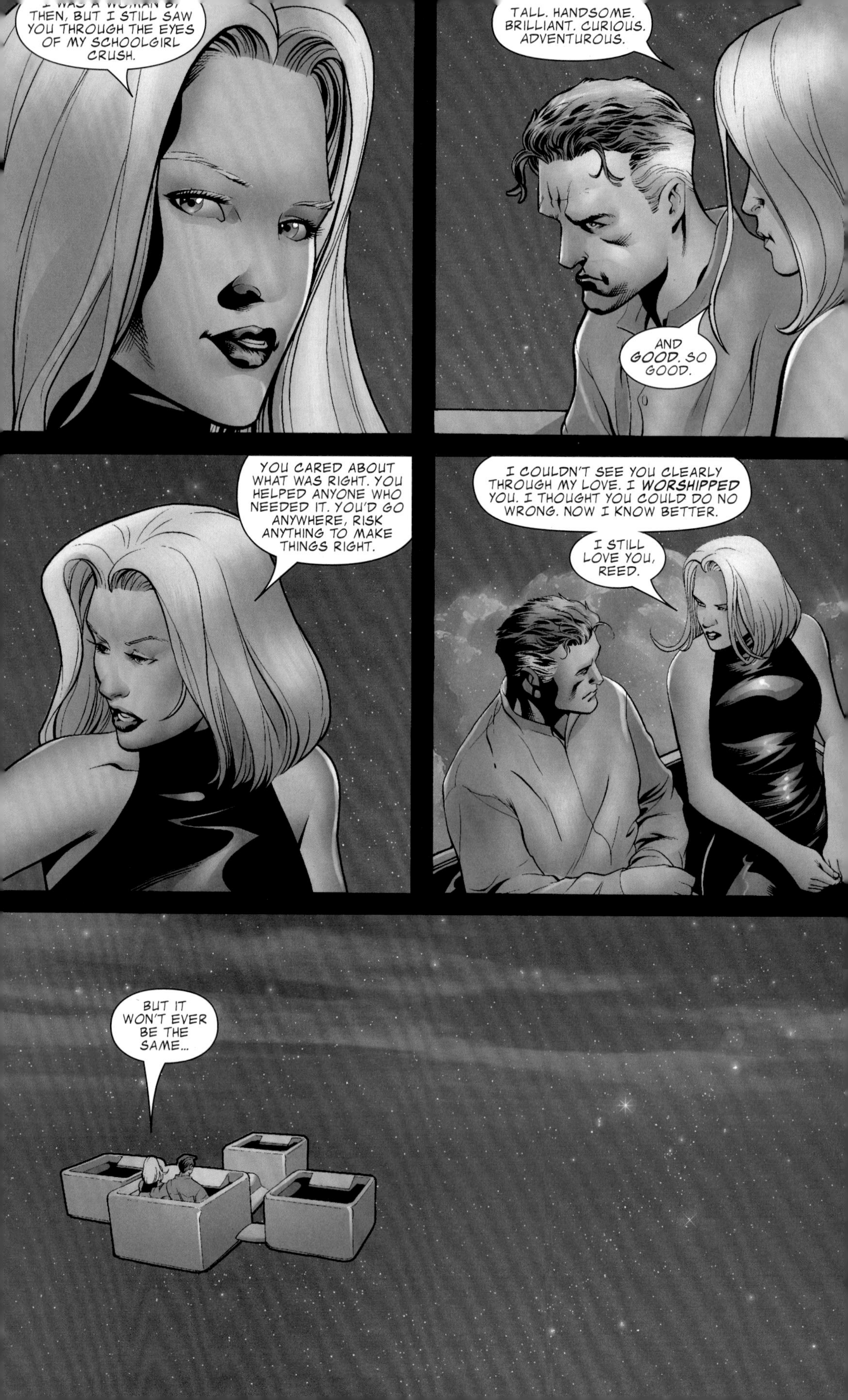
THEN, BUT I STILL SAW YOU THROUGH THE EYES OF MY SCHOOLGIRL CRUSH.
TALL. HANDSOME. BRILLIANT. CURIOUS. ADVENTUROUS.
AND GOOD. SO GOOD.
YOU CARED ABOUT WHAT WAS RIGHT. YOU HELPED ANYONE WHO NEEDED IT. YOU'D GO ANYWHERE, RISK ANYTHING TO MAKE THINGS RIGHT.
I COULDN'T SEE YOU CLEARLY THROUGH MY LOVE. I WORSHIPPED YOU. I THOUGHT YOU COULD DO NO WRONG. NOW I KNOW BETTER.
I STILL LOVE YOU, REED.
BUT IT WON'T EVER BE THE SAME...

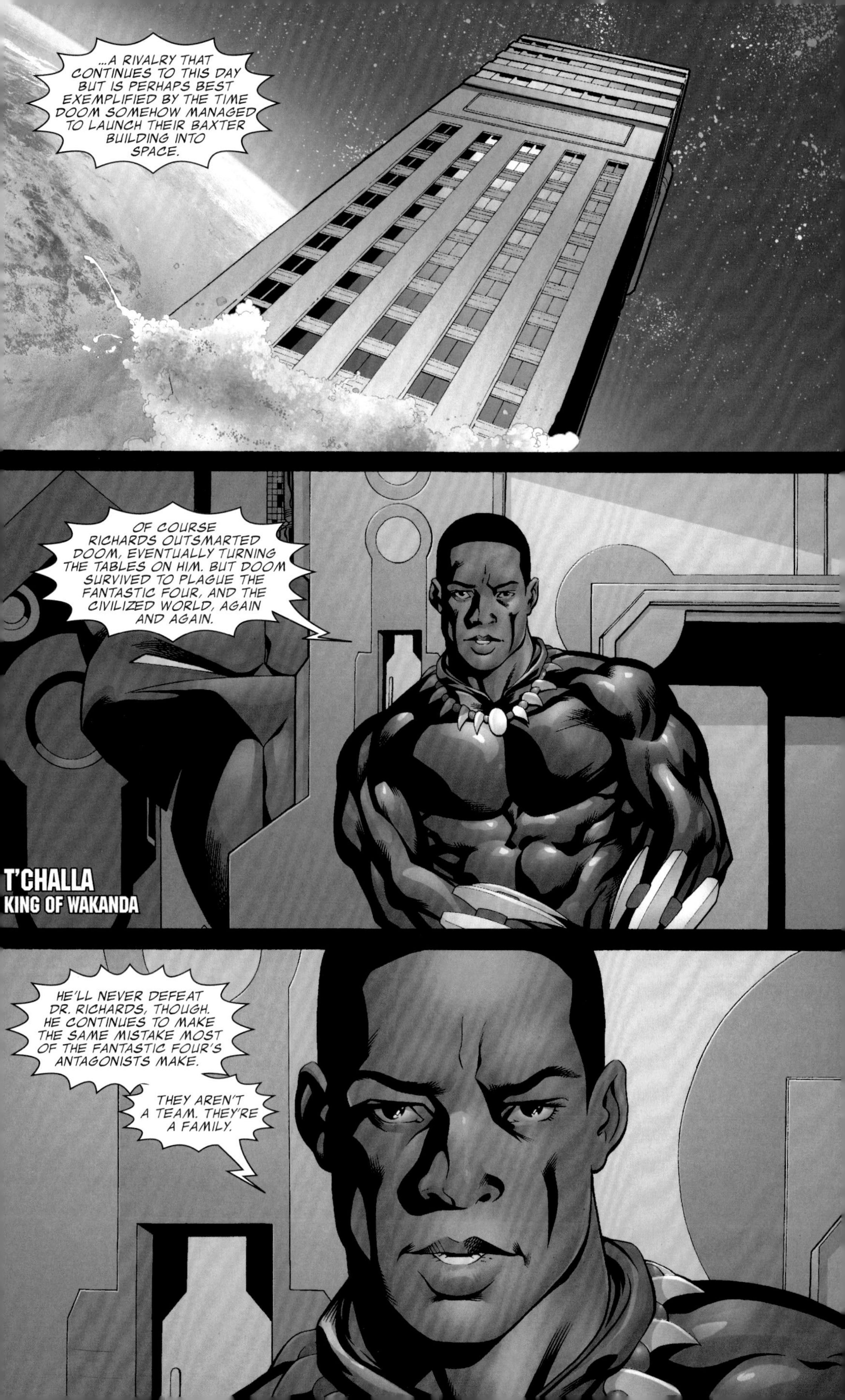
...A RIVALRY THAT CONTINUES TO THIS DAY BUT IS PERHAPS BEST EXEMPLIFIED BY THE TIME DOOM SOMEHOW MANAGED TO LAUNCH THEIR BAXTER BUILDING INTO SPACE.
OF COURSE RICHARDS OUTSMARTED DOOM, EVENTUALLY TURNING THE TABLES ON HIM. BUT DOOM SURVIVED TO PLAGUE THE FANTASTIC FOUR, AND THE CIVILIZED WORLD, AGAIN AND AGAIN.
T'CHALLA
KING OF WAKANDA
HE'LL NEVER DEFEAT DR. RICHARDS, THOUGH. HE CONTINUES TO MAKE THE SAME MISTAKE MOST OF THE FANTASTIC FOUR'S ANTAGONISTS MAKE.
THEY AREN'T A TEAM. THEY'RE A FAMILY.

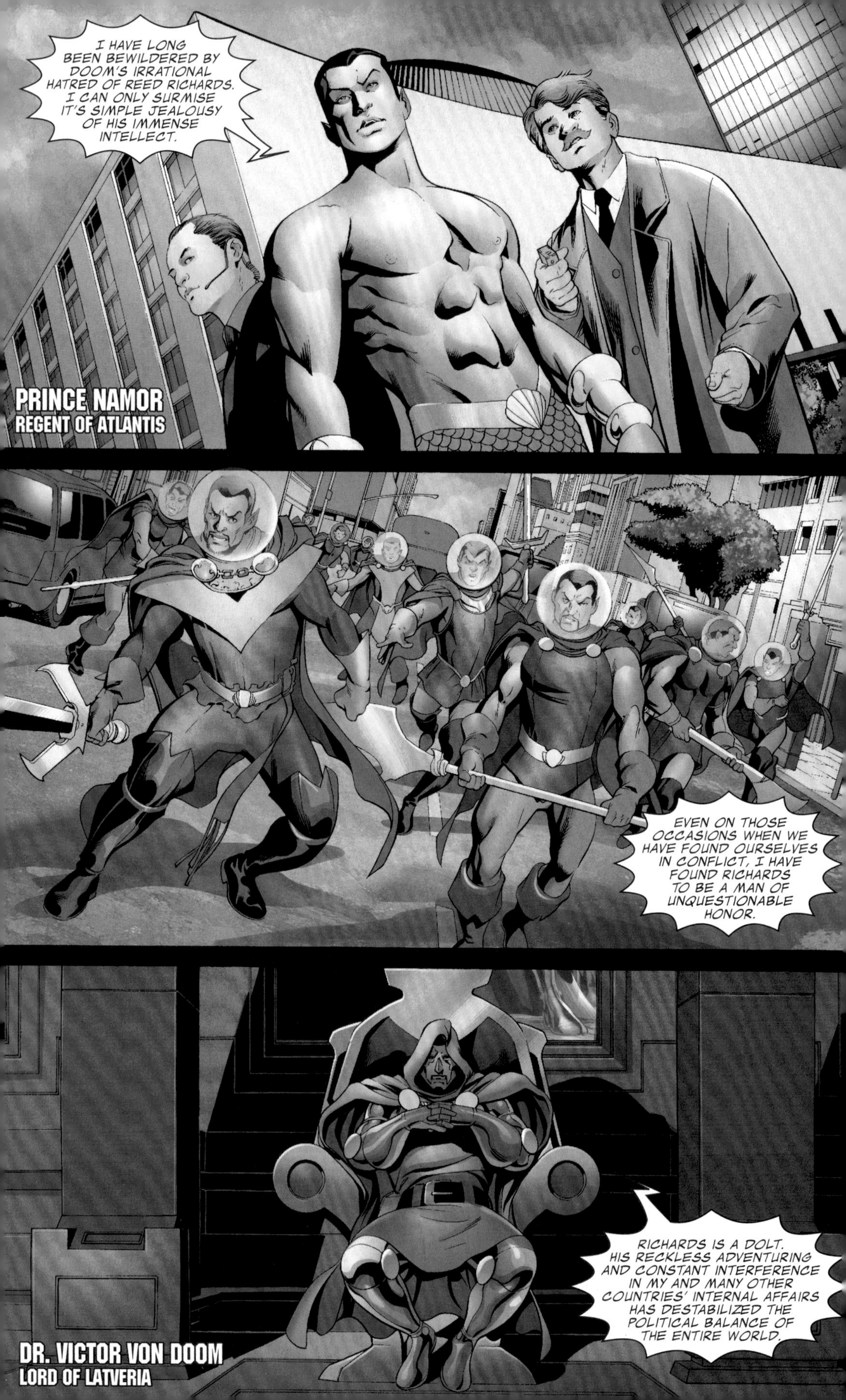

I HAVE LONG BEEN BEWILDERED BY DOOM'S IRRATIONAL HATRED OF REED RICHARDS. I CAN ONLY SURMISE IT'S SIMPLE JEALOUSY OF HIS IMMENSE INTELLECT.
PRINCE NAMOR
REGENT OF ATLANTIS
EVEN ON THOSE OCCASIONS WHEN WE HAVE FOUND OURSELVES IN CONFLICT, I HAVE FOUND RICHARDS TO BE A MAN OF UNQUESTIONABLE HONOR.
RICHARDS IS A DOLT. HIS RECKLESS ADVENTURING AND CONSTANT INTERFERENCE IN MY AND MANY OTHER COUNTRIES' INTERNAL AFFAIRS HAS DESTABILIZED THE POLITICAL BALANCE OF THE ENTIRE WORLD.
DR. VICTOR VON DOOM
LORD OF LATVERIA

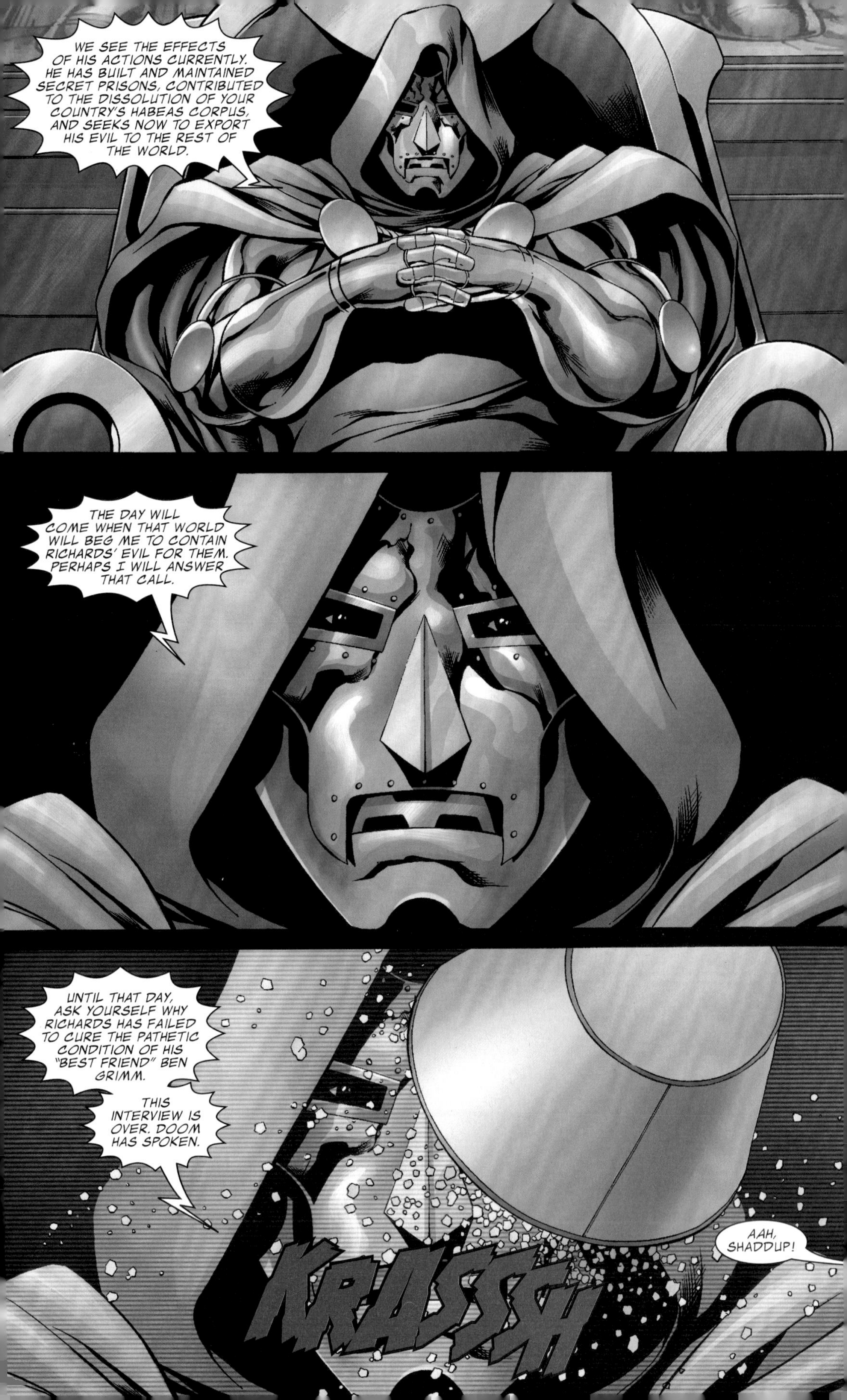
WE SEE THE EFFECTS OF HIS ACTIONS CURRENTLY. HE HAS BUILT AND MAINTAINED SECRET PRISONS, CONTRIBUTED TO THE DISSOLUTION OF YOUR COUNTRY'S HABEAS CORPUS, AND SEEKS NOW TO EXPORT HIS EVIL TO THE REST OF THE WORLD.
THE DAY WILL COME WHEN THAT WORLD WILL BEG ME TO CONTAIN RICHARDS' EVIL FOR THEM. PERHAPS I WILL ANSWER THAT CALL.
UNTIL THAT DAY, ASK YOURSELF WHY RICHARDS HAS FAILED TO CURE THE PATHETIC CONDITION OF HIS "BEST FRIEND" BEN GRIMM.
THIS INTERVIEW IS OVER. DOOM HAS SPOKEN.
KRASSH
AAH, SHADDUP!

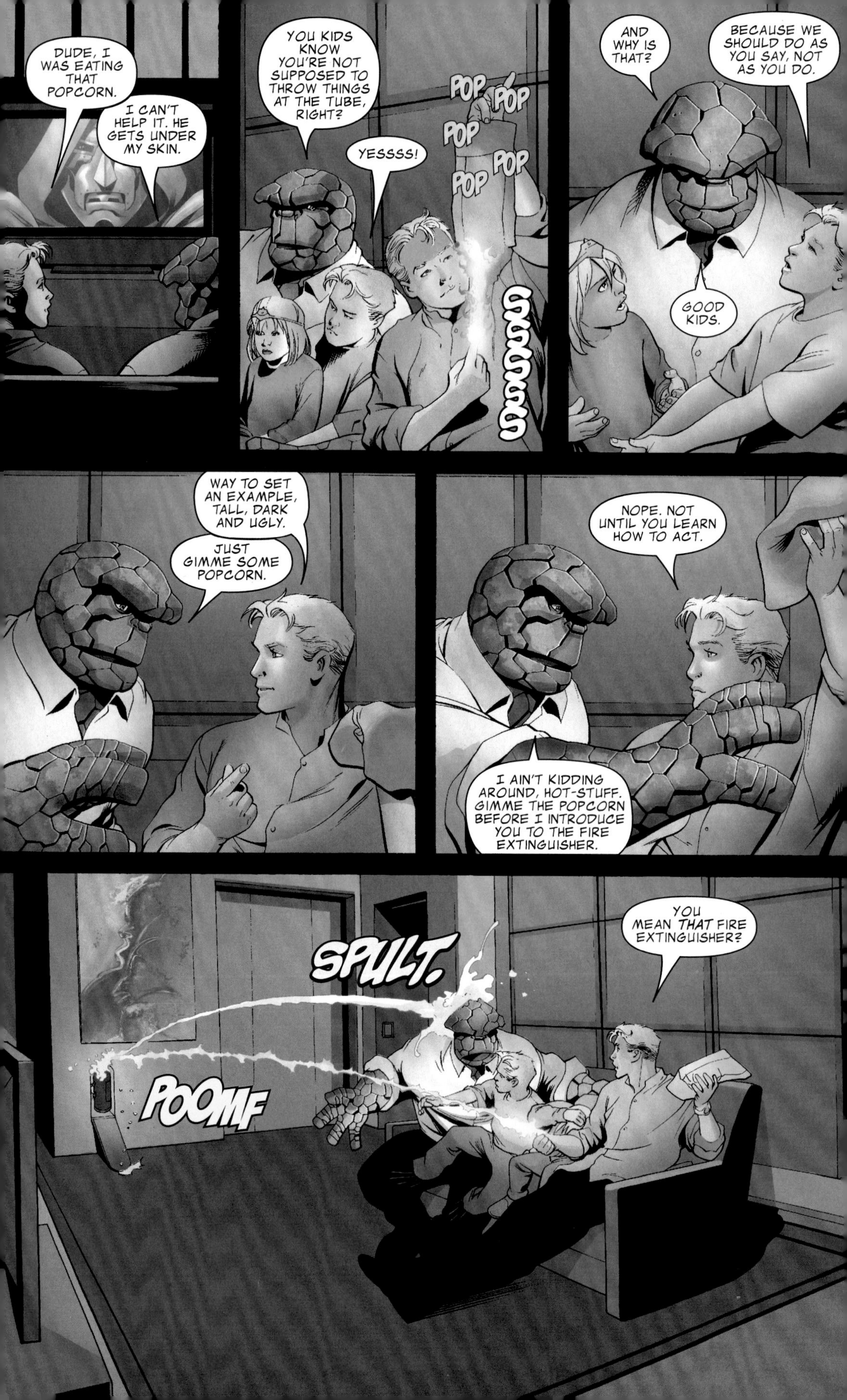
DUDE, I WAS EATING THAT POPCORN.
I CAN'T HELP IT. HE GETS UNDER MY SKIN.
YOU KIDS KNOW YOU'RE NOT SUPPOSED TO THROW THINGS AT THE TUBE, RIGHT?
YESSSS!
POP POP POP POP POP POP
AND WHY IS THAT?
BECAUSE WE SHOULD DO AS YOU SAY, NOT AS YOU DO.
GOOD KIDS.
WAY TO SET AN EXAMPLE, TALL, DARK AND UGLY.
JUST GIMME SOME POPCORN.
NOPE. NOT UNTIL YOU LEARN HOW TO ACT.
I AIN'T KIDDING AROUND, HOT-STUFF. GIMME THE POPCORN BEFORE I INTRODUCE YOU TO THE FIRE EXTINGUISHER.
SPULT.
POOMF
YOU MEAN *THAT* FIRE EXTINGUISHER?

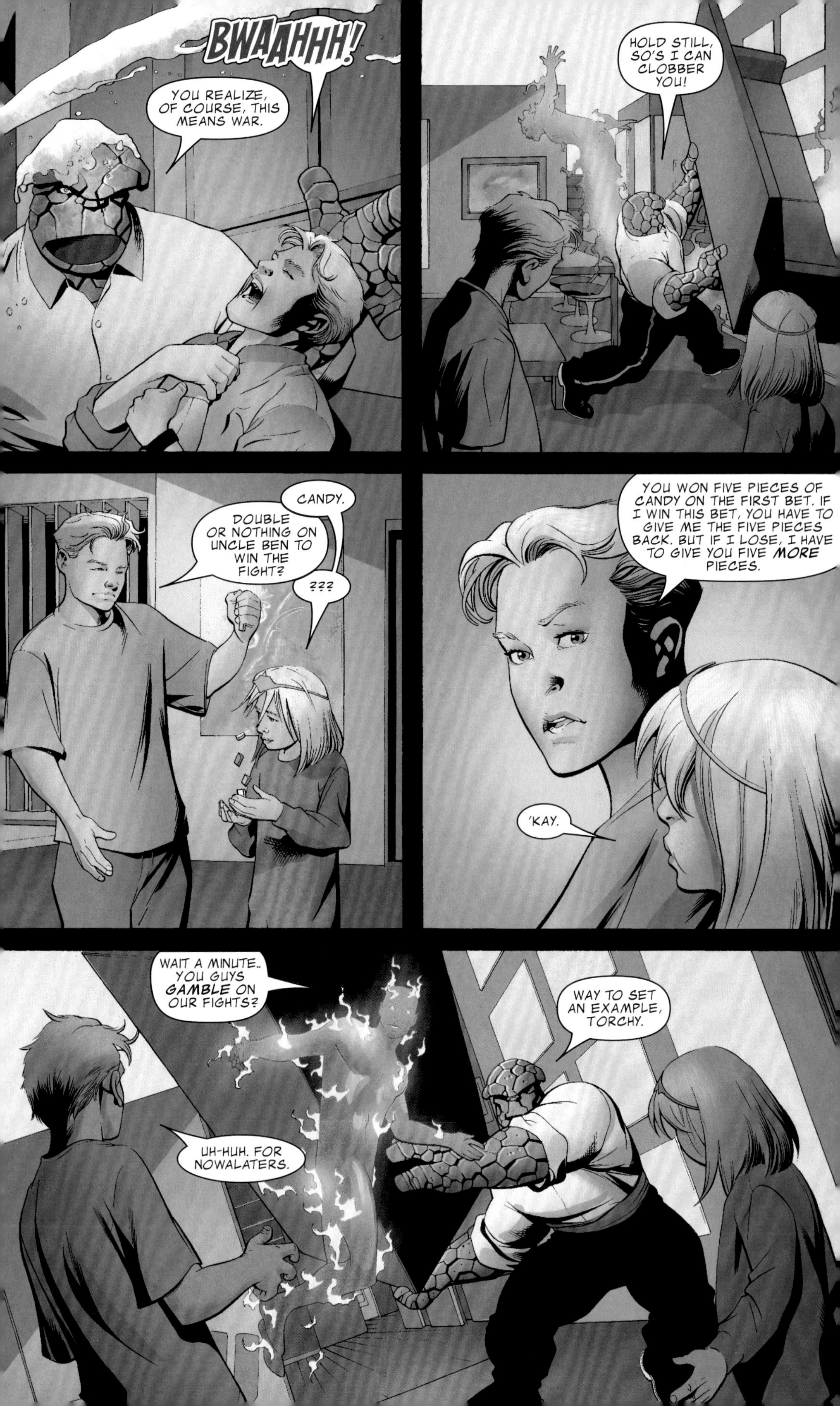
BWAAHHH!
YOU REALIZE, OF COURSE, THIS MEANS WAR.
HOLD STILL, SO'S I CAN CLOBBER YOU!
DOUBLE OR NOTHING ON UNCLE BEN TO WIN THE FIGHT?
CANDY.
???
YOU WON FIVE PIECES OF CANDY ON THE FIRST BET. IF I WIN THIS BET, YOU HAVE TO GIVE ME THE FIVE PIECES BACK. BUT IF I LOSE, I HAVE TO GIVE YOU FIVE MORE PIECES.
'KAY.
WAIT A MINUTE.. YOU GUYS GAMBLE ON OUR FIGHTS?
UH-HUH. FOR NOWALATERS.
WAY TO SET AN EXAMPLE, TORCHY.

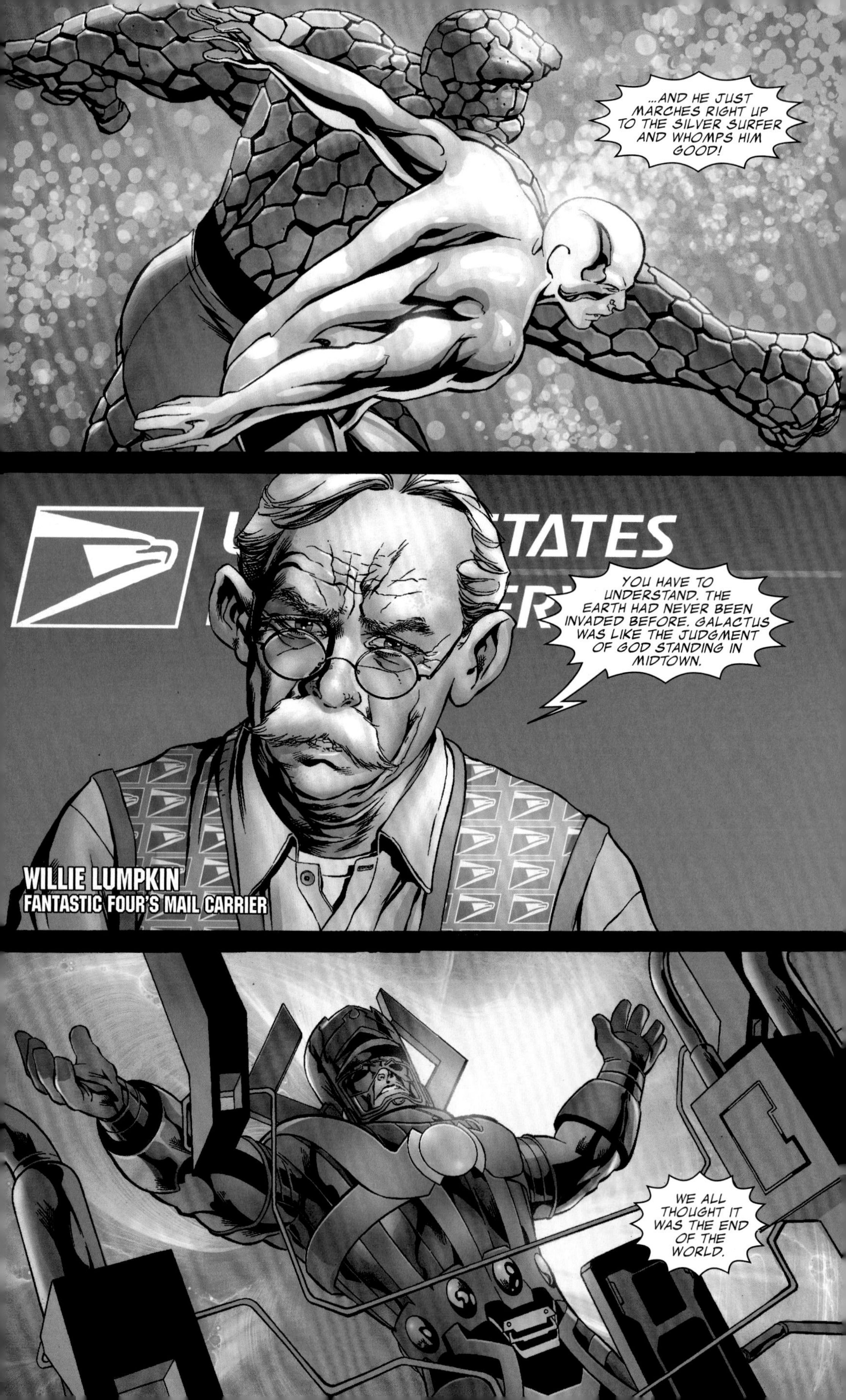
...AND HE JUST MARCHES RIGHT UP TO THE SILVER SURFER AND WHOMPS HIM GOOD!
YOU HAVE TO UNDERSTAND. THE EARTH HAD NEVER BEEN INVADED BEFORE. GALACTUS WAS LIKE THE JUDGMENT OF GOD STANDING IN MIDTOWN.
WILLIE LUMPKIN
FANTASTIC FOUR'S MAIL CARRIER
WE ALL THOUGHT IT WAS THE END OF THE WORLD.

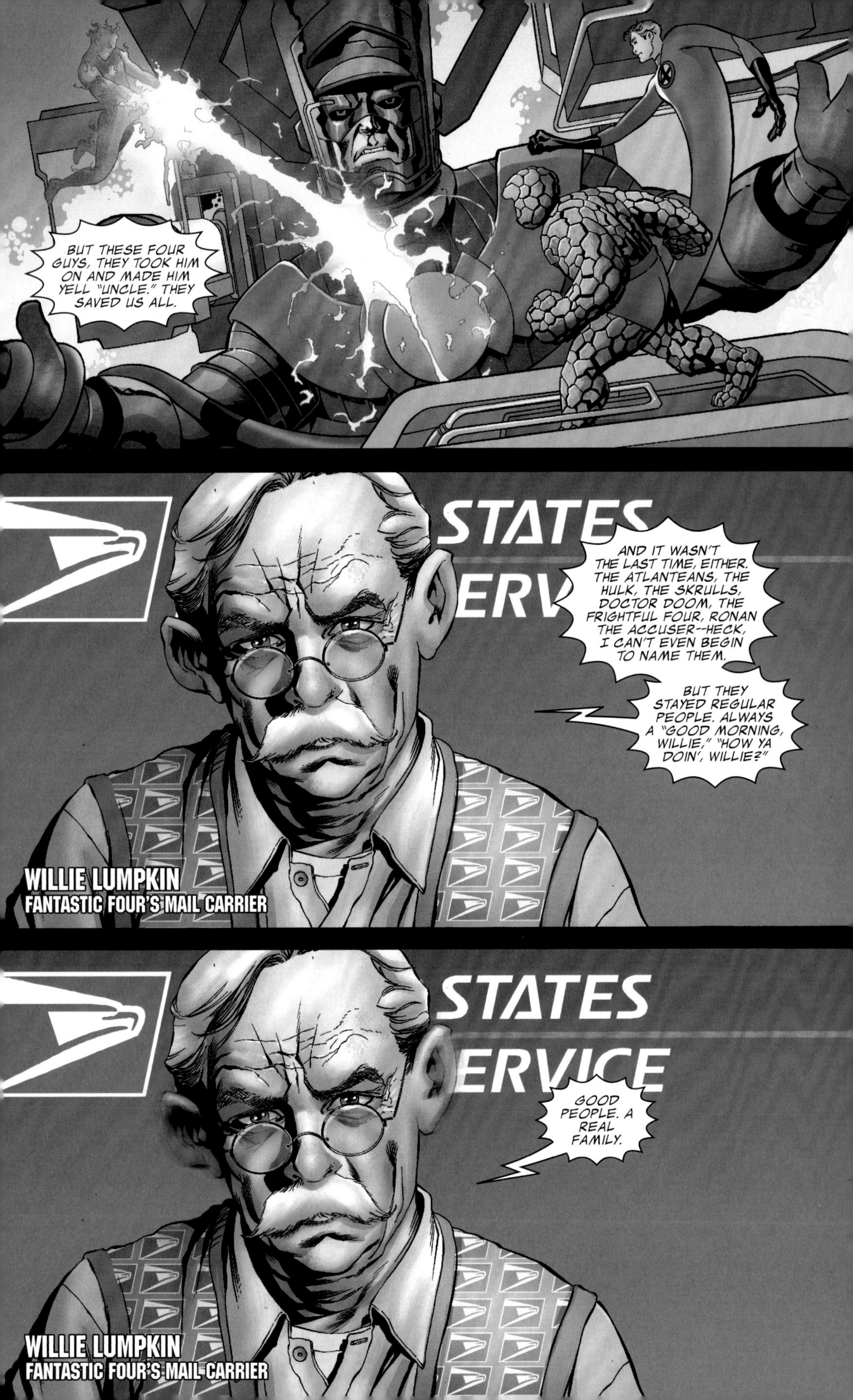
BUT THESE FOUR GUYS, THEY TOOK HIM ON AND MADE HIM YELL "UNCLE." THEY SAVED US ALL.
STATES
ERV
AND IT WASN'T THE LAST TIME, EITHER. THE ATLANTEANS, THE HULK, THE SKRULLS, DOCTOR DOOM, THE FRIGHTFUL FOUR, RONAN THE ACCUSER--HECK, I CAN'T EVEN BEGIN TO NAME THEM.
BUT THEY STAYED REGULAR PEOPLE. ALWAYS A "GOOD MORNING, WILLIE," "HOW YA DOIN', WILLIE?"
WILLIE LUMPKIN
FANTASTIC FOUR'S MAIL CARRIER
STATES
ERVICE
GOOD PEOPLE. A REAL FAMILY.
WILLIE LUMPKIN
FANTASTIC FOUR'S MAIL CARRIER

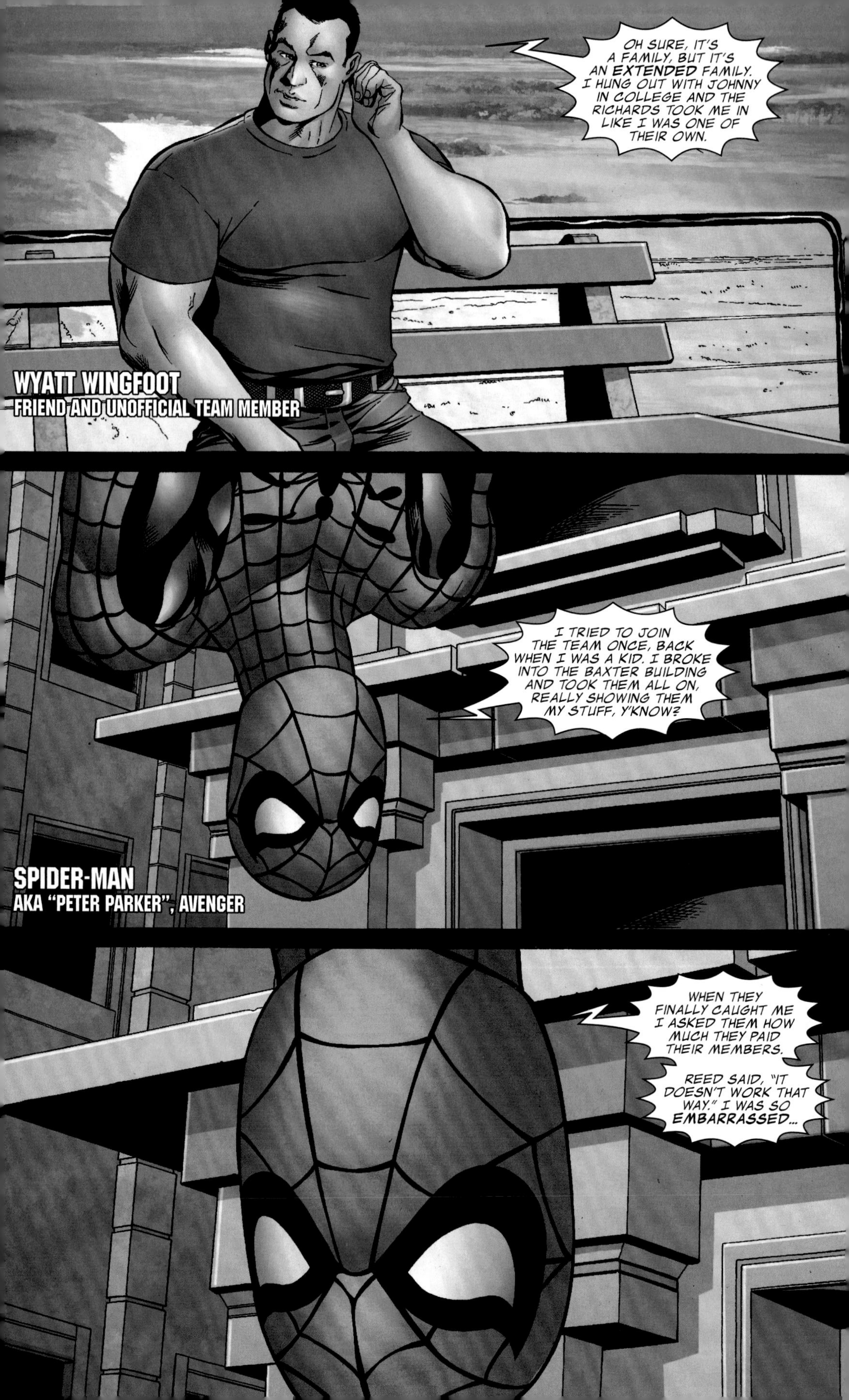
OH SURE, IT'S A FAMILY, BUT IT'S AN **EXTENDED** FAMILY. I HUNG OUT WITH JOHNNY IN COLLEGE AND THE RICHARDS TOOK ME IN LIKE I WAS ONE OF THEIR OWN.
WYATT WINGFOOT
FRIEND AND UNOFFICIAL TEAM MEMBER
I TRIED TO JOIN THE TEAM ONCE, BACK WHEN I WAS A KID. I BROKE INTO THE BAXTER BUILDING AND TOOK THEM ALL ON, REALLY SHOWING THEM MY STUFF, Y'KNOW?
SPIDER-MAN
AKA "PETER PARKER", AVENGER
WHEN THEY FINALLY CAUGHT ME I ASKED THEM HOW MUCH THEY PAID THEIR MEMBERS.
REED SAID, "IT DOESN'T WORK THAT WAY." I WAS SO **EMBARRASSED**...

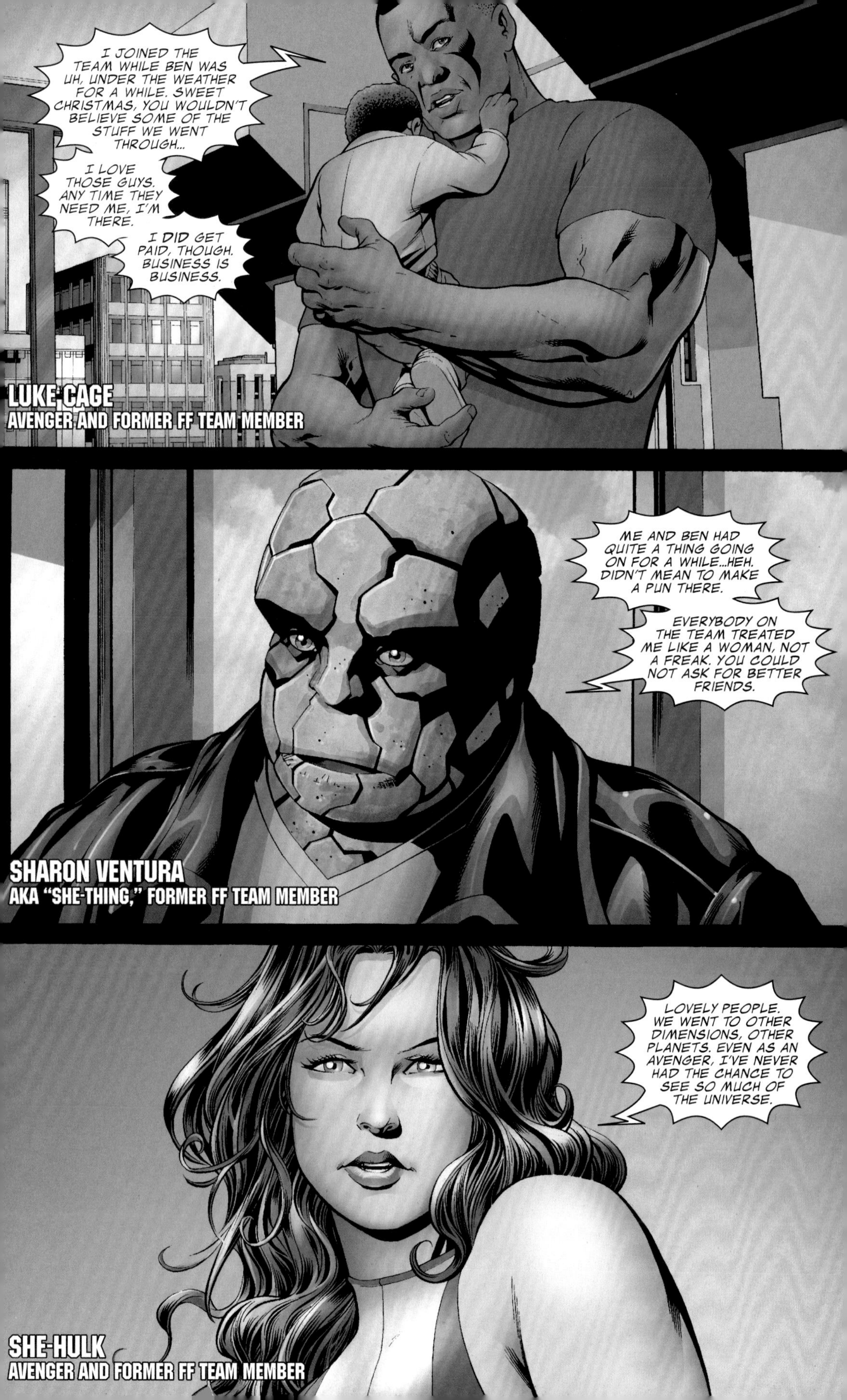
I JOINED THE TEAM WHILE BEN WAS UH, UNDER THE WEATHER FOR A WHILE. SWEET CHRISTMAS, YOU WOULDN'T BELIEVE SOME OF THE STUFF WE WENT THROUGH...
I LOVE THOSE GUYS. ANY TIME THEY NEED ME, I'M THERE.
I **DID** GET PAID, THOUGH. BUSINESS IS BUSINESS.
LUKE CAGE
AVENGER AND FORMER FF TEAM MEMBER
ME AND BEN HAD QUITE A THING GOING ON FOR A WHILE...HEH. DIDN'T MEAN TO MAKE A PUN THERE.
EVERYBODY ON THE TEAM TREATED ME LIKE A WOMAN, NOT A FREAK. YOU COULD NOT ASK FOR BETTER FRIENDS.
SHARON VENTURA
AKA "SHE-THING," FORMER FF TEAM MEMBER
LOVELY PEOPLE. WE WENT TO OTHER DIMENSIONS, OTHER PLANETS. EVEN AS AN AVENGER, I'VE NEVER HAD THE CHANCE TO SEE SO MUCH OF THE UNIVERSE.
SHE-HULK
AVENGER AND FORMER FF TEAM MEMBER

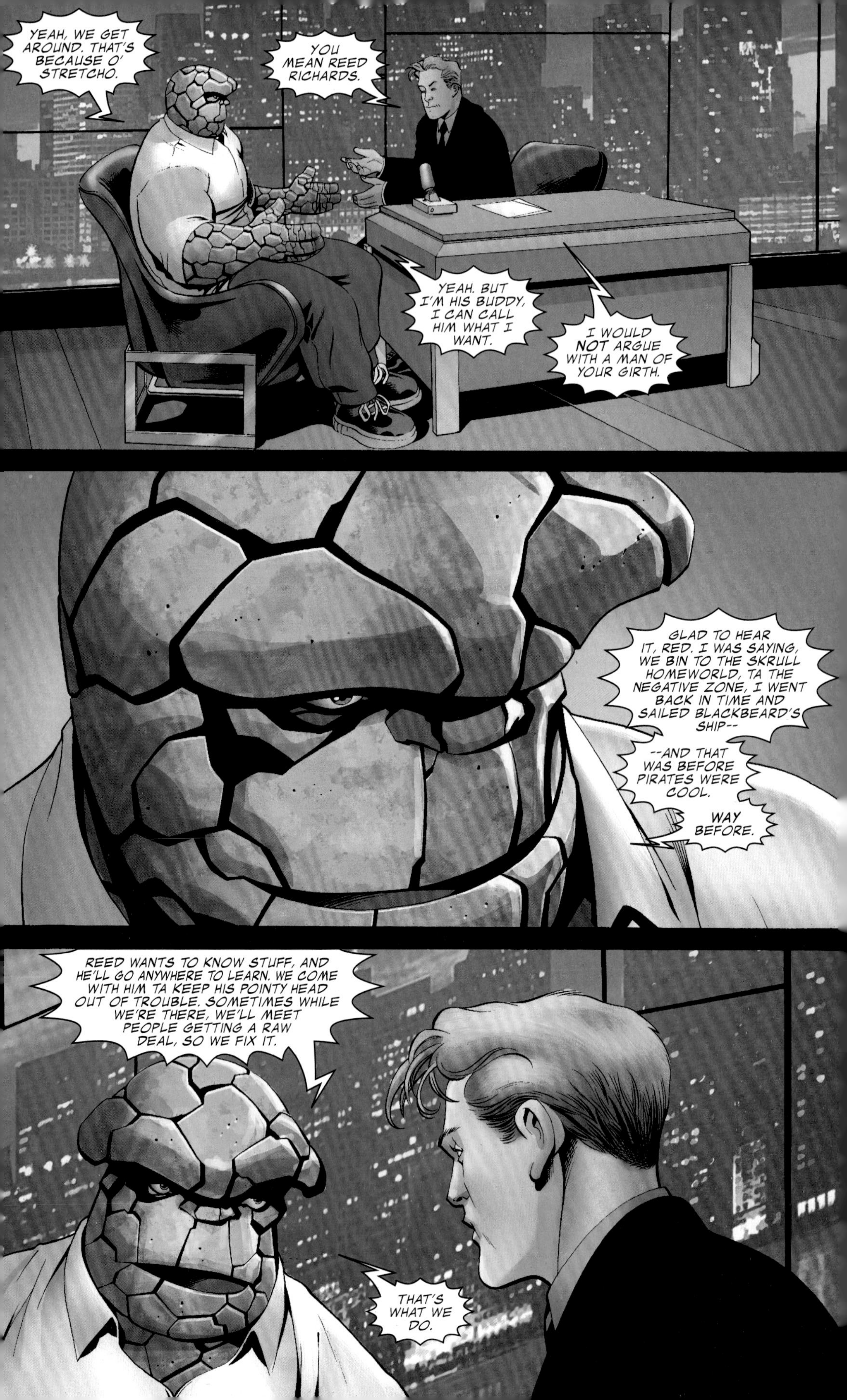
YEAH, WE GET AROUND. THAT'S BECAUSE O' STRETCHO.
YOU MEAN REED RICHARDS.
YEAH. BUT I'M HIS BUDDY, I CAN CALL HIM WHAT I WANT.
I WOULD NOT ARGUE WITH A MAN OF YOUR GIRTH.
GLAD TO HEAR IT, RED. I WAS SAYING, WE BIN TO THE SKRULL HOMEWORLD, TA THE NEGATIVE ZONE, I WENT BACK IN TIME AND SAILED BLACKBEARD'S SHIP--
--AND THAT WAS BEFORE PIRATES WERE COOL.
WAY BEFORE.
REED WANTS TO KNOW STUFF, AND HE'LL GO ANYWHERE TO LEARN. WE COME WITH HIM TA KEEP HIS POINTY HEAD OUT OF TROUBLE. SOMETIMES WHILE WE'RE THERE, WE'LL MEET PEOPLE GETTING A RAW DEAL, SO WE FIX IT.
THAT'S WHAT WE DO.

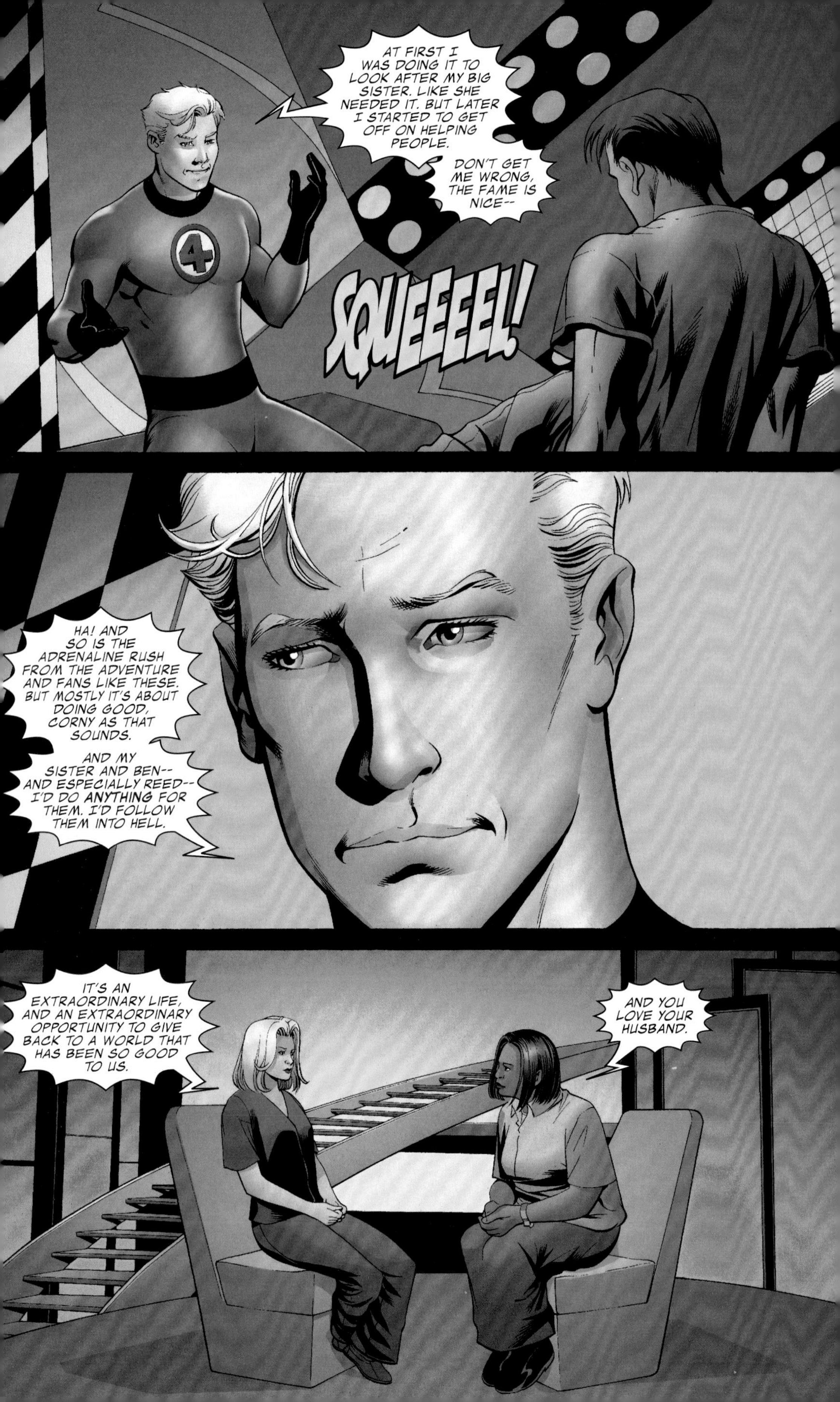
AT FIRST I WAS DOING IT TO LOOK AFTER MY BIG SISTER. LIKE SHE NEEDED IT. BUT LATER I STARTED TO GET OFF ON HELPING PEOPLE.
DON'T GET ME WRONG, THE FAME IS NICE--
SQUEEEEL!
HA! AND SO IS THE ADRENALINE RUSH FROM THE ADVENTURE AND FANS LIKE THESE. BUT MOSTLY IT'S ABOUT DOING GOOD, CORNY AS THAT SOUNDS.
AND MY SISTER AND BEN-- AND ESPECIALLY REED-- I'D DO ANYTHING FOR THEM. I'D FOLLOW THEM INTO HELL.
IT'S AN EXTRAORDINARY LIFE, AND AN EXTRAORDINARY OPPORTUNITY TO GIVE BACK TO A WORLD THAT HAS BEEN SO GOOD TO US.
AND YOU LOVE YOUR HUSBAND.

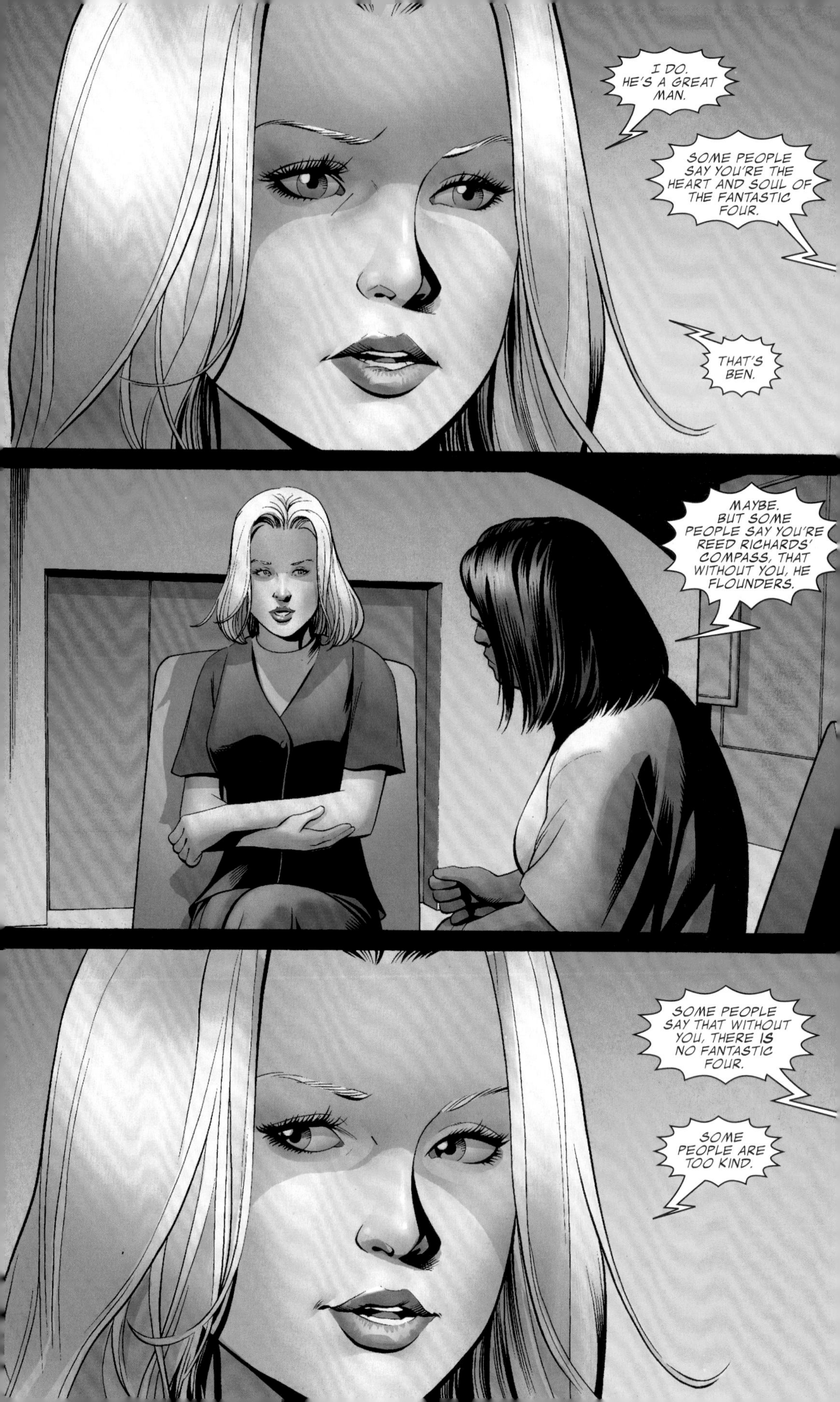
I DO. HE'S A GREAT MAN.
SOME PEOPLE SAY YOU'RE THE HEART AND SOUL OF THE FANTASTIC FOUR.
THAT'S BEN.
MAYBE. BUT SOME PEOPLE SAY YOU'RE REED RICHARDS' COMPASS, THAT WITHOUT YOU, HE FLOUNDERS.
SOME PEOPLE SAY THAT WITHOUT YOU, THERE **IS** NO FANTASTIC FOUR.
SOME PEOPLE ARE TOO KIND.

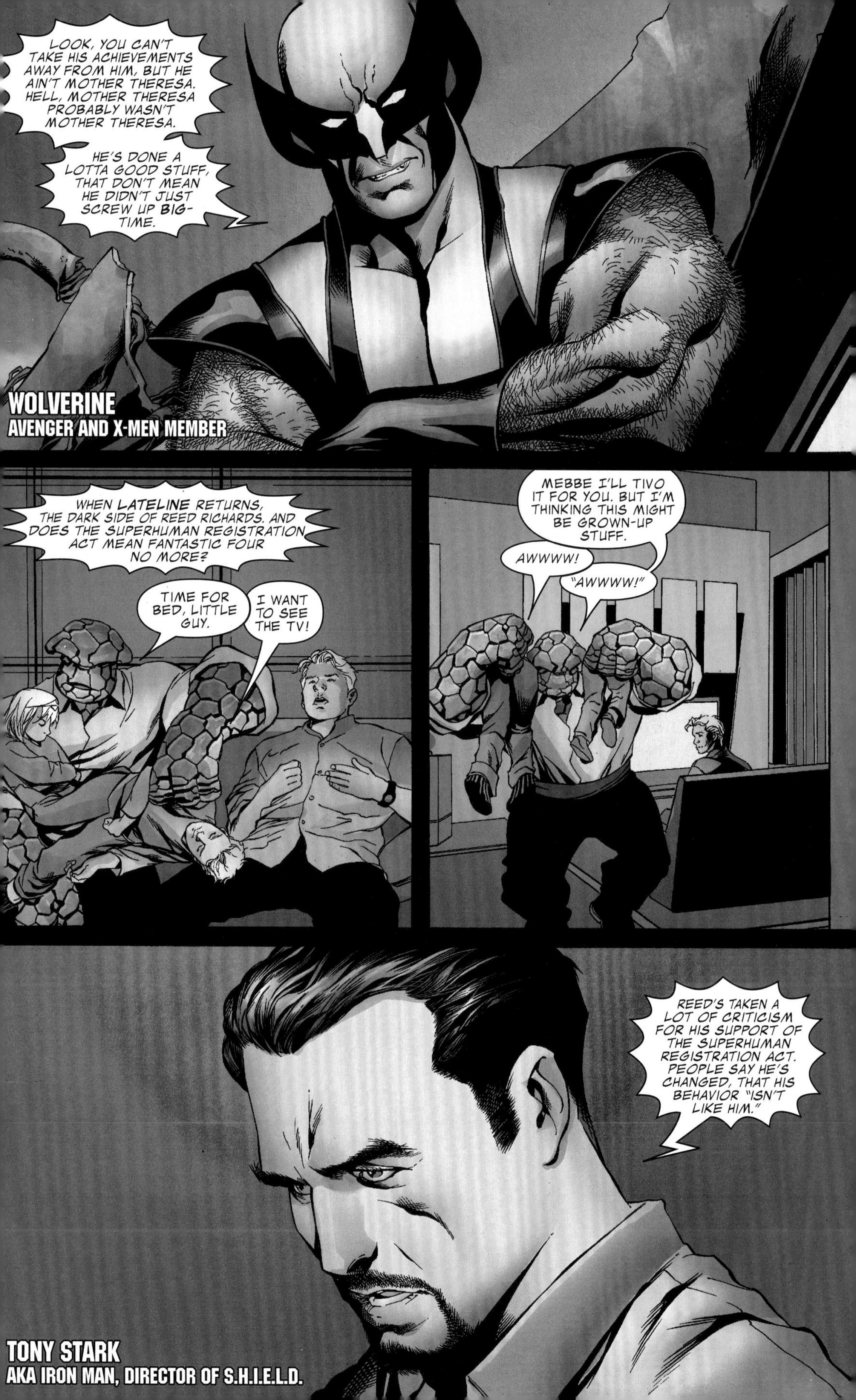
LOOK, YOU CAN'T TAKE HIS ACHIEVEMENTS AWAY FROM HIM, BUT HE AIN'T MOTHER THERESA. HELL, MOTHER THERESA PROBABLY WASN'T MOTHER THERESA.
HE'S DONE A LOTTA GOOD STUFF, THAT DON'T MEAN HE DIDN'T JUST SCREW UP BIG-TIME.
WOLVERINE
AVENGER AND X-MEN MEMBER
WHEN LATELINE RETURNS, THE DARK SIDE OF REED RICHARDS. AND DOES THE SUPERHUMAN REGISTRATION ACT MEAN FANTASTIC FOUR NO MORE?
TIME FOR BED, LITTLE GUY.
I WANT TO SEE THE TV!
MEBBE I'LL TIVO IT FOR YOU. BUT I'M THINKING THIS MIGHT BE GROWN-UP STUFF.
AWWWW!
"AWWWW!"
REED'S TAKEN A LOT OF CRITICISM FOR HIS SUPPORT OF THE SUPERHUMAN REGISTRATION ACT. PEOPLE SAY HE'S CHANGED, THAT HIS BEHAVIOR "ISN'T LIKE HIM."
TONY STARK
AKA IRON MAN, DIRECTOR OF S.H.I.E.L.D.

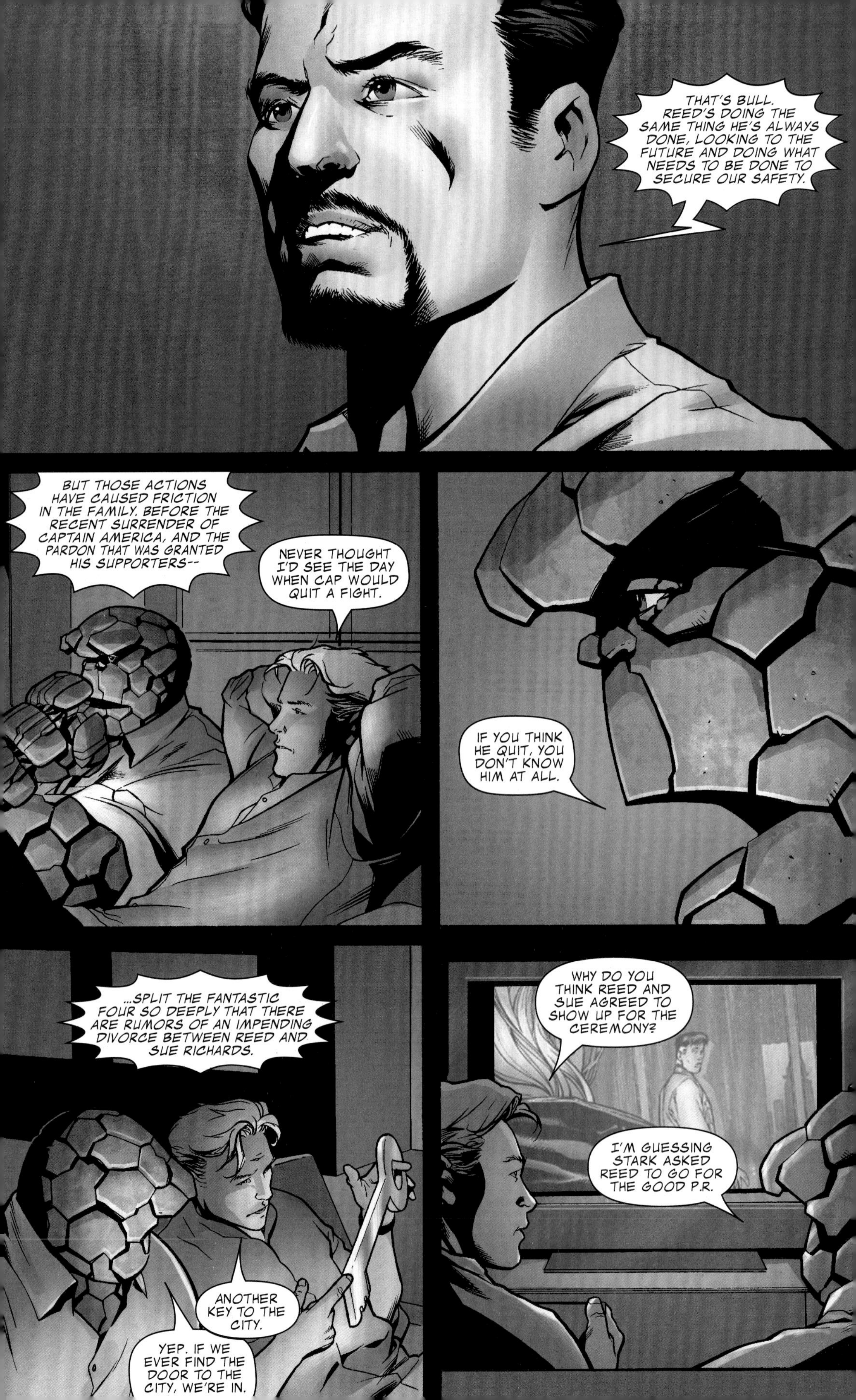
THAT'S BULL. REED'S DOING THE SAME THING HE'S ALWAYS DONE, LOOKING TO THE FUTURE AND DOING WHAT NEEDS TO BE DONE TO SECURE OUR SAFETY.
BUT THOSE ACTIONS HAVE CAUSED FRICTION IN THE FAMILY. BEFORE THE RECENT SURRENDER OF CAPTAIN AMERICA, AND THE PARDON THAT WAS GRANTED HIS SUPPORTERS--
NEVER THOUGHT I'D SEE THE DAY WHEN CAP WOULD QUIT A FIGHT.
IF YOU THINK HE QUIT, YOU DON'T KNOW HIM AT ALL.
...SPLIT THE FANTASTIC FOUR SO DEEPLY THAT THERE ARE RUMORS OF AN IMPENDING DIVORCE BETWEEN REED AND SUE RICHARDS.
ANOTHER KEY TO THE CITY.
YEP. IF WE EVER FIND THE DOOR TO THE CITY, WE'RE IN.
WHY DO YOU THINK REED AND SUE AGREED TO SHOW UP FOR THE CEREMONY?
I'M GUESSING STARK ASKED REED TO GO FOR THE GOOD P.R.

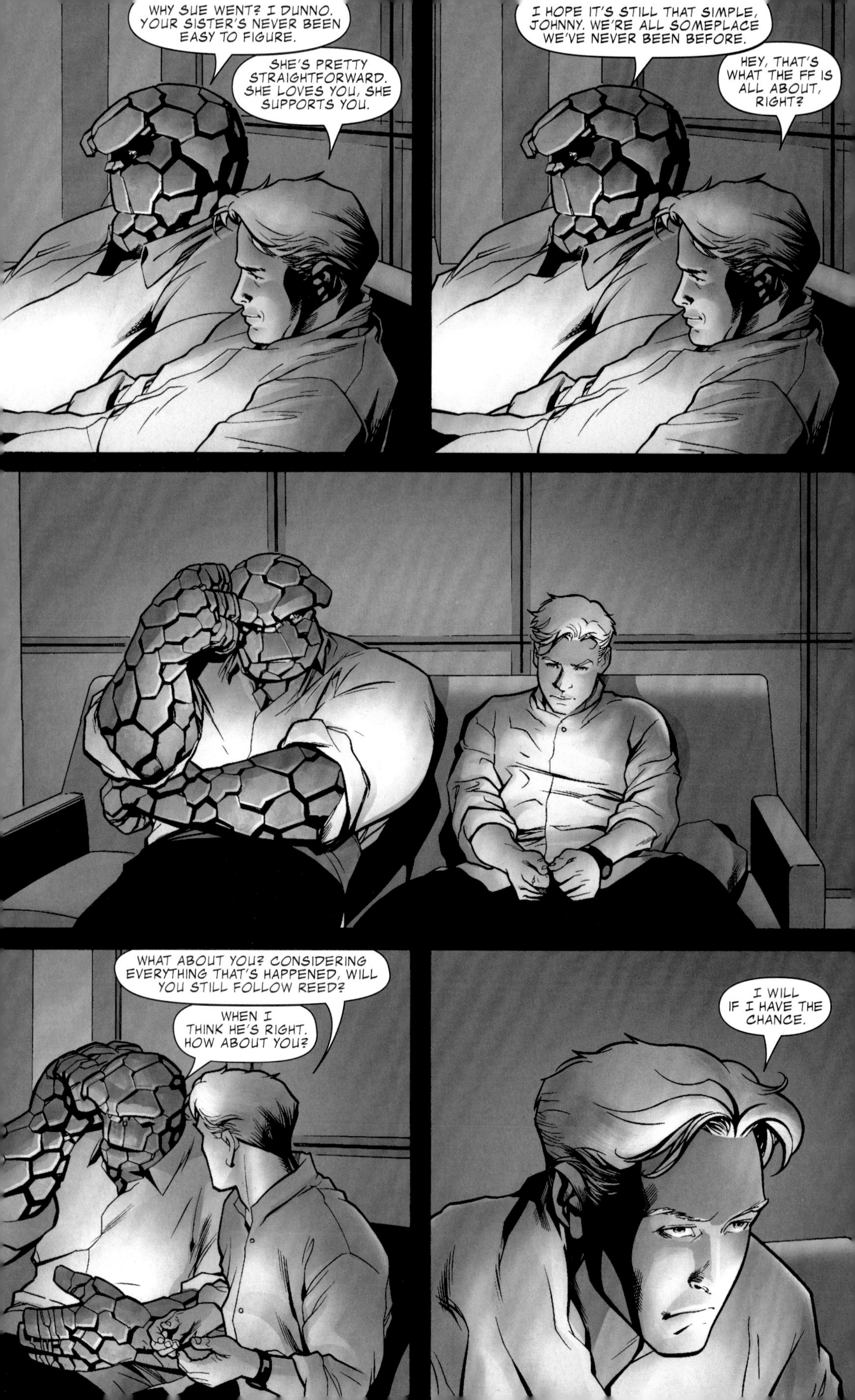
WHY SUE WENT? I DUNNO. YOUR SISTER'S NEVER BEEN EASY TO FIGURE.
SHE'S PRETTY STRAIGHTFORWARD. SHE LOVES YOU, SHE SUPPORTS YOU.
I HOPE IT'S STILL THAT SIMPLE, JOHNNY. WE'RE ALL SOMEPLACE WE'VE NEVER BEEN BEFORE.
HEY, THAT'S WHAT THE FF IS ALL ABOUT, RIGHT?
WHAT ABOUT YOU? CONSIDERING EVERYTHING THAT'S HAPPENED, WILL YOU STILL FOLLOW REED?
WHEN I THINK HE'S RIGHT. HOW ABOUT YOU?
I WILL IF I HAVE THE CHANCE.

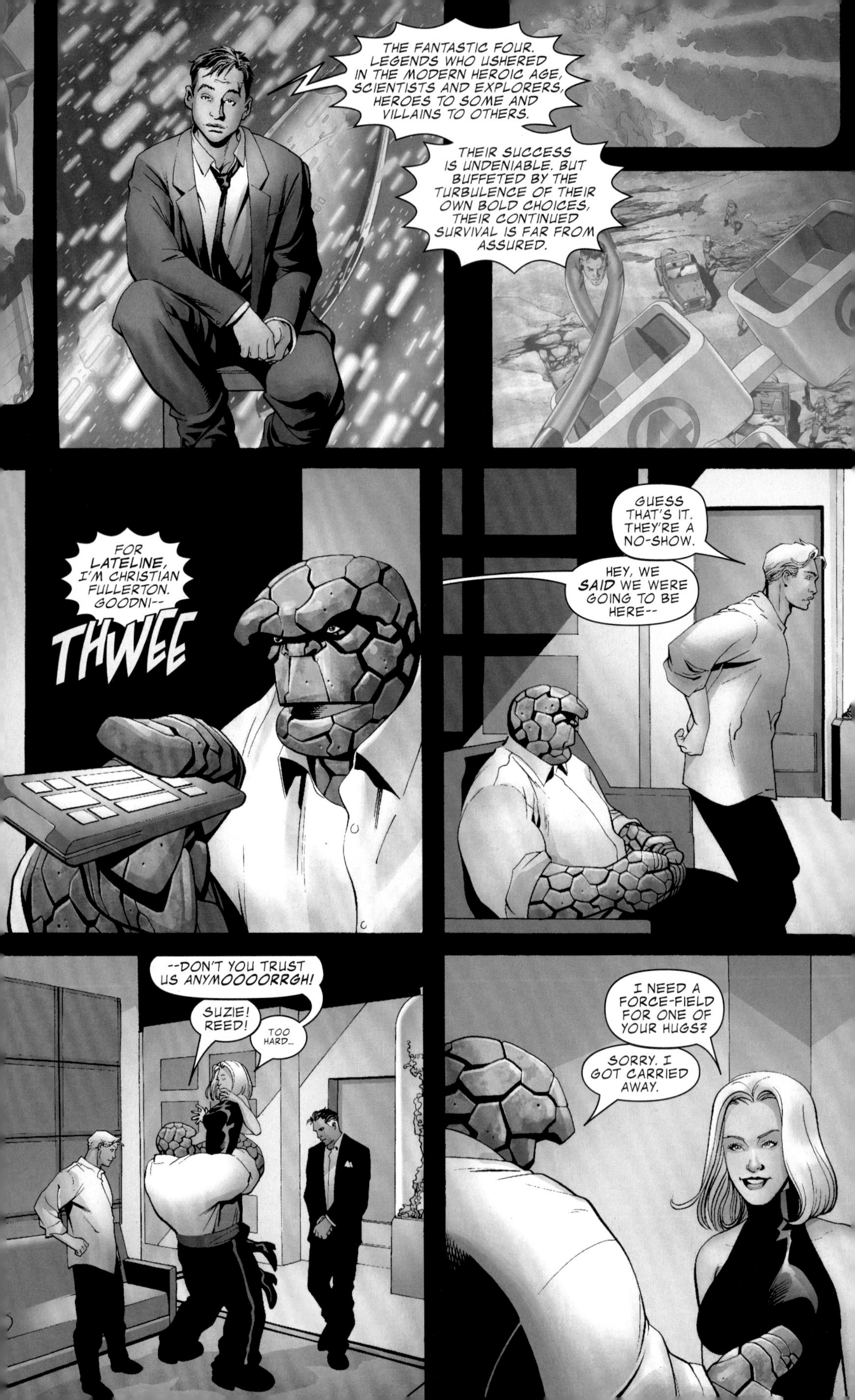
THE FANTASTIC FOUR. LEGENDS WHO USHERED IN THE MODERN HEROIC AGE, SCIENTISTS AND EXPLORERS, HEROES TO SOME AND VILLAINS TO OTHERS.
THEIR SUCCESS IS UNDENIABLE. BUT BUFFETED BY THE TURBULENCE OF THEIR OWN BOLD CHOICES, THEIR CONTINUED SURVIVAL IS FAR FROM ASSURED.
FOR LATELINE, I'M CHRISTIAN FULLERTON. GOODNI--
THWEE
GUESS THAT'S IT. THEY'RE A NO-SHOW.
HEY, WE SAID WE WERE GOING TO BE HERE--
--DON'T YOU TRUST US ANYMOOOORRGH!
SUZIE! REED!
TOO HARD...
I NEED A FORCE-FIELD FOR ONE OF YOUR HUGS?
SORRY. I GOT CARRIED AWAY.

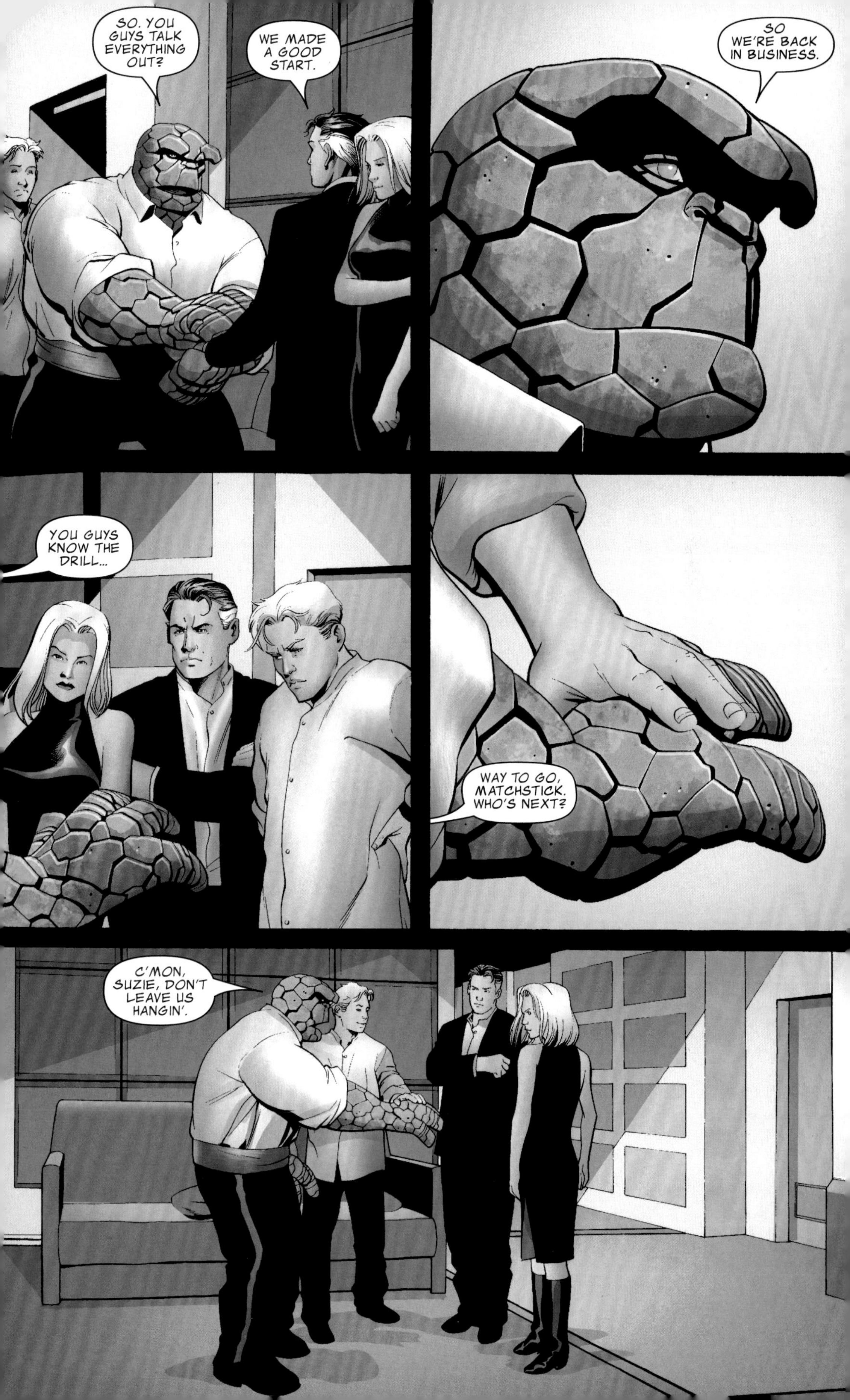
SO. YOU GUYS TALK EVERYTHING OUT?
WE MADE A GOOD START.
SO WE'RE BACK IN BUSINESS.
YOU GUYS KNOW THE DRILL...
WAY TO GO, MATCHSTICK. WHO'S NEXT?
C'MON, SUZIE, DON'T LEAVE US HANGIN'.

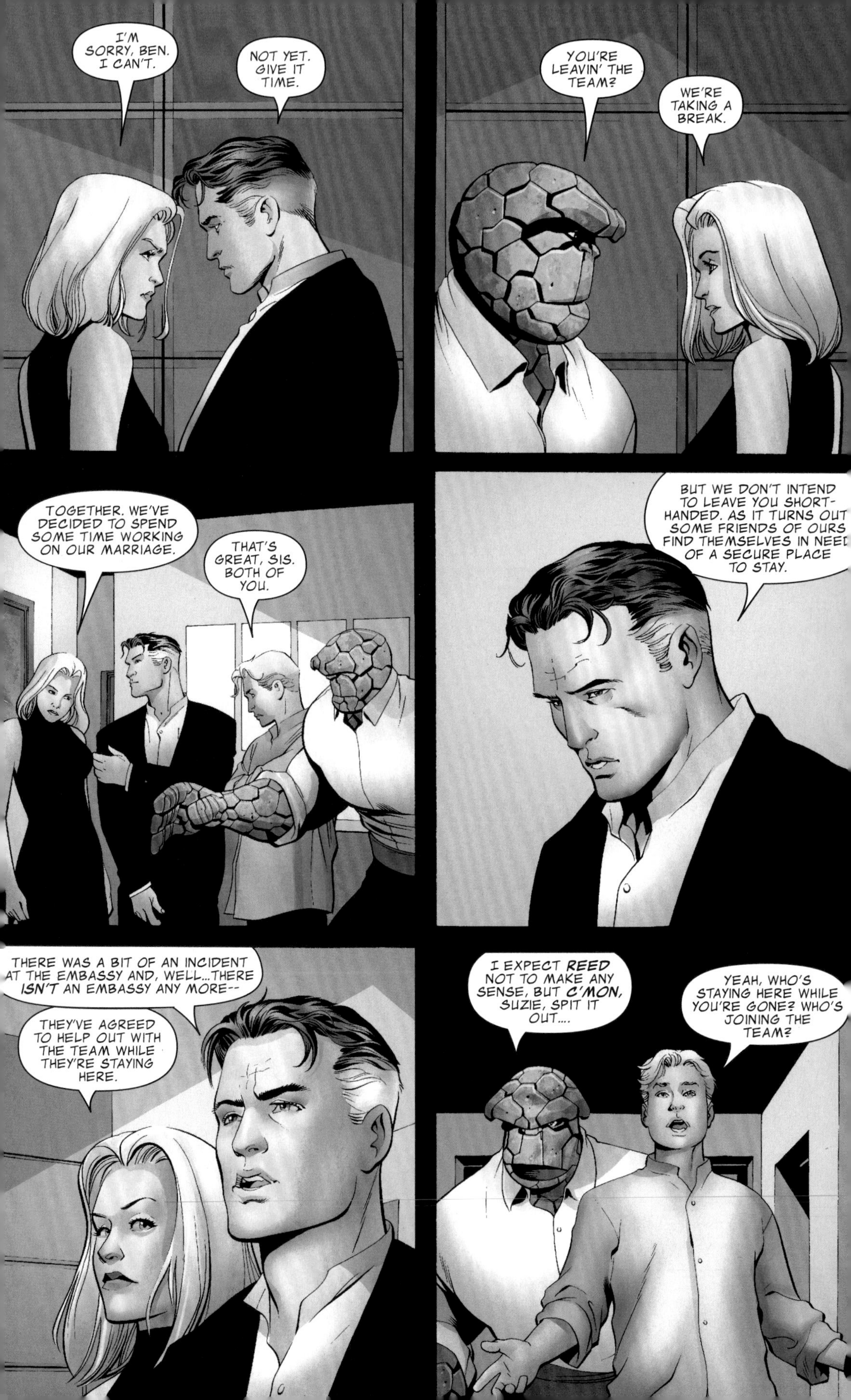
I'M SORRY, BEN. I CAN'T.
NOT YET. GIVE IT TIME.
YOU'RE LEAVIN' THE TEAM?
WE'RE TAKING A BREAK.
TOGETHER. WE'VE DECIDED TO SPEND SOME TIME WORKING ON OUR MARRIAGE.
THAT'S GREAT, SIS. BOTH OF YOU.
BUT WE DON'T INTEND TO LEAVE YOU SHORT-HANDED. AS IT TURNS OUT SOME FRIENDS OF OURS FIND THEMSELVES IN NEED OF A SECURE PLACE TO STAY.
THERE WAS A BIT OF AN INCIDENT AT THE EMBASSY AND, WELL...THERE *ISN'T* AN EMBASSY ANY MORE--
THEY'VE AGREED TO HELP OUT WITH THE TEAM WHILE THEY'RE STAYING HERE.
I EXPECT **REED** NOT TO MAKE ANY SENSE, BUT **C'MON**, SUZIE, SPIT IT OUT....
YEAH, WHO'S STAYING HERE WHILE YOU'RE GONE? WHO'S JOINING THE TEAM?

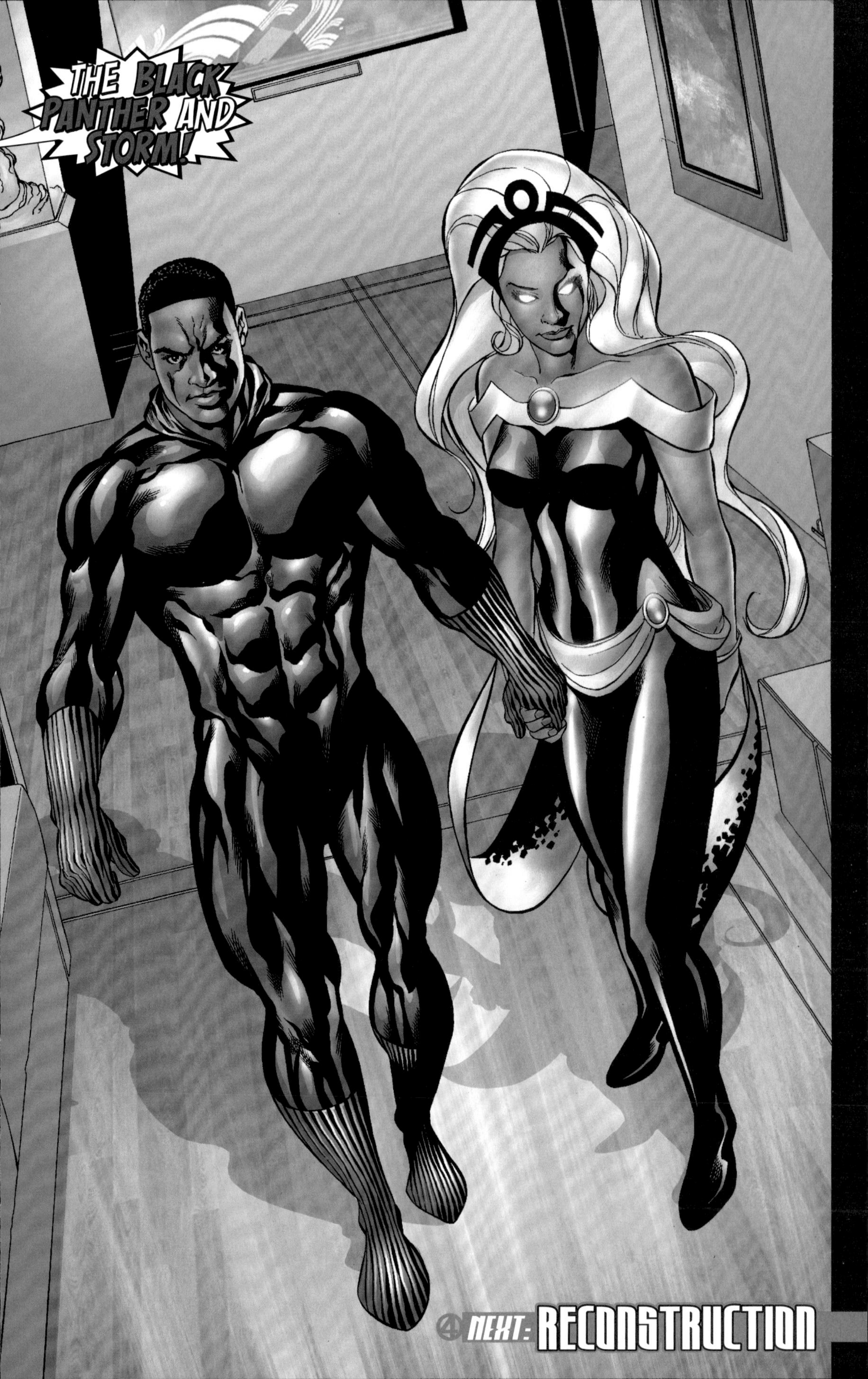
THE BLACK PANTHER AND STORM!
NEXT: RECONSTRUCTION

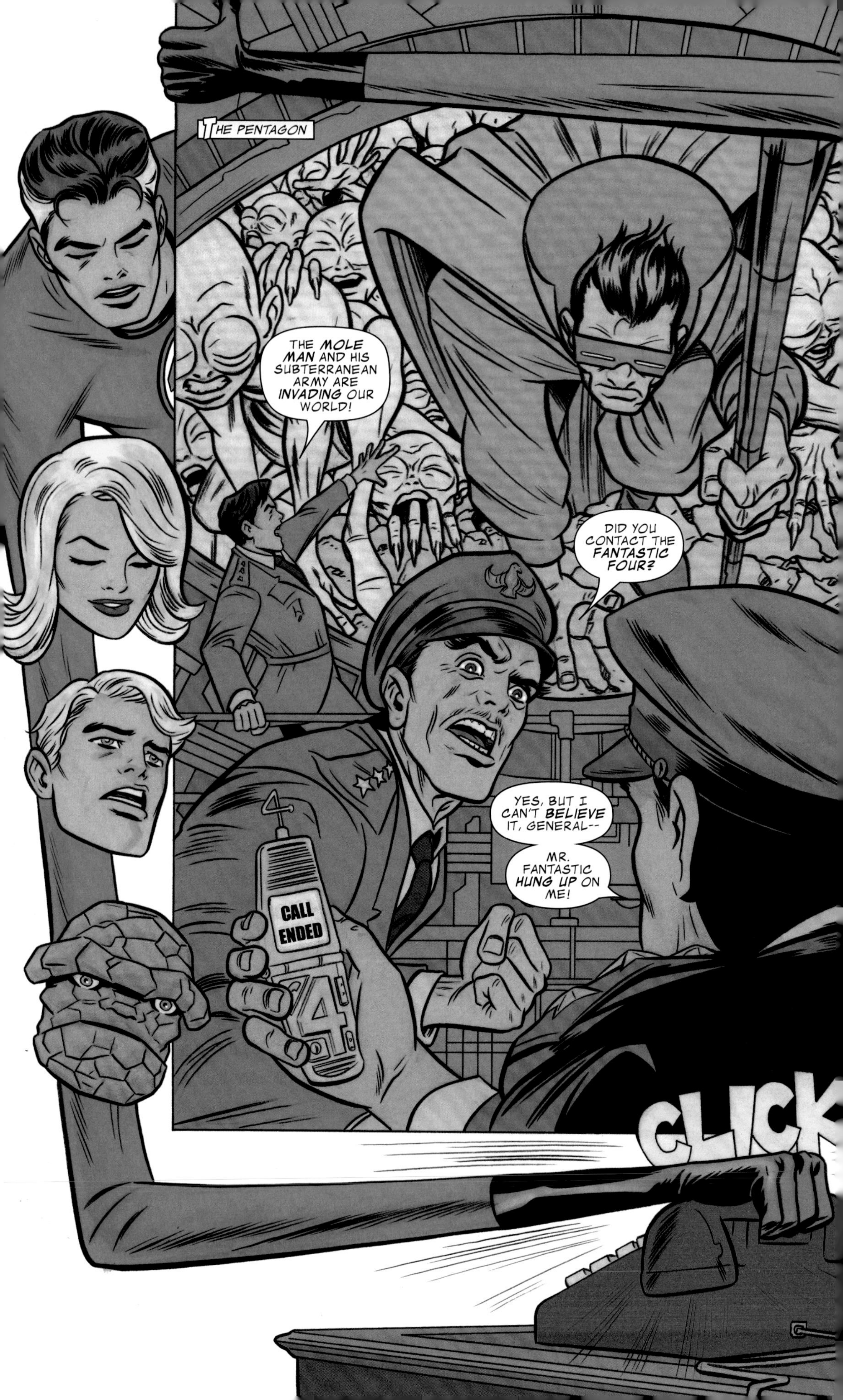
THE PENTAGON
THE MOLE MAN AND HIS SUBTERRANEAN ARMY ARE INVADING OUR WORLD!
DID YOU CONTACT THE FANTASTIC FOUR?
YES, BUT I CAN'T BELIEVE IT, GENERAL--
MR. FANTASTIC HUNG UP ON ME!
CALL ENDED
CLICK

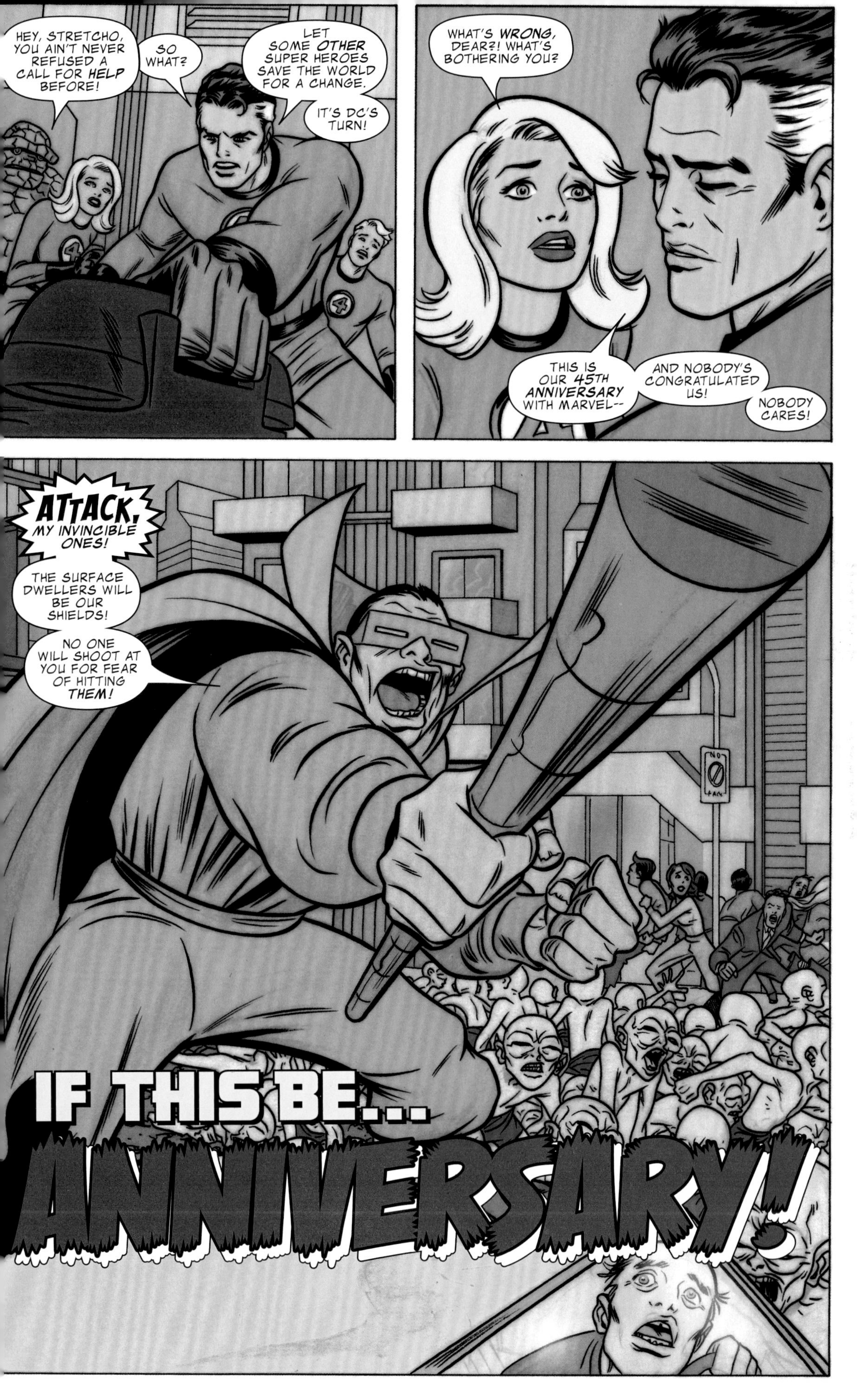
HEY, STRETCHO, YOU AIN'T NEVER REFUSED A CALL FOR HELP BEFORE!
SO WHAT?
LET SOME OTHER SUPER HEROES SAVE THE WORLD FOR A CHANGE.
IT'S DC'S TURN!
WHAT'S WRONG, DEAR?! WHAT'S BOTHERING YOU?
THIS IS OUR 45TH ANNIVERSARY WITH MARVEL--
AND NOBODY'S CONGRATULATED US!
NOBODY CARES!
ATTACK, MY INVINCIBLE ONES!
THE SURFACE DWELLERS WILL BE OUR SHIELDS!
NO ONE WILL SHOOT AT YOU FOR FEAR OF HITTING THEM!
IF THIS BE... ANNIVERSARY!

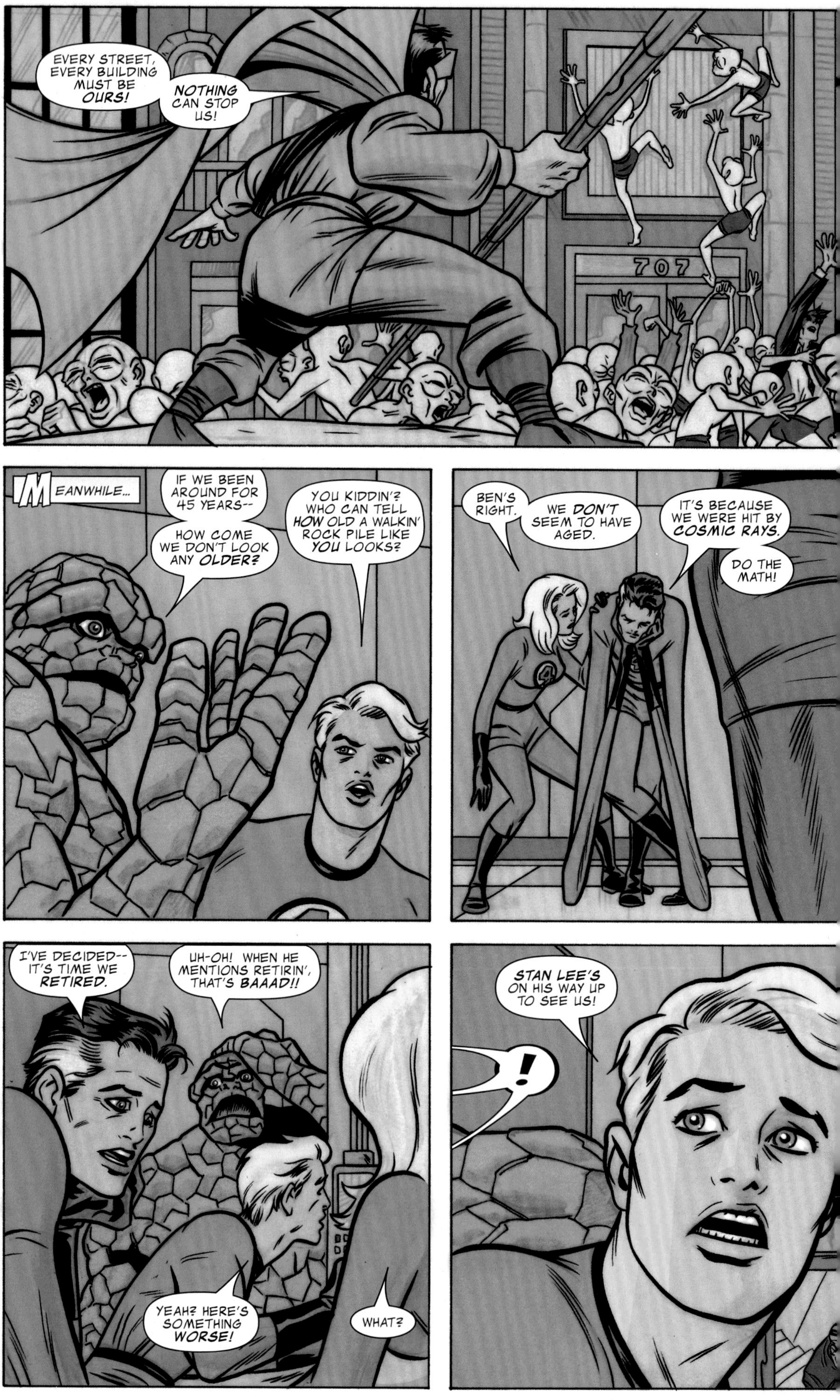
EVERY STREET, EVERY BUILDING MUST BE OURS!
NOTHING CAN STOP US!
707
MEANWHILE...
IF WE BEEN AROUND FOR 45 YEARS--
HOW COME WE DON'T LOOK ANY OLDER?
YOU KIDDIN'? WHO CAN TELL HOW OLD A WALKIN' ROCK PILE LIKE YOU LOOKS?
BEN'S RIGHT.
WE DON'T SEEM TO HAVE AGED.
IT'S BECAUSE WE WERE HIT BY COSMIC RAYS.
DO THE MATH!
I'VE DECIDED-- IT'S TIME WE RETIRED.
UH-OH! WHEN HE MENTIONS RETIRIN', THAT'S BAAAD!!
YEAH? HERE'S SOMETHING WORSE!
WHAT?
STAN LEE'S ON HIS WAY UP TO SEE US!
!

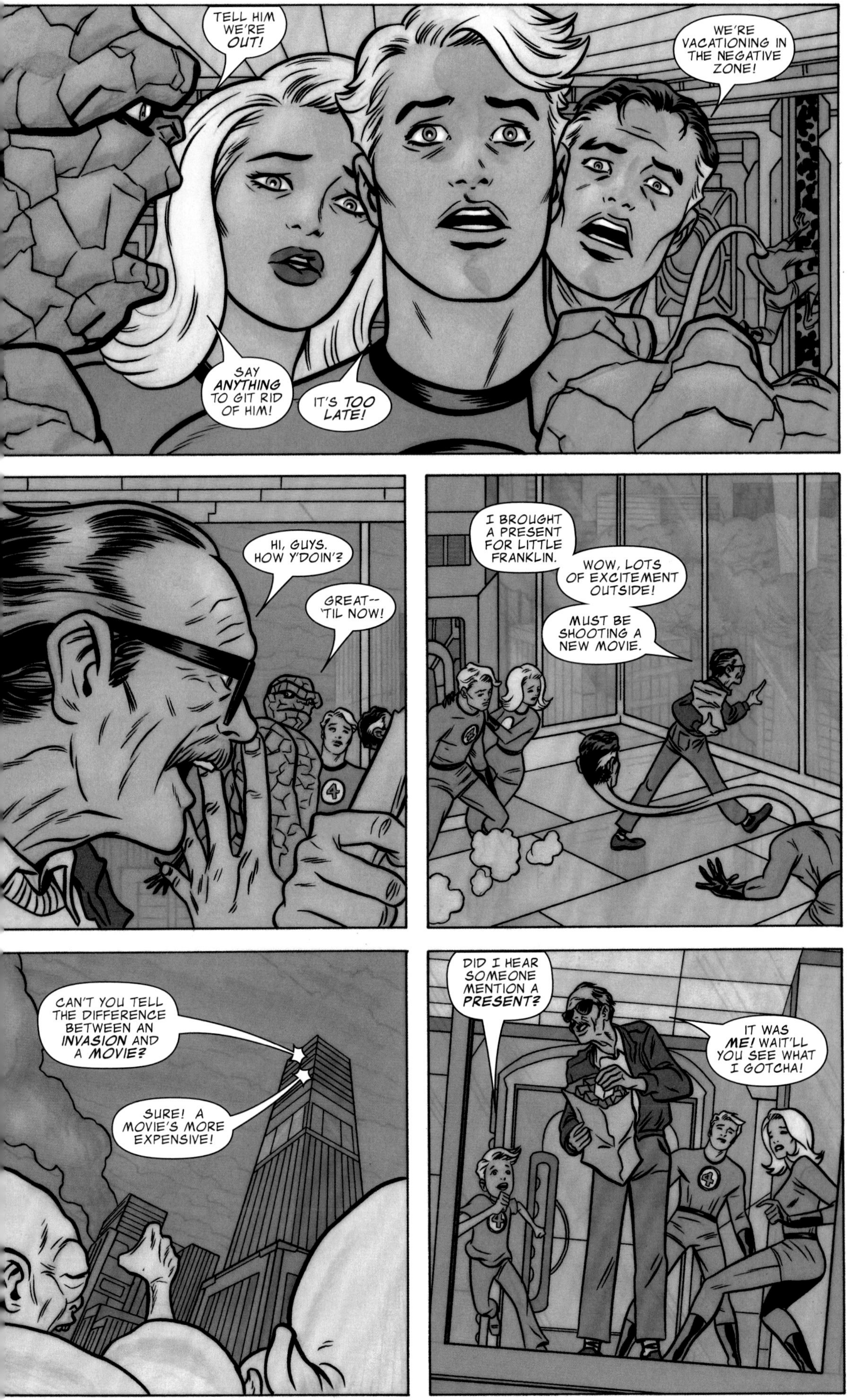

TELL HIM WE'RE *OUT!*
WE'RE VACATIONING IN THE NEGATIVE ZONE!
SAY *ANYTHING* TO GIT RID OF HIM!
IT'S *TOO LATE!*
HI, GUYS. HOW Y'DOIN'?
GREAT-- 'TIL NOW!
I BROUGHT A PRESENT FOR LITTLE FRANKLIN.
WOW, LOTS OF EXCITEMENT OUTSIDE!
MUST BE SHOOTING A NEW MOVIE.
CAN'T YOU TELL THE DIFFERENCE BETWEEN AN *INVASION* AND A *MOVIE?*
SURE! A MOVIE'S MORE EXPENSIVE!
DID I HEAR SOMEONE MENTION A *PRESENT?*
IT WAS *ME!* WAIT'LL YOU SEE WHAT I GOTCHA!

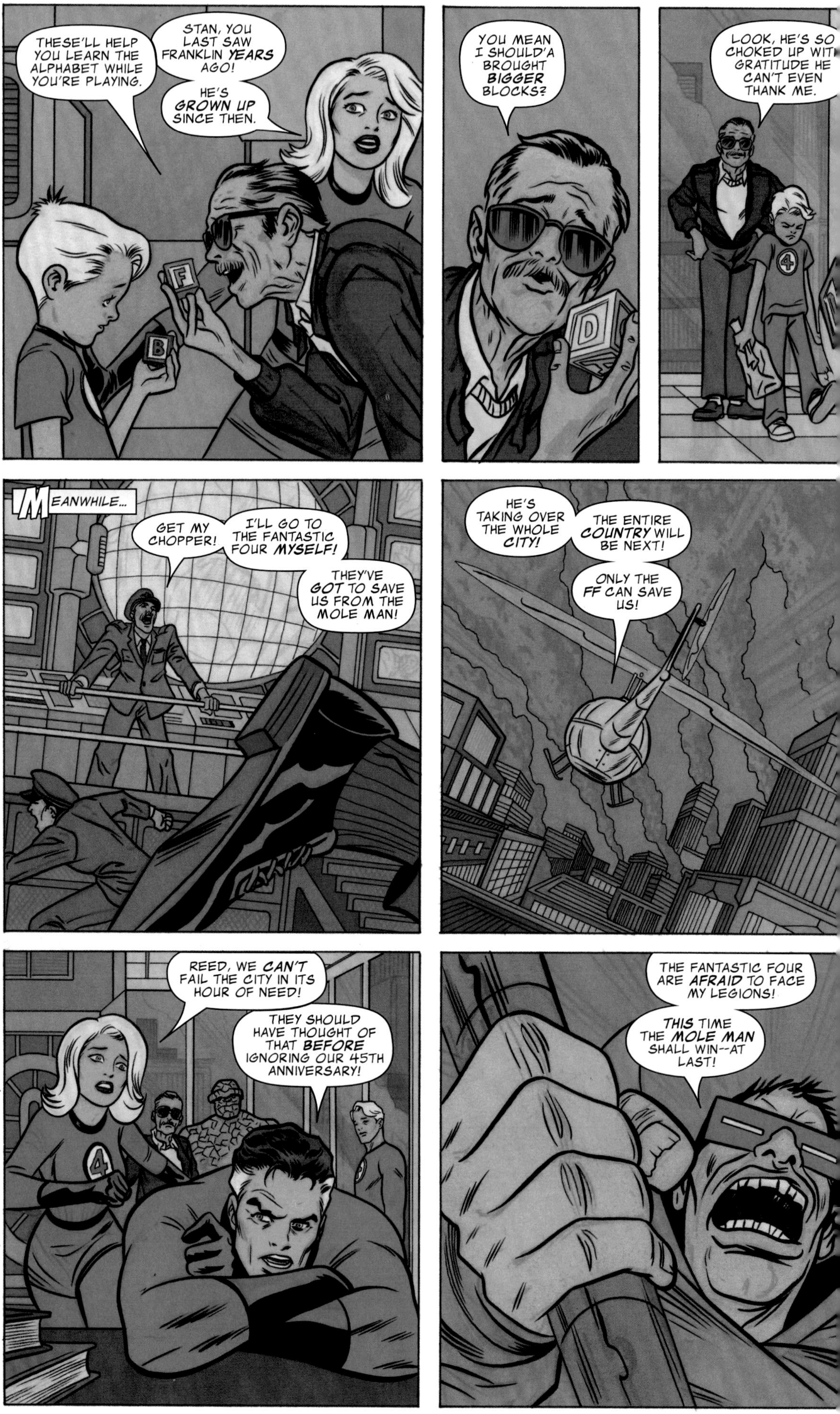

THESE'LL HELP YOU LEARN THE ALPHABET WHILE YOU'RE PLAYING.
STAN, YOU LAST SAW FRANKLIN YEARS AGO!
HE'S GROWN UP SINCE THEN.
YOU MEAN I SHOULD'A BROUGHT BIGGER BLOCKS?
LOOK, HE'S SO CHOKED UP WIT GRATITUDE HE CAN'T EVEN THANK ME.
MEANWHILE...
GET MY CHOPPER!
I'LL GO TO THE FANTASTIC FOUR MYSELF!
THEY'VE GOT TO SAVE US FROM THE MOLE MAN!
HE'S TAKING OVER THE WHOLE CITY!
THE ENTIRE COUNTRY WILL BE NEXT!
ONLY THE FF CAN SAVE US!
REED, WE CAN'T FAIL THE CITY IN ITS HOUR OF NEED!
THEY SHOULD HAVE THOUGHT OF THAT BEFORE IGNORING OUR 45TH ANNIVERSARY!
THE FANTASTIC FOUR ARE AFRAID TO FACE MY LEGIONS!
THIS TIME THE MOLE MAN SHALL WIN--AT LAST!

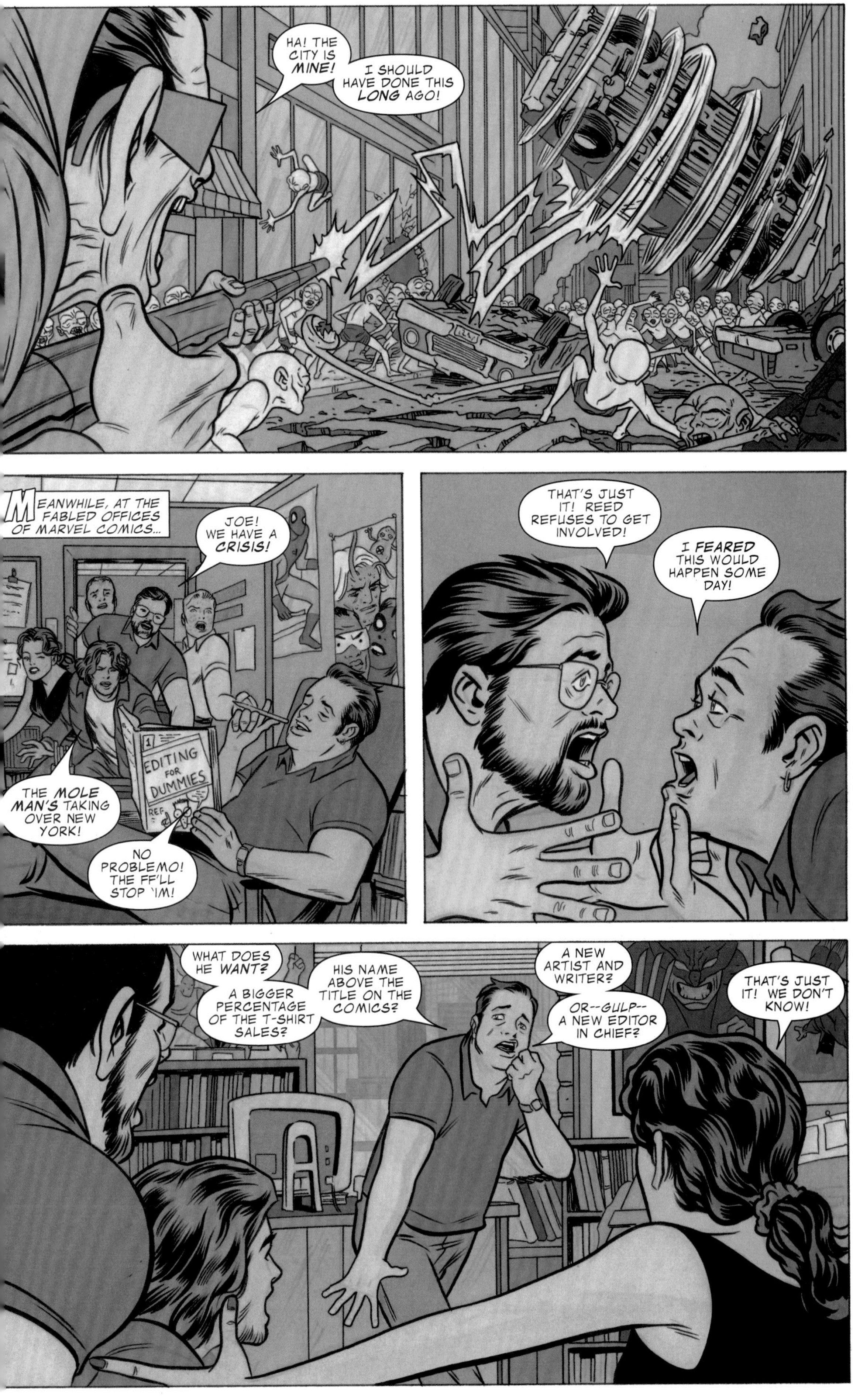
HA! THE CITY IS MINE!
I SHOULD HAVE DONE THIS LONG AGO!
MEANWHILE, AT THE FABLED OFFICES OF MARVEL COMICS...
JOE! WE HAVE A CRISIS!
EDITING FOR DUMMIES
THE MOLE MAN'S TAKING OVER NEW YORK!
NO PROBLEMO! THE FF'LL STOP 'IM!
THAT'S JUST IT! REED REFUSES TO GET INVOLVED!
I FEARED THIS WOULD HAPPEN SOME DAY!
WHAT DOES HE WANT?
A BIGGER PERCENTAGE OF THE T-SHIRT SALES?
HIS NAME ABOVE THE TITLE ON THE COMICS?
A NEW ARTIST AND WRITER?
OR--GULP-- A NEW EDITOR IN CHIEF?
THAT'S JUST IT! WE DON'T KNOW!

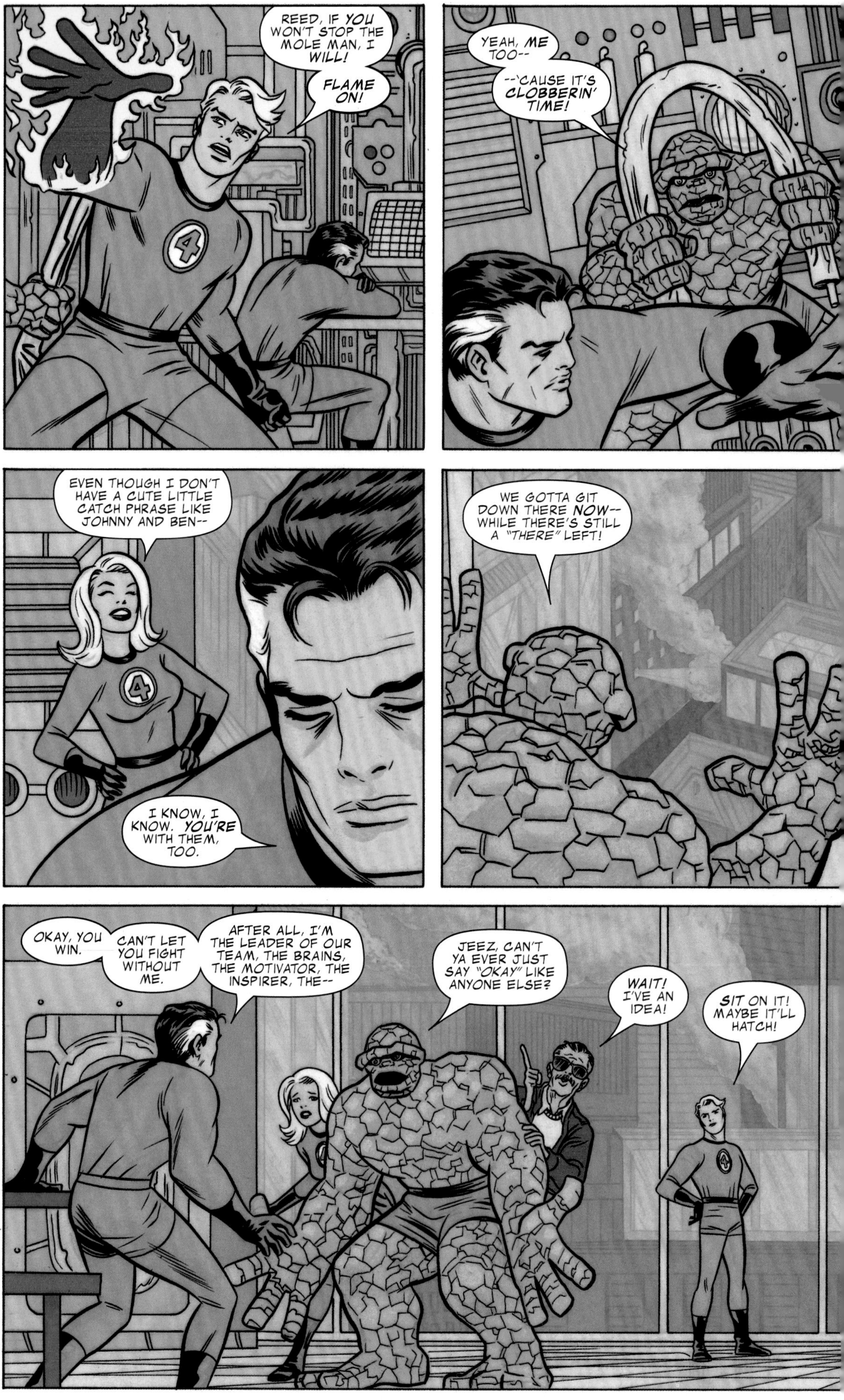

REED, IF YOU WON'T STOP THE MOLE MAN, I WILL!
FLAME ON!
YEAH, ME TOO--
--'CAUSE IT'S CLOBBERIN' TIME!
EVEN THOUGH I DON'T HAVE A CUTE LITTLE CATCH PHRASE LIKE JOHNNY AND BEN--
I KNOW, I KNOW. YOU'RE WITH THEM, TOO.
WE GOTTA GIT DOWN THERE NOW-- WHILE THERE'S STILL A "THERE" LEFT!
OKAY, YOU WIN.
CAN'T LET YOU FIGHT WITHOUT ME.
AFTER ALL, I'M THE LEADER OF OUR TEAM, THE BRAINS, THE MOTIVATOR, THE INSPIRER, THE--
JEEZ, CAN'T YA EVER JUST SAY "OKAY" LIKE ANYONE ELSE?
WAIT! I'VE AN IDEA!
SIT ON IT! MAYBE IT'LL HATCH!

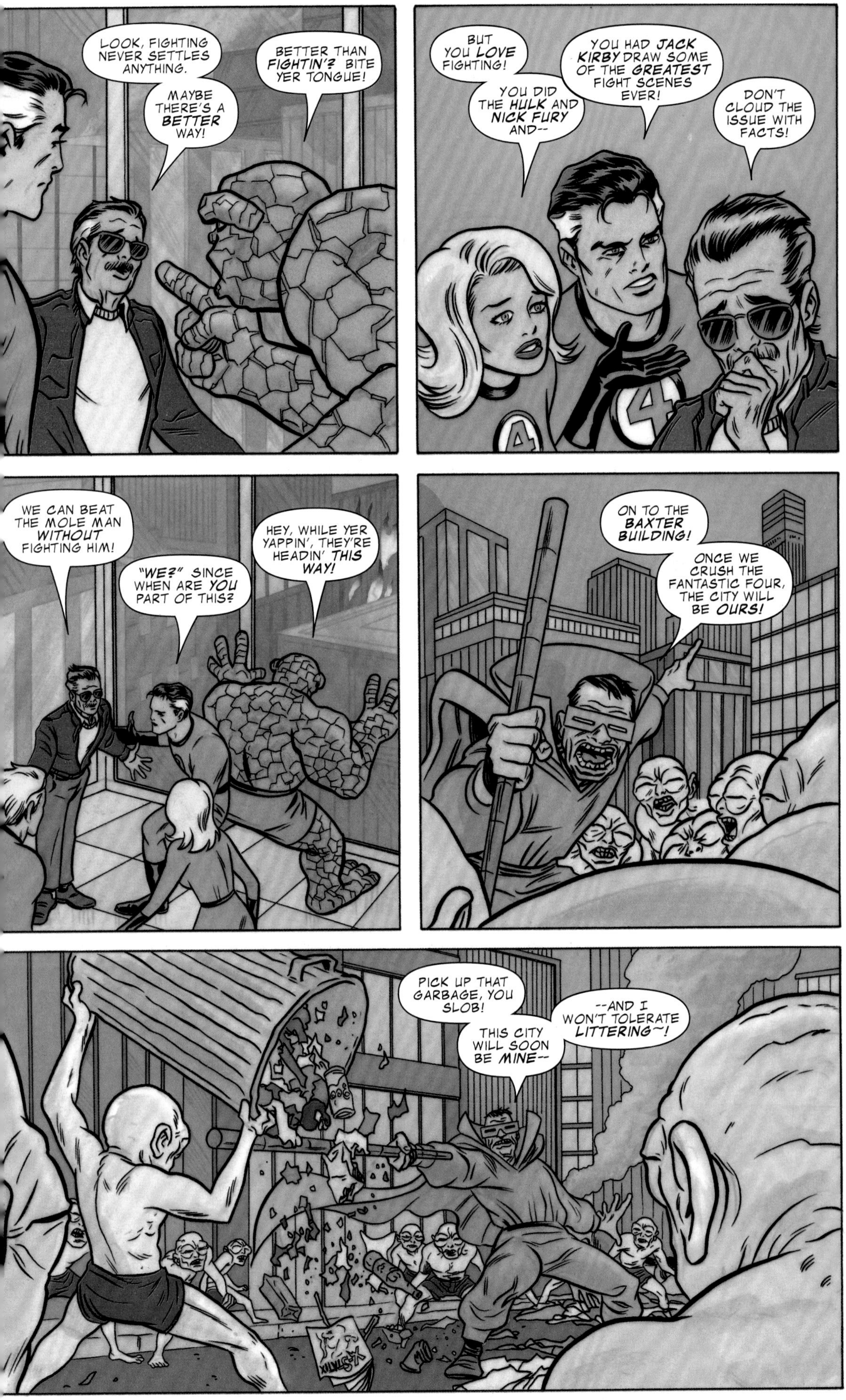
LOOK, FIGHTING NEVER SETTLES ANYTHING.
MAYBE THERE'S A BETTER WAY!
BETTER THAN FIGHTIN'? BITE YER TONGUE!
BUT YOU LOVE FIGHTING!
YOU DID THE HULK AND NICK FURY AND--
YOU HAD JACK KIRBY DRAW SOME OF THE GREATEST FIGHT SCENES EVER!
DON'T CLOUD THE ISSUE WITH FACTS!
WE CAN BEAT THE MOLE MAN WITHOUT FIGHTING HIM!
"WE?" SINCE WHEN ARE YOU PART OF THIS?
HEY, WHILE YER YAPPIN', THEY'RE HEADIN' THIS WAY!
ON TO THE BAXTER BUILDING!
ONCE WE CRUSH THE FANTASTIC FOUR, THE CITY WILL BE OURS!
PICK UP THAT GARBAGE, YOU SLOB!
THIS CITY WILL SOON BE MINE--
--AND I WON'T TOLERATE LITTERING~!

THING: I'M JUST GONNA *TALK* TO THE MOLE MAN.

THING: WHAT'S YOUR PLAN-- TO *BORE* HIM TO DEATH?

THING: LET 'IM GO. IT'S ONE WAY TO GIT RID'A HIM!

MR. FANTASTIC: GIVE ME FIVE MINUTES. IF I'M NOT BACK BY THEN--

MR. FANTASTIC: WE'LL CELEBRATE!

MR. FANTASTIC: I GUESS FIVE MINUTES WON'T MATTER.

INVISIBLE WOMAN: IT'S NOT AS BAD AS-- *45 YEARS!*

MR. FANTASTIC: AW, HONEY, YOU'VE GOT TO GET OFF THAT KICK.

THING: *SONUVAGUN!* LEE'S RIGHT IN THE MIDDLE OF THE FIGHTIN'--

THING: HEADIN' TOWARDS THE MOLE MAN!

INVISIBLE WOMAN: EVEN *HE* DOESN'T DESERVE TO DIE LIKE THAT!

MR. FANTASTIC: RIGHT. THERE ARE PEOPLE *MORE* ANNOYING THAN STAN.

INVISIBLE WOMAN: YEAH? LIKE WHO?

MR. FANTASTIC: HMMMM.

MR. FANTASTIC: OKAY, MAYBE IT'S JUST AS WELL HE WENT.

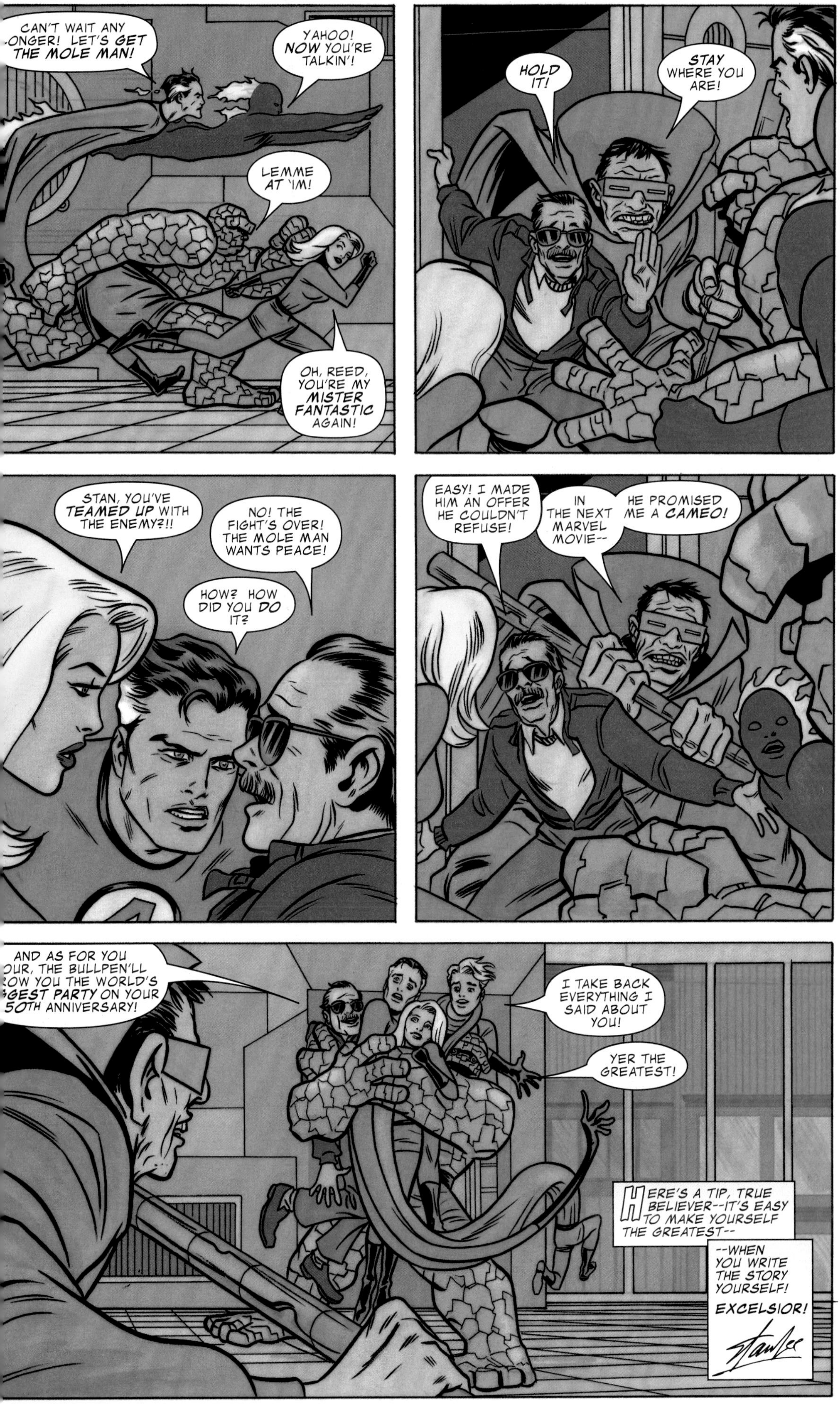
CAN'T WAIT ANY ONGER! LET'S GET THE MOLE MAN!
YAHOO! NOW YOU'RE TALKIN'!
LEMME AT 'IM!
OH, REED, YOU'RE MY MISTER FANTASTIC AGAIN!
HOLD IT!
STAY WHERE YOU ARE!
STAN, YOU'VE TEAMED UP WITH THE ENEMY?!!
NO! THE FIGHT'S OVER! THE MOLE MAN WANTS PEACE!
HOW? HOW DID YOU DO IT?
EASY! I MADE HIM AN OFFER HE COULDN'T REFUSE!
IN THE NEXT MARVEL MOVIE--
HE PROMISED ME A CAMEO!
AND AS FOR YOU OUR, THE BULLPEN'LL ROW YOU THE WORLD'S GEST PARTY ON YOUR 50TH ANNIVERSARY!
I TAKE BACK EVERYTHING I SAID ABOUT YOU!
YER THE GREATEST!
HERE'S A TIP, TRUE BELIEVER--IT'S EASY TO MAKE YOURSELF THE GREATEST--
--WHEN YOU WRITE THE STORY YOURSELF!
EXCELSIOR!
Stan Lee

A DAY AT THE RACES

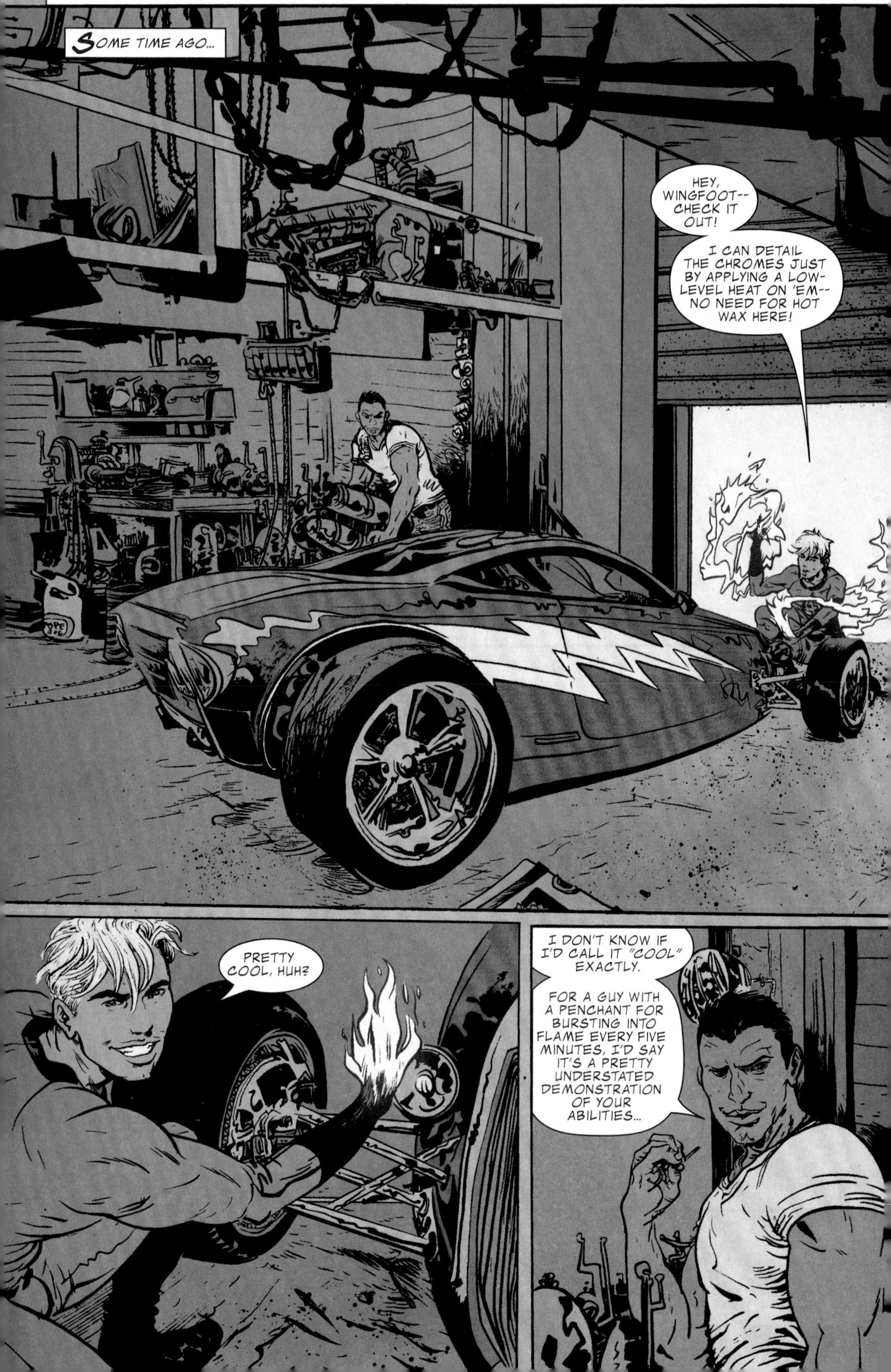
SOME TIME AGO...
HEY, WINGFOOT-- CHECK IT OUT!
I CAN DETAIL THE CHROMES JUST BY APPLYING A LOW-LEVEL HEAT ON 'EM-- NO NEED FOR HOT WAX HERE!
PRETTY COOL, HUH?
I DON'T KNOW IF I'D CALL IT "COOL" EXACTLY.
FOR A GUY WITH A PENCHANT FOR BURSTING INTO FLAME EVERY FIVE MINUTES, I'D SAY IT'S A PRETTY UNDERSTATED DEMONSTRATION OF YOUR ABILITIES...

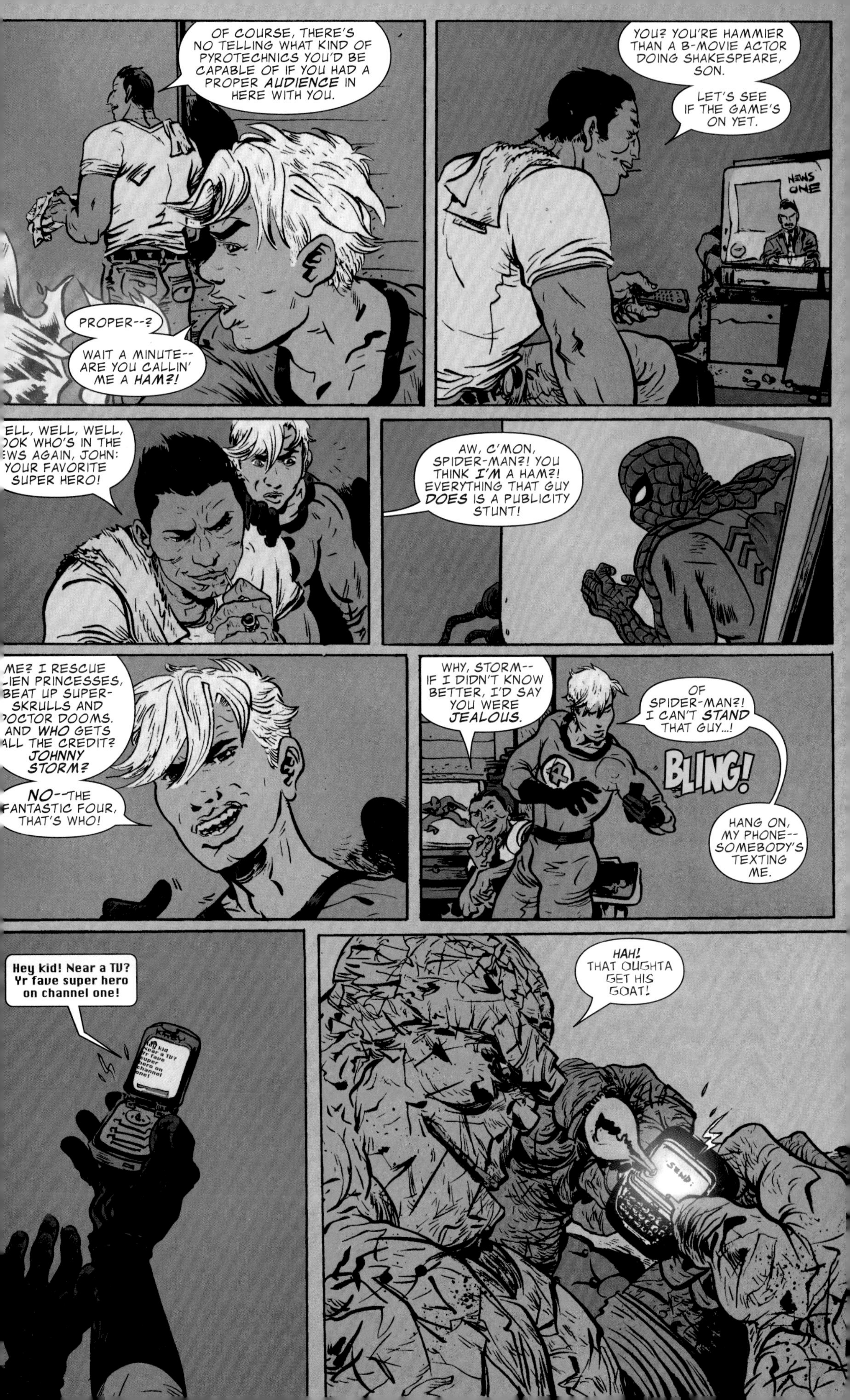
OF COURSE, THERE'S NO TELLING WHAT KIND OF PYROTECHNICS YOU'D BE CAPABLE OF IF YOU HAD A PROPER AUDIENCE IN HERE WITH YOU.
PROPER--?
WAIT A MINUTE-- ARE YOU CALLIN' ME A HAM?!
YOU? YOU'RE HAMMIER THAN A B-MOVIE ACTOR DOING SHAKESPEARE, SON.
LET'S SEE IF THE GAME'S ON YET.
NEWS ONE
ELL, WELL, WELL, OOK WHO'S IN THE EWS AGAIN, JOHN: YOUR FAVORITE SUPER HERO!
AW, C'MON, SPIDER-MAN?! YOU THINK I'M A HAM?! EVERYTHING THAT GUY DOES IS A PUBLICITY STUNT!
ME? I RESCUE LIEN PRINCESSES, BEAT UP SUPER-SKRULLS AND OCTOR DOOMS. AND WHO GETS ALL THE CREDIT? JOHNNY STORM?
NO--THE FANTASTIC FOUR, THAT'S WHO!
WHY, STORM-- IF I DIDN'T KNOW BETTER, I'D SAY YOU WERE JEALOUS.
OF SPIDER-MAN?! I CAN'T STAND THAT GUY...!
BLING!
HANG ON, MY PHONE-- SOMEBODY'S TEXTING ME.
Hey kid! Near a TV? Yr fave super hero on channel one!
HAH! THAT OUGHTA GET HIS GOAT!
SEND

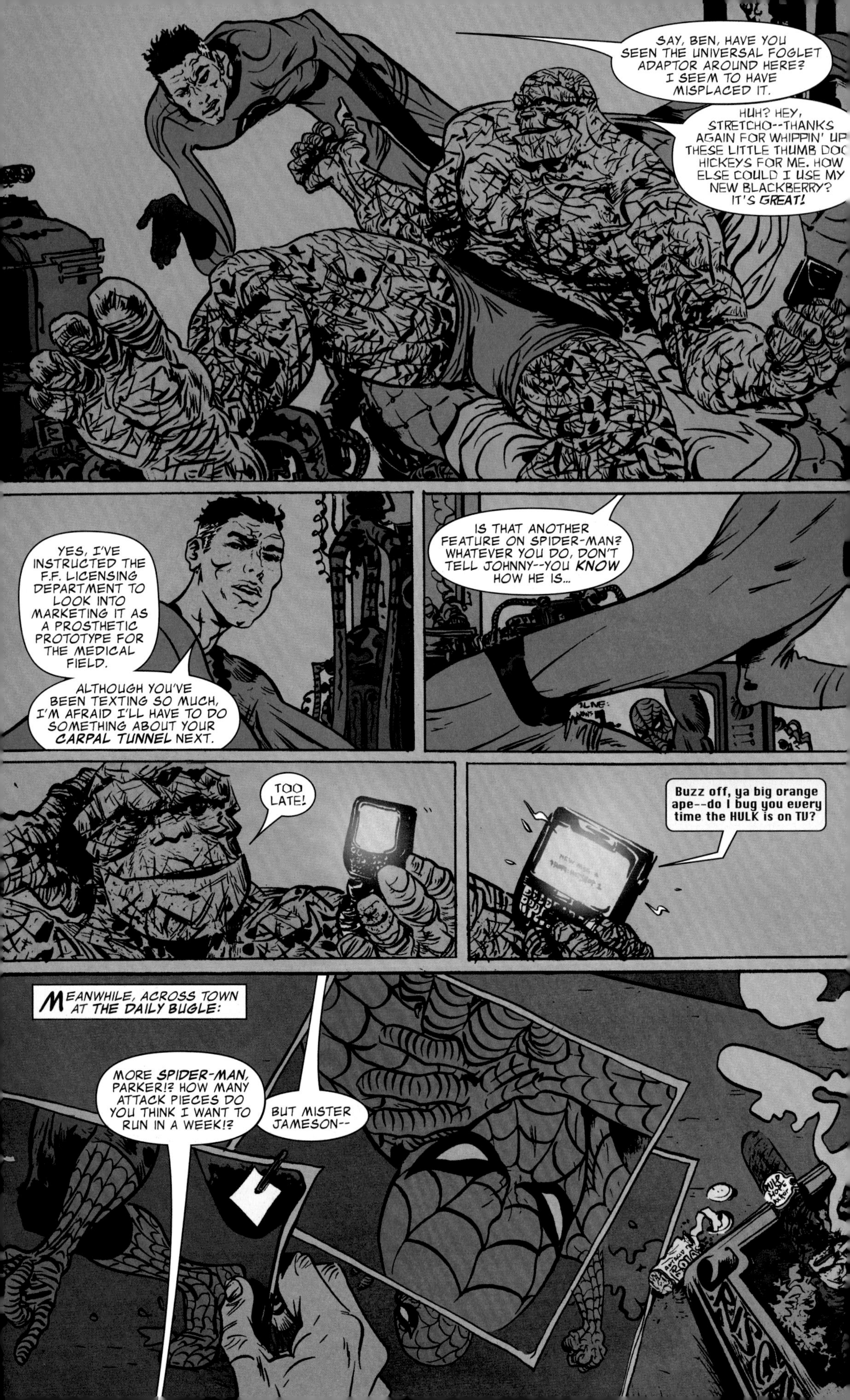
SAY, BEN, HAVE YOU SEEN THE UNIVERSAL FOGLET ADAPTOR AROUND HERE? I SEEM TO HAVE MISPLACED IT.
HUH? HEY, STRETCHO--THANKS AGAIN FOR WHIPPIN' UP THESE LITTLE THUMB DOO HICKEYS FOR ME. HOW ELSE COULD I USE MY NEW BLACKBERRY? IT'S GREAT!
YES, I'VE INSTRUCTED THE F.F. LICENSING DEPARTMENT TO LOOK INTO MARKETING IT AS A PROSTHETIC PROTOTYPE FOR THE MEDICAL FIELD.
ALTHOUGH YOU'VE BEEN TEXTING SO MUCH, I'M AFRAID I'LL HAVE TO DO SOMETHING ABOUT YOUR CARPAL TUNNEL NEXT.
IS THAT ANOTHER FEATURE ON SPIDER-MAN? WHATEVER YOU DO, DON'T TELL JOHNNY--YOU KNOW HOW HE IS...
TOO LATE!
Buzz off, ya big orange ape--do I bug you every time the HULK is on TV?
MEANWHILE, ACROSS TOWN AT THE DAILY BUGLE:
MORE SPIDER-MAN, PARKER!? HOW MANY ATTACK PIECES DO YOU THINK I WANT TO RUN IN A WEEK!?
BUT MISTER JAMESON--

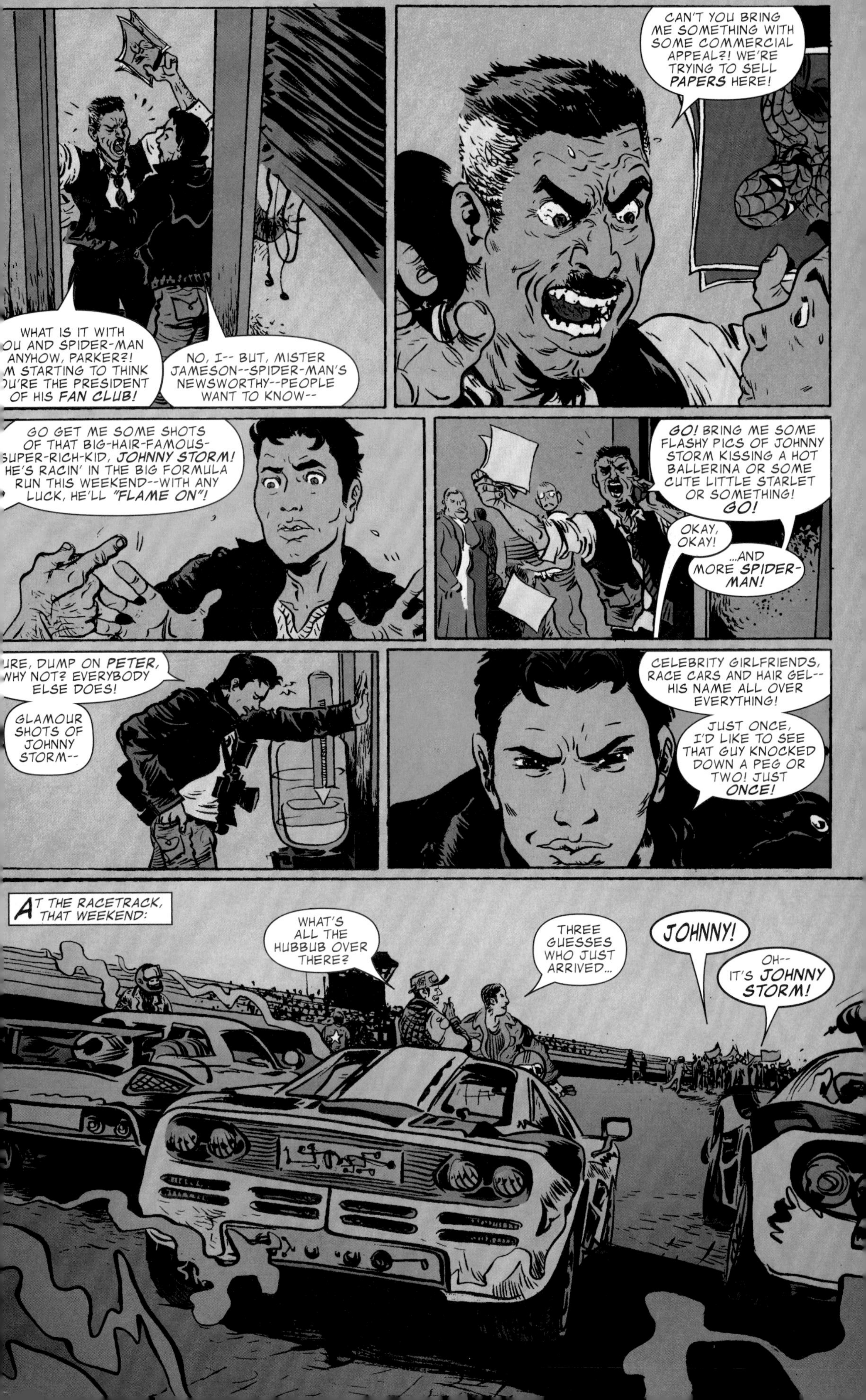

WHAT IS IT WITH OU AND SPIDER-MAN ANYHOW, PARKER?! M STARTING TO THINK OU'RE THE PRESIDENT OF HIS FAN CLUB!
NO, I-- BUT, MISTER JAMESON--SPIDER-MAN'S NEWSWORTHY--PEOPLE WANT TO KNOW--
CAN'T YOU BRING ME SOMETHING WITH SOME COMMERCIAL APPEAL?! WE'RE TRYING TO SELL PAPERS HERE!
GO GET ME SOME SHOTS OF THAT BIG-HAIR-FAMOUS-SUPER-RICH-KID, JOHNNY STORM! HE'S RACIN' IN THE BIG FORMULA RUN THIS WEEKEND--WITH ANY LUCK, HE'LL "FLAME ON"!
GO! BRING ME SOME FLASHY PICS OF JOHNNY STORM KISSING A HOT BALLERINA OR SOME CUTE LITTLE STARLET OR SOMETHING! GO!
OKAY, OKAY!
...AND MORE SPIDER-MAN!
URE, DUMP ON PETER, WHY NOT? EVERYBODY ELSE DOES!
GLAMOUR SHOTS OF JOHNNY STORM--
CELEBRITY GIRLFRIENDS, RACE CARS AND HAIR GEL--HIS NAME ALL OVER EVERYTHING!
JUST ONCE, I'D LIKE TO SEE THAT GUY KNOCKED DOWN A PEG OR TWO! JUST ONCE!
AT THE RACETRACK, THAT WEEKEND:
WHAT'S ALL THE HUBBUB OVER THERE?
THREE GUESSES WHO JUST ARRIVED...
JOHNNY!
OH-- IT'S JOHNNY STORM!

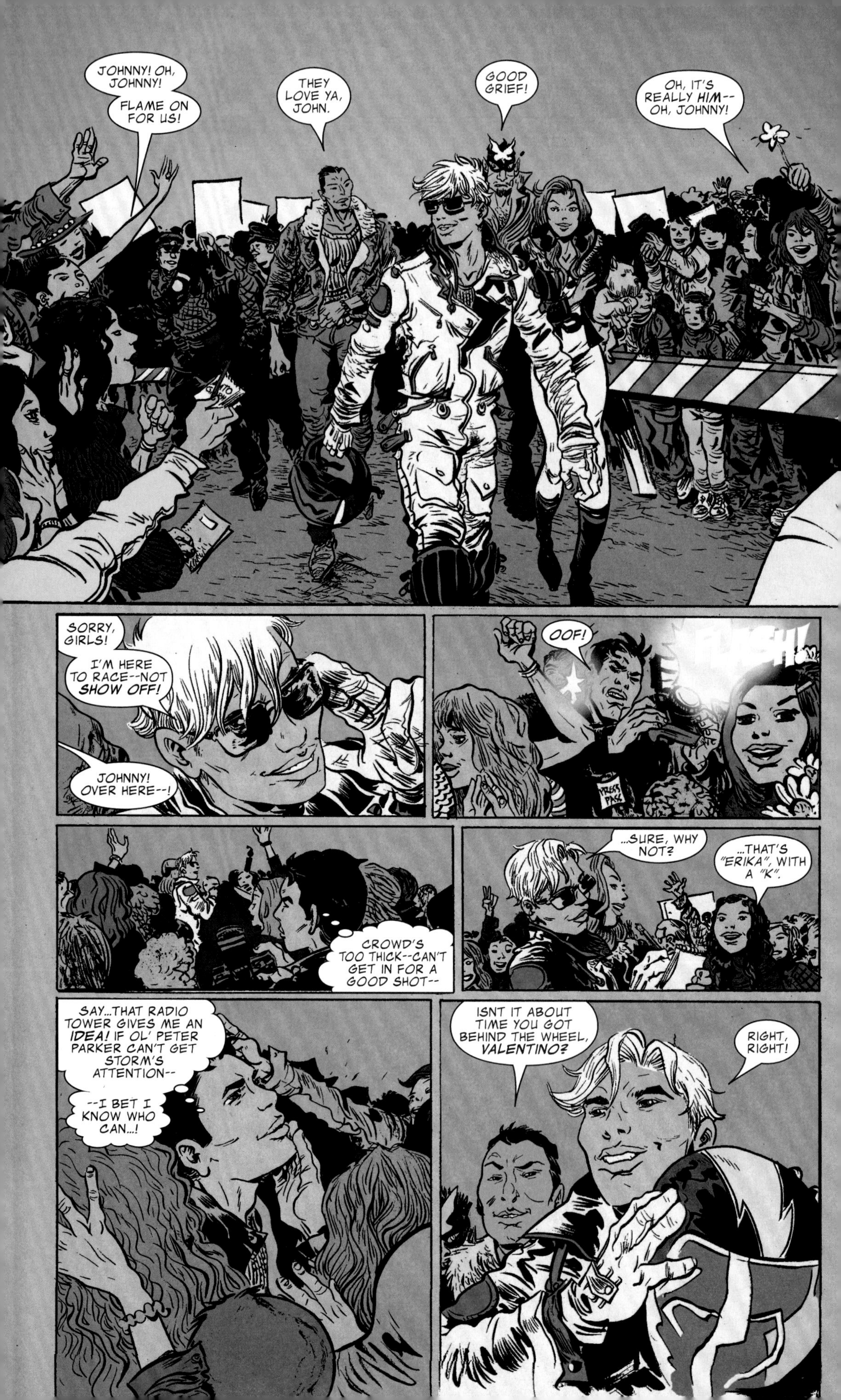
JOHNNY! OH, JOHNNY!
FLAME ON FOR US!
THEY LOVE YA, JOHN.
GOOD GRIEF!
OH, IT'S REALLY HIM--OH, JOHNNY!
SORRY, GIRLS!
I'M HERE TO RACE--NOT SHOW OFF!
JOHNNY! OVER HERE--!
OOF!
PRESS PASS
CROWD'S TOO THICK--CAN'T GET IN FOR A GOOD SHOT--
...SURE, WHY NOT?
...THAT'S "ERIKA", WITH A "K".
SAY...THAT RADIO TOWER GIVES ME AN IDEA! IF OL' PETER PARKER CAN'T GET STORM'S ATTENTION--
--I BET I KNOW WHO CAN...!
ISNT IT ABOUT TIME YOU GOT BEHIND THE WHEEL, VALENTINO?
RIGHT, RIGHT!

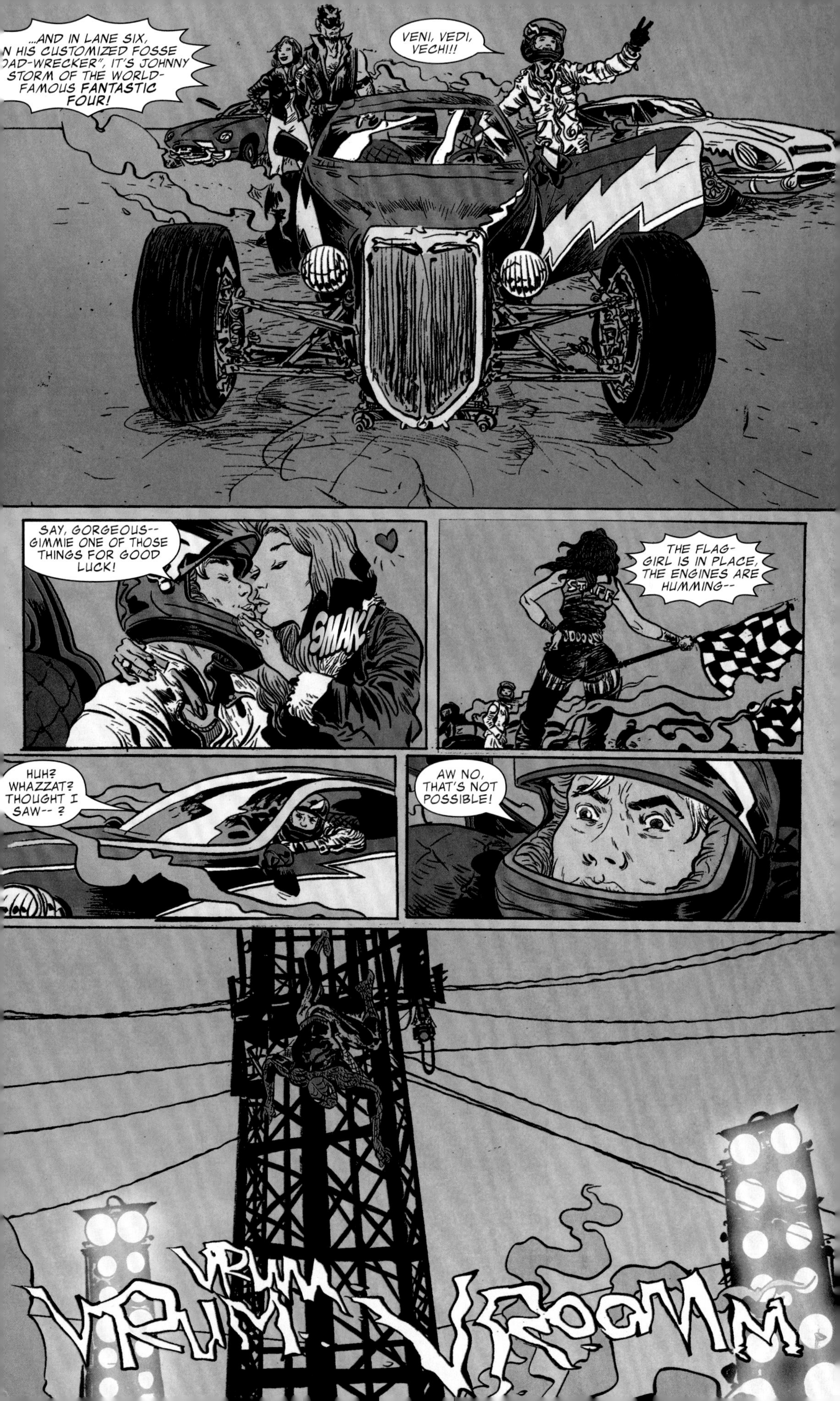

...AND IN LANE SIX, N HIS CUSTOMIZED FOSSE "OAD-WRECKER", IT'S JOHNNY STORM OF THE WORLD-FAMOUS FANTASTIC FOUR!
VENI, VEDI, VECHI!!
SAY, GORGEOUS-- GIMMIE ONE OF THOSE THINGS FOR GOOD LUCK!
SMAK!
THE FLAG-GIRL IS IN PLACE, THE ENGINES ARE HUMMING--
HUH? WHAZZAT? THOUGHT I SAW-- ?
AW NO, THAT'S NOT POSSIBLE!
VRUM
VRUM VROOMM

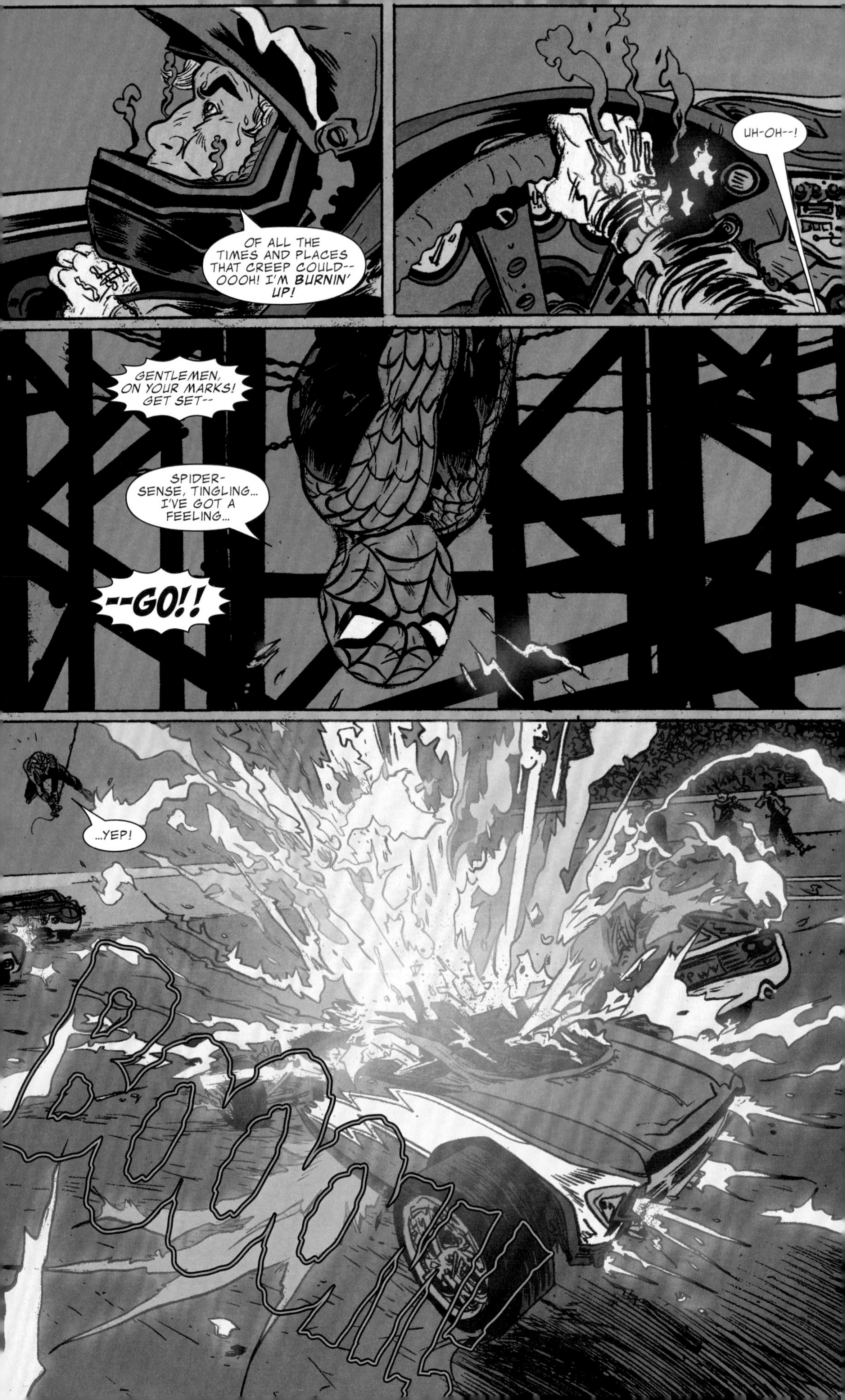
OF ALL THE TIMES AND PLACES THAT CREEP COULD-- OOOH! I'M BURNIN' UP!
UH-OH--!
GENTLEMEN, ON YOUR MARKS! GET SET--
SPIDER-SENSE, TINGLING... I'VE GOT A FEELING...
--GO!!
...YEP!
BOOOOM!!

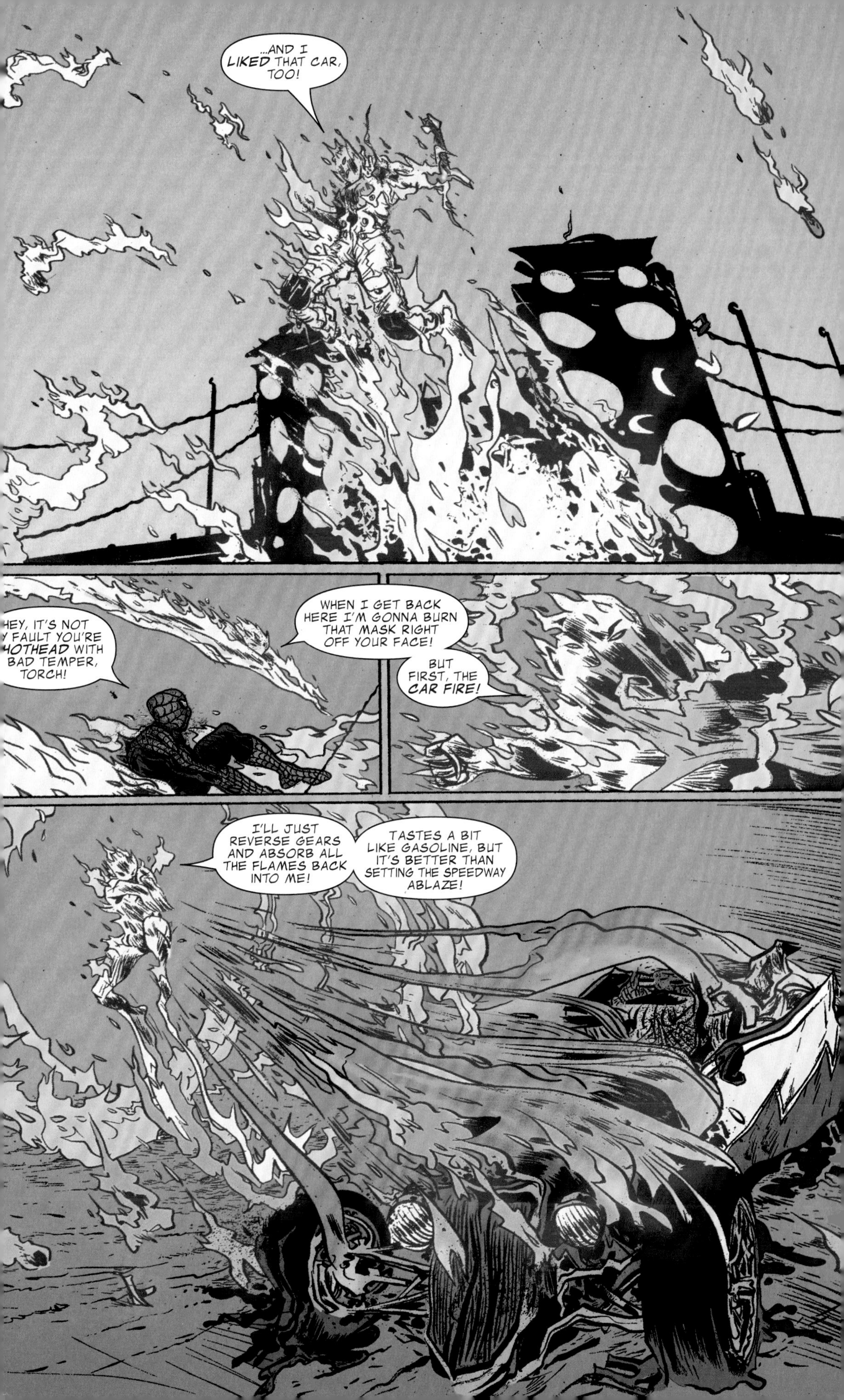
...AND I LIKED THAT CAR, TOO!
HEY, IT'S NOT Y FAULT YOU'RE HOTHEAD WITH BAD TEMPER, TORCH!
WHEN I GET BACK HERE I'M GONNA BURN THAT MASK RIGHT OFF YOUR FACE!
BUT FIRST, THE CAR FIRE!
I'LL JUST REVERSE GEARS AND ABSORB ALL THE FLAMES BACK INTO ME!
TASTES A BIT LIKE GASOLINE, BUT IT'S BETTER THAN SETTING THE SPEEDWAY ABLAZE!

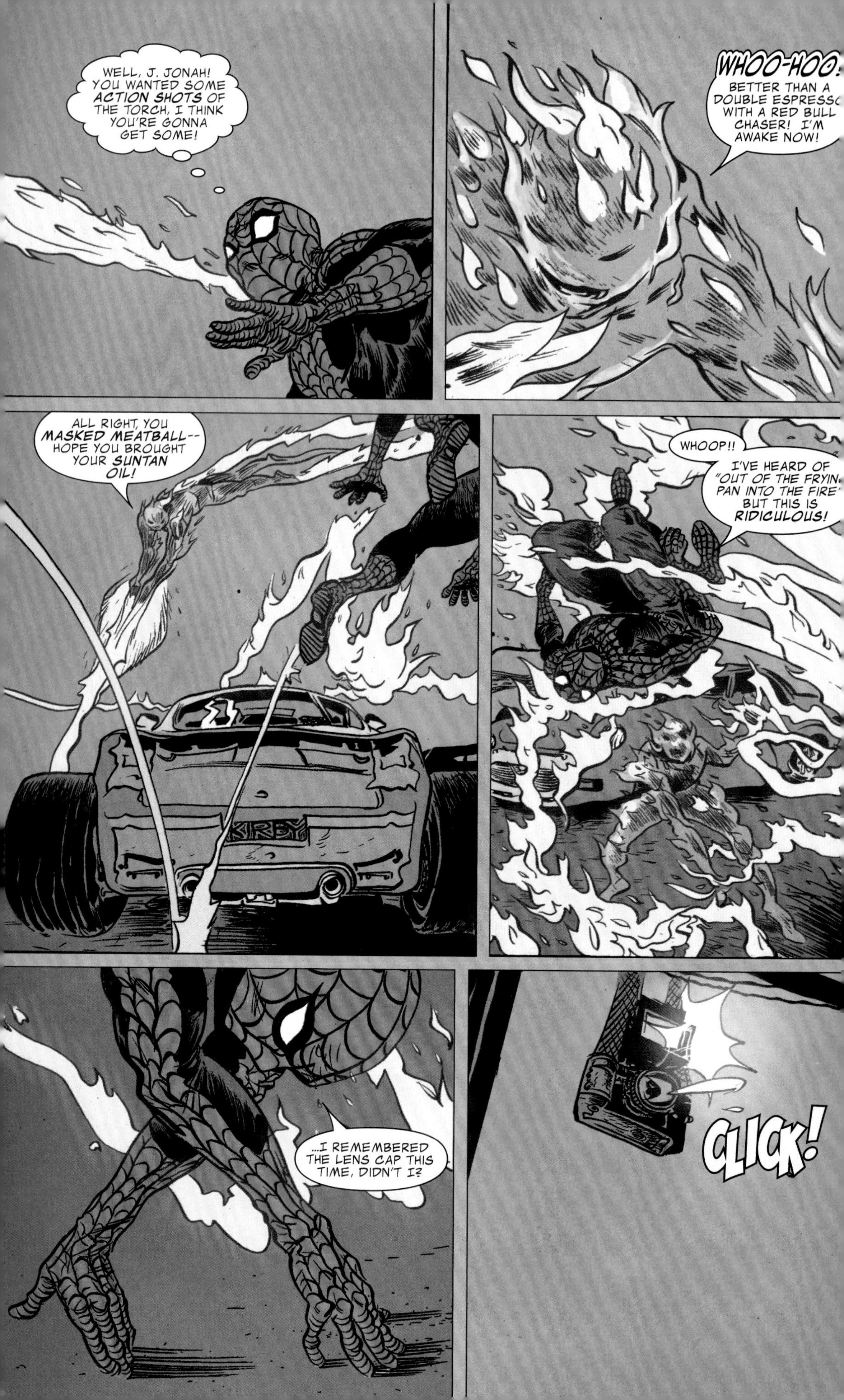
WELL, J. JONAH! YOU WANTED SOME ACTION SHOTS OF THE TORCH, I THINK YOU'RE GONNA GET SOME!
WHOO-HOO!
BETTER THAN A DOUBLE ESPRESSO WITH A RED BULL CHASER! I'M AWAKE NOW!
ALL RIGHT, YOU MASKED MEATBALL-- HOPE YOU BROUGHT YOUR SUNTAN OIL!
KIRBY
WHOOP!!
I'VE HEARD OF "OUT OF THE FRYING PAN INTO THE FIRE" BUT THIS IS RIDICULOUS!
...I REMEMBERED THE LENS CAP THIS TIME, DIDN'T I?
CLICK!

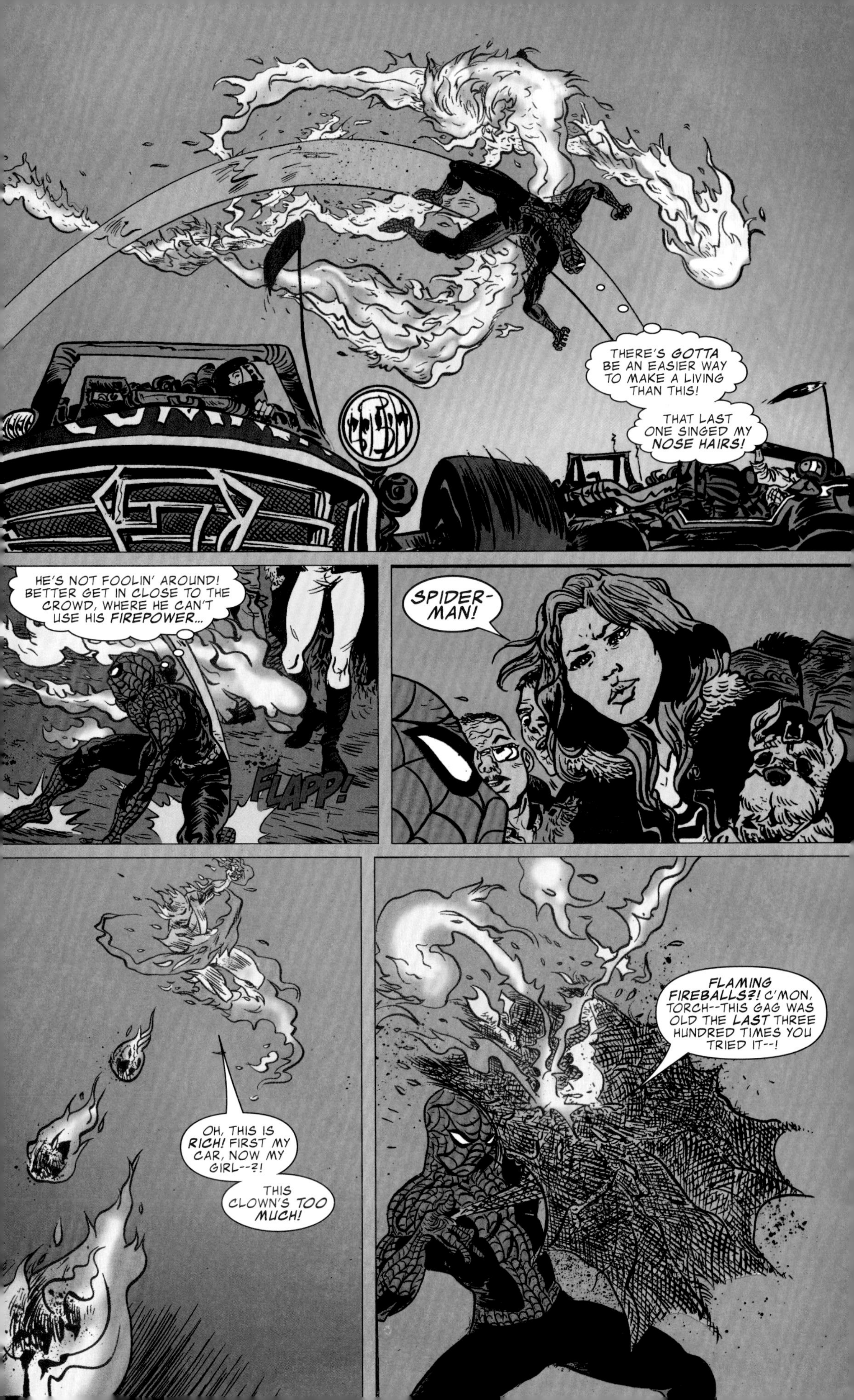

THERE'S GOTTA BE AN EASIER WAY TO MAKE A LIVING THAN THIS!
THAT LAST ONE SINGED MY NOSE HAIRS!
HE'S NOT FOOLIN' AROUND! BETTER GET IN CLOSE TO THE CROWD, WHERE HE CAN'T USE HIS FIREPOWER...
FLAPP!
SPIDER-MAN!
OH, THIS IS RICH! FIRST MY CAR, NOW MY GIRL--?!
THIS CLOWN'S TOO MUCH!
FLAMING FIREBALLS?! C'MON, TORCH--THIS GAG WAS OLD THE LAST THREE HUNDRED TIMES YOU TRIED IT--!

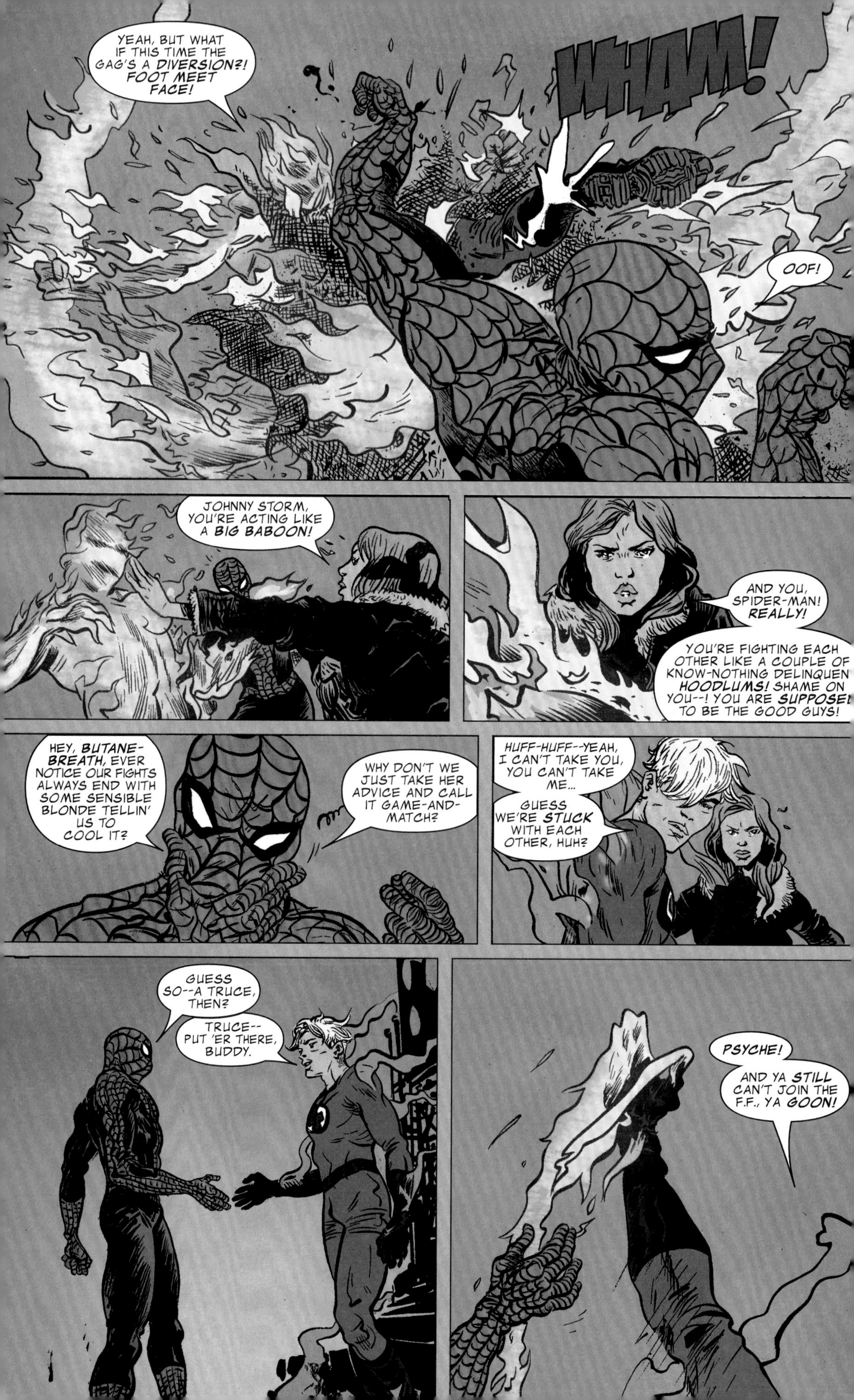
YEAH, BUT WHAT IF THIS TIME THE GAG'S A DIVERSION?! FOOT MEET FACE!
WHAM!
OOF!
JOHNNY STORM, YOU'RE ACTING LIKE A BIG BABOON!
AND YOU, SPIDER-MAN! REALLY!
YOU'RE FIGHTING EACH OTHER LIKE A COUPLE OF KNOW-NOTHING DELINQUEN HOODLUMS! SHAME ON YOU--! YOU ARE SUPPOSE TO BE THE GOOD GUYS!
HEY, BUTANE-BREATH, EVER NOTICE OUR FIGHTS ALWAYS END WITH SOME SENSIBLE BLONDE TELLIN' US TO COOL IT?
WHY DON'T WE JUST TAKE HER ADVICE AND CALL IT GAME-AND-MATCH?
HUFF-HUFF--YEAH, I CAN'T TAKE YOU, YOU CAN'T TAKE ME...
GUESS WE'RE STUCK WITH EACH OTHER, HUH?
GUESS SO--A TRUCE, THEN?
TRUCE--PUT 'ER THERE, BUDDY.
PSYCHE!
AND YA STILL CAN'T JOIN THE F.F., YA GOON!

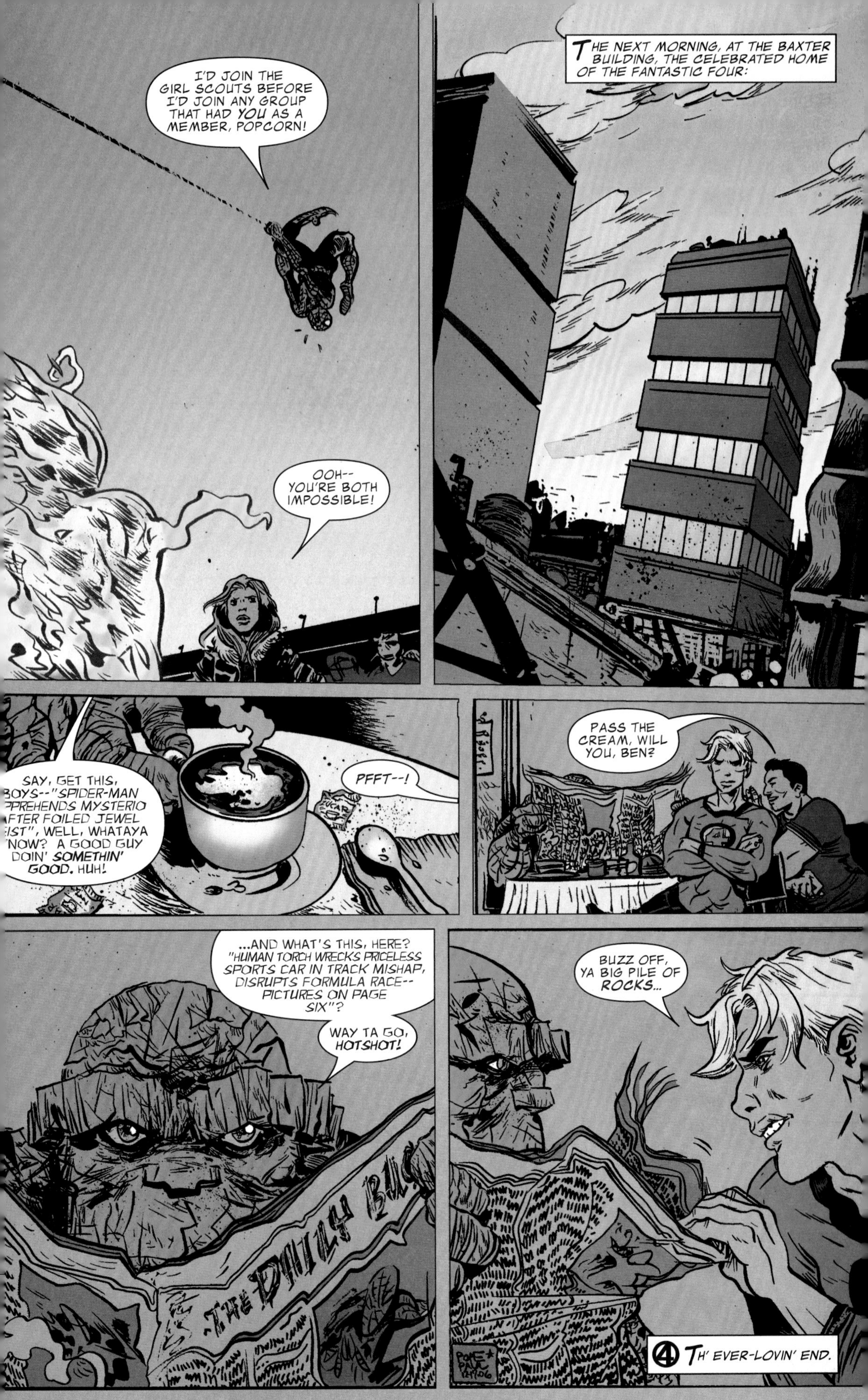
I'D JOIN THE GIRL SCOUTS BEFORE I'D JOIN ANY GROUP THAT HAD *YOU* AS A MEMBER, POPCORN!
OOH-- YOU'RE BOTH IMPOSSIBLE!
THE NEXT MORNING, AT THE BAXTER BUILDING, THE CELEBRATED HOME OF THE FANTASTIC FOUR:
SAY, GET THIS, BOYS--"SPIDER-MAN APPREHENDS MYSTERIO AFTER FOILED JEWEL HEIST", WELL, WHATAYA KNOW? A GOOD GUY DOIN' **SOMETHIN'** **GOOD.** HUH!
PFFT--!
PASS THE CREAM, WILL YOU, BEN?
...AND WHAT'S THIS, HERE? "HUMAN TORCH WRECKS PRICELESS SPORTS CAR IN TRACK MISHAP, DISRUPTS FORMULA RACE-- PICTURES ON PAGE SIX"?
WAY TA GO, **HOTSHOT!**
BUZZ OFF, YA BIG PILE OF **ROCKS...**
TH' EVER-LOVIN' END.

FANTASTIC FOUR 45TH ANNIVERSARY TOAST

Happy 45th Anniversary to Reed, Sue, Johnny and Ben! Who ever thought back in 1961 that Stan Lee and Jack Kirby's fabulous foursome would still be around to see the 21st Century? As a special treat, we've gathered messages from some of the folks involved with chronicling the Fantastic Four's amazing lives throughout the years. Take it away, guys!

Wow, the 45th Anniversary of the Fantastic Four! I was only a one year old when this story came to life in 1961, and it's amazing that it is still going strong today! That in itself signifies that great characters and story line can endure the test of time.

When I was young, I looked upon Jack Kirby as my "dad", not Jack Kirby the artist, comic book creator. I knew what he did for a living was a little different from most other dads, but still it wasn't till later on in life that I started to view him differently. He wasn't just my father, but an amazing artist and story teller!

I would have to say that the Fantastic Four caught my attention because I loved the character "The Thing." Ben Grimm, the tough guy with the Brooklyn accent, reminded me of where my father grew up.

I feel what makes these characters so intriguing is that their human personalities go along with their super powers. They are very human, make mistakes, and have problems like the rest of us. These special qualities I feel endear them to the reader.

Also, there are some very memorable characters that have come out of the Fantastic Four, such as the evil Dr. Doom, and one of my favorites, the Silver Surfer! I am glad that there are very talented people who have carried the torch so future generations can still enjoy these wonderful characters.
It is quite an honor that my father is still getting recognition for his work, and for his contribution to the comic book industry. My hope is that his legacy will continue and not be forgotten.

Happy 45th Anniversary, Fantastic Four!

Lisa Kirby

The year was 1961. I was an eleven year old comics fan making his weekly trek to the local drugstores. There were three drugstores in my hometown and not all of them carried all the comics I wanted. In those days it was all DC for this kid. Then I noticed something new and different staring at me from the comics rack. FANTASTIC FOUR #1. I purchased that issue and fell in love with the characters. The art was exciting and dynamic. The writing was so real and three-dimensional. And for the first time there were names attached to the work. Stan Lee and J. Kirby! They were my heroes.

Flash forward thirty years. Marvel Editor Ralph Macchio offers me the penciling chores on, sound the trumpets, FANTASTIC FOUR. I initially turned down the offer due to an overly committed schedule. I thought about the FF all weekend and remembered that day back in '61 when I first met Reed, Sue, Ben and Johnny. I called Ralph very, VERY early Monday morning and accepted the job. Teamed with writer Tom DeFalco, I enjoyed a wondrous ride for nearly five years. Thanks to Ralph for the job. Thanks to Stan and Jack who built the ride.

FF Fan for life,
Paul Ryan
FF Penciler, 1991-1996

Dear all,

I'm old enough, only just, to remember the very first appearance of the Fantastic Four...and as I recall, although I was immediately won over by the novelty, I didn recognize their uniqueness. Su they were odd and quirky but the weren't that different from th other costumed adventurers wh in the tradition of noble heroic fought evil whenever it reare its ugly head. However, as tim passed I realized how wrong I ha been. The thrill of novelty didn fade, it grew as the FF's univers expanded and their adventure became ever more...well, Fantasti But, the most inexplicable thin was that four characters at th center of the alien wonder becan more ordinary...More "real" And somewhere along the way realized I had developed a genuir affection for this singular foursom Now, forty-five years later, I hav accepted that it is pointless to eve attempt to rationalize the how o why. I just thank the "The Mar and "The King" for magic th filled my youth with wonder an dreams.

With respect and admiration,
Alan Davis
FF Penciler, 1998
FF: THE END Writer an Penciler

The FANTASTIC FOUR began revolution and changed the wa we think about comic books. It wa also the result of a mistake becaus Stan Lee didn't really listen to hi boss. Martin Goodman owned th company that would eventuall become Marvel Comics. Afte learning that a new comic calle The Justice League of America wa selling well for his competitio Martin told Stan to copy th formula. The JLA was a tradition team book that featured 196 versions of some Golden Age super heroes. I assume Martin expecte Stan to resurrect Captain Americ Human Torch, Sub-Mariner, Mis America and Whizzer to produce modern version of the company' old All-Winners Squad. It didn' happen. Instead, Stan create four new characters (okay, on was an update) and introduced eam that was far from traditional. They didn't have costumes, secret identities and weren't particularly nice to each other. Their stories featured big monsters and bug-eyed aliens. The plots were simple, the characterizations complex, and the dialogue sarcastic. It was a super hero team book for people who hated super hero team books and it laid the foundation for the mighty Marvel style of storytelling. It also inspired quite a few of us to become comic book creators.

By the way, Stan eventually gave Martin the book he requested. It was called the AVENGERS, and we all know how traditional that team turned out!

Tom DeFalco
FF Writer, 1991-1996

Dear FF Fans,

Is this still Earth-616? Is it possible? How could it be the 45th Anniversary of the Fantastic Four? Sheesh.

In my alternate dimension, about half that time has passed, so I can still remember those halcyon days at Merry Marvel with Stan and Jack bouncing around the office when they met for their (now fabled) "story conferences." Definitely two of the finest people I've ever met.

What a wild and wacky time! The four members of the FF family were so real to us that they seemed like fellow co-workers, each so unique and three-dimensional. Such amazing powers: would you choose to become invisible at will? Be impermeable to weapons and attackers? S-T-R-E-TC-H any which way? (Maybe best to leave the "Flame On!"s alone—too much paper around.)

I'm saddened that Jack and Roz aren't here to toast this milestone with us. I wish the FF and their current Marvel caretakers the best

for the next 45. Oddly enough, they don't seem to have aged. Neither has Stan. Me, either. =)

'Nuff Said,
Flo Steinberg
Stan's Secretary, 1963-1968

I well remember the summer day in 1961 when I came upon a copy of FANTASTIC FOUR #1 in a store in Cape Girardeau, Missouri, soon after graduating from college. It was as if Plastic Man, the Human Torch, and Invisible Scarlett O'Neil had teamed up with one of those monsters from Strange Journeys of Astonishing Suspense--with art by Jack Kirby of the old Simon & Kirby team, yet! From that day to this, FF has remained my favorite concept of all those devised by Stan Lee with Kirby, Ditko, or whoever. Spider-Man? He never even came close.

In the 1970s, when my turn came to write FF, I found myself paralyzed in a way I'd never been when scripting X-MEN, AVENGERS, et al. I could play around with the edges of FF, but I couldn't bring myself to change anything about the mag, not really. It was already perfect, just the way it was! It really was, for a very long time, "The World's Greatest Comic Magazine!"

Best wishes,
Roy Thomas
FF Writer, 1972-1973, 1975-1977

Dear Jack, Stan, Tom and Marvel,

Back in the early-mid 70s when I was transitioning from reading the FANTASTIC FOUR comics my father had bought and started buying them for myself, it might have been a dream of mine to draw their adventures...but I never had an inkling that it would ever be something that would truly happen. The FF comic was always a favorite of mine for the utter wonder of imagination and talent that was on exhibition by the

creative folks involved over the years. The book that gave birth to the Marvel Universe held a special place in my heart from the first time I read an issue. Fast forward almost 30 years--and I find myself actually drawing the book, working with one of my favorite writers and friends, Mark Waid. It's no wonder I have to keep pinching myself from time to time to make sure I'm really awake. So I'd like to thank Jack Kirby and Stan Lee for creating such a wonderfully timeless and inspiring book--and I'd like to thank Tom Brevoort and Marvel Entertainment for giving me the opportunity to be a part of such a special legacy in super hero comics. It's a special experience I'll never forget.

Mike Wieringo
FF Penciler, 2002-2005

Needless to say, any book that has Jack Kirby, John Buscema, John Byrne, George Perez, John Romita, Rich Buckler, Keith Pollard, Ron Frenz, and others working on it, can't be anything but a success.

Putting it all together was the incomparable Stan Lee and I'll always be grateful that he chose me to be a big part of the FF. Fortunately, I had work published in 209 FF stories, plus 202 covers. I also worked on 21 specials, annuals, and GIANT SIZE FANTASTIC FOUR issues; 9 WORLD'S GREATEST COMICS; 40th Anniversary comics; and 8 new covers for MARVEL'S GREATEST COMICS. How could it help being, arguably, the greatest comic of its time? I'm proud to have been a part of it.

Joe Sinnott
FF Inker, 1962, 1965-1981

J. MICHAEL STRACZYNSKI'S

ORIGINAL PLOT OUTLINE FOR CIVIL WAR: FANTASTIC FOUR, WRITTEN ON THE BACK OF A MENU AT A MARVEL CONVENTION DINNER.

FF COVER + ARC CONCEPT —
YANCY STREET GANG IS
PROTESTING/AGAINST THE
REGISTRATION ACT.
INFILTRATED BY THE FEDS,
INVESTIGATED, HARASSED
ARRESTED.
(METAPHOR FOR THE ASSAULT
ON CURRENT PROTEST
GROUPS, CIVILIAN
ASPECT.)
THEY NEED SOMEONE TO HELP
GET THEM OUT OF THE
POLICY, THEY GO TO
BEN FOR HELP.
THIS RUNS PARALLEL/AS A
RELIEF FROM THE
REED/SUE/JOHNNY STORY.